STIFFED

*A True Story
of MCA, the
Music Business,
and the Mafia*

STIFFED

WILLIAM KNOEDELSEDER

HarperCollins*Publishers*

HarperCollins books may be purchased for educational, business, or sales promotional use. For information, please write: Special Sales Department, HarperCollins Publishers, Inc., 10 East 53rd Street, New York, NY 10022.

FIRST EDITION

Designed by Jessica Shatan
Photo insert designed by Kristin Tobiassen

Library of Congress Catal⟨   ⟩n Data

Knoedelseder, William, 1947–
    Stiffed :   a true story of MCA, the m⟨   ⟩ the Mafia / by William Knoedelseder. — 1st ed.
        p.   cm.
    Includes index.
    ISBN 0-06-016745-9
    1. Sound recording industry—United States—Corrupt practices. 2. MCA Inc. 3. Mafia—United States. I. Title.
ML3790.K56 1993
364.1'68—dc20   92-53329

93 94 95 96 97 ❖/HC 10 9 8 7 6 5 4 3 2 1

To Irv Letofsky,
to whom I owe my writing career,
and to my family
—Bryn, Matt, and Colin—
to whom I owe my life and happiness

Contents

PART II MUSCLE

PART III JUDGMENT DAYS

Photographs appear after page 176

Acknowledgments

During the more than five years it took to research and write this book, I was aided and abetted by scores of people in law enforcement, the legal profession, and the music industry. Many of them are mentioned in these pages, while many others prefer to remain anonymous.

I would like to single out for special acknowledgment the following individuals:

My dear friend and tireless agent, Alice "The Velvet Hammer" Martell, who gave birth to two children while awaiting the birth of this book, which she managed to sell twice; my HarperCollins editor, Craig Nelson, who bought the book once, edited it deftly, and came up with a great title; my reporting colleagues who kept me company for weeks at a time in courthouse hallways and kept the story going when the road got rough—Chris Blatchford, Henry Schipper, Jeff Ressner, Michael Goldberg, and Chris Morris on the West Coast and Dan Moldea, George Anastasia, Charlie Wolfson, and Fred Dannen on the East; my former *Los Angeles Times* teammates Ron Soble and Kim Murphy, who helped me see the story through to the end and made my last year at the newspaper fun (I miss you guys); and my former *Times* editors Steve West, Harry Anderson, and Dennis Britton, who banged their heads against the bureaucratic wall on my behalf.

My thanks to you all.

Cast of Characters

THE MUSIC MEN

Irving Azoff: President of MCA Records Group and MCA Music Entertainment from 1983 to 1988 and chairman of Music Entertainment from 1988 to 1989; formerly manager of the Eagles, Steely Dan, Boz Scaggs, and a dozen other big-name rock acts from the 1970s; practitioner of "rock 'n' roll rules."

    Sidney Sheinberg: President of MCA, Inc., who wanted to turn his weakling record company into a heavyweight contender; hired Irving Azoff to do the job.

    Lew Wasserman: Chairman of MCA, Inc., who disliked the music business but went along with Sheinberg's plan; for years Ronald Reagan's Hollywood agent and still his close friend.

    Gene Froelich: President of MCA Records Group before Azoff; part of the old guard that was swept out when Azoff took over.

    Al Bergamo: President of MCA Distributing who also lost his job under the Azoff regime.

    Sam Passamano, Sr.: For years vice president in charge of selling MCA's cutout records, until he was replaced by Sal Pisello.

    George Collier: MCA Distributing executive who was fired after raising questions about the shipment of thousands of free records to several accounts.

    Myron Roth: Hired away from CBS by Azoff to be executive vice president of MCA Records; later promoted to the office of president and given a big raise after supposedly approving a series of misbegotten business deals with Sal Pisello, including the cutout sale and the distribution agreement with Sugar Hill Records.

    Dan McGill: Vice president and chief financial officer of MCA Records who took rubber checks from Sal Pisello and kept them in his desk drawer; the only MCA executive to testify at Pisello's trial.

John Burns: Took over Al Bergamo's job as president of MCA Distributing; asserted the Fifth Amendment before the grand jury in the Pisello case.

Zach Horowitz: Vice president of legal affairs for MCA Records; said he would not testify in the Pisello case without immunity.

Larry Solters: A longtime Azoff publicist whom Azoff brought along to MCA Records as vice president of artistic development; credited with developing teen singer Tiffany.

Richard Palmese: Former seminarian with a party-animal reputation who was hired by Azoff to be MCA's vice president of promotion; turned to members of the independent promotion "Network" with a vengeance.

Allen Susman: MCA's outside legal counsel for decades; told the prosecutor in the Pisello case, "We can make life difficult for you."

Eugene Giaquinto: President of MCA's home video division who came under federal investigation for allegedly funneling company funds to a member of Philadelphia's Bufalino crime family; his wiretapped phone conversations led authorities to believe he was connected to Gambino family boss John Gotti.

Morris Levy: Legendary president of Roulette Records; considered by law enforcement officials to have been the Mafia's front man in the record business; investor in Sugar Hill Records; Sal Pisello's partner in buying cutouts from MCA.

Joe Robinson: President of tiny Sugar Hill Records who lost his company in the aftermath of the Pisello debacle; longtime business associate of—and debtor to—Morris Levy.

THE MIDDLE MEN

John LaMonte: Owner of a small Philadelphia budget record distributorship who bought four million MCA cutouts through Sal Pisello in 1984, claimed he was cheated in the deal, and had his jaw broken as a result.

John Gervasoni: Owner of Scorpio Music; a competitor of LaMonte's who claimed that he, too, was cheated in an MCA cutout sale orchestrated by Sal Pisello; sued MCA but lost.

Ranji Bedi: Sometime actor-singer-songwriter who dabbled in the cutout record trade just enough to wind up in the middle of two MCA cutout sales with Sal Pisello.

Joe Isgro: Most conspicuously successful member of the Network, an influential group of independent record promoters that the government believed orchestrated a nationwide payola scheme in the 1980s; the target of the Los Angeles grand jury investigation.

Fred DiSipio: Isgro's Network counterpart on the East Coast, based in Cherry Hill, New Jersey.

Ralph Tashjian: Independent record promoter and employee of Isgro who became one of the few people ever successfully prosecuted under the federal payola statute.

THE MOBSTERS

Salvatore Pisello: Reputed member of the Gambino crime family and suspected drug trafficker who operated out of MCA Records between 1983 and 1985; his failure to pay income taxes kicked off the entire scandal.

Gaetano ("Corky") Vastola: Reputed acting boss of the DeCavalcante crime family; convicted extortionist; lifelong friend of Morris Levy; owner of Video Warehouse and a number of other businesses; breaker of John LaMonte's jaw.

Sonny Brocco: Vastola's cousin and business associate; learned the cutout record business from John LaMonte; got LaMonte involved in the MCA cutout deal.

Lew Saka: Vastola's "left-hand man" at Video Warehouse; ordered by Vastola to take over LaMonte's business.

Nicholas ("Nicky") Massaro: Bookmaking associate of Vastola whose wiretapped phone conversations led to the broader investigation of the Vastola organization and the Genovese crime family; sold cocaine to LaMonte while under surveillance by the FBI.

Federico ("Fritzy") Giovanelli: Reputed capo in the Genovese crime family; Sal Pisello's partner in a company called Consultants for World Records; convicted killer of New York police detective Anthony Venditti.

Rocco ("Rocky") Musacchia: Reputed member of the Genovese crime family; another of Pisello's partners in Consultants for World Records; the muscle that Morris Levy threatened to apply to John LaMonte; feigned a heart attack on the witness stand during the Vastola trial.

Rudolph ("Rudy") Farone: Reputed Genovese family member and longtime associate of Sal Pisello.

Vincent ("the Chin") Gigante: Boss of the Genovese crime family; Morris Levy's controlling partner in a myriad of business deals over the years, including the MCA cutout sale and, at one time, the Strawberries record store chain.

Dominick ("Baldy Dom") Canterino: Gigante's most trusted capo; presided over a sit-down to settle the dispute between Gaetano Vastola and Morris Levy over the MCA-LaMonte cutout deal.

Joseph ("Joe Piney") Armone: Convicted narcotics trafficker and reputed underboss of the Gambino crime family whose meeting with record promoter Joe Isgro in the lobby of New York's Helmsley Palace hotel sparked the nationwide payola investigation.

THE G-MEN

Marvin Rudnick: Tenacious Organized Crime Strike Force prosecutor who twice convicted Sal Pisello for tax evasion, but ran afoul of his Justice Department superiors when he tried to push the investigation inside the doors of MCA Records.

John Dubois: Strike force colleague and supporter of Rudnick who was in charge of the early stages of the Joe Isgro payola investigation.

Ted Gale: Los Angeles strike force chief who backed the MCA-Pisello investigation in the beginning.

John Newcomer: Gale's successor as strike force chief who backed out of the MCA-Pisello investigation in the end.

Mike Defeo: Deputy chief of the strike force in Washington, D.C.; pulled Rudnick off the payola investigation.

David Margolis: Chief of the strike force in Washington, D.C.; told Rudnick he was becoming "too high-profile" in the Pisello case.

Richard Stavin: Los Angeles strike force prosecutor who was put in charge of the payola investigation after Rudnick's removal; later clashed with Newcomer, Defeo, and Margolis over his investigation of MCA home video president Eugene Giaquinto.

John Mahoney: FBI agent who, with his partner *Jeff Dossett*, convinced John LaMonte to become a protected witness and testify against Morris Levy and Gaetano Vastola.

Bruce Repetto: Federal prosecutor in Newark, New Jersey, who convicted Levy and Vastola; took up Marvin Rudnick's refrain, "How did Sal Pisello wind up inside MCA Records?"

Part I

A SIMPLE TAX CASE

1

"I've got more money than God"

On the morning of April 23, 1983, Irving Azoff was savoring a level of material comfort and professional prestige that few men ever attain, even in Hollywood, where success is measured in exaggerated terms.

Dressed in tennis whites, Azoff was sitting on the veranda of his newly redecorated $2.5 million Beverly Hills mansion overlooking his brand new world-class tennis court equipped with stadium lights for nighttime play. Over his shoulder, he could hear his kitchen staff preparing a nouvelle cuisine brunch that he'd selected from a typed menu of the day. Upstairs, a nanny tended to his two young daughters. Out in front of the house, a team of Japanese gardeners was laying in flower beds along the semicircular driveway, where a charcoal-gray Ferrari crouched behind a Mercedes sedan.

The lord of all he surveyed, Azoff was also attended on this particular morning by a reporter from the *Los Angeles Times*. In the dappled sunlight of the veranda, the reporter scribbled down notes as Azoff sounded off with trademark bravado about the industry that had made him a multimillionaire before his thirtieth birthday.

"It's not the record business anymore, it's the music delivery business," he said. "It's music videos and cassettes and compact discs and even T-shirts. The record companies have to wake up to the fact that the black vinyl disc they've been selling for the last thirty years is a dinosaur, it's history."

At age thirty-five, Azoff was the most successful manager of rock 'n' roll talent in the entertainment industry. The company he'd founded ten years earlier, Front Line Management, guided the careers of some of the most popular recording artists to emerge from the 1970s—the Eagles, Jimmy Buffett, Dan Fogelberg, Boz Scaggs, Steely Dan, Stevie Nicks, and Chicago, among others.

The company's name was derived from Azoff's view that managing artists was like going to war. "Everyone on that side of the line is the enemy, everyone on this side of the line I'll kill for," was how he described his philosophy of doing business. And Azoff, if not a General Patton, was a five-foot-three bespectacled version thereof. What he lacked in physical stature he made up for in aggressiveness and bombast. In the executive suites of the record companies he was renowned for explosive fits of temper that were alternately childish, funny, and frightening, but usually effective.

Even Azoff's enemies—and they were legion—conceded that he was a brilliant negotiator who always got his clients every penny they were worth, and more. For the Eagles, he negotiated what was then the highest royalty rate in the history of the record business—$1.50 per album on the group's fourteen-million-selling *Hotel California* LP.

Front Line's cut of the Eagles alone would have made Azoff a very rich man. "I've got more money than God," he liked to boast. But he'd parlayed the popularity of his talent stable into more than personal wealth—he'd turned it into political power. Taking advantage of post-Watergate election laws that provided candidates with matching public funds for any money raised by benefit concerts, Azoff had enlisted his clients in the reelection campaigns of Senator Alan Cranston and Governor Jerry Brown, both of California. The

Eagles' last concert before they broke up in 1980 was a benefit for Cranston.

With clients capable of raising more than $1 million for a candidate in a single night, Azoff quickly became a Democratic political force in the state. Brown appointed him to the board of one of his pet projects, the California Entertainment Commission. The two men attended a Los Angeles Lakers game together. Senator Edward Kennedy was among the famous and powerful who played tennis at Azoff's house. John McEnroe gave him pointers on his serve.

Azoff had also used his clients as stepping stones into another exclusive club, the Hollywood movie community. Following the phenomenal success of *Saturday Night Fever* and *Grease,* the major film studios had begun a fevered courtship of the music business aimed at marrying their movies to the proven youth market drawing power of rock 'n' roll. One of the first people they went to was Azoff, who soon had movie projects in development—featuring his artists and his name attached as executive producer—with every studio in town. "Irving Azoff is Juggling 10 Pic Prod'n Slate," proclaimed a headline in *Daily Variety.*

The release of *Urban Cowboy* in 1979 firmly established Azoff as a creative and deal-making force to be reckoned with in Hollywood. The movie—which he produced from scratch based on an *Esquire* magazine article—turned out to be a box-office blockbuster. Starring John Travolta, hot on the heels of his *Saturday Night Fever* success, it pulled in more than $50 million for Paramount Pictures and made a star out of its previously unknown female lead, Debra Winger. The *Urban Cowboy* soundtrack album—which Azoff packed with such Front Line artists as the Eagles, Dan Fogelberg, Jimmy Buffett, and Boz Scaggs—sold more than four million copies on Azoff's own Full Moon record label. The album kicked off a cowboy music craze around the country that pumped several hundred million dollars into the record business.

So in April 1983 it would have appeared that Irving Azoff had no worlds left to conquer in show business. But as he sat talking to a reporter over lunch that morning, he was about to make the most ambitious and most fateful move of his career.

The next day, he was appointed president of MCA Records Group and was made a high-ranking vice president of its parent company, MCA, the giant entertainment conglomerate that also owned Universal Studios. The announcement caught the industry by surprise—"the most dramatic boardroom development in the record business in a decade," wrote one Hollywood columnist. Many show business observers predicted the marriage wouldn't last.

Indeed, it was difficult to imagine Azoff—the abrasive, outspoken, free-wheeling counterculture entrepreneur—operating within the gray corporate confines of MCA, where a coat-and-tie dress code remained in effect even for executives of the entertainment divisions, a jarring anomaly in Hollywood. Despite the disparate styles, however, both sides had good reasons for wanting the union.

MCA had long been perceived as the weak sister of the so-called Big Six U.S. record distributors (the others were CBS, Warner Communications, RCA, Capitol-EMI, and Polygram). MCA Records was marginally profitable but it suffered from a severe image problem, that of a loser label, the last name on the list if you were a promising performer shopping for a recording contract. MCA was finding it increasingly difficult to attract new artists and keep its established stars. Neil Diamond, Elton John, and The Who had recently left the label, leaving only Olivia Newton-John and Tom Petty as guaranteed million-plus sellers. Petty had agreed to stay only on the condition that his albums be released on his own vanity label, Backstreet Records. The MCA corporate thought was that if anyone could bring new talent and excitement to the nearly moribund record company, it would be Azoff.

For Azoff, the case for taking the job was equally compelling. Aside from salary and stock compensation amounting to about $1 million a year, it would provide him with a high-profile forum and put him on equal footing with such industry heavyweights as his mentor David Geffen, with whom he competed maniacally, and CBS Records president Walter Yetnikoff, whose reckless style he emulated and whose power he envied.

The way Azoff figured it, the MCA job was virtually a no-risk venture: the record label had been so poorly managed in recent years that anything he did would look good in comparison. Most important, he knew that the parent corporation was gorged with cash from the box-office success of Steven Spielberg's *E.T.: The Extra-Terrestrial* and that MCA's chief executive, Sid Sheinberg, was determined to spend whatever it took to make his record company a competitive force in the industry.

In a sense, Azoff was walking into the best-stocked candy store in Hollywood, and he reveled in the possibilities. As he began assembling his staff to run what he dubbed "the new MCA Records," Azoff's constant refrain was, "We're gonna shake 'em up."

That would turn out to be an understatement.

2

"... a pushing,

screaming,

raving lunatic"

The call came at 8:00 A.M.

As usual, Gene Froelich was already at his desk in MCA's corporate offices, an hour before his secretary and the rest of the staff would arrive. Picking up the receiver, he knew instinctively it was MCA's chief executive, Sid Sheinberg, on the line. Who else in Hollywood would be making calls at that hour of the morning?

"Gene, it's Sid. I just wanted you to know we have a new Records Group president. There'll be an announcement later today. We've hired Irving Azoff."

Froelich was dumbfounded at the news, but he took his cue from Sheinberg and managed to sound upbeat. "Gee, Sid, that's great. He's very bright and certainly has great credibility in the artist community." Privately, Froelich had grave misgivings about Azoff's hiring. He'd been expecting a new Records Group president to be named for the last three months, ever since Sheinberg relieved him of the position after three years at the job. Previously, Froelich had been an MCA corporate vice president and assistant treasurer, known around the company as Sheinberg's fix-it man; some said he was Sheinberg's heir apparent. The Records Group had been losing money and credibility steadily for years when Sid asked him to step in and turn it around. Going in, Froelich had looked at it as a short-term trouble-shooting assignment.

Froelich was not a record man, he was an accountant. His particular area of expertise was corporate acquisitions. But he'd learned a lot about the record business when he oversaw MCA's purchase of ABC Records from its parent corporation, the American Broadcasting Company, in 1979. He didn't like much of what he learned. He thought it was a dirty business—tough to make profitable, easy to lose your shirt in, with huge potential for executive corruption.

ABC proved what Froelich believed. The company had lost more than $100 million in the two years prior to the MCA acquisition. It was a victim of classic record company mismanagement, in Froelich's view—overstaffed and overextended by too many multi-million-dollar contracts with supposed superstars whose records subsequently stiffed. He also saw how ABC had been practically looted by some of its own executives. One former ABC president, Jay Lasker, had negotiated an employment contract that paid him bonuses based on sales. The problem was, the contract defined "sales" as what was manufactured and shipped to the distribution centers, not what was actually sold to consumers. As a result, Lasker pressed records far in excess of any market demand, eventually filling up ABC's own warehouses and having to lease more space from independent distributors, which he paid for by giving the distributors the equivalent in free records. Lasker made a lot of money and ABC ultimately joined the list of entertainment companies that, awash in red ink, abandoned the record business— Paramount, MGM, United Artists, Twentieth Century Fox. In the end, ABC sold its record company to MCA at a fire-sale price of $30 million.

When Froelich took over the MCA Records Group in 1980, he was determined not to make the traditional mistakes. He bore down hard on expenditures such as promotion and advertising, pushed pricing programs aimed at increasing sales of MCA's older catalog product, and resisted getting into expensive bidding wars for big-name acts. He saw the record business as a flat, no-growth prospect throughout the 1980s, and he didn't think smaller record companies like MCA could be profitable operating in the same spendthrift manner as the two industry giants, CBS Records and Warner Communications. The others could afford to take the losses on a $10 million contract with someone like a James Taylor or a Paul Simon—MCA couldn't.

Froelich felt he'd done a good job with the Records Group, taking it from a loss of $10 million in 1979 to profits of $16 million in 1980, $25 million in 1981, and $24 million in 1982, a better showing that year than industry sales leader CBS Records.

Under Froelich, some of MCA's premiere artists—Tom Petty, the Oak Ridge Boys, Barbara Mandrell, and Olivia Newton-John—had scored their biggest successes.

Unfortunately, none of the new artists signed under Froelich had broken through big on the pop charts, so the company's image as a "loser" label hung on.

Part of the image problem may have been Froelich's personal style. In the novelty-driven, oh-so-hip world of the record business, he was an oddball: soft-spoken and serious, with immaculately trimmed gray hair and investment-banker suits. It was impossible to imagine him smoking dope or knocking back shots of Southern Comfort backstage with the Heartbreakers. As such, he was a perfect foil for the creative folks who liked to grumble that "the business has been taken over by the bottom-liners." Froelich just didn't look or sound rock 'n' roll.

Azoff, on the other hand, seemed to personify it. Long-haired and bearded when that was the fashion in the 1970s, he was as colorful and quotable as the acts he managed. If a hotel room was trashed on the concert trail, Azoff was right there joining in the fun, armed with a wad of cash to pay for the damages the next morning. Not surprisingly, his artists loved him, expressing their loyalty in the liner notes of practically every album they released.

Outside the artist community, however, Azoff had a colored reputation. The book on Azoff was that he couldn't be counted on to keep his word. One of his most often quoted sayings—usually uttered with a shrug—was "So I lied. It's rock 'n' roll rules: I win, you lose." He'd even earned the nickname Swerving Irving.

What puzzled Froelich about Azoff's hiring was that Sheinberg knew about his reputation firsthand. Back in 1978, Azoff served as executive producer of the Universal movie *FM*, about a group of

wild and crazy deejays who take over their radio station and do battle with their straight-laced management. Azoff's role was to convince the cream of the rock world to contribute their songs and performances to the movie and its soundtrack album. But two weeks
before *FM* was released, Azoff publicly disavowed the movie, saying "It's not an authentic representation of the music business . . .
it's an AM movie." He also announced that he'd asked to have his
name removed from the film's credits.

FM went on to stiff at the box office and Sheinberg said of Azoff,
"I never want to deal with that guy again."

But now, five years later, here was Sid gushing like a schoolgirl,
giddy over the fact that this same man was in charge of his cherished
record company and was positioned as the fourth-ranked officer in
the parent corporation.

Perhaps he should be relieved, Froelich thought as he hung up
the phone that morning. Ever since he was removed as Records
Group president, he'd been given no new responsibilities, just a big
office, a secretary, and a title. He was a vice president without profile. But with Sid in this state of euphoria, maybe the internal ban-
ishment would finally end.

Still, the whole thing troubled him. In his precise CPA's mind, it
just didn't balance out. There had to be some other set of facts he
didn't know about that was affecting the equation.

Al Bergamo, president of MCA Distributing, the distribution
arm of the record company, got the news about an hour after
Froelich. Bergamo was visibly upset when he called Sam Passamano into his office a few minutes later. "I just got off the phone
with Sheinberg. He hired Irving Azoff to be group president!"
Bergamo practically shouted.

As president of MCA Distributing for six years, Bergamo had
hoped to land the group presidency himself. Sheinberg had hinted
as much to him on several occasions.

Passamano was stunned. Within the company rumor mill, Bergamo had been considered the front-runner ever since Froelich's
ouster. He knew that Al had been angling for the job for more than
a year and may have even contributed to Froelich's demise with his
constant complaints to Sheinberg that all his penny-pinching was
making it impossible for the company to compete in the marketplace.

Passamano and Bergamo held different opinions of Froelich.

Passamano thought he was a brilliant financial manager who'd done the best he could in a thankless job. Gene made the record division profitable, after all, and no one else had managed to do that in a long time. He agreed with Froelich's go-slow approach—that it was better to develop ten new acts than spend $2 million to buy an established one. Most of all, he respected Froelich for his utter lack of Hollywood pretense and for his honesty—rare qualities in the record business. Passamano's only disagreement with Froelich was on the issue of cutouts.

Largely due to the ABC Records acquisition, MCA had a huge backlog of records that had been cut out of the company's sales catalog because they weren't selling. Usually, record companies dispose of their cutout inventory on an annual or a semiannual basis by selling it off in bulk to a network of budget record distributors around the country at severely distressed prices, ranging from ten cents to a dollar a unit. The major record companies sold an estimated two hundred million records a year as cutouts. Because by contract they usually didn't have to pay any artist royalties on this so-called schlock product, companies used the cutout market as a way of recouping manufacturing costs on records they overproduced.

Sam Passamano was in charge of MCA's cutout inventory. In the cutout trade he had a reputation for being scrupulously honest. Some executives who oversaw cutout sales at other companies were known to demand kickbacks of as much as five or ten cents a unit from buyers. That could amount to a small fortune for a corrupt executive on a single sale of a million or more units, which was not uncommon in the business. But the word on Passamano was, "You can't even buy the guy lunch."

Under Passamano and Froelich, MCA's cutouts were sold on the strict basis of sealed bids, with the sale going to the highest per-unit bidder who could handle the largest quantity. There was never any "sweetening," the common practice of mixing in current or non-cutout records—unbeknownst to the artists—as a way of enticing buyers into paying more for a load.

Even with those strict guidelines, Passamano had managed to reduce MCA's cutout inventory from sixteen million after the ABC acquisition down to ten million, at a tidy profit. Now, however, he was having difficulty unloading the remainder at the price Froelich had set—eighty cents apiece.

Froelich was suspicious of the whole cutout business. He knew it was rife with sleazy operators, record counterfeiters, and Mafia types who seemed to make an awful lot of money reselling the supposedly worthless records, most of which wound up back in record store budget bins priced at $2.99 to $3.99. As an accountant, he just couldn't see selling records for less than it cost to manufacture them, which in MCA's case was fifty-seven cents each. He agreed to drop the price of the cutouts to sixty-five cents. Still no sale.

So MCA had more than ten million old records clogging up its warehouses—pallet upon pallet of Guy Lombardo, Lawrence Welk, the Harmonizing Four, the Pilgrim Jubilee Singers.

Whatever their differing views on Froelich, Bergamo and Passamano were of a single mind on his replacement. "Sid's gotta be nuts," said Bergamo. "Azoff doesn't know the first thing about running a record company. I had to deal with the guy a bunch of times when I was with Epic Records and I thought he was a joke—a pushing, screaming, raving lunatic. That's the only side of him I ever saw."

Passamano nodded. He'd dealt with Azoff only once, back in 1978, right after the release of *FM*. The movie was bombing, but the soundtrack album was selling reasonably well for MCA Records. The company had shipped about three hundred thousand copies in the first few weeks of release. But that apparently wasn't good enough for Azoff, who had packed the soundtrack with Front Line artists—Jimmy Buffett, the Eagles, Dan Fogelberg, Boz Scaggs, Steely Dan, Randy Meisner, and Joe Walsh.

"He was nonstop pressure," Passamano recalled. "Calling me everyday, hollering, 'We have to have more product out there, more product, more product.' I tried to explain to him that the market just couldn't handle it, that it wasn't selling through that well, but he didn't give a damn. All he cared about was going gold, then platinum, then double platinum, so he'd look good in *Billboard* magazine. It meant little to him if the company had to take all those records back."

In the case of *FM*, Azoff put so much pressure on MCA that the company eventually shipped more than a million albums into the marketplace, of which nearly half came back unsold. Four years later, when Azoff took over the record company, hundreds of thousands of *FM* albums were still gathering dust with the rest of the cutouts in MCA's warehouses.

Unlike Al Bergamo, Sam Passamano wasn't concerned about losing his job under the new regime. At fifty-five, he'd been with the
company thirty-two years—from Bing Crosby to Oingo Boingo—
and he'd seen a dozen presidents come and go. He'd started out as a
shipping clerk and had worked his way up to become an officer of
the company, executive vice president of MCA Distributing, with a
salary of $2,200 a week. Now his son was following in his footsteps,
only faster—at twenty-six, Sam, Jr., was already director of marketing for the record company.

So Sam Passamano was a company man to the core, a loyal MCA
soldier. MCA had been very good to him over the years and he
couldn't imagine that things would change simply because there
was a new kid in charge of the record division.

Besides, he figured, Sheinberg and Wasserman had to know that
he was greatly responsible for the recent profits at the Records
Group. He was the one who'd come up with the idea of taking all
MCA's older million-selling albums by Elton John, The Who,
Olivia Newton-John, and the like, putting them together in a new
line called Platinum Plus, and offering them at the reduced price of
$5.98 retail, $3.21 wholesale. As a result of that move, sales of those
albums had skyrocketed. For the last three years the Platinum Plus
line had accounted for about 35 percent of all MCA's record sales.
Passamano considered it the crowning achievement of his career.
Froelich had rewarded him with shares of MCA stock that would be
worth nearly $500,000 when it became fully vested in two years. So
he wasn't worried about job security.

As he sat in Bergamo's office that day, Passamano remembered
one more indirect encounter he'd had with Azoff. He'd never mentioned it to Al before because it had seemed like no big deal at the
time. One morning back in January or February, Froelich came into
his office with a puzzled look on his face. "I just had a call from Irving Azoff at Front Line Management and he said that he and his
partner, Sam Nassi, were interested in buying our cutouts. He
wants us to send the inventory list to Nassi's office."

Like Froelich, Passamano thought it was odd that Azoff would be
interested in cutouts, or that he would be in business with Nassi, a
coarse, cigar-chomping Beverly Hills businessman who'd made
millions buying and selling the product inventories of companies
going out of business. Known as "the King of the Liquidators,"

Nassi had recently disposed of a fleet of DeLorean cars he'd purchased in that company's bankruptcy.

Still, Passamano wasn't about to question anyone's interest in buying MCA's cutouts. He sent the list to Nassi's office, quoting sixty-five cents a unit. Apparently Azoff and Nassi thought the price was too high, since Passamano never heard anything from them.

On April 26, 1983, three days after Azoff's appointment, all the MCA Records Group vice presidents and department heads were gathered in the conference room just off Gene Froelich's old office for what would be their first and only full staff meeting with the new president.

Azoff walked in wearing casual slacks and an open-neck sport shirt—in contrast to the white shirts, suits, and ties around the oval conference table. Most of those present knew him only by reputation or from terse, unpleasant telephone conversations. For them, discovering the physical presence behind the legend was a bit like pulling back the curtain and finding a gnome at the controls of the Great Oz. "He's even shorter than me," thought Sam Passamano, who was five-foot-five and had pictured Azoff as being at least six feet tall, judging from the power of his vocal cords.

Azoff quickly launched into a spirited pep talk about how the new MCA Records was going to shake up the industry. He told them that, with their help, he was going to turn the label into a serious competitor, no more "that joke of a record company in the Valley that nobody wants to sign with."

He told them exactly what they wanted to hear—that he was very pleased with the caliber of executives already in place, that there would be no major staff changes, that their jobs were safe.

He was swerving again. Within a year, most of them would be gone.

3

The "Food Consultant"

In the fall of 1983, federal authorities in Los Angeles began picking up information that Salvatore James Pisello—date of birth May 17, 1922, aka Sal the Baker, Sal the Swindler, and Big Sal—was back in town.

Considered by law enforcement agencies on both coasts to be an accomplished con artist and high-ranking soldier in the Gambino crime family of New York, Pisello had disappeared from Los Angeles four years earlier while being investigated by a task force of FBI, IRS, and Drug Enforcement Administration agents for suspected heroin trafficking.

On the legitimate side, Pisello was in the food business. Over the years, he'd owned a couple of restaurants, which had burned down under suspicious circumstances. He was also a food importer-exporter. In 1972, he'd proposed a plan to a group of Maine farmers, bankers, and state officials to fatten and export two hundred thousand head of cattle to Italy for the purpose of introducing a new kind of veal to Europe. The proposal prompted a summit meeting of investigators from the New York State Police, the U.S. Customs Service, the New England Organized Crime Intelligence Division, the Bureau of Narcotics and Dangerous Drugs, and the Securities and Exchange Commission. Noting that Pisello had recently been tracked by the Italian National Police traveling through Europe in the company of two Sicilian Mafia drug lords, the investigators concluded that Pisello had ulterior motives for the veal-exporting plan that would not be in the interest of the state of Maine. The Italian authorities didn't care much for Pisello's plan, either. They refused to let him bring the cattle into the country.

According to government records, in 1979, Pisello had approached Marianno ("Marty") Antoci, the owner of the Fulton Fish Market in West Los Angeles, with a plan to use his store as a cover for importing narcotics from Italy in airline-safe lobster tanks. Frightened at the idea, Antoci went to the authorities and agreed to cooperate in a sting operation to nab Pisello. He was given $15,000 in cash to set up the drug deal. He gave the money to Pisello, but Pisello never delivered the drugs. Instead, he pocketed the cash and disappeared, leaving the task force frustrated and embarrassed. They'd been taken by Sal the Swindler.

The case was turned over to the IRS, which quickly ascertained that Pisello had filed only four personal tax returns between 1965 and 1979 and had paid a total of only $2,500 in taxes during that time. But with Pisello nowhere to be found, the IRS investigation languished. Now that Pisello had returned to the city, official interest in the investigation was rekindled.

Why would Pisello return to Los Angeles, where he knew the authorities were probably looking for him? Sal supposedly was working as a $500-a-week "food consultant" for the Oh Boy Pizza chain in the San Fernando Valley. That couldn't be it. Pisello was a reputed money-maker for the mob, and he loved the good life. He drove a Cadillac and had a charge account at the most exclusive men's store in Beverly Hills. He gave Piaget watches to girlfriends as presents. Hell, $500 was Sal's daily walking-around money.

No, it had to be something else, something very big that had brought him back to town. Something too good to pass up, or perhaps an assignment he couldn't refuse.

What the government would eventually discover was that Sal

Pisello was now working in the record business, earning a high-six-figure income operating out of Irving Azoff's new MCA Records.

That revelation would prove Pisello's undoing and kick off one of the most embarrassing scandals in the history of the record business.

4

*"Either
I win,
or I win"*

When Irving Azoff took over MCA Records, the music business was just starting to emerge from a devastating four-year slump. Prior to 1979, the industry had enjoyed a twenty-year period of uninterrupted growth—annual sales ballooned from less than $1 billion to more than $4 billion. The increases had been so steep and so steady that many record executives had come to believe their industry was recession proof—like the liquor business. Then the bottom fell out. Sales plummeted nearly 20 percent between 1979 and 1982.

Consumer researchers said it was because the baby boomers—now in their late twenties to early thirties—were buying refrigerators and baby carriages, while teenagers—a rapidly declining segment of the overall population—were spending more of their limited income on the newest entertainment craze, video games. To hear the record companies tell it, just about everyone in the country was either taping borrowed records at home or buying counterfeit copies at the record stores. Music critics complained that the record companies were simply putting out crummy records that nobody wanted to hear.

Whatever the reasons for the dramatic downturn, it caught the major companies unawares. Coming off a banner year in 1978, when sales hit an all-time high of $4.1 billion, they were spending money like the sultan of Brunei on a Beverly Hills bender. The *Saturday Night Fever* soundtrack had sold more than twenty million copies, and *Grease* and Fleetwood Mac's *Rumors* had each sold more than twelve million. A dozen other albums had sold more than five million copies each. Gold or platinum record certifications were no big deal anymore. Now it was megaplatinum. The Recording Industry Association of America [RIAA], a trade group funded by the major record labels, was even toying with the idea of establishing a new certification for sales of more than ten million copies—a titanium record?

Convinced that the good times would continue to roll in 1979, the big companies handed out huge advances on recording contracts and shoveled more and more copies of each new record into the marketplace. Initial pressings and shippings of a million units of a record were not uncommon, so confident were the companies that buyer demand would be there.

By mid-1980, however, their warehouses were filled with untold millions of returned records and their financial statements reflected frightening losses. They quickly began slashing costs through massive staff layoffs, deep cuts in artist rosters, and branch office closings. CBS Records shut down half its manufacturing plants and let go nearly two thousand employees between 1980 and 1982. CBS Records president Walter Yetnikoff diagnosed the industry as "in the intensive care ward."

Only the strongest companies survived the carnage, saved by the deep pockets of the entertainment conglomerates that owned them. A number of once-prominent independent record labels went under, including Georgia-based Capricorn Records, which had pioneered Southern rock with the Allman Brothers and Marshall Tucker bands, and RSO Records, which had released both *Saturday Night Fever* and *Grease* just two years earlier. Other independents were forced by falling sales to give over their distribution to the bigger firms—they could no longer afford to maintain large distribution staffs and branch office operations. A&M Records, which recorded such 1970s superstars as Peter Frampton and the Carpenters, joined RCA. So did Arista Records, home of Barry Manilow. Chrysalis Records went to CBS. Casablanca Records, which exploded onto the scene in the late 1970s with Donna Summer, the Village People, and Kiss, disappeared into European-owned Polygram, itself staggering from $200 million in losses since entering the U.S. market ten years earlier.

When it was all over, the landscape of the record industry was radically altered. Six companies now controlled nearly 90 percent of the record distribution in the United States. A group of about twelve men—chief executives of the major labels—was effectively deciding what music would be recorded, promoted, and distributed to the American public. The number of new recordings released by the major labels had dropped from more than four thousand in 1978 to about two thousand in 1982.

Of the Big Six, CBS and Warner were dominant, accounting for 45 percent of all record sales between them. Another 39 percent of sales was roughly equally divided among RCA, Capitol-EMI, and Polygram. That left MCA, the littlest of the big guys, with about 6 percent of record sales in the country.

In his announced plan to make MCA a serious competitor to CBS and Warner within five years, Azoff had his work cut out for him. Prevailing wisdom in the industry was that it couldn't be done, and certainly not within Azoff's time frame.

But Azoff wasn't one to be daunted by a David-and-Goliath undertaking. He'd come of age with the record business. Born in Chicago, where the Beatles first bounded off a plane in America in 1964, he started booking and managing local bands in high school in Danville, Illinois. In 1970, he dropped out of the University of Illinois and went to Los Angeles with his college roommate, a wispy-voiced singer-songwriter named Dan Fogelberg. Brash and cocky, Azoff talked his way into a job working for a talent agency owned by rock wunderkind David Geffen, who also owned a hot new company, Asylum Records, that had recently signed Jackson Browne, Joni Mitchell, Linda Ronstadt, and a fledgling group called the Eagles.

When Azoff left the Geffen organization three years later, he took Fogelberg and the Eagles with him as clients at Front Line Management. At that time, the Eagles had released two moderately successful albums. By 1976, under Azoff's tutelage, they were the most successful rock group in America, and one of the most critically acclaimed. Other clients began lining up at Front Line's door as Azoff's reputation grew as a man who recognized talent and could exploit it to its maximum earning potential.

During his fifteen-year career in the music business, Irving Azoff had not known failure, and he wasn't about to learn now. "Either I win, or I win," he liked to say.

During the early months of the Azoff regime, the mood inside MCA Records was schizophrenic. Some of the younger staffers, like Sam Passamano, Jr., were excited at the prospect of the hip young leader bringing some badly needed excitement to the company. They were embarrassed working for MCA, the Music Cemetery of America, as the joke went. They were frustrated from years of having to promote the disappointing results of the artists signed by top executives and then getting blamed when the records bombed. It seemed that too many creative decisions were made by the distribution side of the company, where middle-aged managers toiled away on pricing programs aimed at squeezing sales out of albums released in the 1970s by artists who didn't even record for the company anymore—Elton John, The Who, Neil Diamond. Middle-aged acts, yesterday's news.

In the view of this group of employees, Azoff blew in like a breath of fresh air. He was a dynamo: walking through the hallways at all hours of the day and night—fresh off an airplane from somewhere, dragging his luggage along behind; handling eighty to ninety phone calls a day from people ranging from Walter Yetnikoff to Jerry Brown; entertaining reporters with outrageous bon mots and off-the-record industry gossip, issuing directives from the phone in his car cruising down Benedict Canyon on the way to the office. Azoff brought a new looseness to the traditionally stuffy operation.

Some of the older executives found that looseness disturbing, however. They weren't amused by the new president running through the office dressed in a red hood and squirting people with a water machine gun or his returning from lunch with several of his new hires in the legal department one day, laughing about having thrown eggs at cars. One of Azoff's bright new promotion men regularly walked through the office loudly exhorting his staff, including several sixty-year-old secretaries, "Fuck 'em up the ass and make 'em bleed."

This was what Sheinberg and Wasserman were paying a million a year for?

The old guard was also troubled by the deals Azoff was making. In his first month on the job, he signed Joan Jett to a recording contract. The twenty-three-year-old former leader of the all-girl rock band the Runaways, Jett was a legitimate signing. Her most recent solo album, *I Love Rock 'n' Roll*, had sold more than a million copies for Boardwalk Records. Still, some people at MCA thought Azoff paid far too much to get her—$4.5 million for three albums, with $3 million of that up front.

Azoff also paid dearly for Barry Gibb. As a member of the BeeGees, Gibb had played a hand in what was then the most successful album in history, *Saturday Night Fever.* As an untried solo artist, however, he was a gamble, especially at $2.5 million for two albums, with $1.5 million in advance. Triumph, a moderately successful heavy metal band from Canada, received $3 million for the rights to its four previous albums on another label plus a new one to be recorded for MCA. Azoff chose Triumph over the well-known female duo Heart, which was shopping for a recording contract at the time.

Azoff likewise spent a fortune acquiring executives from other record companies, often paying them double their previous salaries. He hired Richard Palmese away from Arista and made him senior vice president of promotion at $250,000 a year—as much as the presidents of some bigger labels. When Nashville record producer Jimmy Bowen was hired to head up MCA's country music division, Azoff gave him $250,000 a year plus a $1 million lump payment for Bowen's claimed rights to the master recordings of the First Edition, a folk-rock group of the mid-1960s that featured then-unknown Kenny Rogers. The $1 million was in effect a signing bonus for Bowen, since the First Edition's old records were moving slowly on the cutout market at ninety-nine cents, making the masters next to worthless.

Azoff made one deal in June 1983 that was widely regarded in the industry as a shrewd move. He signed a distribution agreement with Motown Records, the Detroit-based company that exploded onto the music scene in the 1960s with the Supremes, the Temptations, the Four Tops, Stevie Wonder, and Smokey Robinson and the Miracles. The acquisition of Motown's distribution gave MCA a strong presence in the black music field, which it never had before, and it immediately doubled MCA's share of U.S. record sales to about 12 percent. Motown was considered a plum, the last of the independently distributed major labels, and it was expected to do well in the coming year with new albums from Stevie Wonder and Lionel Richie.

But some of those inside MCA who were familiar with the terms of the Motown contract saw it as another Azoff giveaway. For one thing, it called for MCA to receive a distribution fee of only 16 percent of sales, whereas the industry standard was anywhere from 20 percent to 30 percent. MCA figured that it cost about 8 percent of sales to distribute its own records. So the company would net only 8 percent on Motown, and out of that it would have to deduct the cost of twenty or so new salespeople to handle the Motown product, plus office space, plus the $5 million that Azoff advanced to Motown upon signing the agreement. MCA would do well if it broke even on the Motown deal.

The most troubling aspect of the agreement—to Froelich at least—was that it allowed Motown to continue manufacturing its own records. Before Azoff came on board, MCA had had several discussions with Motown about taking over the company's distribution, but the negotiations always broke down over the issue of manufacturing. Motown insisted on pressing its own records, but Froelich flatly refused, arguing that if MCA was going to take over distribution, it should be in control of how much product went out into the market in the first place.

Froelich had reasons to be wary of Motown. There were serious questions about product security at the company. Motown subcontracted much of its record and cassette manufacturing to small independent plants, several of which were suspected by the FBI of back-dooring Motown product—that is, secretly manufacturing more than they'd contracted for and selling the excess for cash.

Froelich was also aware that Motown's president, Jay Lasker, had a reputation for playing fast and loose with product when he had been president of ABC Records. Froelich knew about the warehouses full of leftover ABC recordings the auditors found after MCA bought ABC in 1979—Sam Passamano was still trying to unload that stuff on the cutout market.

Azoff apparently didn't share the previous administration's concern about Motown. On June 30, MCA issued a press release that began, "In a dramatic move in which two towers of strength in the record industry have joined forces, Motown and MCA have reached an accord whereby MCA will exclusively distribute all Motown product in the U.S. effective immediately."

"It's a license to steal," Froelich thought when he learned the details of the distribution agreement. He was glad he had nothing to do with the record division anymore. He sensed trouble ahead.

Sam Passamano got his first hint of things to come when he was called to a meeting in Azoff's office on June 1, 1983. Al Bergamo was there, along with Myron Roth, Azoff's newly hired executive vice president and right-hand man. Also present were Sam Nassi and a man named Fred Tarter. Azoff announced that Nassi and Tarter, through a New York company they owned called Deerfield Communications, were going to take more than nine million cutouts off MCA's hands at a price of thirty-five cents a unit. MCA would get $250,000 in cash and the balance—about $2.9 million— would be in the form of "barter credits" on an array of products and services that Deerfield could provide through its other barter clients.

Deerfield billed itself as an "inventory asset management firm." What it did was buy one manufacturer's excess inventory—its cutouts—for a combination of cash and credit on other manufacturers' excess inventories. Deerfield arranged trades of companies' unsold goods.

The MCA-Deerfield deal was done, Azoff said; Sheinberg had already approved it. The only thing to be worked out was exactly how MCA would utilize its barter credits.

Passamano was taken aback by the announcement and a little pissed off. He was supposed to be in charge of cutouts, but he wasn't even consulted on this. And it was a very unusual deal. Even though record companies normally didn't have to pay artist royalties on records sold as cutouts, they still had to pay a reduced royalty to the music publishing companies that own the copyrights to the songs performed on the records. The reduced royalty usually amounted to only a few cents per record, but those pennies added up when you were unloading nine million records. At best, the $250,000 would barely cover it.

What's more, as far as Passamano could tell, Deerfield didn't have anything that MCA needed in the way of barter goods. "Barter at thirty-five cents is zero if they don't have anything we can use," he complained to Bergamo after the meeting. "What are we gonna do with Air Florida tickets? We don't even have a branch office in Florida. With the cost of handling this stuff in the warehouse, we're losing money. We'd be better off digging a big hole and burying it."

The whole deal smelled badly to Passamano, especially since he knew that Azoff and closeout king Sam Nassi had been trying to buy the same cutouts themselves just four months earlier. The asking price then was sixty-five cents a unit. Now Azoff was selling them to his friend Nassi for next to nothing.

Neither Passamano nor Bergamo objected strongly to the Deerfield sale, however. Not to Azoff anyway. With all the new people he was bringing in, they didn't feel it was a good time to challenge the new boss, especially over something as inconsequential as cutouts. Besides, they were damn glad to get rid of the stuff.

By the fall of 1983, Al Bergamo could see there was little future for him at the company. He was still head of MCA Distributing, holding the title of president. But Azoff had gone to Sid Sheinberg in August and convinced the chief executive that the distribution company should no longer report its profit and losses separately but they should all be lumped together with operations of the record label—artist acquisitions, marketing, promotion, and so on.

It was a slick maneuver on Azoff's part. Distribution had long been the most profitable division of the Records Group. Now those profits would be reflected on the bottom line of the record label, helping offset any losses there. Azoff made it known that, in his words, "I'm the only president around here." So Bergamo's title meant nothing. The power in the company had shifted completely to the record label side, where Azoff had assembled a new team of vice presidents whose loyalty was to Azoff, not MCA. The new team included the following men:

• Myron Roth, formerly a business affairs attorney for CBS Records, now second in command at the label, the man charged with putting into effect whatever plans the boss came up with. "Take care of it, Myron, make it work," was Azoff's refrain.

• Richard Palmese, a rumpled, overweight, former Jesuit seminarian who'd made a reputation in the industry by promoting records the old-fashioned way—he threw parties with plenty of pretty girls and free refreshments. Palmese brought along Harold Sulman, his immediate subordinate at Arista Records.

• Zach Horowitz, an idealistic young lawyer brought in by Roth from CBS. Now vice president of business and legal affairs.

• Larry Solters, for years Azoff's public relations chief and all-around errand boy at Front Line Management. More than a loyal retainer, Solters was practically a cult devotee of Azoff. He supposedly once took a copy of a Hollywood trade magazine that contained an unflattering item on his boss, set it on fire and jumped up and down on it. Now Azoff was rewarding him with the title of Vice President of Artist Development.

In addition to this group, two holdovers from the previous administration seemed to have been picked to play on the new team—Dan McGill, the tight-fisted controller who scrutinized executive expense accounts with the zeal of an IRS auditor bucking for a promotion, and John Burns, the vice president of MCA Distributing who was looking more and more like Bergamo's soon-to-be successor.

Bergamo was particularly rankled because he was increasingly being asked to report to Myron Roth, a man he supposedly outranked in the corporation. It was a frustrating, humiliating situation.

In late October 1983, Roth instructed Bergamo to set up a meeting with Joe Robinson, the president of Sugar Hill Records, a small, New Jersey label whose rhythm and blues–flavored dance records appealed to a largely urban black audience. Roth said MCA wanted to acquire Sugar Hill's distribution, and Bergamo should work out the details of an agreement.

Bergamo was less than enthusiastic about Sugar Hill. He'd researched the company several years earlier for a possible distribution deal and wasn't impressed with what he'd found. Sugar Hill was owned by Robinson and his wife, Sylvia, formerly of the singing duo Mickey and Sylvia, whose only hit was "Love Is Strange." The Robinsons' previous company, All-Platinum Records, had gone into bankruptcy in the mid-1970s in the midst of a Newark federal grand jury investigation into payola practices in the industry. Joe Robinson ultimately was convicted of tax evasion in that investigation and paid a fine.

The Robinsons started Sugar Hill in 1979 with financial backing from Morris Levy, the owner of New York–based Roulette Records and a legendary figure in the recording industry. Levy was one of the pioneers of the music business, formerly owner of the famous Broadway jazz club Birdland and a patron of the careers of such jazz greats as Dizzy Gillespie, Count Basie, Duke Ellington, and George Shearing, who wrote "Lullaby of Birdland" in honor of the club. Levy was a friend of Frank Sinatra and Bob Hope, Francis Cardinal Spellman and Israeli prime minister Menachem Begin, CBS Records president Walter Yetnikoff and Atlantic Records vice chairman Sheldon Vogel. He'd also been friends with a number of notorious mobsters over the years. He once owned the dominant cutout record distributorship in the country, Promo Records, in partnership with Thomas ("Tommy Ryan") Eboli, the boss of New York's Genovese crime family until he was gunned down gangland-style on a Brooklyn street in 1972.

In the recording industry, as well as in law enforcement circles, Morris Levy was considered to be "mobbed up," inextricably linked with the underworld. Because Sugar Hill Records president Joe Robinson was inextricably linked with Levy, some in the record business held a similar view of him. In fact, Robinson was a tough customer in his own right. Physically imposing at well over six feet and 200 pounds, he was known in earlier years to carry a gun (not a common practice among record executives) and, according to one New Jersey newspaper report, was rumored to have once been involved in the Harlem numbers racket—though Robinson denied it. No matter. When CBS Records looked into the possibility of taking on Sugar Hill's distribution in 1983, one CBS executive argued against the deal by opining in a memo that Sugar Hill was "the Black Mafia."

Bergamo's dim view of Sugar Hill was based more on bottom-line considerations, however. The company had enjoyed a splash of success in 1981 and 1982 with several records—*Rapper's Delight* by the Sugar Hill Gang and *Funk You Up* by Grandmaster Melle Mel and the Furious 5—that featured a new kind of fast talk-and-rhythm music that became known as rap. But although Sugar Hill had pioneered the growing trend to rap music, from what Bergamo could see the company was not in good shape financially. Its sales were running at about $2 million a year and its independent distributors claimed they were owed more than $500,000 from advances they'd given Robinson. Sugar Hill said it held the rights to the old Checker Records and Chess Records master recordings of such blues and early rock 'n' roll legends as Muddy Waters, Howlin' Wolf, and Chuck Berry. But in the tangle of bankruptcy litigation and tax liens that lay behind the company, it was difficult to determine exactly who owned what.

Bergamo knew that Robinson had been shopping around for a distribution deal for some time and had recently been turned down by Capitol-EMI. He'd probably take whatever was offered. Bergamo felt his main responsibility was to keep MCA clear of any hidden financial entanglements Sugar Hill might have.

The first official negotiating session took place in Bergamo's office during the first week of November 1983. John Burns and Zach Horowitz were there, and Azoff sat in briefly. Joe Robinson was accompanied by a tall, distinctly Italian-looking man in his early sixties whom he introduced as Sal Pisello. "He represents me," Robinson said. "He's here to make sure I don't do a bad deal." During the course of the meeting it became apparent to everyone that Pisello didn't know diddley about the record business. His presence was both baffling and unsettling. With his rough-and-tumble speech, expensive silk suit, and $200 shoes he came across like a character straight out of *The Godfather*. At one point, Bergamo asked him, half-jokingly, "Are you Mafia, Sal? Have you ever broken anyone's legs?" There was nervous laughter around the room. Horowitz almost fell out of his chair at the question. Pisello laughed, too, but didn't answer.

Gradually, an agreement was hammered out. It was to be a straight pressing and distribution deal. MCA would get a fee of 25 percent of gross sales. MCA would not accept any returns on previously manufactured Sugar Hill records. MCA would advance Sugar Hill no money to sign artists or produce records. That way, if Sugar Hill went under, MCA would be out only the manufacturing costs on the records it pressed. And those losses would be collateralized by the rights to the Checker/Chess master recordings. It was a safe deal, Bergamo thought. MCA probably wouldn't make much money, but it certainly wouldn't lose any either.

Several weeks after the agreement was signed, Pisello asked Bergamo to lunch at the Palm, a pricey show business hangout in West Hollywood where Pisello was treated with a deference that included a reserved table near the front of the restaurant. The stated purpose of the lunch was to discuss the schedule for releasing Sugar Hill's upcoming albums, but the conversation never got around to that. Pisello first chatted idly about his love of good food and how he liked to cook gourmet Italian dishes for special guests at the Los Angeles restaurant he once owned, Roma di Notte on La Cienega Boulevard. He steered the discussion into the record business by saying he was part owner of a record-pressing plant in South Los Angeles. He wondered if MCA might be interested in having his plant press some of the Sugar Hill records. "No way," said Bergamo. "We never go outside for manufacturing, for security reasons."

Pisello finally got around to what Bergamo suspected was the real reason for the lunch. There was a problem with the MCA–Sugar Hill distribution deal, Pisello said. Sugar Hill owed Morris Levy $1 million on the Checker/Chess masters, and unless MCA paid off the indebtedness the deal could fall through. If Bergamo could convince MCA to pay Levy, "I'll take care of you," Pisello said.

It sounded to Bergamo like he was being offered a bribe. "This guy's poking around our underbelly trying to find someone who'll play ball with him," he thought. "He figures I'm a likely candidate because my name ends with a vowel."

Bergamo was furious that Levy's security interest had not been mentioned before. The deal was done, it was collateralized by those masters and now he was hearing for the first time that Sugar Hill didn't hold clear title to them. He told Pisello he thought it was a material breach of the contract, that he never would have made the deal if he'd known the masters were encumbered. He left without finishing his meal.

Back at MCA, Bergamo immediately told Roth what had transpired at lunch. "They sandbagged us. I think we should get out right now," he said. To his amazement, Roth didn't seem at all upset about the $1 million. He waved the whole issue aside disinterestedly, mumbling something to the effect that, "We'll cross that bridge when we come to it."

In early December 1983, Pisello threw a dinner party for MCA executives at the Palm. Roth, Horowitz, Burns, and McGill were among those who attended the dinner to celebrate the Sugar Hill agreement. Pisello brought a date, a busty blonde showgirl type who was half his age.

Bergamo didn't go to the dinner. By that time he'd had enough. He asked MCA to buy him out of his employment contract, which ran until October 1984. The company offered to pay him half his salary if he resigned, but Bergamo refused. Instead, he just stopped going to the office. For the next ten months, he played golf and collected his full salary—$180,000—while John Burns took over his job.

Bergamo wouldn't find out until two years later—when he was being questioned by a federal prosecutor—that the MCA–Sugar Hill distribution agreement he signed with Roth and Azoff in November 1983 was a sham.

5

"I don't want
to go down
for this"

I n 1983, all Irving Azoff really wanted for Christmas was a big hit to close out his rookie year. He'd spent a fortune in his eight months at MCA, but the label had scored only one bona fide hit album. *Reach the Beach,* by the rock group The Fixx, sold more than one million copies, but since the group was signed and the album was recorded under Froelich's tenure, Azoff couldn't take credit.

As Azoff's first major artist signing, Joan Jett was seen as a real test of the new administrations's effectiveness. Her debut MCA album, titled simply *Album,* was released in the final weeks of the year, just in time for the big Christmas selling season. To ensure the record's success, Richard Palmese hired a network of high-powered independent record promoters around the country to hype it to program directors at key radio stations and convince them to add it to their playlists. Anticipating widespread airplay and subsequent strong consumer demand, John Burns shipped more than 500,000 copies into the marketplace, enough to assure the record would be certified gold by the RIAA.

But *Album* turned out to be a financial and psychological disaster for the company. It sold only about 300,000 copies, a fraction of Jett's previous album's sales. Nearly that number of copies came back to MCA unsold. Considering that Jett had been paid $3 million in advance for the record, it was an embarrassing black eye for Azoff and crew.

When MCA's 1983 annual report came out, it showed a loss of $7 million for the Records Group—a $31 million turnaround from the previous year, when Froelich had guided the group to profits of $24 million.

The annual report told only part of the story, however. The group's year-end results included an estimated $8 million in earnings from the distribution of Motown, which had a phenomenal year in 1983, with sales of about $100 million. Also included were approximately $5 million from MCA's music publishing division and a like amount from the distribution of MCA's home video products, which was handled by MCA Distributing for a 20 percent fee. None of those figures was broken out in the annual report. Had they been, simple subtraction would have shown that MCA Records lost more like $25 million in 1983, its worst performance ever.

Still, the view in the record industry in 1984 was that Azoff had at least begun to turn the company into a player. With the kind of money he was putting out, MCA was becoming more appealing to recording artists and their managers and lawyers. He had signed two promising new rock acts, New Edition and Night Ranger, and an up-and-coming country singer named Reba McEntire. He was negotiating with Boston, a rock group whose 1977 debut album sold nearly seven million copies. Boston was technically under contract to CBS for its long-awaited third album, but the group was locked in a bitter legal battle with the label over back royalties and was suing for breach of its contract. CBS was suing back. In entering negotiations with the group prior to a settlement of the lawsuits, Azoff was going head to head with CBS chief Walter Yetnikoff. If nothing else, he was making MCA Records more interesting to watch.

The coming year also held promise for the company. Barry Gibb was in the studio finishing up his debut solo album, which was due out in the summer. If a little of that BeeGee magic remained, the album might reach platinum status. Olivia Newton-John, MCA's longtime pop mainstay, was working on the follow-up to her 1982 six-million-seller, *Physical.* Only an act of God could keep Olivia's next release from going over a million units. Tom Petty and the Heartbreakers also were due to deliver an album, already two years in the making. Azoff had been hanging out with Petty in the recording studio, apparently shoring up the label's historically strained relations with the rock star. Azoff also had made a deal for MCA to release the soundtrack to an upcoming Eddie Murphy movie called *Beverly Hills Cop.* With Murphy's box office appeal and Azoff's track record for putting together soundtracks—*FM, Urban Cowboy,* and *Fast Times at Ridgemont High*—the *Beverly Hills Cop* album might prove to be a sleeper hit.

Through his longstanding relationships with the Hollywood trade press and entertainment reporters around the country, Azoff was able to put his own spin on the state-of-MCA-Records story. In interviews, he stressed that the company was in the midst of a difficult and necessarily expensive period of rebuilding. "We were forced to be aggressive," he told the *Los Angeles Times.* "We had to rebuild this company the way George Allen used to put together football teams. We were forced to beg, borrow, and steal because we had nothing to release, an empty schedule. When I first came here we went for two and a half months without releasing a record."

He took every opportunity to blame the poor showing in 1983 on the previous administration. "My first six months here were spent kicking myself and saying I never would have taken this job if I had known it was this bad," he said. "As bad as I thought it was beforehand, I had no idea."

He scoffed at rumors that his free spending and poor sales had put him in the doghouse with chief executive Sheinberg, challenging, "Check with Sid." Sheinberg backed him up. "I think Irving and his staff have done an incredible job," he said. "I'm thrilled with the way things are going."

Veterans inside MCA Records hooted at that one. Sheinberg could read a balance sheet as well as anyone, but what else could he say publicly—"Oops, looks like I screwed up?" His credibility was on the line, too. Azoff was his hand-picked boy. Sid had convinced MCA chairman Lew Wasserman, who had little interest in the

record business, that MCA Records could be to the music industry
what Universal Studios was to the film industry, and that Azoff was
the man who could make it happen.

Sheinberg had something to prove with the new MCA Records.
In 1978, under his direction, MCA had launched a New York–based
label called Infinity Records, which, Sheinberg predicted, was
going to put the company's record division at the forefront of the
industry. Eighteen months, $25 million, and zero hit records later,
Wasserman ordered him to shut the label down.

The Infinity fiasco was a personal defeat for Sheinberg, a man of
no small ego. Industry insiders still chuckle about the time Infinity
president Ron Alexenburg—Sheinberg's man—signed a deal to
release an album of music by Pope John Paul II just prior to the
pontiff's first visit to America. MCA shipped a million copies of
John Paul II, which turned out to be all in Polish. It reportedly
moved like gangbusters in the Polish-speaking neighborhoods of
Milwaukee, Detroit, and Chicago, but three-fourths of the copies
still came back to MCA unsold.

After Infinity, Sheinberg wasn't about to admit to Wasserman
and the rest of the industry that he'd made a mistake with Azoff.
He still believed that Infinity would have worked if only Lew
hadn't pulled the plug too soon. So despite the 1983 losses and over
the objections of some executives in MCA's corporate financial
department, the money kept flowing to the record label in 1984.
Azoff seemed to be able to get anything he wanted from Sheinberg,
including $750,000 to decorate a new suite of offices for himself and
his team of executives. The president's quarters included a conference room with an immense stone conference table, a mirrored bar,
and a private bathroom with a full shower and gold-plated fixtures.
Neither Wasserman nor Sheinberg had a private bathroom in their
offices on the fifteenth floor of the Black Tower, as MCA's corporate
office building is commonly called. But across the lot at the record
company, Richard Palmese now had one in his.

The new executive suite was dubbed the Taj Mahal by the longtime employees, who were separated from the inner sanctum by
heavy glass doors. Outside the doors, the atmosphere in the office
was charged with fear and loathing as, one by one, veteran department heads and vice presidents were either fired or quit in frustration—Vince Duffy in purchasing, Joan Bullard in publicity, George
Osaki in creative services, Vince Cosgrave in marketing, Pat Pippilo

and practically his entire promotion staff. Sam Passamano had been stripped of all his responsibilities in the distribution company and placed in charge of putting together a new budget line of records that would sell for $1.50 wholesale, a lowly task for a man with his title and experience. Passamano wasn't even in charge of selling cutouts anymore. For reasons that no one clearly understood, Myron Roth had turned that responsibility over to Sal Pisello, who'd become a fixture in the office since the Sugar Hill agreement was signed.

Pisello's presence was a puzzlement to most people on the staff. He wasn't an MCA Records employee, yet he was in the office almost every day, usually arriving around 8:30, before anyone else, to use the phone in any open, unoccupied office. He was outgoing, charming, and deferential to the secretaries, whom he cajoled into taking phone messages for him, handling his mail, and even typing occasional letters. But he was a little too friendly with everyone, overly familiar, given to shouting greetings across the office, "Hey, Myron, how's it going?" No one else did that. Nor did they breeze in and out of Roth's office the way Sal did. He had complete run of the place, which was unique for a nonemployee. Artist managers and even Motown executives weren't allowed to come and go as freely as Pisello. They had to call ahead for an appointment, they couldn't just come in and hang out.

Pisello was comical in a way—always elegantly attired in hand-tailored suits from Bijan's, an ultra-exclusive, appointment-only men's clothier on Rodeo Drive, but still carrying the unmistakable cachet of a hustler up from the mean streets of Brooklyn. He wore a diamond ring so large that the standing joke around the office was, "Do you shake Sal's hand or kiss it?" He drove a bronze Cadillac Eldorado convertible with special gold trim and gold wire wheels. There was nothing else remotely like it in MCA's parking lot. Pisello just plain stuck out. You couldn't miss him. Everyone knew who Sal was, they just didn't know exactly what he did.

Pisello told people various stories about his business at MCA. He was the "West Coast representative" of Sugar Hill Records, as well as a part owner, he said. He was there to watch over things—release schedules, sales reports, promotion, whatever. Just a businessman protecting his interest, "keeping the niggers in line," he told distribution vice president John Burns. Pisello was also president of his own company, called Consultants for World Records, which was now handling the sale of MCA's cutouts. Consultants had a number of other deals going, too, several with MCA, he said. Sal oozed confidence, claiming that he represented a number of recording artists that he was trying to "place with different record companies." He told Bill Isaacs, MCA's director of special markets, that he'd been negotiating for some time with Myron Roth, Zach Horowitz, and Dan McGill about selling Sugar Hill's Checker/Chess master recordings to MCA. He was looking to get around $6 million for the whole catalog, which he claimed contained nearly one hundred thousand tapes, priceless stuff.

Isaacs had to laugh. He was an expert in repackaging and marketing old music. His job was to squeeze income from the company's vaults of inactive material—its catalog—by licensing recordings for use in TV commercials, movies, mail order, and telemarketing programs. Isaacs prided himself on his encyclopedic knowledge of music catalogs dating back to the 1930s. He could, for example, rattle off in chronological order every early rock 'n' roll record released on the Brunswick or Scepter labels, complete with the names of the songwriters and current copyright holders. Isaacs knew the Checker/Chess catalog well. He told Pisello he didn't think it was worth anywhere near $6 million. He said that of the purported one hundred thousand tapes, at most two hundred were usable album masters, and of the artists contained on those tapes only Chuck Berry had any commercial potential in today's market.

Pisello pestered Sam Passamano constantly with questions about cutouts, and it galled Passamano. At Myron Roth's instruction, he'd given Pisello the cutout inventory list and a list of cutout buyers around the country. "We're going to give Sal a chance to sell the stuff, you just handle the administration," Myron said. Now Passamano was having to instruct Pisello in the rudiments—billing and shipping forms, purchase orders, credit approval, legal clearances, the whole paper chase through the corporation. He was spending more time than if he were selling the stuff himself. He couldn't understand why it was being handled this way, why they were putting an outsider with no experience in charge of a potential million-dollar transaction that previously had required the written approval of at least three company officers. It didn't make any sense. Myron wouldn't discuss it with him. "This is the way we're going to handle it," was all he'd say.

Passamano didn't push too hard. As angry as he was at seeing some of his responsibilities turned over to a neophyte like Pisello, he was afraid to make too many waves right then. His employment contract was up the following November. If it were going to be renewed, the company would begin negotiations with him six months prior to its expiration, which would be in May, two months away. There weren't a lot of job openings in the industry for fifty-five-year-old executives with thirty-five years at the same company. Al Bergamo was gone. Gene Froelich was leaving in April—he had been offered a new position in the company that would have required relocating his family to London and when he turned the job down his employment contract was not renewed. Passamano figured his future with the company was hanging by a thread as it was. So he shut up about Pisello and the cutouts.

He didn't shut up for long, however. In mid-February, Passamano and Kent Crawford, the newly hired vice president of national distribution, were in John Burns's office for a conference call with the regional sales managers around the country. Passamano was there to explain the pricing program and advertising plan for the new budget line of records he'd put together. Burns was on the phone discussing the fall program for Platinum Plus, MCA's bread-and-butter line of about 150 albums, most recorded in the 1970s, that were perennial sellers at the midline price of $5.98 retail. With a dearth of new album releases coming up, Burns needed to move a lot of Platinum Plus units in order to pump up the overall sales figures for the first-quarter financial report. The problem was that MCA's pricing program on Platinum Plus, offering customers a 3 percent discount on the normal price of $3.21 a unit, hadn't stirred up much interest among the big national accounts. CBS Records had just come out with a unit price of $2.25 on its midline catalog. MCA just wasn't competitive; the big buyers wanted a lower price. So Burns said MCA would offer an additional 10 percent discount in the form of free records—one free record for every ten they buy, ten free on one hundred, and so on.

There was nothing unusual about the offer. The practice of giving so-called free goods went back a long way in the record industry. Most artists' contracts contained a clause allowing the record company to give away 15 percent of their recordings free of charge, without paying a royalty, as a way of inducing sales.

But despite not paying a royalty, record companies could come up a loser on a free goods deal, especially if, like MCA, they had a

100 percent buyer return policy. A buyer could place a big order just to get the free goods, then return the bulk later for full credit, leaving the buyer with 15 percent of the original quantity—perhaps thousands of records—at no cost. It was the record industry's version of a free lunch.

Burns knew the risk of his one-on-ten Platinum Plus proposal. But he probably weighed it against the new administration's desperate need for billings in the first quarter, coming on the heels of the 1983 losses. He'd worry about returns later. The boys in the Black Tower were bound to start getting nervous if the record division didn't show a measurable improvement soon. Heads could roll, conceivably his own.

No doubt with that in mind Burns decided to sweeten the Platinum Plus offer to several large accounts, like Minneapolis-based Handleman Company, which stocks hundreds of department stores all over the country. If Handleman would order 250,000 or more units, MCA would throw in another 10 percent free goods, for a total of 20 percent.

Passamano couldn't believe what he was hearing. "We can't do that, John," he said after Burns got off the phone with the sales managers. "It's price discrimination. If we offer the deal to Handleman, it has to be offered in writing to everybody."

"We can do what we need to do to meet the competition," Burns responded testily.

"Then we need to be competitive across the board, with every account," Passamano said.

Burns ended the conversation. "Let me worry about that. You're not involved in distribution anymore, Sam, remember?"

After Passamano left the room steaming, Kent Crawford weighed in on his side, telling Burns that in his ten years with Warner Brothers Records, it had been drilled into him by the company's attorneys, "No price preferences, you just don't do it, it's not worth the risk."

The risk was running afoul of the Federal Trade Commission, which had come down hard on the record industry for its pricing practices just a few years earlier.

But it wasn't just the potential antitrust aspect of the proposal that bothered Kent Crawford, it was the way MCA planned to pass along the extra 10 percent free goods to Handleman. First of all, the free records wouldn't be tied directly to the titles purchased.

Normally, in order to qualify for one hundred free copies of an Olivia Newton-John album, for example, a buyer had to order one thousand copies of that particular album. What was being proposed was that Handleman could order whatever it wanted and then cherry pick the best titles for its free goods.

That meant big-selling artists like Newton-John, The Who, and Elton John would bear the brunt of the program. In effect, their records would be used as bait to sell records by less popular artists.

Further, MCA was planning to ship Handleman's extra 10 percent carried on the books as promotional records rather than free goods. That meant it would be difficult for an artist's accountant to pick up on it in an audit.

Crawford objected to the plan, but there wasn't much he could do except go along. He'd only been with the company for a little more than a month, and Burns was his boss. As he left the meeting, he thought to himself, "I guess they can do what they want, but I don't want to go down for this."

6

"I've got to take care of them that take care of me"

Every year in the spring, the National Association of Record Merchandisers (NARM), a trade group of wholesalers and retailers around the country, hosts a three-day convention that attracts about one thousand recording industry professionals, scores of hookers, and a contingent of drug dealers to some tolerant hotel in a warm-weather city like Miami, Los Angeles, or Las Vegas.

The NARM convention is an all-industry affair, attended by everyone from cassette box manufacturers to cutout distributors to independent record promoters to the presidents of the smallest and largest record companies. Like most conventions, it features company-sponsored presentation booths and hospitality suites, cocktail parties and dinners with a dais, keynote speakers, Executive of the Year awards, live entertainment, and lukewarm entrées.

For the major companies, NARM is pretty much a see-and-be-seen event, about the only time home-office executives get to meet face-to-face with the people who actually sell their records to the public. The big companies spend a lot of money hosting receptions and hyping their new releases, but they actually do very little business during the three days—except for one area of commerce. The NARM convention is where most of the major cutout sales are made each year, usually negotiated in the off-hours between official events, out by the pool or in smoke-filled hotel rooms late at night.

The 1984 NARM convention was held at the Diplomat Hotel in Hollywood, Florida, long a favorite of NARM officials and, coincidentally, vacationing mobsters from New York City. Among the MCA executives who made the trip were Irving Azoff, Myron Roth, Richard Palmese, John Burns, Harold Sulman, Larry Solters, and Sam Passamano, the sole survivor of the old guard at the company. Sal Pisello was there, too, though not as part of the official MCA delegation. Ostensibly, Pisello was representing Sugar Hill Records; but his real purpose at the convention was to sell a load of about five million MCA cutouts.

The 1984 convention was to be the industry's first up-close look at Azoff and his new MCA Records team. And they certainly created a lasting impression. Azoff's plan was to make a grand showing, something commensurate with MCA's hoped-for new standing in the business, first class all the way. When they arrived at the Diplomat, however, they found that MCA's accommodations were not as commodious as those of the bigger companies. The conference room and hospitality suite were smaller than CBS's and Warner's and were located on the basement floor of the hotel, way in the back by the service elevator.

Azoff was furious. At a luncheon staff meeting the first day, he announced that MCA would boycott all evening functions in protest; the reserved table that the company had paid for was to remain empty throughout the weekend. Midway through his diatribe against NARM officials, he picked up a ketchup bottle, unscrewed the top, and began splattering the contents all over the conference room, sending his executives scrambling for the door. Azoff's anger often came out in the form of mischievousness, but with a destructive edge. An oft-repeated story in the record business had it that once, when the Eagles were on a concert tour and one of their hotels was unable to provide the band members with connecting suites, Azoff went to a hardware store and bought a chain saw, which he and guitarist Joe Walsh used to carve a passage between the rooms. Later, Azoff supposedly had a carrying case made for the chainsaw so that Walsh could take it with him whenever he went on the road.

(Food seems to be a recurring theme in Azoff lore. On another Eagles road trip, Azoff entertained the staff and customers at a Midwestern diner by ordering every item on the menu and then throwing it at Walsh, who was sitting in another booth across the room. Azoff once boasted to a reporter that he and Larry Solters had been kicked off more than one airplane for having a food fight in First Class.)

Azoff's demonstration with the ketchup bottle set the tone of behavior for the rest of the weekend, as members of the MCA entourage staged repeated displays of sophomoric high jinks. During a company presentation by Sulman and Burns later that day, Azoff and Solters began pelting the speakers' table with muffins. Late one night, Solters put Super Glue on the receivers of the hotel's house phones. (Solters apparently had a thing about telephones—back at the home office he was known for bashing them to bits with a baseball bat whenever he got angry.) Even Azoff's wife, Shelli, got into the act, carrying around a clear plastic bag full of flour that was supposed to look like cocaine. The flour ultimately ended up being thrown all over a hallway.

Sam Passamano was mortified by the antics; he hated being associated with these people. Sam hadn't wanted to make the trip in the first place but couldn't avoid it. He had to present the new budget line—repackaged old recordings by the likes of Pete Fountain, Lawrence Welk, and the McGuire Sisters—to the rack jobbers, wholesalers who stock the racks of $2.99 and $3.99 records in drugstores, supermarkets, and other nonrecord outlets. Beyond his presentation, he put in only perfunctory appearances at company functions and otherwise tried to keep to himself as much as he could.

Passamano saw Pisello only once during the weekend, on the last day, sunning himself by the pool. Pisello called him over and announced excitedly that he'd made a deal to sell the MCA cutouts to Morris Levy of Roulette Records. Passamano was surprised to hear that Levy would be interested in cutouts—he'd been out of that business since Promo Records folded in the late 1970s. "That's great, Sal," he said. "Be sure you get a purchase order on it."

"No problem," Pisello replied. "Send me a memo to remind me when we get back to the office."

Later that day, in the hotel lobby, Passamano ran into Myron Roth, who was on his way to play tennis with Azoff. "I see that Sal sold the cutouts to Morris Levy," he said, by way of making idle conversation. Roth indicated that he was aware of the sale but didn't want to discuss it right then. "You just be sure to take care of the paperwork, Sam," he said over his shoulder as he hurried off to the courts.

Returning to his room, Passamano had an uneasy feeling about the cutout sale. MCA was getting into bed with Pisello and Levy—an unholy alliance if there ever was one—on a deal that he had no say in. And yet, the way things were lining up, his name was going to appear on all the documents as having approved it and pushed it through. He couldn't shake the fear that he was going to wind up as the fall guy if the deal went bad.

Among the attendees at the 1984 NARM convention was John LaMonte, the owner of a small budget record and oldies distributorship called Out of the Past, which was located in the Philadelphia suburb of Darby. LaMonte came to NARM, as he did every year, hoping to buy cutouts directly from one of the big record companies. He knew he didn't stand much of a chance, however.

The problem was that the big record companies sold their cutouts primarily to the three largest cutout buyers in the country—Great Atlantic and Pacific in St. Louis, Surplus Records and Tapes in New York, and Countrywide in Neptune, New Jersey. The public reasoning for this sweetheart arrangement with the Big Three is that they were the only cutout distributors with sales volume and cash flow enough to buy multimillion-unit inventories, without cherry picking for just the good titles. Little guys like LaMonte and his across-town competitor, Scorpio Music, consequently had to buy their cutouts from these middlemen, at a substantial markup. Understandably, they chafed under the system. Scorpio president John Gervasoni once found out what one of the big buyers had offered for a load of cutouts from Capitol Records and put in a higher bid, only to be told by the record executive in charge, "Sorry, but I've got to take care of them that take care of me."

LaMonte had another problem in buying from the big companies. He was a convicted record counterfeiter, one of the lowest forms of life in the minds of record executives, right down there with kiddie pornographer. And LaMonte was no run-of-the-mill bootlegger. He was a notorious, near legendary character.

LaMonte's father, Bob LaMonte, was something of a legend, too. Back in the 1950s and 1960s, when Dick Clark's "American Bandstand" was televised from Philadelphia, the city was the boom town of the budding rock 'n' roll music business, with dozens of successful little independent record labels popping up seemingly overnight then disappearing just as quickly—Chancellor Records with Frankie Avalon and Fabian; Cameo-Parkway with Chubby Checker and Bobby Rydell; Swan Records with Freddie Cannon; Imperial Records; Gamble Records, and so on. And it was in this heady atmosphere that the elder LaMonte pioneered the cutout record business. He arranged a deal with all the local companies to buy their excess product and he bought up all the leftovers whenever they went belly up. In a matter of a few years, his Coast-to-Coast records was buying cutouts from companies all across the country. One thing Bob LaMonte taught his son was that there is a lot of money to be made in old records, even if the record companies themselves were too dumb to realize it.

John LaMonte opened up his own cutout and oldie business in 1970, when he was twenty-five. Called the House of Sounds, it was located in a six-story warehouse at the corner of Quarry and Hamilton Streets in Darby. The business prospered, going from gross sales of $100,000 that first year to $4.5 million in 1976. At its peak, the House of Sounds warehouse bulged with nearly twenty million old records. In addition to buying and selling cutouts, LaMonte began dabbling in counterfeiting. His first big score came in 1972 with the album *Introducing the Beatles*. Although the group would go on to become the biggest seller in the history of recorded music, at the time *Introducing the Beatles* was released in 1963, the Fab Four had not yet made their big splash on the Ed Sullivan show, so no major record company would pick up the U.S. distribution rights to their first LP. Tiny Philadelphia-based VeeJay Records took the gamble and distributed the record until the company went broke in the late 1960s. (All subsequent Beatles albums were released in the United States through Capitol Records, including the group's second introduction album, *Meet the Beatles*.)

Following the VeeJay bankruptcy, *Introducing the Beatles* went out of distribution and, for a time, it was unclear who owned the rights. Knowing there was still a market for the record—and being friendly with a Philadelphia-area record presser who still held a copy of the master recording—LaMonte began putting the record out himself, priced to budget record distributors at $2. He sold several million of them, more than VeeJay ever did, netting himself about $500,000.

In a way, LaMonte built his business on the Beatles. Several years later, when United Artists Records (which was owned at the time by Capitol) dumped several million copies of the group's final album, the soundtrack to *Let It Be*, on the cutout market, he used the sale as a cover to counterfeit several million copies of the record. With all the legitimate copies floating around the back alleys of the business, it was easy for LaMonte to sell his counterfeits to distributors at a low price without raising suspicions. He simply cut off one corner of the record jacket, just as the record company did, and said he'd picked them up on the cheap from the big cutout sale. At $2 apiece, the stuff flew out of his warehouse.

Even though he operated constantly in the area of illegality, LaMonte never considered that what he was doing was a crime. Rather, he viewed it as a game of one-upsmanship with the big record companies, getting even with them for their heavy-handed business tactics when dealing with small operators like himself. LaMonte knew that every big company had started just the way House of Sounds had, with one guy wheeling and dealing from a garage, storefront, or tiny recording studio, hoping for the elusive big score. But as records became big business in the late 1960s and 1970s, the more successful companies had conglomerated, bought each other up, consolidated manufacturing and distributing, and, in LaMonte's opinion, squeezed the entrepreneurial spirit out of the industry. Now a few major firms controlled virtually everything, from which undiscovered band would get a recording contract to who would be awarded the honor of disposing of the leftover records from their bad investments and overproduction. They set the prices and dictated the cost of doing business, in effect determining the amount of profit small independent operators could make (legally at least).

As a result of this control by the consolidated companies, the underbelly of the record business was filled with businessmen who delighted in sticking it to the big companies any way they could—short of hijacking their trucks at gunpoint. Among this group, John LaMonte was considered something of a hero, for his inventiveness as well as his brass.

There were many classic LaMonte stories. Like the time in 1974 when he managed to get hold of about twenty tractor-trailer loads of cutouts and overstocks from the Capitol Records plant in Jacksonville, Illinois. In those days, Capitol's policy was to scrap its cutouts—sell them to vinyl reprocessing centers to be ground up, melted down into compound, and ultimately reused. So LaMonte bought nearly ten million records—including several million Beatles albums—through a man he knew who owned a vinyl reclamation company in New Jersey. Capitol assumed the records were going to be destroyed. Instead, they were routed directly to LaMonte's warehouse, with LaMonte paying the truckers an extra $100 a trailer load to get the shipments from Jacksonville to Darby in a single day, trying to hurry up the process before the company caught on to what was happening. The overloaded trucks traveled the back roads late at night to avoid speed traps and weigh stations.

The unloading at House of Sounds went on twenty-four hours a day for more than a week. In the end, on an investment of about $100,000, LaMonte netted nearly $1 million. It was a perfect scam: he hadn't broken any law, he'd made a bundle of cash, and put one over on one of the most powerful record companies in the world. He didn't lose any sleep over the fact that the artists received no royalties on the records. He wasn't under any contractual obligation to pay them—that was Capitol's problem. If the record company didn't pay artists royalties when it sold their records as cutouts, then why should he?

LaMonte stung Capitol a number of times over the years. On one occasion he purchased, for a few pennies each, several million Beatles singles the company thought it had destroyed by cutting into each fifty-count box with a band saw, leaving a half-inch dink in the discs. Never one to underestimate the stupidity of a big company, however, LaMonte simply slipped each ruined record into a crisp new white sleeve, packed them in new boxes, and sold them for forty cents apiece to rack jobbers who were able to return them to Capitol for a ninety-cent credit. The scam wasn't discovered until later when a Capitol auditor determined the company was taking back more returns on some singles than it had sold. Only then did someone at the return center look inside the sleeves—just as LaMonte had figured.

Capitol eventually traced the scheme back to LaMonte and reported the incident to the FBI, alleging counterfeiting. But when several agents visited his warehouse to question him, LaMonte challenged them to find the illegality—there was no law against counterfeiting plain white record sleeves, and he hadn't returned them to Capitol for credit, he'd sold them legitimately on the open market for the highest price he could get.

The Capitol scam marked the beginning of the end for LaMonte, however, because it brought him to the attention of the FBI. Under intense lobbying from the RIAA, the Justice Department had begun putting a high priority on music copyright infringement. With help from the RIAA's gung-ho new antipiracy squad, which was staffed by former FBI agents at more than double their government salaries, the department launched a three-year undercover investigation of what it described as a "massive, nationwide counterfeiting operation of unparalleled dimensions." FBI agents from New York, Los Angeles, Philadelphia, Minneapolis, Albany, and San Diego were assigned to a task force, which numbered LaMonte among its key targets.

On February 11, 1977, the agents raided House of Sounds and arrested LaMonte on charges of racketeering, wire fraud, and copyright infringement—135 counts in all. It was the first big bust by the newly forged forces of the FBI and the RIAA, and they played it for all it was worth, sending out press releases that described the House of Sounds case as "the single most important breakthrough ever in the investigation of illegal sound recordings."

LaMonte eventually pleaded no contest to the charges and was sentenced to eighteen months in prison. He served eleven months in the minimum security federal prison at Lewisburg, Pennsylvania. It wasn't exactly hard time, but for LaMonte the whole experience was devastating. He had a wife and three children who attended Catholic schools. He was a state handball champion who had been honored by several local charities for devoting his time to teaching the sport to underprivileged children. He'd been a successful businessman. Now he was a convict, forced by the government to forfeit his interest in a business he'd built from scratch. He was financially ruined and publicly disgraced. "Music Forger Jailed," read a headline in the *Philadelphia Inquirer* the day he was sentenced. "Disc Pirate Gets Jail, $25,000 Fine," said the *Philadelphia Daily News*.

LaMonte got out of prison in 1980 determined never to go back there. Since records were the only business he knew, he started up a new company, Out of the Past, specializing in old hit singles (from the 1950s through the 1970s) and cutout and imported albums and cassettes. His mail-order catalog featured only oldies—priced at

$1.50 each, minimum order of three, everything from "Yakety Yak" by the Coasters to Michael Jackson's just-off-the-charts "Billie Jean." LaMonte's seventy-five-year-old mother, Jane, oversaw the singles business, which she'd learned from her husband, who died in 1972. John ran the cutout and import side, mostly by phone— buying, selling, swapping, hipping, and dipping around the same old network of underbelly entrepreneurs that serves the host industry by feeding on its discarded waste. He bought from foreign exporters laying off production that outstripped their country's population and from financially strapped retailers looking for quick off-the-books cash. He sold to rack jobbers who stocked the budget bins in grocery stores, truck stops, and discount department stores like Target and Jem. He sold scrap albums by the pound to vinyl reprocessors and plastic cassette boxes, tape cartridges, and even used magnetic tape to salvage companies that wiped it all clean for recycling. Although he often dealt in goods the major record companies disapproved of—particularly import albums—he stayed clean and within the copyright laws.

Slowly, steadily, LaMonte had built up his new business to the point where, in the spring of 1984, he was making a comfortable living—enough to pay for a new car, his kids' tuition, and the mortgage on his rambling home on a leafy two-acre plot in the suburb of Landsdowne. Still, he was looking for the big deal that would put him back into the real money and perhaps the mainstream of the business. He was hoping the 1984 NARM convention would present an opportunity.

On the second day of the convention, LaMonte got a call in his hotel room from his sometime business partner, Sonny Brocco, saying that a large load of MCA cutouts was available. "I just talked to the MCA guy," Brocco said. "He's ready to deal with anybody. We're across the street at the Hilton, out by the pool."

LaMonte practically bolted out of his room. A chance to deal directly with a major label didn't come along that often. This could be it, he thought, as he rode down in the elevator. A direct buy from a big company would not only mean a heftier profit than going through Surplus or Countrywide, it might also up his credibility in the industry, perhaps help erase some of the stigma of his counterfeiting conviction.

LaMonte and Brocco had met in prison, where the stocky, white-haired Brocco was serving time for securities fraud, "passing bad paper," as he called it. Following Brocco's release from Lewisburg, LaMonte had given him a job at Out of the Past, paying $500 a week. He taught Brocco the record business and let him invest in a few cutout deals. They'd flown down to Florida together for the NARM convention.

Out beside the pool, Brocco introduced Sal Pisello as "the MCA man." LaMonte was curious about Pisello. He knew practically everyone in the cutout business, but he'd never heard of this guy before. Sam Passamano had been MCA's cutout man for years—everybody knew Sam. Pisello reeked of wise guy, conversationally crude but slickly packaged—deep tan, dark sunglasses, fancy threads—like Brocco's cousin, Gaetano "Corky" Vastola, who was supposedly a made guy, an initiated member of the DeCavalcante crime family of New Jersey. Before LaMonte could ask any questions, however, Pisello produced a computer printout of MCA's cutout inventory. That was bona fide enough for LaMonte. There was no way Pisello could get hold of MCA's inventory list unless he was legit, LaMonte thought. He must be Passamano's new boss or something.

LaMonte told Pisello he was definitely interested in the cutouts but needed to price out the list, go over the numbers and titles with his customers before coming up with a dollar bid. He took the printout back to his hotel room and spent the rest of the day and night on the phone preselling with his buyers, finding out how much he could get for the merchandise in advance so he knew how much to offer, figuring in his profit, which is standard operating procedure in the cutout trade. Since record companies don't demand payment until sixty to ninety days after delivery, a smart cutout distributor lays off his risk by selling the cream of the shipment in advance, thereby guaranteeing his profit, or at least his break-even point, before putting out a dime.

LaMonte met with Pisello by the Hilton pool the next morning and offered a nice round figure, $1 million, for the approximately four million cutouts. Pisello was noncommittal. "I'll have to check with my record expert," he said. He got up and walked into the hotel. When he came out fifteen minutes later LaMonte was horrified to see the burly figure of Morris Levy walking behind him. LaMonte shot Brocco a look. "Holy shit, his expert is fuckin' Morris. Did you know about this?" Brocco shrugged. He knew that LaMonte probably would not have met with Pisello in the first place if he'd been told that Levy was involved.

LaMonte first met Morris Levy when he was only twelve years old. His father took him along on a business trip to New York to buy cutouts from Roulette Records. "The man we're seeing today is a bad man," his father told him. "He's a mobster." At the time, young LaMonte didn't know exactly what "mobster" meant, only that it was scary. In the ensuing years, he learned just how scary.

In the early 1970s, LaMonte was importing counterfeit Motown product pressed by a renegade licensee of Motown in Puerto Rico. Levy, who had an exclusive on Motown cutouts through his company Promo Records, found out about it and called LaMonte to a meeting at the Roulette Records offices in New York to discuss the problem. LaMonte knew that one of his friends, Fat Freddie Kaplan, had once had his jaw broken in Levy's office for counterfeiting a record by a group called the Channels. Freddie had spent a month in the hospital with his mouth wired shut. In the years before the RIAA's antipiracy unit, the big record companies often went to Levy for help in solving their counterfeiting problems. Levy would dispatch a "goon squad" to the suspected counterfeiter's place of business and they would bust his equipment or his head or both. Levy provided the service to the record companies free of charge, but sometimes he exacted payment from the counterfeiter.

LaMonte went to the meeting because he felt he had no choice—if he didn't go, they'd come after him sooner or later. Besides, he was a cocky young kid in those days and thought he could talk his way out of the situation. "How quick can you come up with $100,000 in cash?" was Levy's opening line. LaMonte's jaw dropped. "You better kill me now," he responded. Levy lowered the figure to $25,000. The threat was unspoken. LaMonte agreed to pay and to stop bringing in the records from Puerto Rico. He borrowed the money from the parents of a friend in Philadelphia.

On another occasion, LaMonte was counterfeiting albums by the rock groups Cream and Vanilla Fudge on the Atlantic Records label Atco, with which Promo Records also had an exclusive cutout arrangement. This time, LaMonte was visited in his office by one of Levy's henchmen, a six-foot-four, 240-pound man named Nate McCalla. McCalla demanded that La-Monte turn over the master tapes and artwork for the Vanilla Fudge and Cream albums. He also placed an empty suitcase on

LaMonte's desk and told him to fill it with $40,000 in cash to be taken back to New York.

LaMonte felt he had no choice but to comply. McCalla had a fearsome reputation for violent behavior. Legend had it that in a fit of rage he once ripped the door off an automobile. Although he was nominally a vice president of Levy's Promo Records, along with Genovese crime boss Tommy Eboli, McCalla functioned as an enforcer and bodyguard to Levy—the captain of the goon squad. In June 1975, McCalla and Levy were indicted for blinding an off-duty police officer, Lt. Charles Heinz, in an altercation outside the Blue Angel nightclub in New York. According to police reports, McCalla held the officer's hands behind his back while Levy punched him several times in the face, putting out his left eye. The case was later mysteriously dismissed and the court files remain sealed.

McCalla's violent ways came to an appropriate end in 1981. He was found by police in a vacant house in Pompano Beach, Florida, badly decomposed, with three bullets in his head. The murder has never been solved, though investigators suspect it may have had something to do with a falling out McCalla had with Morris Levy.

Out by the Hilton pool at the NARM convention, Levy strode directly up to LaMonte, who immediately got up out of his chair and instinctively took a few steps backward. Thick-necked and barrel-chested, with a booming rasp of a voice straight out of a 1930s gangster movie, Levy was an intimidating figure from across a room, much less standing directly over someone sitting in a low-slung chair. He seemed to have a lot more at stake in the cutout deal than just being Pisello's record expert. In fact, he was Pisello's partner in the transaction.

"What are you trying to do, rob us?" Levy growled.

"Morris, this is my bid, it's the same thing any of my competition would offer," LaMonte said. "If you don't think it's enough, that's your business."

"It's no good," Levy snapped, waving LaMonte away. "Get out of here."

LaMonte was all too happy to oblige. Back at the Diplomat he berated Brocco for nearly getting him involved with "that cocksucker Super Jew." But he was bitterly disappointed about not being able to make the MCA deal. "I'm telling you, Broc, that cutout list was pure gold, we coulda made a fortune on it."

Four days after the NARM convention, with the missed MCA deal still gnawing at him, LaMonte got a phone call from Sal Pisello in Los Angeles. Would LaMonte still be interested in the MCA cutout list at the same price if the company threw in some sweeteners? Like a few hundred thousand copies of good titles?

"It depends on what the sweeteners are," LaMonte replied. "Send me the list of new stuff and I'll price it all out again."

"Better yet, why don't you fly out here to California tomorrow and we'll do this in person," Pisello said.

LaMonte agreed. Even though it would be easier to have Pisello Federal Express the new list to him, he liked the idea of concluding the deal with the MCA man face-to-face. It made him feel more secure, less likely to get cheated, what with Morris Levy lurking in the background. Besides, he thought he'd found a way to neutralize Levy. He'd bring in Brocco's cousin, Gaetano Vastola, as his partner in the deal, sort of an equalizer. Whatever Levy might do to LaMonte, he'd never rip off Vastola, who was not only physically large—his associates referred to him as "the Galoot"—but according to Brocco also very high up in the Mafia hierarchy, at least a capo, maybe even underboss of the DeCavalcante family. Levy had some heavyweight mob connections, but he was no made guy, he was just a Jewish front man. Vastola.was the genuine article.

What LaMonte didn't know at the time was that Morris Levy and Gaetano Vastola went back a long way together. In fact, they were lifelong friends.

LaMonte felt even better about the deal five minutes after he and Brocco sat down with Pisello the next evening in the bar of the Palm restaurant in West Hollywood. The sweeteners were good— lots of big-name country artists like Loretta Lynn, Conway Twitty, and Don Williams, stuff that sells like hotcakes along the truckstop circuit. Of the approximately 4.2 million units, nine hundred thousand were priced at fifteen cents and the rest at forty cents, for a total of about $1.3 million. Even before the sweeteners, LaMonte held guaranteed orders for more than $1 million worth of the best merchandise from just three customers. It didn't seem like he could lose. He figured his profit could be in the ballpark of $750,000.

Further cementing the transaction, Pisello had been followed into the restaurant by a handful of men that he introduced to LaMonte and Brocco as MCA Records executives. The names and titles were a blur to LaMonte, but one of them stood out from the others because of his size—he couldn't have been much more than five feet tall. The name Azoff meant nothing to LaMonte. All he knew was he was now definitely dealing directly with a big record company. He shook hands with Pisello and the deal was sealed, along with his fate.

7

"Kid, I just made you in this business"

S everal weeks after the Palm restaurant meeting, John LaMonte drove to New York City for a meeting in Levy's office to tie up all the loose ends on the MCA cutout deal.

Entering the Roulette Records building at 1790 Broadway, a block off Central Park, he felt a familiar chill of fear, remembering the last time he'd been summoned by Morris on the Motown matter. Unaware of the longstanding relationship between Vastola and Levy, however, LaMonte figured he now had a protector in Vastola, who was attending the meeting as his and Brocco's partner. Pisello was flying in from California with the final list of merchandise. If everything was in order, MCA would begin shipping the goods in about two weeks.

Morris Levy's office didn't look like that of a multimillionaire. It was homey and funky-comfortable with a fireplace, a couple of tattered easy chairs, and a well-worn rug. Hung on the walls and resting on the mantelpiece were numerous testimonials to his public life as a liberal-minded philanthropist. There was a large photograph of Levy standing on the steps of St. Patrick's Cathedral shaking hands with the late Catholic leader John Cardinal Spellman. Roulette recorded two albums of the cathedral choir and Levy helped raise money for the Cardinal's pet charity, the Foundling Hospital. There was a framed citation from the Black Congressional Caucus citing Levy's chairmanship of a 1973 fund-raiser that netted $3 million. It was signed by Atlanta mayor Andrew Young, Congressman Ron Dellums, and Congresswoman Shirley Chisholm. Levy had long been involved in civil rights issues. As a patron of such legendary black jazz performers as Dizzy Gillespie, Count Basie, Duke Ellington, Charlie Parker, and Sarah Vaughan when he owned the famous Birdland nightclub in the late 1950s and early 1960s, Levy booked concert tours that played to nonsegregated audiences in the South during the infancy of the civil rights movement.

Ironically, despite his liberal Democratic bent, he detested John and Robert Kennedy. "That's because that little prick Bobby had the Justice Department wiretap me in the 1960s because I was dating Judy Exner at the same time she was fucking his brother the president," Levy once told a reporter, on the record. "One night I had her call and ask for Jack through the White House switchboard while she was with me at my apartment, just because I knew they would be listening and it would fuck up their minds," he said, breaking into a raucous, rasping laugh. "Judy put me in her book." (In her autobiography, Exner confessed to having simultaneous affairs with John Kennedy and Chicago mob boss Sam Giancana, but claimed that her relationship with Levy was platonic.)

In Levy's office, there were plaques recognizing his longstanding service to a number of Jewish organizations, including his ten years as chairman emeritus of the United Jewish Appeal. Above his desk was a framed wooden plaque with the invocation, "O Lord, give me a bastard with talent."

On the mantelpiece was a mounted check in the amount of $3 from Walter Yetnikoff, with the designation, "for mental health consultation." Levy liked to tell the story of how he first met Yetnikoff when the future CBS Records president was fresh out of Harvard Law School and toiling in obscurity in CBS's legal affairs department. "They sent him over to negotiate on a $300,000 bill that we'd been disputing. When he walked into the room I handed him a check for the full amount and said, 'Kid, I just made you in this business.'" The two men had been close friends ever since. Yetnikoff called him regularly to complain about his ongoing hassles with CBS board chairman Thomas Wyman. "Aw, booby, what's that fucking goy doing to you now?" Levy would commiserate.

There were no hints in Levy's office of his other, less public life, however—his more than forty years of close association with the rulers of the East Coast underworld: Tommy Eboli, Tommy ("Three Fingers Brown") Luchese, Johnnie Dio, Angelo ("Gyp") DeCarlo, Joseph ("Joe the Wop") Cantaldo, Federico ("Fritzy") Giovanelli, Anthony ("Fat Tony") Salerno, Vincent ("the Chin") Gigante, Dominick ("Swatsy Mulligan") Chiafone, John ("Sonny") Franzese, Gaetano ("Corky") Vastola—murderers, loan sharks, heroin smugglers, extortionists, numbers racketeers, gambling czars, money launderers, bank robbers, securities fraud artists, and corrupters of union officials, judges, and politicians. Levy knew them all and had done business with quite a few.

Levy had practically grown up in the company of mobsters, beginning his business career at age fourteen working in Broadway nightclubs that were frequented, and in some cases owned, by organized crime figures. While still in his teens, he was running the hat check and photography concessions at a number of clubs on New York's East Side. By his mid-twenties, Levy either owned or was partnered in a string of successful cabarets and restaurants—the Roundtable, a favorite Mafia lunch spot; the Embers nightclub; the Royal Roost, the first modern sit-down jazz club, nicknamed "the Metropolitan Bopera House" for a new form of jazz called bebop that was born there. In 1949, Levy opened Birdland in the basement of a building on Broadway at Fifty-third, dubbed "the jazz corner of the world" by New York music critics. Named in honor of the legendary sax man Charlie "Bird" Parker, Birdland became perhaps the most famous and successful American jazz club of all time, the New York after-hours hangout of such jazz age celebrities as Frank Sinatra, Jane Russell, and Tennessee Williams. Birdland's cool, hipster-haven ambiance was immortalized in the timeless jazz piece "Lullaby of Birdland," which was composed by George Shearing as he sat noodling at the club piano one night.

Birdland and its owner gained notoriety one night in late January 1959 when Levy's older brother Zachariah, the manager of the club, was stabbed outside the bar, then staggered back inside and

died in full view of one hundred horrified patrons, including ban-
dleader Woody Herman. The New York newspapers covered the
story with lurid headlines, referring to it as the "bebop killing."
Police speculated at the time that it was the result of a drug deal
gone sour and may have been a case of mistaken identity, noting
that Morris Levy, a dead ringer for his brother, had disappeared
shortly after the murder, having provided investigators with very
little information. That scenario was never proven, however, and a
small-time hood named Lee Schlesinger was eventually convicted
of killing the elder Levy in an act of revenge for the ejection of his
prostitute wife from the club.

Birdland became the cornerstone of a musical entertainment
miniconglomerate that included Roulette Records and a score of
smaller record labels, seven music publishing companies, and an
assortment of artist management, concert production, direct mail,
and radio promotion firms. From the mid-1950s through the mid-
1960s, Roulette was one of the hottest independent record labels in
the business, scoring a string of hits with Jimmy Rogers ("Honey-
comb," "Kisses Sweeter than Wine," "Uh-oh, I'm Fallin' in Love
Again"), Frankie Lyman and the Teenagers ("Why Do Fools Fall in
Love"), Joey Dee and the Starlighters ("Peppermint Twist"), and
Tommy James and the Shondells ("Hanky Panky," "Mony, Mony,"
"Crimson and Clover").

At age thirty-two, Levy was one of the richest and most powerful
men in the music business. Referring to his swift rise in the entertainment world, New York police investigators called him "Won-
derboy" in their intelligence reports. They'd begun looking into his
business activities after his brother's murder. What they found
throughout Roulette and its sister companies were wise guys, lots of
them. According to the records of the New York Crime Commission, Roulette provided jobs for a steady stream of low-level Mafia
soldiers who received early releases from prison based on their
employment at the company. "We also used to record all the hoods'
girlfriends," said one record producer who worked at Roulette in
the 1960s. "We musta spent $250,000 a year recording big-titted
phony blondes and hookers for these guys that Morris was doing
favors for, using the best bands and backup you could find. It was
amazing all the hoods coming in and out of Morris's office."

In addition to Tommy Eboli, who was part owner of Promo

Records, there was Dominick Chiafone, a Genovese family soldier involved in labor racketeering who was said to have had a financial interest in both Roulette and the Roundtable. Chiafone was a fixture in the Roulette office for years, until his death in 1980 at age eighty-two, after which Levy continued to support his widow.

By 1975, state and local law enforcement officials in New York were convinced that Levy's operation was actually controlled by the Genovese crime family, whose members were using their association with him to obtain a foothold in the record industry. Angelo DeCarlo "owned a piece" of the Four Seasons singing group "in association with Roulette Records," according to the 1973 Senate testimony of Gerald Zelmanowitz, a convicted stolen securities trader who was the first person placed in the federal Witness Protection Program. New York Police Department intelligence files noted that Genovese family members "have a reputation of aggressively expanding operations through the use of legitimate front men who have successfully assumed control of many business ventures connected with the local entertainment industry." The New York State Crime Commission reported in a 1972 intelligence memo, "It is suspected that Levy is the front man for the syndicate in the record business, and it is alleged that Levy was the main person behind the disk jockey scandal several years ago."

The organized crime figure who used Levy's music business connections to the best advantage was Gaetano Vastola, a nephew of Chiafone and a friend of Levy's dating back to their teenage days. As a young man, Vastola had risen rapidly through the ranks of New Jersey's DeCavalcante family, earning the respect of family boss Sam ("the Plumber") DeCavalcante with his ability to earn money through loan-sharking, bootlegging whiskey, robbery, and extortion. In 1965 he was arrested for burglary, grand larceny, and coercion in connection with the theft of a shipment of fur coats from the Chelsea Warehouse. According to transcripts of FBI wiretaps placed on DeCavalcante's phone at the time, Vastola's partners in the fur theft—Michael ("Mikey D.") D'Allessio, Rocky Infelice, and Frank Cocchiaro—suspected that he had become a stool pigeon for the police and discussed putting out a contract on him. They were both suspicious and jealous of his dealings with Levy, which prompted a phone conversation between DeCavalcante and his cousin Bobby Basile: "Sam, this Corky sticks in Frank's craw. This guy is tied up with a guy by the name of Levy. This guy's got his own airplane. They go here, they go there. The whole thing is like a fantastic movie production."

Basile went on to discuss his suspicions that Vastola might have been cooperating with authorities in exchange for their looking the other way on a counterfeit record scam he ran with Levy.

"See, this kid was in a bad situation with those counterfeit records, Sam. He walked away clean. Sam, if nothing else, the Internal Revenue Service should have crucified this guy. He made a half a million dollars. And he walked away. He paid a $215 fine. And walked away. How do you do things like this? He was in a national swindle, remember, with the counterfeit records. This guy moves around like he's got a license. What is he, a genius, and we don't know it? Let's not underestimate the Treasury men, the FBI, the Internal Revenue Service. Sam, these people know what they are doing. And this guy's getting away with murder. I said to Frank, 'Did this kid ever do any work for you?' He said, 'No, he just smacked a couple of guys around. But he ain't got the guys.' I said 'Frank, maybe this should have been brought to light a long time ago.' This kid moves in with everybody. You name a friend and this guy knows him. Sam, we might be 100 percent wrong, but can we check it?"

DeCavalcante nixed the proposed hit on Vastola, saying that if anyone touched him they'd "have their heads blown off." The question of Vastola having some sort of immunity with the police was answered in May 1968 when he and DeCavalcante were indicted for extorting four men who had been running a rigged dice game at the American Hotel in Trevose, Pennsylvania. According to trial testimony, Vastola and his brother-in-law, Daniel Annunziata, held up the game at gunpoint, knocked one man unconscious, forced the others to remove their pants, took $2,800 from them, and demanded that they pay $300 a week from then on. Later, the four men were called to a meeting with DeCavalcante, who told them he had persuaded Vastola to accept a $12,000 cash settlement from them to drop the matter. "As mad as this guy is, you are lucky not to be in the river," DeCavalcante told the gamblers. DeCavalcante, Annunziata, and Vastola were convicted in September 1970. DeCavalcante was sentenced to the maximum—three consecutive five-year prison terms. Annunziata received a three-year sentence, and Vastola got five years. Vastola was released from prison after only a year because an appeals court overturned the convictions of the three men. But he didn't have much time to enjoy his freedom. He was back in prison in September 1972, serving a two-year stretch in the Atlanta penitentiary for conspiracy to commit a $500,000 extortion of a Georgia businessman. Vastola's lawyer in that case was the late, unlamented Roy Cohn.

By 1980, with the extortion charges behind him, Vastola was the wealthy head of his own crime organization centered in Union County, New Jersey. As a capo in the DeCavalcante family, he collected a share of all monies earned by his crew in such traditional Mafia activities as bookmaking, loan-sharking, drug dealing, insurance fraud, and arson for hire. On the legitimate side, he had financial interests in a number of diverse businesses, including a Long Island carpet company; a chain of sandwich shops called Stuff Yer Face; a video manufacturing and distributing company in Neptune, New Jersey, called the Video Warehouse; a New York talent agency called Mecca Artists; and a concert-booking firm called Queens Booking that had managed the performing schedules of such popular black artists as Ray Charles and Aretha Franklin. He played golf with Sammy Davis, Jr., and maintained high-level contacts throughout the record industry, often flying between New York, Atlantic City, Las Vegas, and Los Angeles to confer with the likes of United Artists Records president Artie Mogull. At age fifty-six, Vastola was a millionaire with a mortgage-free, million-dollar home in Colt's Neck, New Jersey; a daughter just graduating from law school; and a son just breaking into the music business. And one of his best friends in the world was Morris Levy.

John LaMonte didn't know that, however, as he sat in Levy's office in early June 1984, finalizing the MCA cutout deal. As it was explained to him, Levy's involvement was as an adviser to Pisello, who didn't know the record business, and as guarantor of payment for the cutouts. LaMonte understood that to mean if he didn't pay MCA, then Levy would send a couple of goons to see him. Instead of being billed at the selling price of forty and fifteen cents a unit, he was told, he would receive invoices for thirty-seven and twelve cents a unit. He was supposed to pay Levy the other three cents per record off the books, in cash. As soon as he'd received the cutouts and had begun selling them, Levy would expect a $15,000 cash payment every week until the full amount of $120,000 was paid.

LaMonte looked at Brocco and Vastola for guidance. They nodded their approval of the deal, so he agreed to it.

LaMonte didn't mention it during the meeting, but he noticed that the list of MCA cutouts on Levy's desk was all marked up, with certain titles highlighted. He'd seen that before; it was exactly the way one of his competitors, Charlie Sutton, marked up a list when he was ordering cutouts. As he left Levy's office with Vastola, sure enough, he saw Sutton sitting in the reception area, along with Pete Hyman, one of the owners of Surplus Records and Tapes.

In the elevator, Vastola rubbed his hands together and said, "Whaddya think, kid, are you happy with the deal?"

LaMonte replied, "Let me get this straight. I'm responsible to you for an accounting of what we sell, and then you, me, and Brocco whack up the profits, right? What about Morris, what's his cut?"

"No, no, Morris and Sal is that side of the deal, we don't split nothing with them," Vastola said.

"Did you see those two guys sitting in the office as we left?" LaMonte asked. "They're gonna sell off the good stuff to them, Morris is going to cream our load and screw us."

Vastola assured him he'd never let that happen. LaMonte shrugged, "If you say so, okay." He headed back to Philadelphia not entirely reassured.

Within weeks, LaMonte's worst fears had been confirmed. By the middle of July he'd received sixty tractor-trailer loads of cutouts from MCA—representing freight bills to Out of the Past totaling nearly $100,000. But none of the good titles were there—no Bing Crosby, no Loretta Lynn or Conway Twitty, no Joe Walsh. He complained to Brocco, who was supposed to relay the complaint to Levy and Pisello through Vastola. "Tell them that MCA ain't sending us any of the good stuff, they're fucking us. Tell 'em I'm not paying for this shit until I get the cream, which I got customers waiting for."

Next, LaMonte found out that at least one of his customers, John Gervasoni of Scorpio Music, had purchased many of the same titles that were missing from his MCA shipments. Gervasoni had bought them from a small cutout distributor in Los Angeles called Betaco Enterprises, owned by a fellow named Ranji Bedi. Gervasoni let LaMonte see his purchase order from Betaco. LaMonte's stomach turned. It listed the same titles and same quantities that Out of the Past hadn't received from MCA. Worse, Scorpio had paid only sixty-five cents a unit for more than three hundred thousand cutouts that LaMonte had presold to Scorpio for $1.50 a unit. That represented nearly $300,000 profit to LaMonte wiped out. He called

Brocco, screaming, and was told that Pisello was claiming that, as far as he knew, Out of the Past had received everything it was supposed to from MCA.

LaMonte finally put in a call to MCA, asking for Sam Passamano, the only person he knew at the company. When Passamano came on the line, LaMonte told him, in a barely controlled voice, "Sam, I've never made any money doing business with you over the years, but you always seemed like an honorable gentleman. So I just want you to know that your guys are creaming my load of cutouts and I ain't ever going to pay for this stuff unless they put the sweeteners back in."

Passamano said he knew nothing about it, since cutouts were now being handled exclusively by Pisello. He'd check on it and get back to him. He called back the next day. "John, if it ever comes up I'll deny that this conversation took place, but you're right, you're getting screwed." He told LaMonte that, according to MCA's internal records of the sale, more than six hundred thousand units from his order had been sold to Betaco and had been shipped, at Betaco's instruction, to Scorpio and one other buyer, Last Chance Records and Tapes, in Little Rock, Arkansas.

"Bingo," LaMonte thought. "Now I got the goods on that fuckin' Super Jew Morris. Good ol' Sammy."

LaMonte hoped that, with the information he had from both Passamano and Gervasoni about the diversion of records from his order, he could convince Vastola that they were being cheated by MCA, Sal, or Morris, just as he'd suspected all along. He hoped that Vastola could then get everything straightened out. He thought there was still a chance to save the deal and most of his potential profits.

He thought wrong. A year later, he would say, "I musta been sittin' on my brains or something not to see what was coming."

8

"Get it in writing; save all memos; cover your butt"

Working out of MCA's branch office in Sun Valley, California, twelve miles northwest of Los Angeles, George Collier was comfortably removed from all the paranoia and intrigue of the home office. He'd heard about Pisello but hadn't met him. He knew about all the firings and about Sam Passamano's demotion. It was pretty shabby treatment for a man who'd given all those years to the company, he thought.

Passamano was a mentor, something of a father figure to Collier—he'd given George his first job in the record business back in 1966. Collier remembered the day, years earlier, when Sam taught him the value of records. They were supervising the transportation of inventory from Camden, New Jersey, to a new warehouse in Cherry Hill, and Sam told him to put armed guards on the trucks. Collier laughed and said he thought that was a bit dramatic. "You don't understand, George," Passamano said. "That truckload of records is worth $250,000—cash, negotiable tender. In fact, those records are better than gold, because you and I and the old lady down the street can't buy and sell gold. But anyone can sell records, even old records, faster than you can spit." Collier never forgot the lesson. From that day on he'd always thought of records as $5 bills made out of vinyl.

As bad as he felt about what had happened to Passamano and the others, Collier had no complaints about the way he'd been treated under the new Azoff regime. In August 1983, he'd been promoted from New York branch manager to West Coast regional director of MCA Distributing. He was given a $15,000 raise, a company car, and generous moving expenses to relocate his family to the Los Angeles area. In February, he received a Branch of the Year award for his performance in the new position and was given $14,000 worth of bonuses and stock. Things had never looked better for him.

In early April 1984, Jerry Eggert, the warehouse manager at MCA's West Coast shipping depot in Sun Valley, walked into Collier's office one morning with a handful of documents. "George, I wanted to be sure you were aware of this," he said. "It's been going on for a few months now and I'm starting to get a little concerned."

Collier looked at the stack of papers that Eggert thrust at him. They were telexes from Harold Sulman, the vice president of sales in the home office, requesting that records be shipped from the warehouse at no charge to two local accounts—Show Industries, which supplied the 134-store Music Plus chain, and Nottingham Industries, a small wholesaler that stocked a single retail store on Hollywood Boulevard. The telexes were marked "QRP Order," which stood for Quick Response Program, a priority system for getting small amounts of brand new releases into the marketplace in a day or two as a stop-gap measure, to make sure that at least a few copies were in the stores while the bulk of the shipment was on its way. The names of two vice presidents of promotion, Steve Meyers and John Schoenenberger, were also on the telexes, indicating to Collier that they had approved the requests. All three men reported to Richard Palmese, the head of promotion.

It all looked in order to Collier, except for the amount of records being shipped—six hundred to fifteen hundred copies at a crack, both 45s and cassettes. Those were big numbers, especially for Nottingham, which did very little business with MCA, only about

$50,000 a year. MCA often sent free 45s to accounts as both a reminder and an encouragement for the retail stores to log and report MCA sales to trade publications such as *Billboard* magazine that survey them in putting together the weekly best-seller charts. Every record company did that. Normally, however, MCA sent only a handful of 45s per store, amounting to a couple hundred copies at a time. A shipment of a thousand copies of a single album to one account was excessive. "This is more than a reminder for store reports," Collier thought. "This is dumping them."

The number of cassettes was even more troubling. Record companies commonly send free promotional copies of cassettes to accounts for in-store play, the playing of the recording on the store's stereo system as a means of stimulating impulse buying. MCA usually sent only one copy per store, which would be 134 in the case of Show Industries. Sulman was sending out ten times that amount.

At the bottom of each telex was a word that set a warning bell ringing in Collier's head—"cleans." In record industry parlance, a clean is a recording without the markings that indicate it's a promotional copy and not for sale. Without such markings—a drill hole in a cassette box, a stamp or a cut corner on an album jacket—a recording can be sold for full price or returned for full credit. Collier knew there was no good reason for any shipping document to specify that recordings be cleans. If they were part of a regular sale or free goods program, it wasn't necessary, because that's all wholesalers purchased. Nobody bought promotional copies. And if they really were being used for a proper promotional purpose, then they shouldn't be cleans.

He flipped through the telexes Eggert had given him: one thousand singles, six hundred cassettes, sixteen hundred singles—all cleans, all sent to Nottingham at no charge in a period of sixty days. That was more than $5,000 worth of merchandise that Nottingham didn't pay for but could sell or return for credit. If there was a legitimate reason for the shipments, Collier couldn't imagine what it would be.

Collier called his boss, Kent Crawford, and asked if there was some special promotion going on with the two accounts that he wasn't aware of, something that would explain the shipments. Crawford said he didn't know of any promotion, but since he'd only been on the job a few months, maybe Collier should check with

John Burns. Collier asked Burns about the telexes—were they properly authorized? Burns said he knew nothing about them but would check with the promotion department and get back to him.

Collier was concerned that telexes are not official documents routed through the company. There would be only two copies of each, the one in his hand and the original. Neither Sulman nor Meyers nor Schoenenberger had signed the telexes. If something funny was going on and someone had to answer for the telexes somewhere down the line, Collier feared it would be his ass, or Eggert's.

With that in mind, Collier told Eggert that further shipments of cleans to Nottingham or Show were to be hand-delivered by a sales-man who would insist on a signed bill of lading as a receipt. That way there could be no suspicion that the records had been siphoned off or sold out the back door of the warehouse by any Sun Valley employees. It was the kind of thing that Passamano had taught him about corporate survival: "Get it in writing; save all memos; cover your butt."

Burns called back the next day and said everything was okay, the telexes were properly authorized. But he gave no explanation about why the cleans were being sent out. Collier thought Burns sounded a little unsure of the situation, however. Before he hung up, he said, "Keep me informed about what's going on with this, will you, George?"

Several days later, Sulman called to complain that the shipments to the two accounts had taken too long in the past. Wasn't there something Collier could do to expedite things in the future? Collier said he'd see what could be done. Again he called Burns and again Burns said he'd look into it.

This time, Collier didn't wait for Burns to get back to him; he started doing some detective work on his own. He did an analysis of Nottingham's and Show's returns for the year to date and what he found shocked him. Nottingham's rate of return on 45s was 264 percent, meaning it had returned 164 percent more than it had pur-chased. Its rates of return on albums and cassettes were 61 percent and 118 percent, respectively. Show Industries had purchased $59,000 worth of 45s and had returned $87,000 worth, a rate of 147 percent.

Collier next called one of the salesmen who handled the two accounts and asked if there was some promotion going on that distribution hadn't been told about. The salesman said there wasn't. When Collier told him about the telexes and the alarmingly high rate of returns, the salesman warned, "I'd stay away from that one if I were you, George. The word on the street is that Nottingham is a big nose-candy connection. You know, cocaine."

Was that it? Collier wondered. Was someone trading records for coke? Were the company and its artists paying for someone's drug habit? Collier had no intention of staying away from it. He decided immediately that he was going to try to bust the operation. But he knew he had to be careful. If he went off half-cocked now and started making allegations, it could cost him his job. He would bide his time, collect evidence, and build a solid case before taking it to the higher-ups. He started putting together a file, which he kept locked in his desk drawer.

Collier never got a chance to use the file. At noon on June 8 he got a call from John Burns telling him he'd been fired. The reason given was that the record stores in his region were not stocked with MCA product in a manner that Azoff considered "visibly persuasive," whatever that meant. Collier's firing was so abrupt that it wasn't even cleared with Kent Crawford, who was out of town on business and didn't hear about it until three days later.

Two and a half hours after Collier's firing, a QRP order was sent from Harold Sulman to Jerry Eggert in Sun Valley authorizing the shipment of another eleven hundred cleans to Nottingham Industries.

A week after Collier's firing, the paperwork from John Burns's free goods deal with Handleman Company, the nation's biggest rack jobber, began coming across Sam Passamano's desk. It wasn't supposed to. When the new administration demoted him, no one realized that, years earlier, Passamano had sent a letter to all shipping depots and factories directing that any invoices for sending "gratis" or no-charge records to an account were to be routed to him. He'd installed the policy as a safeguard against payoffs to employees.

"I can't believe they're really doing it," Passamano thought as he sifted through the documents. Mostly, he couldn't believe the way it was being done. They were billing the merchandise internally as promotional records, so no artists, songwriters, or music publishers would be paid a royalty. It was all Platinum Plus LPs and cassettes—Olivia Newton-John, The Who, Elton John, Neil Diamond—the best-selling midline titles. And at the bottom of each document, on the line marked "Special Shipping Instructions," were the hand-written words "clean copies." Lots of them—2,148 to Handleman's Detroit depot, 2,976 to Cincinnati, 2,610 to Addison, Illinois. Passamano stopped counting at 50,000 units, $250,000 worth of records, at no charge.

This time Passamano complained to Dan McGill. The deal was, in his opinion, nothing more than a giveaway to a favored customer and raised serious antitrust questions. He got the same reaction he'd gotten earlier from Burns: "You're not in distribution anymore, Sam, let them handle it. They know what they're doing."

Passamano was beginning to wonder if anyone in the company knew what they were doing anymore, he'd seen so many crazy things going on in recent months.

Sal Pisello was all over the place, making deals that defied logic. MCA was paying him a fee of 3 percent of Sugar Hill's gross sales, off the top. Any time there was anything to be done with regard to Sugar Hill manufacturing, distribution, promotion, or record releases, MCA middle managers were instructed by upper management to "check with Sal," "run it by Sal," or "ask Sal." But Pisello still didn't seem to know the first thing about the record business. He was always asking the most rudimentary questions about how things worked. Nonetheless, MCA had advanced him $30,000 supposedly to help the company establish a Latin music label. He'd been given another $100,000 for researching a cockeyed plan he'd come up with for marketing a line of plastic mats to be used for break dancing. There were no signed contracts on any of these ventures. Sal had even convinced Myron Roth to give some of MCA's record jacket printing work to a small New York company called Modern Album, of which Pisello claimed to be part owner.

The cutout sale was Byzantine: the customer was supposedly Morris Levy's Roulette Records, which was being billed at thirty-five cents and ten cents per unit on the 4.2 million pieces. But the actual records were being shipped to two other cutout distributors, billed at forty cents and fifteen cents. So Levy was making a nickel a record profit for simply having the Roulette Records name on the purchase order. MCA was being paid for the cutouts by a fourth company, Consultants for World Records, of which Pisello was president. As a down payment for the cutouts, Pisello had written two checks, one for $150,000 and one for $100,000, drawn on a small bank in Astoria, New York. The first check bounced and the second had been returned because Pisello hadn't signed it. Consultants for World Records had been exempted from the normal financial background check by MCA's credit division. Credit director Larry Hariton was told by Dan McGill that the Consultants account was being handled "at the executive level."

Passamano was appalled by it all. Since Froelich left, there seemed to have been a complete breakdown of internal financial controls.

9

". . . has been known to carry a weapon"

The first week of August 1984 marked the beginning of the Summer Olympics in Los Angeles. With the downtown courts closed in anticipation of the crush of traffic and all available federal law enforcement personnel detached to special security assignments for the extravaganza, Marvin Rudnick, a special attorney with the Justice Department's Organized Crime Strike Force, was looking forward to a lull in his hectic workload and maybe even a chance to use the tickets he held to several Olympic events.

No such luck. On his desk when he arrived that Monday morning were three large cardboard boxes of background documents on his next assignment, already approved by the chief, a two-count income-tax-evasion prosecution. Another boring, make-work, low-priority case, he thought, and one that had been kicking around for quite some time, judging from the coating of dust on the boxes. He grabbed a handful of documents, slumped into his chair, put his feet up on the desk and began reading:

Salvatore James Pisello—age, sixty-two. Recommended to be charged with lying on his 1977 corporate income tax return, a felony. Claimed no income that year from a meat brokering company he owned called Cal-Bro, when in fact he earned $50,000. To be charged additionally with failing to file a 1978 personal tax return, a misdemeanor.

Rudnick had just completed a case involving a convicted bank robber named Jack Cantella who'd set up a soup kitchen for the needy in downtown Los Angeles. Cantella and his kitchen had been the subject of several heartwarming human-interest stories in the local news media. He'd received a letter of recognition from U.S. Attorney General Edwin Meese, citing his selfless service to the underprivileged, and he'd been given a humanitarian award by the wife of Los Angeles mayor Tom Bradley. But the money to set up the kitchen had come from the Los Angeles Mafia, and investigators from the U.S. Agriculture Department believed Cantella was operating it in violation of federal agriculture laws. Rudnick thought the agents were joking when the case was first assigned to him. Talk about a piddly-ass prosecution.

Nonetheless, Rudnick eventually convicted Cantella on fraud charges for illegally trafficking in $130,000 worth of food stamps that he'd bought from an undercover agent, believing they were stolen. Rudnick's superiors in the office had expected the conviction to draw a six-month prison sentence. But prior to sentencing, in the course of a background check on Cantella, Rudnick dug up two more armed robbery charges against him that had been sitting in the district attorney's office since 1982 without ever going to court. Armed with that information in Rudnick's presentencing report, the judge slapped Cantella with the maximum five years in prison on the fraud charges, plus seven more years for violating his probation on his previous bank robbery conviction. Cantella then got six more years on the bank robbery charges that were reactivated because of Rudnick's inquiry—making a grand total of eighteen years in prison for what had started out as a borderline prosecutable case.

The whole thing was typical Rudnick. During his four years with the strike force, he'd earned a reputation as a tireless investigator and relentless prosecutor who made the most out of every case, no matter how small or seemingly insignificant. His career conviction rate was better than 90 percent and the jail sentences he obtained were invariably longer than average. In 1982, he obtained a twenty-four-year sentence for the head of a local Colombian cocaine ring, the longest in the history of the Los Angeles office.

Rudnick's specialty was white-collar crime and his particular talent was tracing laundered funds. No one could follow a paper trail to dirty money better than Marvin, his colleagues would say. He possessed a bulldog-like tenacity that seemed to be reflected in his appearance—short, stocky, gap-toothed, and perpetually rumpled-looking.

Rudnick also had a reputation for being outspoken and sometimes bumptious when dealing with defense attorneys and their recalcitrant clients. Immunity? Forget about it. "Tell your guy not to send you back down here again looking for a deal unless he's prepared to give up his boss!" he once shouted at a stunned defense attorney in the hallway outside the strike force offices. Even some of his own people thought he was at times too aggressive. One FBI agent who'd dealt with him on a case referred to him as "Mad Man Muntz."

Rudnick dismissed such criticism. How could anyone be too aggressive in getting bad guys off the streets? he argued. He saw his role as one of the good guys whose nearly sacred trust it was to protect honest citizens from those who preyed upon them and got rich by cheating, stealing, and influence peddling. It wasn't a game to him, it was more of a mission, "Trying to keep society from becoming a sewer," as he put it. He had little sympathy for white-collar criminals, who he believed received lenient treatment too often from investigative agencies and the courts because of their education, social connections, and ability to hire high-priced legal counsel. People in positions of power and public trust often turned out to be the most corrupt of all, he'd found, and, unlike many of the less fortunate, they had no excuse for breaking the law.

Rudnick's views on power and criminality grew naturally out of his background. He was born Lipe Mendel Rudnicki in a German refugee camp in 1947. His mother and father were Polish Jews who'd survived the Nazi death camps—the only members of their respective families who did—and who'd met and married shortly after the war. When he emigrated to America with his parents and twin brother, Joseph, in 1949, little Lipe received an official welcoming letter from the U.S. Justice Department, which now hung on a wall in his office at home. "The last good letter I ever got from the government," he would joke later. The name Marvin was bestowed by the pediatrician who first examined him in this country.

The family settled in Glens Falls, New York, a small town in the Adirondacks, where Abraham Rudnicki became a plumber's apprentice and eventually opened up his own plumbing supply business. Marvin eventually graduated from Syracuse University, then the University of Kentucky School of Law.

Rudnick's first job out of law school was working as an aide to Florida's governor, Reuben Askew. From there, he became staff counsel to the Florida State Legislature. There, his first two investigations led to the convictions of the state education commissioner and the state treasurer for misappropriation of funds and taking kickbacks, respectively. At age twenty-seven, Rudnick was made head of his own fraud division in the St. Petersburg state attorney's office, where he promptly unearthed the biggest consumer fraud in the state's history, involving the Florida Power Corporation, the state's second largest utility, with more than a billion dollars a year in revenues.

Acting on a complaint from the owner of a single share of Florida Power stock and an item in a story by syndicated columnist Jack Anderson, Rudnick turned up evidence that the utility had been overcharged for fuel purchased during the 1973–74 Arab oil embargo with the complicity of its former chairman, Angel Perez, who'd received several hundred thousand dollars in kickbacks from the operators of a "daisy chain" of Texas oil distribution companies that had artificially inflated the price. Florida Power had passed the cost of the price hike along to consumers, adding millions of dollars to their electricity bills. Rudnick's revelations to the state's Public Service Commission caused such a storm of outrage that the Department of Justice launched a federal grand jury investigation and appointed him a special prosecutor in the case. Before the trial was over he'd been named an assistant U.S. attorney.

The Florida Power "daisy chain" oil swindle case culminated in 1979 with jail sentences for four Houston oil men, a fuel purchasing agent, and former chairman Perez. Shortly after the story was aired on a segment of CBS's "60 Minutes," Rudnick was called to Washington to testify before Congress. The legislators wanted to know why his was the only prosecution by the federal government for manipulating oil prices during the Arab embargo. Hadn't this same scam gone on all over the country? he was asked. "We don't know because we haven't looked into it," he responded.

The answer was truthful, direct, and impolitic. Rudnick's Justice Department superiors in Washington had urged him not to testify in the first place. Now they were furious, feeling that his comment made it appear that they weren't really interested in going after the politically powerful oil industry and had prosecuted the Florida case only because they were forced to by the extensive media coverage of his investigation and the resultant hue and cry from the public.

Rudnick did not say that to the committee, but privately he believed it was true.

Rudnick's testimony branded him a maverick within the Justice Department—not a team player, not a company man, a grandstander. Making matters worse, he was engaged to Kathryn Harris, a bright young reporter for the *St. Petersburg Times*. In the tight-lipped world of federal investigatory agencies, publicly consorting with a member of the press was looked upon as collaborating with the enemy. This Rudnick kid would bear some watching. He was talented all right, but with his tendency to shoot his mouth off and embarrass the department, he obviously had to be kept under tight control.

Whatever the view in Washington, back home in Florida Rudnick was a genuine hero, celebrated in the local news media as a giant-killer and defender of the downtrodden. For the thirty-two-year-old prosecutor, who'd come to Florida seven years earlier with no investigative experience and vague plans of getting into politics, it had been a dizzying ride. But when his fiancée was offered a job as a business reporter for the *Los Angeles Times* in the fall of 1979, he resigned his position in the U.S. attorney's office to go with her to the West Coast. His resignation prompted the *St. Petersburg Times* to publish an unabashedly fond farewell article. "Marvin L. Rudnick, the tough young prosecutor who helped lay bare some of the state's biggest scandals, is leaving Florida to start a new career in California," it began, continuing in a detailed litany of his successes.

In Los Angeles, Rudnick quickly landed a job with the Organized Crime Strike Force. Established during the 1960s in eighteen major U.S. cities, the force was envisioned as elite units of skilled government attorneys supported by investigators from the FBI, IRS, Drug Enforcement Administration (DEA), and local police. Since they reported directly to the Justice Department's Organized Crime and Racketeering Section in Washington, the strike force units operated autonomously from the politically appointed U.S. attorneys in their regions. The idea was to protect them from being buffeted by political winds. Rudnick became one of six special attorneys in the Los Angeles office.

Historically, organized crime activity in Los Angeles has differed from that in New York, Philadelphia, and Chicago—cities where the traditional Mafia first flowered in this country as the enforcement arm of racketeers exploiting the waves of Italian immigrants that arrived after the turn of century. In a number of large Eastern cities, dense concentrations of highly structured, competing crime families have produced periodic violent wars for control of bootlegging, narcotics, gambling, loan-sharking, and prostitution, as well as recurring political corruption scandals.

In Los Angeles, organized crime has always operated as a more subtle, almost invisible force, employing more lawyers, bankers, and investment brokers than leg breakers and button men. The indigenous Mafia "family" has traditionally been weak, both in numbers and organization. With no dominant local crime group, the second largest metropolitan area in the country has become what's known as an "open city" for the mob, a sort of free zone where anyone can operate without fear of treading on another family's turf. L.A. is the place where Eastern mobsters have always come to invest, or launder, their ill-gotten gains and retire.

Following Prohibition, several hundred million dollars from Al Capone's Chicago crime syndicate was funneled into southern California real estate by supposedly legitimate local businessmen operating as fronts. Hollywood has also been a favorite depository of mob money over the years, attractive for both its attendant glamour and its murky accounting practices. In the late 1930s, two transplanted associates of the Chicago mob, Willie Bioff and George Browne, shook down the all-too-willing major Hollywood movie studios for millions of dollars in exchange for labor peace. Bioff and Browne were convicted in the labor racketeering scheme in 1943, along with former Capone confidantes Frank Nitti and Johnny Roselli, who'd become a movie producer by then.

In the 1970s, members of New York's Colombo crime family ran untold millions in cash profits from the porno movie *Deep Throat* through a legitimate Hollywood movie company they set up called Bryanston Pictures, which released the modern horror classic *Texas Chainsaw Massacre* as well as *Devil's Rain,* the debut film of John Travolta, and *Echoes of a Summer,* which starred a precocious pre-teen named Jodie Foster. Bryanston president Louis ("Butchie") Peraino, a graduate of the Times Square peep-show school of moviemaking, became a well-known Hollywood figure for a time, employing scores of legitimate film executives, writers, and producers. He gave speeches to gatherings of movie theater owners and distributors and was quoted constantly in the trade papers announcing his plans to make "family-oriented movies," including one about the Pope. Instead, Bryanston went out of business owing millions in 1976, and, three years later, Peraino went to prison on pornography charges.

Bryanston is an example of how organized crime is often virtually indistinguishable from legitimate business in Los Angeles. One of the strike force's most difficult tasks is keeping the two separate—preventing outside crime groups from penetrating local industry and rooting them out when they do manage to penetrate. How well the Los Angeles office has done its job is open to debate.

In 1981, the strike force took down the entire top echelon of the L.A. Mafia family on racketeering charges stemming from a bungled bookmaking operation. The boss, underboss, consiglieri, and several lieutenants were sentenced to long prison terms, prompting the strike force chief at the time, James Henderson, to announce that they'd "broken the back" of the "Mickey Mouse Mafia."

On the other hand, as Rudnick soon learned, the Los Angeles office rarely tackled cases of more sophisticated, high-level mob infiltration of legitimate business. They'd never gone after Sidney Korshak, for example. He was a former Chicago syndicate lawyer—representing Bioff and Browne in the racketeering case—who'd moved to Los Angeles in the late 1940s and set up a law practice in Beverly Hills. In the ensuing years he'd become widely recognized in law enforcement circles as the principal link between organized crime and legitimate business, a high-powered fixer who could—for a fat fee—quickly settle a labor dispute on any issue anywhere in the country. Korshak had also become quite a social lion in Los Angeles, numbering among his closest friends MCA chairman Lew Wasserman, once actor Ronald Reagan's agent and for forty years the most powerful man in Hollywood. Wasserman not only remained close to President Reagan, he also was one of the most effective Democratic fund-raisers west of the Potomac.

Perhaps it was Wasserman's political connections that made his pal Korshak seemingly untouchable in the eyes of local law enforcement. Rudnick didn't know. But he did know that the strike force had never even attempted to take a peek at Korshak's activities.

The first case Rudnick worked on in Los Angeles involved the president of an Orange County aerospace company who spent his weekends working for the Dunes Hotel in Las Vegas. Investigators found company money going into a slush fund and then into cashier's checks—nearly $300,000 worth—that were laundered through the Dunes and eventually wound up in the hands of a Las Vegas gambling junketeer named Big Julie Weintraub. The case was dropped, however, after the company president hired a New York attorney who was a friend of former strike force chief Stephen P. Crane. (Crane had quit the strike force in 1979 to become a 5 percent owner of a Las Vegas casino named the Barbary Coast.)

As it turned out, most of Rudnick's early prosecutions were in Las Vegas, which fell under the jurisdiction of the Los Angeles office. In 1983, he convicted a man named Sorkis Webbe, a well-known St. Louis attorney and Democratic fund-raiser, on tax evasion charges stemming from a kickback on a construction project at the Aladdin Hotel, which had been financed with a loan from the longtime mob-controlled Teamsters Central States Pension Fund. Prior to Webbe's sentencing, a number of prominent St. Louisans had written letters to the judge attesting to Webbe's character—among them Missouri senator Thomas Eagleton and Lt. Col. John A. Doherty of the St. Louis Police Department, supposedly the city's top fighter of organized crime. The letters were to no avail—Webbe got three years in prison. In the court hallway after the sentencing, Rudnick and Doherty got into an argument and Rudnick shouted, within earshot of the press corps, "You oughta quit hanging around with organized crime." The St. Louis newspapers had a field day with that, Doherty was censured, and Rudnick was once again in hot water with his superiors for publicly stating the obvious.

Since the Webbe incident, Rudnick felt he'd been assigned to only "scrap" cases in the office. Like the one he held in his hand that morning: borderline prosecutable and unlikely to draw a jail sentence, since Salvatore Pisello had no prior convictions. That's probably why the case had been banging around in the system since 1979, he thought. It took that long to get approved because nobody really cared much about it. He was the fourth prosecutor assigned to handle the case.

As Rudnick plowed through the documents in the cardboard boxes on his desk, however, Pisello began to emerge as an interesting character: Born in Brooklyn in 1922, six-foot-three, 220 pounds, blind in the right eye. A high-ranking soldier in the Gambino crime family, part of Aniello Dellacroce's crew, according to the FBI. "Subject suspected narcotics and precious gem smuggler . . . close associates are among the top drug violators in organized crime . . . two separate reports, considered reliable, indicate Pisello had drug related contacts with Mexico and Panama . . . a major narcotics supplier of heroin from Mexico City . . . On two occasions, Pisello reportedly 'ripped off' other narcotics dealers for $250,000 . . . has been known to carry a weapon."

Sal definitely got around. He appeared to have spent the early 1970s hopscotching through Switzerland, France, South America, Mexico, Japan, and especially Italy, with the authorities tracking him all the way, even monitoring his phone calls.

"Italian National Police indicate that Pisello was described as an international swindler in 1969–70 for having committed fraud in the amount of 60 million lire (approximately $102,000) to the damage of a jeweler named Gerard at the Hotel di Paris at Monte Carlo."

Sal the Swindler.

"On September 25, 1974, (informant) NY T-1 advised Pisello had resided intermittently at the Hotel Flora, Rome, Italy, during the past two years."

"On Sept. 19, 1974, Lorenzo Di Gesu, an alleged member of the Palermo Mafia registered at the Hotel Flora. Pisello and Di Gesu failed to meet. However, before checking out of the hotel, Pisello paid the Di Gesu bill."

"On 10/7/74, DEA, NY., advised that on 9/23/74 Charles Alaimo and Edward Lino (two well-documented narcotics traffickers) were positively identified by the DEA surveillance in Rome associating with Salvatore Pisello. DEA surveillance determined that Pisello rented two apartments, one for Alaimo and one for Lino, in Vive Mardie. . . . Surveillance indicates that the three were constantly together and spending large amounts of money. They had a regular

table at the Piccolo Mondo Restaurant. . . . Surveillance was terminated when the subjects entered France on Sept. 28, 1974. . . . Information was received from a reliable source that the subjects were
definitely in Italy and France to arrange for a multi-kilo shipment
of heroin."

On the personal side, Pisello was described as a "boisterous, lik-
able extrovert" and a "good dresser who always wore dark glasses."
Married for more than forty years to Assunta (nee Morlano), he also
had a longtime mistress in New York, a wealthy Jewish divorcée
named Lucille Barrie who was formerly married to the founder of
Fabergé Cosmetics and was still a large shareholder in the company.
Barrie once lent Sal $150,000, which he promptly lost at the track.
Despite years of high living around the globe, Pisello "does not
have a documented visible means of income," according to the
intelligence reports. In 1972, he "exhibited the abilities of an excel-
lent confidence man when he convinced Maine farmers, Maine
state officials, and a charter airline president of his sincerity in a
highly questionable business venture."

That was the ambitious veal cattle export proposal that prompted
a summit meeting of investigators from the New York State Police,
New England Organized Crime Intelligence Division, U.S. Customs Service, the Bureau of Narcotics and Dangerous Drugs, and
the Securities and Exchange Commission at the strike force office
in New York on June 6, 1972. Notes of the meeting indicate the
investigators were "skeptical" of the plan in part because they
"could find no address or telephone number for Regency Beef,"
Pisello's alleged exporting firm. Nonetheless, Pisello did manage to
ship one load of eighty-five veal cattle from Bangor, Maine, to Italy
on June 15, 1972. The shipment was stopped at the airport by Italian officials, however, because it was not accompanied by a required
document from federal veterinarians in the U.S.

According to a DEA intelligence report, Pisello flew to Italy on
June 16 to "straighten out" the matter and deliver the necessary
documents. "He brought incomplete documents of questionable
authenticity, and he was advised by the U.S. Agriculture Attaché
not to present them to the Italian Ministry of Health. In spite of the
advice, Pisello presented the documents and then proceeded to
cause a scene. He was ushered out of the offices as soon as possible
and informed that the U.S. Attaché would meet and discuss the

importation problem with Italian officials at a later date.... The U.S. Embassy has not heard from him since."

Pisello apparently moved to Los Angeles sometime in the mid-1970s, when FBI agents began picking up information about his local business dealings. "U.S. Customs reported that David Esses is a jewelry fence for Pisello. Esses resides at 1155 La Cienega Blvd., Los Angeles, and is owner of Jade East Importer, 202 Beverly Drive. Esses is well documented in DEA files and was allegedly involved in the 600 lbs of heroin smuggled into Florida from Hong Kong."

Pisello appeared to be particularly active in the Beverly Hills area. "Informant said that Pisello told him the male Negro who has assisted Pisello in collection of 'protection payments' to Pisello by Bijan's Clothiers in Beverly Hills is named Benny Shells and is described as approximately 6' 7", 265–270 lbs, in his mid 30s. According to the informant, Benny Shells has worked for Pisello in the past and is often used for collection of debts because of his appearance."

The informant went on to tell FBI investigators about a phone conversation he heard between Pisello and a New York mobster named Rudy Farone regarding Aladena ("Jimmy the Weasel") Fratianno, who was then in the federal Witness Protection Program and informing on his mob associates all over the country. "Pisello stated that they would kill Fratianno whether he was under the protection of the U.S. government or not ... and Farone, in a laughing manner, described what they had done to a 'canary who could sing but could not fly.' Both Pisello and Farone considered this a humorous incident where they eliminated a witness to their criminal activities."

In November 1977, another informant told an FBI agent he'd had dinner with Pisello at the pricey La Scala restaurant and later met with Tony Roma at Tony Roma's Restaurant in Beverly Hills. While in the presence of the informant, according to the FBI report, "Pisello and Roma discussed their involvement in using 'mob' money to purchase restaurants in the Los Angeles area, and that the money was coming from Meyer Lansky, through Jack Rosen, Lansky's son-in-law. Later that evening, according to the informant, Pisello used a pay telephone at Tony Roma's and placed a call to a person Pisello said was Aniello Dellacroce. The informant spoke with the individual and was told, 'Anything my friend Sal says to you, you better believe, because Sal, he's number one.'"

Pisello opened up his own Los Angeles restaurant in 1978, La Roma di Notte ("Rome by Night"), on La Cienega Boulevard just outside Beverly Hills. It drew a rave review from *Los Angeles Times* restaurant critic Lois Dwan: "The lightest hand that has been set to Italian cooking in this city for many a moon," she enthused. Rudnick had to chuckle at Dwan's description of Pisello: "A Sicilian out of New York, he is a big, graceful, smiling man with great energy and no untoward modesty. . . . At one time he worked with the U.S. Department of Agriculture in experimenting with a new crossbreed of cattle for Italy."

Sal the Baker.

Dwan no doubt would have choked on her veal cutlet à la millanese if she'd known what else Pisello was up to at the time:

"In 1977–78 Pisello was subject of a Los Angeles FBI-DEA Task Force Title 3 investigation . . . based on allegation that Pisello was directing large scale narcotics transactions involving Aniello Dellacroce, acting boss of the Carlo Gambino crime family."

"On 10/27/77, a confidential informant jointly developed by FBI and DEA, who is a wholesale fish and lobster merchant, advised he had been approached by Pisello on that date to use his business of importing fish from Europe to include the importation of narcotics. Pisello advised he had recently returned from Europe where he had established a contact in Turkey for a large quantity of narcotics. Pisello advised he desired several loads of fish to be imported to establish a routine and thereafter one load would be primarily narcotics."

The informant, Marty Antoci, agreed to help the task force nail Pisello. He was given $15,000 in government funds, which he gave to Pisello as a loan to help launch the smuggling operation, and he was fitted with a hidden microphone to record his conversations with Pisello. On October 28, as Pisello was getting ready to fly to New York to set up a drug purchase, he gave Antoci a small vial containing what later proved to be 84 percent pure cocaine.

"That's my whole thing," Pisello said. "Ever since I've been coming here, that's my whole thing. See, I'm involved with you to make money, only for that reason and no other. But out of one condition. The condition is that you open your mouth to anybody, Marty, I swear to God . . . "

"You told me, I'm dead," Antoci replied.

"Marty, I'll take an oath on my children, I shouldn't see them alive anymore, too, and my mother, who I buried. I'll tell you now, Marty."

When Antoci expressed concern that he would end up losing his money on the deal, Pisello replied, "Yeah, but you see, you shouldn't worry or nothing, you see, when you do business with a man—remember, a man. When you do business with punks in the street, then you do what you wanna do—understand? But you'd never blow your money with me, you see, cause I'm a man. You understand what a fucking man is?"

Big Sal.

Pisello apparently never set up the drug smuggling scheme, possibly because he learned that the authorities were watching him, and he never returned the $15,000 to Antoci. A few weeks later, Antoci reported that he'd received a phone call from Pisello saying he'd learned that his conversations had been electronically intercepted by the government. "You're a dead man," Pisello told him.

The drug investigation petered out after that, with investigators deciding there was "insufficient evidence to prosecute Pisello." They turned the matter over to the IRS because of the $15,000 in government funds that Pisello had pocketed.

To Rudnick, the Pisello story read like a classic case of a career racketeer who'd always managed to slip through the cracks in the system. Despite countless man-hours and hundreds of thousands of dollars spent dogging his tracks over a fifteen-year period, he'd never even been arrested for anything, much less convicted.

And unless Rudnick moved quickly on the case at hand, Pisello would skate again—the statute of limitations was due to run out on September 9. He had approximately five weeks to bring an indictment.

He called Mike McCormick, the IRS agent assigned to the case, and asked where Pisello was—there was nothing in the files after 1979. "We don't know where he is; we lost him," McCormick said.

"Well, I don't want to indict somebody just for the hell of it if we don't know where he is," Rudnick said.

McCormick didn't seem very interested. "Last we heard, he'd gone back to New York," he said, as if that was the end of it.

The official lack of interest in Pisello just made Rudnick more determined to find him. On his lunch hour, he went over to federal court and began a search through the case files to see if his name came up anywhere subsequent to 1979. Nothing. Next he tried the bankruptcy court. Zero. Finally, he went to the county court and looked for the name *Pisello* on the microfilmed list of plaintiffs and defendants in civil cases. He got a hit—*Tuchinsky* v. *Pisello,* a 1984 lawsuit. He pulled the file for the case and there it was—Salvatore James Pisello was being sued by Joseph Tuchinsky, a San Fernando Valley businessman, for failure to repay a $65,000 loan. Rudnick called Tuchinsky's lawyer and got Pisello's address, 949 Larabee Street. He'd been missing for nearly five years and yet he was living—and apparently doing business—right here in Los Angeles.

Rudnick issued a subpoena for Pisello, who showed up at the strike force office a few days later with his lawyer "to see what this is all about," he said.

Rudnick showed him a copy of the indictment he intended to bring for tax evasion. Pisello claimed he didn't know anything about his 1977 corporate tax return, an accountant had handled all that for him. He said he was unaware the IRS had been looking for him. It was all a mistake that could be easily cleared up, he said. He was cool, seemingly unconcerned.

Two weeks later, on August 23, Pisello was indicted by the federal grand jury in Los Angeles. It was all very undramatic. Pisello wasn't even arrested. Trial was set for October 30, 1984. Rudnick knew he had a weak case going in, but in the two months he had before trial, he would try to build it into something more substantial. The first thing he would do would be to try to find out what Sal had been up to since he dropped out of sight in 1979.

He was in for the surprise of his life.

10

"It sounds like you might be a victim here"

n mid-September 1984, John LaMonte was summoned back to Morris Levy's New York office for a "sit-down" to straighten out the problems with the MCA cutouts. Pisello flew in from California. Brocco and Vastola met him there.

Levy wanted to know when LaMonte was going to start paying for the records. "MCA is bugging me for the money," he said. "I guaranteed the payment on this deal, so I'm responsible."

LaMonte came to the meeting with all his documentation—a copy of the original MCA inventory list Pisello had given him to order from, a copy of his purchase order, and an inventory list of what he had actually received from MCA. From the three documents, it was clear that MCA had not shipped him some 600,000 units of the best titles he'd ordered. He was supposed to have received 122,000 Olivia Newton-John albums but got only 2,000. There were no Mamas and Papas albums, no Joe Walsh, no Barbara

Mandrell, none of the two-record Impulse jazz sets. He ordered 144,000 units of Crystal Gale but received only 2,000. He was missing 83,000 *Bing Crosby's Greatest Hits* albums. "You sold me apples and I got pears," he said to Pisello. "Somebody creamed my load."

Pisello feigned ignorance. LaMonte had to be mistaken, he said. "My guys at MCA say everything was shipped that was ordered. The goods must be in your warehouse somewhere."

"Who else is involved in this deal?" LaMonte asked, pulling from his briefcase the bills he'd received that week for the cutouts—not from MCA but from some cockamamie company he'd never heard of, Consultants for World Records. "What's this shit?"

"That's my company," Pisello said. "You pay me and then I pay MCA; that's the way we're handling it."

"Well I ain't paying anybody, MCA or Consultant World or whatever, until I get what I ordered," LaMonte shot back.

There were two other men at the meeting that day whom LaMonte had never met before. Introduced simply as Fritzy and Rudy, they'd been sitting in the corner of the room behind LaMonte, saying nothing, their presence unexplained. When the exchange between LaMonte and Pisello grew heated, the one identified as Fritzy stood up and walked slowly to the middle of the room between the two combatants. "It sounds like you might be a victim here, kid," he said in a conciliatory tone. "Maybe we can work something out with MCA."

LaMonte was asked to leave the room while the others discussed a possible solution to the problem. Sitting in the hallway outside Levy's office, his mind raced. "I see what's going on here," he thought. "They're gonna run the money through this phonyass company, bankrupt it, and not pay MCA for the goods. It's a bust out."

"Who were these other two characters?" he wondered. "They must be heavyweight wise guys, since everyone in the room seemed to show them a lot of respect. Vastola said nothing the whole time, like he was afraid of them or something."

After a few minutes, Fritzy came out into the hallway. "What do you think this deal is worth, John, as is?" he asked, sounding sympathetic.

"Without the cream? A million dollars tops," LaMonte replied.

"What if we could work out a deal with MCA to send you some more records, would you be willing to pay the full amount?"

"If they send me about three hundred thousand albums, good artists, and good titles. There's fourteen million units of MCA stuff on the market already, and I got mediocre stuff and shit. So if I call up a customer and say I got MCA, he's gonna hang up on me. I need leaders."

Fritzy patted him on the shoulder and said it was no problem. Walking LaMonte to the elevator, hand on his shoulder, he said, "Don't worry, kid, you'll get your records."

LaMonte would later recognize Fritzy from police mug shots as Federico ("Fritzy") Giovanelli, a member of the inner circle of Genovese family boss Vincent ("the Chin") Gigante.

Rudy, he would learn, was Rudolph Farone, the New York mobster Marvin Rudnick read about in the Sal Pisello file—the one who, according to an unidentified informant, laughed about "eliminating" a witness to his and Pisello's criminal activities.

11

*"The jury
has a
question"*

The week before Sal Pisello's tax evasion trial in October 1984, Marvin Rudnick was poring over Pisello's financial records when he found documents of a $10,000 loan from Bank of America to a company Pisello owned called Cal-Bro. The money had been deposited in an account at South Coast Bank that had been opened with the assistance of Jack Catain, a well-known Los Angeles organized crime figure.

Rudnick was looking for business operations in 1977—Pisello claimed on his corporate tax return that Cal-Bro had none. A connection to Catain would be a bonus, a lead on another case—the strike force had been investigating Catain for years.

The bank documents showed that a local man named Robert Berglass had guaranteed the loan for Pisello. Rudnick called Berglass, who told him that Pisello was the boyfriend of his mother,

Lucille Barrie, who lived in New York. "Talk to my sister, Carol Kaplan. She knows more about it than I do," Berglass said.

Carol Kaplan was reluctant to discuss Pisello when Rudnick called, saying she was too busy that week to meet with him for an interview. After some cajoling, however, she agreed to come to his office on Saturday morning, October 27.

She arrived with her husband in a red Porsche. She didn't know much about Pisello either, she said, except that her mother had lived with him in New York for years. When Rudnick asked what Pisello was doing for a living now, she replied off-handedly, "He's got some sort of deal with MCA Records. He's involved with making album covers. He works with a guy named Sam Passamano over there."

Trying hard to conceal his excitement, Rudnick scribbled down the information. Finding a reputed New York Mafia figure operating inside a publicly traded, Fortune 500 company like MCA was a significant development. Based on his reading of Pisello's background, he assumed a crime was being committed at the company, he just had to find out what the crime was. "Call Passamano," he wrote.

Pisello's trial began three days later, Tuesday, October 30. From the outset, Rudnick sensed that U.S. District Court Judge Harry L. Hupp either didn't like the case or just wasn't very interested in it. He could hardly blame him. Like most tax cases, *U.S.* v. *Pisello* was less than riveting stuff, filled with dry testimony about small-time financial transactions and arcane tax law.

Of course, the real story of Pisello's business activities in 1977 was more colorful: his company, Cal-Bro (California Brokers), was just a shell through which he passed the commissions he'd earned as a sales representative for Consolidated Foods, a Cincinnati company that marketed Hillshire Farms sausage. The company fired Pisello after it learned he'd been threatening the supermarket meat managers in his territory, in effect telling them they'd better order the smoked kielbasa, or else. Pisello's former partner in Cal-Bro was prepared to testify that when he sought his share of the company's income, Pisello displayed a gun and said, "You ain't getting nothing."

The judge ruled, however, that such testimony was irrelevant to the tax charges and would be too prejudicial to the defendant. So the jury never heard it. Nor did they hear anything about Pisello's reputed Mafia background. And since Pisello didn't take the stand to testify in his own defense, Rudnick wasn't able to question him about his dealings with MCA.

On the third day of the trial, an odd thing happened that, once again, the jury missed. During the fifteen-minute morning recess, instead of disappearing into his chambers while the jury went to the jury room, Judge Hupp strolled out into the courtroom and bummed a cigarette and a light from Pisello. Both men stood there together for a moment, puffing. Rudnick was slack-jawed. Never mind that the Municipal Code forbade smoking in the courtroom, a judge having a cigarette with a defendant in the middle of a trial was something he had never before witnessed. "What the hell is going on here?" he wondered.

Rudnick finished his closing arguments just before noon on the fourth day, Friday, November 2. Back in his office during jury deliberations, he received a phone call from Judge Hupp's clerk. He had to get over to court right away. "The jury has a question," the clerk told him.

When Rudnick arrived in the courtroom, Hupp explained that there'd been a foul-up—documents the defense submitted as a motion had somehow wound up in the jury room mixed in with the trial exhibits. It was his clerk's error, he said. "We may have prejudice in jury deliberations."

Rudnick's antennae went up. He'd seen the defense motion mixed in with the exhibits that morning on the table where the clerk sat. It was easy to spot, since motion papers are backed with a blue sheet of paper. He'd even pointed it out to the clerk, telling him the motion should be pulled out so it wouldn't go to the jury.

Rudnick asked for a poll of the jury to see if there in fact had been any prejudicial effect. Hupp refused. Banging his gavel, he declared a mistrial. The case would have to be retried the following March, he said.

Just like that, it was over. Rudnick turned on his heels and walked quickly out of the courtroom, fighting the urge to say something about the smoking incident, just to get it on the official court record. That'd be foolhardy, he knew, because he had to face Hupp again when the case was retried. No use irritating him further. The only thing to do was use the time to come up with an even stronger case against Sal. He would dig some more.

12

*"Nothing's gonna
move until
they get
half the money
up front"*

The week of the Pisello trial, John Gervasoni, the owner of Scorpio Music in Philadelphia, got a call from Ranji Bedi, a some-time actor and songwriter in Los Angeles who dabbled in the cutout trade through a little company he owned called Betaco Enterprises. Bedi wanted to know if Gervasoni would be interested in MCA's new cutout inventory. He had an "exclusive" on MCA product, Bedi said, and Scorpio could have first pick.

Gervasoni was very interested. He'd made a lot of money on his last buy from Bedi—the cream from LaMonte's MCA shipment. He felt bad that LaMonte had gotten screwed on the deal, but he wasn't the one who'd done the screwing. Besides, he was a hard-nosed businessman and LaMonte was a competitor. He asked Bedi to Federal Express the MCA list to him overnight.

What he received the next day was the best cutout inventory list he'd seen in all his years in the business. It contained 400,000 two-record sets, including 208,000 copies of The Who's *Greatest Hits*, 93,000 copies of The Who's *Hooligans* album, and 36,000 copies of the group's *The Kids Are Alright*. There were ten different Neil Diamond titles, including his greatest hits, and ten different Olivia Newton-John albums, including a greatest-hits package and her biggest seller, *Physical*.

The list went on: 102,000 Steely Dan albums, including 86,000 copies of *Gold*, the group's greatest hits; 64,000 Tom Petty albums; nine different Lynyrd Skynyrd titles, including a double greatest-hits package; eleven different B. B. King LPs; sixteen selections by Elton John, eleven by Barbara Mandrell, twenty-four by Conway Twitty, twenty-two by Loretta Lynn; forty-four different original Broadway-cast albums, including *The King and I, Man of La Mancha,* and *Guys and Dolls;* the Oak Ridge Boys; Willie Nelson; Jimmy Buffett.

Many of the albums on the list weren't actually cutouts; they were still listed in MCA's sales catalog, priced at $3 or better wholesale. The double albums were priced at $6. Gervasoni assumed they were overstocks, excess album inventory that MCA was trying to even out with its cassette inventory. He was on the phone to Bedi before he even finished reading the list.

Bedi wanted him to buy a minimum of one and a half million units at fifty cents apiece. Gervasoni said he only had room in his warehouse for seven hundred thousand. Bedi checked with MCA and countered with a million units at seventy cents each, for a total of $700,000. Gervasoni had to think about it—a million units would be the biggest order his company had ever placed. He'd have to move a lot of his present inventory to make room for the new stuff, or lease more warehouse space to hold it. Of the million units, there would be three hundred thousand pieces of pure junk, worth about a nickel each for recycling.

On the other hand, he knew he could sell the four hundred thousand double-LP sets for $5 apiece. That was $2 million right there. Plus, he could use the good stuff to sell tons of his mediocre goods by requiring his customers to order a mix of good and bad titles. He could make a couple of million dollars easily on the deal. "I'll take it," he told Bedi.

The two cutout men then began a round of haggling over the manner of payment. Bedi said he needed a $50,000 "good faith" down payment to prove to MCA it was a bona fide order. No problem, Gervasoni said. Bedi said he wanted it in cash, placed in a brown paper bag, and brought to Las Vegas. Gervasoni wasn't shocked by Bedi's request, but he didn't like the idea of carrying that much cash to Las Vegas. Besides, drawing $50,000 out of the bank might cause him tax problems at the end of the year, since it could be viewed by the IRS as income to him. Cash was no good, he said. "I'll wire the money to your account; whatever you do with it after that is your business."

After more consultation with MCA, Bedi agreed to the wire transfer but said the company needed more good faith money, another $200,000. So Gervasoni wired it on November 7. A week later, Bedi called and said MCA was insisting on yet another $100,000 in advance. Gervasoni protested—$250,000 was all he could scrape up, any more he'd have to borrow from the bank. Bedi said he was sorry, but, "They say nothing's gonna move until they get half the money up front."

Against his better judgment, Gervasoni took out a loan at his bank and wired the $100,000 to Bedi's account on November 16. Little by little, Bedi had coaxed $350,000 out of him. The terms of the deal were extraordinary, in his experience, but so was the list of cutouts. The deal was just too good to pass up.

13

"The Galoot"

During the same week that Pisello was on trial in Los Angeles and John Gervasoni was negotiating with Ranji Bedi for the MCA cutouts, authorities in Union County, New Jersey, obtained a court order for a wiretap on the telephone of Nicholas John Massaro at 184 Atlantic Avenue in Long Branch, New Jersey.

"Nicky" Massaro was a low-level associate of Gaetano "Corky" Vastola, Union County's most powerful mobster. Detectives from the Union County prosecutor's office in Elizabeth, New Jersey, had evidence that Massaro was running a gambling wire out of the Long Branch address. He was laying off bets from a larger book-making operation on Long Island that was run by the Genovese family. The investigators figured that a tap on Massaro's phone would not only help them gather further evidence on the local gambling scene but would also provide valuable leads into the Vastola organization and its connection to the far more powerful Genovese group.

They never expected the tap on Massaro's phone to lead as far as it did, however.

From the beginning, detectives manning the listening post picked up odd snatches of conversation about the record business between Massaro and Vastola's cousin, Sonny Brocco, who worked at a company called Video Warehouse in Neptune City, New Jersey. There was talk about Black Sabbath albums. Some guy named John "needed 100,000 pieces," but he only wanted *"Greatest Hits* and *Alive at Last."* Brocco told Massaro that Vastola, whom he referred to as "the Galoot," was trying to "expedite the MCA deal."

Detective Sgt. Robert A. Jones was the supervisor of the team monitoring the wiretap and his ears perked up when he heard the reference to MCA. Called "Bobby" by his friends, Jones was a thirty-seven-year-old rock 'n' roll aficionado with a large record collection and a fair knowledge of the record business. He knew that MCA was one of the biggest record companies in the country, located in Los Angeles, part of the same company that owned Universal Studios. "What the hell are these characters doing dealing with a company like MCA?" he wondered.

It seemed there was a problem with the MCA deal. This guy John wasn't paying up and, as a result, Vastola was under pressure from "Levy" and some people in New York. There was talk about Levy sending "Rocky" to see John.

Jones surmised that the "Levy" being discussed was probably Morris Levy of Roulette Records in New York. Jones was familiar enough with Levy's reputation to know he was not a man you wanted mad at you. He knew that Levy had friends at the highest level of organized crime in New York City, men way above Gaetano Vastola in the Mafia hierarchy.

The way Bobby Jones figured it, whoever this John fellow was, he was in some real deep shit.

14

"Psychiatrically
Disabled"

etective Bobby Jones didn't know it at the time, but even as he was eavesdropping on Nicky Massaro, Sonny Brocco, and Gaetano Vastola in New Jersey, FBI agents in New York were beginning an investigation of Morris Levy and his Mafia friends. The main target of the New York investigation was Vincent ("the Chin") Gigante, one-time chauffeur and bodyguard to Vito Genovese, now underboss of the crime family that bore his late employer's name.

Rated by law enforcement officials as one of the most clever and peculiar mob bosses in the annals of organized crime, Gigante had risen to prominence in the Genovese family in the early 1980s. Born in 1928, one of five sons of a Neapolitan watchmaker, he was arrested seven times when he was between the ages of seventeen and twenty-five, on charges of receiving stolen goods, possession of an unlicensed handgun, gambling, and bookmaking. Most of the charges were dismissed, and the longest jail sentence he'd served was sixty days.

In 1957, at the age of twenty-nine, Gigante wrote his name in the Mafia history books when he was arrested for the attempted assassination of New York mob boss Frank Costello. Gigante was acquitted after Costello testified at the trial that he had not seen the gunman who fired the bullet that grazed his scalp. Following the trial, Costello retired and Vito Genovese took over his organization. Two years later, in 1959, Gigante and Genovese were convicted of heroin trafficking and sentenced to seven years in prison. Gigante was released after five years. He was arrested once again in 1973 for conspiracy to bribe the entire five-man police department of Old Tappan, New Jersey. That charge was dismissed, however, when he produced a hospital report saying that he was mentally unfit to stand trial.

The incompetence gambit worked so well that Gigante thereafter made it a permanent part of his routine. Ever since, he'd feigned a mental disorder, authorities believed, to establish a defense in case he was ever arrested again. Investigators had often observed him walking down Sullivan Street near his headquarters in South Greenwich Village, in a seemingly confused state, wearing pajamas, a bathrobe, and slippers, being led by the arm by his confidante and right-hand man, Dominick ("Baldy Dom") Canterino. If he sensed he was being watched, Gigante was known to stop, unzip his pants and urinate on the nearest tree. "He'd just pull out his pecker in broad daylight and pee like a dog," laughs one New York cop.

Once, when FBI agents served Gigante with a subpoena at the home of his mother, they found him standing naked in the shower holding an open umbrella. "Every six months or so, he checks himself into Westchester Mental Hospital for a tune-up," says one agent.

"Psychiatrically disabled" is how Gigante's high-priced lawyer, Barry Slotnick, describes his client. Crazy like a fox, say investigators who've watched him direct the Genovese family's $100 million gambling, loan-sharking, narcotics-trafficking, and labor-racketeering operations from the dingy storefront office of his Triangle Social Club and Civic Improvement Association at 208 Sullivan Street.

Gigante arrived at the Triangle every day around 3:00 P.M. and spent the evening playing cards, watching TV, and listening while his lieutenants conducted business. Tuesday night was usually busy; it was payoff night for the gambling operation. Gigante rarely talked inside the club. Usually he communicated to his most trusted associates—underboss Venaro ("Benny Eggs") Mangano; consiglieri Bobby Manna; Dominick Canterino, his top capo; and Federico ("Fritzy") Giovanelli, a rising star in Canterino's crew—during late-night strolls through the neighborhood. He seldom used a telephone.

One of the few people Gigante talked to outside his small inner circle was Morris Levy. The two had known each other since they were young men and appeared to have grown particularly close in recent years, supposedly because of the kindness that Levy showed to Gigante's retarded son. Levy had been observed regularly in the vicinity of the club, talking with Gigante on the street.

In April 1984, FBI agents were told by a reliable informant that Gigante had developed a "stranglehold" on Levy's recording industry enterprises. Levy was an "earner," a source of ready cash for the organization and a front man in real estate investments, the informant said. He told the agents that a member of Gigante's family owned a substantial interest in Levy's Strawberries record store chain and was receiving large amounts of cash from him. What's more, the informant said that Levy had come to resent the control that Gigante exercised over his business but couldn't do anything about it because he was in too deep. Levy had been beholden to the Genovese family for so many years that there was "only one way out," he said, adding that Gigante had threatened to kill Levy if he refused to purchase real estate properties for Gigante's associates.

Through grand jury subpoenas and a corporate records check, agents quickly learned that much of Levy's business with "the Chin" apparently was conducted through a woman named Olympia Esposito, Gigante's de facto, common-law wife. Levy was the custodian of bank accounts in the names of the three illegitimate children Esposito had borne by Gigante. Esposito was an officer in a Levy record company called Adam VIII, named after Levy's twenty-eight-year-old son, Adam. She was also vice president of the 67 East 77th Street Realty Corporation; Levy was listed as president of the company, whose corporate office was at 1790 Broadway, the same as Roulette Records. Levy had the power of attorney over bank accounts held by Olympia Esposito Realty, which also was located at the Roulette address. Phone company records showed daily calls between Levy and Esposito and between Esposito and Gigante capo Dominick Canterino. Olympia Esposito seemed to function as something of an appointments secretary to Gigante.

In their investigation of Gigante, FBI agents decided they would focus on Levy, Esposito, and the capos Dominick Canterino and Federico ("Fritzy") Giovanelli. They hoped to find a weak link, someone who wasn't as careful or as clever as Gigante. On November 7, a bug was secretly placed in the Triangle Social Club. Two days later, one was installed in Dominick Canterino's 1984 Cadillac. On November 27, a tap was put on Olympia Esposito's phone. That same day, both Levy and Fritzy were observed talking to Gigante on the street near the club.

In the New Jersey investigation, meanwhile, another wiretap had been installed on the phone at Video Warehouse, and the conversations about the record business had grown even more intriguing. Bobby Jones and his teams of wiretap monitors and transcribers heard Brocco complaining to Nicky Massaro, Vastola's underling, about the poor quality of 4.1 million records that a company called Out of the Past had received. "MCA has been sellin' this same shit for five years, all this country and western stuff," he said. "They're talking about running that stuff back [to MCA], but I don't think they'll take it back at this late date." He said that John had "a big Friday meeting with the Galoot."

Things were not good between LaMonte and his creditors in New York. At that November meeting, he paid Levy $30,000, the first installment on the 2 percent cash deal Levy had insisted upon. He carried the cash—three hundred $100 bills—into Roulette's office in a brown paper bag. Levy split the money up with Fritzy Giovanelli and Gaetano Vastola right in front of him—$10,000 each. Levy took $300 from his stack of bills and gave it to his secretary with orders, "go out and get us some good chocolate." LaMonte then watched the three gruff characters gorging themselves on the sweets like greedy little children as he explained to them that unless MCA shipped the three hundred thousand pieces of sweeteners as Fritzy had promised, he wanted to cancel the deal and return all the goods to MCA. The three waved aside his concern and once again assured him that he would get the records. Levy wanted to know if the two $15,000 checks LaMonte had made out to Consultants for World Records would be good the following week. LaMonte promised they would be.

What he didn't tell them was that he already had a contingency plan in case the records didn't come. He'd contacted a man named Alvin Ranglin, whose company, G. G. Records Specialists, in Kingston, Jamaica, was MCA's Jamaican licensee, meaning it had the right to manufacture and distribute MCA's recordings on the island. LaMonte made a deal to import several hundred thousand MCA Platinum Plus cassettes from G. G. to replace the goods that had been creamed from his load of cutouts. Actually, "import" was not exactly the right word. Ranglin was short on cash to buy the parts necessary to manufacture the cassettes—plastic boxes, cartridges, magnetic tape. So LaMonte arranged for the cassettes to be manufactured by a company called Golden Circle Marketing in Stamford, Connecticut. It was to be done under G. G.'s license and all Ranglin had to do was supply the master tapes and the artwork. G. G. would be paid in cassettes. As LaMonte sold the goods to his customers, he would assign the receivables to Levy and Consultants for World Records to pay off his debt.

Once again, LaMonte was operating in the gray area of the law. He knew that when MCA learned of the scheme the company would scream counterfeiting. But he also knew that since G. G. was a bona fide licensee it would be difficult for the authorities to prove criminal intent on his part. The worst that could happen, he figured, was that MCA would sue him. That was better than having his legs broken.

LaMonte was getting very nervous about the way things were going. He'd counted on Vastola as his partner to protect his interests in the cutout sale. But Vastola wasn't coming to his defense. During all the meetings at Roulette, he'd remained pretty much in the background, letting Levy, Fritzy Giovanelli, Rudy Farone, and Sal Pisello do all the talking. Something wasn't right.

As near as Bobby Jones could tell from listening to the wiretaps, MCA was pressuring Levy for payment on the cutout deal and Levy and his New York friends were pressuring Vastola to lean on John.

On December 18 at 10:00 A.M., Vastola called Brocco at the Video Warehouse in an agitated state. "Did you speak to John? You gotta get a hold of this guy. We gotta sit down and talk with him, Sonny. They're holding you responsible, too. Everybody's screaming over these fucking payments, the notes. They're saying you went down to Florida with him and negotiated this deal, so you're partners. They want you to sit in the fucking joint and not let a record go in or out until this thing is paid. You gotta do this, I'm telling you right now it's important."

"I hear you, cousin," Brocco replied.

The next day, Jones learned from the wiretaps that John had bounced a $15,000 check to Levy and the boys. At that point, the investigators decided they'd better find out who John was and what the deal with MCA was all about. It sounded like they had a full-blown extortion on their hands, and this John character obviously didn't know who he was dealing with—either that or he was crazy. He could end up in a river.

15

"What you're doing is extortion"

December 15, 1984, was a black day for Sam Passamano—it was his last at MCA. Six weeks earlier, he'd been called into Myron Roth's office and given the bad news.

"We've decided not to pick up the option on your employment contract; we're giving you early retirement," Roth said matter-of-factly, as if he were relaying some minor administrative decision. It was five minutes to five on November 2—Passamano would always remember. Stone-faced, Roth handed him a two-page letter that effectively ended his thirty-five-year career in the record business.

Though he'd been expecting it, Passamano was unprepared for the coldness of the dismissal.

"Dear Mr. Passamano," the letter began. "This will summarize your employment status with the Company, thereby enabling you to plan ahead accordingly. Your existing employment contract with the Company dated January 1, 1982 for a period of three years expires on December 31, 1984 and, consequently, your employment with the Company terminates on December 31, 1984.

"As a result of termination of your employment with the Company, you will not thereafter be entitled to receive any benefits accruing to employees of MCA Inc. with the sole exception that we agree to let you continue your participation in the Group Medical Plan (Note: this does not include dental and life insurance coverage) for up to 30 days after December 31, 1984.

"Any unvested shares in the MCA Inc. Incentive Stock plan will be forfeited as of December 31, 1984, pursuant to the terms of the plan."

Passamano felt sick. He held 2,960 shares of common stock that would have become vested in three years, when he turned sixty. At the time, MCA shares were trading at $64 a share. So he was losing nearly $200,000 that he'd been counting on for his retirement. Worse, he was losing his medical benefits, which also would have become vested at age sixty. That was a potentially devastating loss for Passamano, who'd suffered two heart attacks in recent years, one at the NARM convention in 1982. At his age and with his heart condition, obtaining individual medical coverage would be difficult and expensive.

He could barely read the rest of the letter. He was to turn in his company car—"1982 Buick Century, Beige, California License 1DUE889"—and his company air travel card by 5:00 P.M. November 15.

"As full and complete consideration to you for executing this agreement, and in lieu of and in settlement of any and all claims arising from your employment by or rendition of services to MCA Inc., and from your employment contract, the Company will make a cash payment of $100,000, less applicable withholding taxes, to you on or about December 31, 1984."

It was signed by Michael Samuel, MCA's corporate secretary, with a space for Passamano's signature agreeing to the terms. He asked Roth if perhaps the $100,000 settlement could be paid to him over the next three years and he could be kept on as a consultant or something, so he wouldn't lose his medical benefits or his stock. Roth told him he would have to take it up with Samuel. That was the end of the conversation. There was no handshake, no words of appreciation for all the years devoted to the company. Roth took a phone call and Passamano left without signing the agreement.

Following the meeting with Roth, Passamano found himself ostracized at the company. As word went around that he'd been fired, no one called or came by his office to offer condolences or wish him good luck in the future. Men he'd talked with every day for years—Dan Westbrook, Dave Clark, John Burns, Dan McGill—suddenly avoided him as if he had a disease they might catch. The only exception was Arnold Stone, the vice president of administration who, at age fifty-seven, was Passamano's only remaining contemporary at the record company. Stone asked Passamano to have lunch with him on his last day. "You don't have to if you don't want to, if you think it will cause problems for you," Passamano said. "What are you talking about?" Stone replied. "I don't care who sees me with you."

They ate at the Universal Studio commissary, where everyone could see them. They talked most about the sad state of affairs at MCA Records. For the second year in a row, the label was losing money. The music division was going to report operating profits of $8.8 million for the year, but that included revenues from the distributing company, music publishing, home video distribution, and Motown. Further disguising the record company's performance was that millions of dollars' worth of expenditures—for the Joan Jett and Barry Gibb advances, among other things—were being carried on the books as an asset instead of being written off as a loss. Historically, such advances were written off quarterly, as soon as it was determined they were worthless. It was easy to see what was going on—MCA couldn't report the advances as a loss and still claim the record label had experienced a dramatic turnaround, which was the story Azoff was putting out through the media.

In truth, the label was hurting. MCA's only platinum album in 1984 was Night Ranger's *Midnight Madness* LP, which sold 1.5 million copies. The Azoff administration couldn't claim full credit for Night Ranger, however, because the group was actually signed to Camel Records, a small label distributed by MCA. After a million-selling debut album in 1983, the Fixx's second album, *Phantoms*, was a disappointment. It was certified gold for sales of 500,000 copies, but it netted only 350,000 after returns. Another new group, New Edition, made a promising debut, scoring a number one single on *Billboard*'s Black Music chart, "Cool It Now," the company's first black hit since 1979. But after signing New Edition away from independently distributed Streetwise Records, MCA learned that Morris Levy owned the rights to the group's name and he was demanding several million dollars for the use of the name. The company's two biggest acts, Olivia Newton-John and Tom Petty, still hadn't delivered their long-awaited albums. Petty had broken his right hand in a freak accident in the recording studio, which pushed back completion of the record indefinitely.

Then there was Pisello. As overseer of the Sugar Hill Records distribution deal, he'd been paid $76,000 by MCA in 1984. In an extremely unusual move, instead of sending Sugar Hill a check each month for its share of net proceeds—less Pisello's 3 percent—MCA gave the check to Pisello for him to hand-carry to Sugar Hill's New Jersey office. Such an arrangement was unique in Stone's and Passamano's experiences in the record business. Pisello wasn't an employee of either company, and yet MCA was entrusting him with monthly checks that ranged from $100,000 to $200,000.

Pisello was a particularly sore point with Passamano. Sam believed he'd been fired because he raised objections to John Burns's unequal Platinum Plus pricing program and also because the administration didn't trust him to keep quiet about Pisello's activities, especially in the area of cutout sales. As keeper of the cutouts for twenty years, Passamano was about the only person at the company who knew how they should be disposed of legitimately. With him gone, there was no one to raise questions about the suspicious way they were being handled now. For example, just two weeks earlier, on December 3, Pisello had made a deal to buy another one million cutouts from an inventory list he was given that included several hundred thousand Platinum Plus albums that were still in MCA's active sales catalog. Passamano had complained to Dan McGill on several occasions that the inventory list contained records that shouldn't be on there, but he was ignored. He only learned of the sale because Pisello had asked Passamano's longtime personal secretary, Sue Ramos, to type up the purchase order to Dan McGill. Sal was buying several million dollars' worth of records for $500,000—a sweetheart deal if there ever was one.

Passamano was shocked that McGill would even consider approving another cutout sale to Pisello after what happened on the first sale to Roulette Records. In the eight months since the 1984 NARM convention, MCA had collected only about $600,000 on the deal, leaving a balance of over $800,000, long overdue. Just a week before the second sale, Pisello gave MCA a $300,000 check from Consultants for World Records as partial payment on the Roulette-LaMonte deal, and the check had bounced! The check was signed by some guy he'd never heard of before, a Rocco Musacchia.

Since Azoff came aboard, the company had sold more than fifteen million cutouts to questionable characters under terms that departed sharply from prior company policy and made little or no economic sense. Was it recklessness, corruption, or a combination of both?

Passamano and Stone discussed the human carnage that had resulted from the Azoff takeover. Firings and early retirements are not uncommon in any company when new leadership is brought in. But in the case of MCA Records, the actions often were abrupt, without explanation, and unnecessarily brutal. "Termination" was a good term—they seemed like executions.

Stone would know. As vice president of administration, it had fallen on him to inform the condemned parties and carry out the sentence on a number of occasions. He hated it. Around the company, they were calling him Azoff's "angel of death." But what could he do? Like Passamano, he had only three years to go until retirement age, when his stock and medical insurance would be fully vested. If he complained or resigned in protest, it wouldn't alter anything except his family's security.

There had been a number of recent firings of executives who balked at carrying out orders they considered unethical. Joe Fiorentino, a promotion man who covered the Philadelphia–Baltimore–Boston–New York region, was canned in October after he complained that he was being asked to engage in what he called "payola."

Under Palmese, the practice of giving free goods to record stores that reported their sales to trade publications such as *Billboard* had increased to the point that, in Fiorentino's opinion, the promotion staff was "buying" inaccurate reports and, therefore, inaccurate positions on *Billboard*'s Hot 100 chart. MCA promotion men were being told to provide the stores with anywhere from twenty-five to fifty free records in exchange for reporting MCA's releases as selling better than they actually were, thereby causing artificial movement up the *Billboard* chart. With more than one hundred accounts, Fiorentino was being asked to hand out thousands of records a month. He felt like some sort of sleazy bag man, so he complained to Harold Sulman, the vice president of sales.

"Maybe you're too old for the job," Sulman told him. "Maybe we should put a younger man in there who'll tear down the walls and buy up everyone."

"When you are in your fifties you have more sense than when you are nineteen or twenty," Fiorentino replied, "and no employer can dictate my integrity."

"Maybe you should have been a priest," Sulman snorted.

Fiorentino was fired without explanation in October. His severance pay amounted to $708 after taxes.

Another promotion man, Frank Falise, an eighteen-year employee, was fired by mail after he complained that independent promoters hired by Palmese were encroaching on his territory.

Passamano was disconsolate. He'd put out feelers for another job but so far there had been no takers. "Who wants a fifty-seven-year-old with a history of two heart attacks?" he said.

He was thinking about suing the company. That's what George Collier was doing. He'd talked with Collier's lawyer, Will Dwyer, who specialized in wrongful termination and who felt he might have a good case under the state's so-called whistle-blower statute, which says that an employee cannot be fired for refusing to carry out orders that violate the law.

But going up against MCA in a legal action was a frightening prospect. The company had something like thirty-two lawyers on staff, enough to spend anybody into the ground, depose them to death. Passamano wasn't sure his heart could handle the stress of a nasty, protracted lawsuit.

And it could be nasty. Back in September, Collier, who now worked for Capitol Records, had run into Azoff backstage at a rock concert. According to Collier, Azoff shouted at him. "What you're doing is extortion. You're a slimy scum bag, and I'll spend the next ten years ruining your career."

Passamano just didn't know if he was up to it. However, had he known, he might have found some solace in the fact that Sal Pisello's tenure at MCA Records was about to come to an end as well.

The *Los Angeles Times* was investigating the cutout record business and a reporter was asking questions about the millions of MCA cutouts that had wound up in the hands of Morris Levy and John LaMonte.

"That was a deal done by a guy who's no longer with the company; we fired him," Azoff said when asked about the sale. He hadn't known anything about the deal in advance, or else he would have stopped it, he said. And it wasn't nearly as large a sale as the reporter had heard—it involved only 350,000 records, according to John Burns.

Who was Sal Pisello? "He was just some guy Sam Passamano brought in," Azoff said.

Back in New Jersey, on December 31, detective Sgt. Bobby Jones heard Sonny Brocco tell Gaetano Vastola in a wiretapped phone conversation, "Sal isn't going to be at the company anymore after the fifteenth of January."

16

"I'll put him in a bucket and I'll ... "

At 1:15 in the afternoon on January 10, 1985, Sonny Brocco answered the phone in the Video Warehouse office.

"Video."

"Sonny?"

"Yes."

"Get in your car, go over to Philadelphia. Pick up a check for $629,000. I called this dirty motherfucker; every time I call, they're out, they're not here, they're not nothing."

It was Brocco's cousin, Gaetano Vastola, calling from a phone booth. His voice trembled with barely controlled rage, directed at John LaMonte.

"I don't like the way this is going with this kid, I'm tellin' you now, I don't like it. I'm gonna be out there tomorrow morning. I'll put him in a bucket and I'll ... "

"If you want to go out tomorrow, we'll go there," Brocco soothed.

"I'm gonna put him in a fuckin' hospital. I'm not even gonna talk to him. I don't like this motherfucker, what he's doing."

LaMonte had been ducking Vastola's calls for several weeks, bobbing and weaving, passing one excuse after another through Brocco as he scrambled to raise the money to pay for the MCA cutouts. Through a combination of cash, promissory notes, and receivables from customers for the MCA Jamaican "imports" that he assigned to Consultants for World Records, LaMonte had come up with nearly $600,000. But the boys in New York were running out of patience waiting for the balance. And so was MCA.

Since Vastola had vouched for Brocco and LaMonte in the deal, it was his responsibility to see that the money got paid, and LaMonte's foot-dragging was making him look bad with the boys from New York—Morris Levy, Fritzy Giovanelli, Rudy Farone, and (Levy's muscle) Rocco Musacchia—whom he referred to sarcastically as "my board of directors." In Vastola's world, losing face was more than humiliating, it was downright dangerous.

"Rudy, Sal—I got everybody calling me," Vastola sputtered over the phone to Brocco. "It's a disgrace over here. Morris Levy. I don't want to pick up the phone for nobody."

Brocco was caught in the middle. On the one hand, he liked LaMonte. They were friends. LaMonte had helped him get an early release from prison by giving him a job, lent him $5,000 to get on his feet, and taught him the record business. He owed LaMonte.

He also knew that LaMonte had been screwed on the MCA deal. Pisello was lying, and so was Levy. But he couldn't get Vastola to believe that his old friend "Moishe" had cheated him. Vastola believed what Levy was telling him—that LaMonte had actually sold the goods he claimed had been creamed from the load and was just trying to weasel out of paying up. Brocco knew that was ridiculous—LaMonte may have been irresponsible, but he wasn't suicidal.

Still, he had to admit that John wasn't handling the situation very well. Under all the pressure, he'd begun doing a lot of cocaine. He was spending at least a $1,000 a week on it, money his business couldn't afford. He was staying up half the night, not going to the office until the middle of the day, then disappearing in late afternoon to score some more coke. He was impossible to reach. Brocco was having trouble getting him to sit still long enough for them to figure out what they were going to do about the problem with the payments and what they were going to tell Vastola. All of which was putting Brocco in a bad position with his cousin.

At 3:06 P.M., Vastola called Video Warehouse again to see if Brocco had gotten hold of LaMonte. He hadn't.

"Sonny, he's making a cocksucker out of me, and that's what I'm gonna be. What the fuck is he gonna do, Sonny? Go over there and pick up the check."

"It's not as easy as going over there and picking up a check."

"Because if it's gonna come to the point, I'm gonna tell Rudy, Sal, everybody, 'Go over there and do what you got to do.'"

Six minutes later, after trying unsuccessfully to reach LaMonte, Brocco called Vastola back.

"Big guy, he left for the day," he said, dispiritedly.

"Go over to John's house and get a check. Or go over to his place and get a check for $629,000."

"Just like that?"

"Just like that. Made out to MCA Records for January 31. Did you hear what I said, Sonny? I'm tellin' you right now, Sonny. Just take a list of everything that's around us and what they are doing to me ... including Sal [Pisello], including the Chin [Vincent Gigante]. Sal's been here for two days waiting for his check to go back to California."

"Is it that important to have it made out to MCA?" Brocco asked. "Can't we make it out to Worldwide Consultants?"

"No, it has to be made out to MCA; that's who the money has to go to."

"For a total of $629,000?" Brocco knew there wasn't a chance in the world that LaMonte could get the money, but he was playing for time. Maybe the Galoot would cool off by tomorrow and listen to reason. It wouldn't be smart to provoke him further today.

"I'm not letting this go no further," Vastola said. "I'm gonna tell them you're picking up the check tomorrow morning."

He hung up.

The check was not picked up the next morning, or the next. LaMonte and Brocco managed to persuade Vastola that just maybe what they were saying was true, that Pisello had ripped them off and perhaps Levy didn't even realize it.

Vastola got Levy to agree, albeit reluctantly, that before any action was taken against LaMonte, a visit should be paid to his warehouse to see exactly what he had there. The main thing, after all, was to collect the money that was owed, and that couldn't be done if La-Monte was in the hospital, or dead. Levy argued that if LaMonte didn't have what he was supposed to have in his warehouse, they should simply take over his company and run it themselves. "I'll put Rocky in there," he said, referring to Rocco Musacchia.

The pressure was getting to LaMonte. "I should quit," he told Nicky Massaro, the bookie whose telephone line tap kicked off the larger investigation. "Corky [Vastola] calls, Morris Levy calls," LaMonte complained. "It's no longer a pleasure to do business. We're not going to make any money, we're working for Morris Levy."

On January 21, Vastola called Brocco at Video Warehouse about the meeting at LaMonte's place that was planned for the next morning. "I've got the kid alerted," he said. "Fritzy's gonna be there with Rocky. I'm picking up Levy at the Mt. Laurel Diner. We're meeting at 9:00 A.M. at the Executive Hotel in Mt. Laurel to go to LaMonte's. If the stuff's not there, maybe we'll have to set up a new company."

At 9:47 A.M. the next morning, a van pulled up in front of Out of the Past in Darby and disgorged a veritable rogues' gallery—Gaetano Vastola, Morris Levy, Fritzy Giovanelli, Rocco Musacchia, and Sonny Brocco. They looked like characters straight out of a Damon Runyon story. Hulking figures, each weighing well over two hundred pounds, their combined weight caused the van to ride low on its suspension.

Hidden in another van parked across the street, FBI agent James Scanlon peered through the telephoto lens of a camera and snapped pictures of the men as they emerged from the van, milled around for a few minutes, and then went inside.

(The FBI was brought in on the Union County investigation following the mention of "the Chin" on the wiretaps twelve days earlier. Vincent Gigante was a bigger fish than the Union County prosecutor's office ever expected to net in the case and it didn't have the manpower to send a surveillance team to Philadelphia. A call was placed to the local office of the FBI in Redbank, New Jersey, and Redbank contacted the New York FBI office, where they learned there was a task force of agents and police already working its own case on Gigante, Levy, and Giovanelli. Approval was given from FBI headquarters in Washington, D.C., for the New Jersey and New

York investigators—a small army, when combined—to cooperate with one another, share intelligence, and build two grand jury cases, one overseen by Rudolph Giuliani, the U.S. attorney in Manhattan, and the other by Thomas R. Greelish, the U.S. attorney for the District of New Jersey, based in Newark. Detective Sgt. Bobby Jones and his crew of Union County cops were deputized as special U.S. marshals.)

As FBI agent Scanlon continued his surveillance outside LaMonte's warehouse, at least ten other men arrived and went inside. The others were there to help with the considerable task of taking inventory of the five-floor, 122,000-square-foot building, which was bursting at the seams with old records. They were looking for a particular batch of old records: the approximately one million MCA cutouts that LaMonte claimed had been creamed from his load and that Levy claimed were either hidden somewhere in LaMonte's warehouse or had been secretly sold by LaMonte. Today's convocation was to determine who was telling the truth.

As the others fanned out through the warehouse, Levy, Giovanelli, and Vastola sat with LaMonte in his cluttered office. "What you're looking for ain't in this warehouse," LaMonte said, directing his comments to Giovanelli, who seemed to be in charge of the expedition. "What you're looking for is here," he said, handing Giovanelli a folder of documents.

Earlier in the week, LaMonte had gone to see John Gervasoni at Scorpio Music. He knew that Gervasoni had purchased from Ranji Bedi and Betaco the same records that were missing from his MCA shipments. So he asked Gervasoni for a copy of his purchase order.

"Well, it wouldn't be right for me to give that to you, John," Gervasoni said with a smile. "But if you just happened to take it off my desk while I was out of the room, then there wouldn't be anything I could do about it." By the time he finished the sentence, Gervasoni was out of the room. LaMonte took the purchase order off the desk and left.

Now Fritzy Giovanelli held the document in his hand. There were the Olivia Newton-John, Mamas and Papas, Joe Walsh, Crystal Gayle, and Bing Crosby albums that LaMonte had ordered but not received. Unit for unit, everything coincided. And while the Scorpio purchase order showed the cutouts had come from MCA through Betaco, it also showed that the billing had gone through Morris Levy's Roulette Records.

"What I have here is all junk," LaMonte said. "There is no profit to be made on this stuff."

As Giovanelli went over the paperwork, Vastola remained silent, while Levy kept grumbling that "the kid is lying." But when the others returned from their search of the building and reported that the missing cutouts were not there and everything else seemed to be in order, Giovanelli turned to Levy and said, "There's only one thief here, Morris, and it's you. This kid didn't do anything."

LaMonte fought the temptation to leap from his chair and thrust his fist into the air in triumph. Instead, he said calmly to Giovanelli, "Do I have any other problems with you fellows?"

"No, this is no longer your problem," Giovanelli replied. "Get the goods back to MCA. Fuck 'em."

With that, the entire entourage filed out of the building, climbed into their vehicles, and drove off as FBI agent Scanlon clicked away with his surveillance camera.

Back in his office, LaMonte relaxed for the first time in months, confident that he'd finally turned the tables on "Super Jew" and that Levy and Sal Pisello would soon get their comeuppance for cheating their own Mafia buddies.

Wrong again.

17

"I'm looking for
Sal Pisello.
Is he there?"

W hile the FBI was dogging Morris Levy and the boys on the East Coast, out on the West Coast, unaware of the New York–New Jersey investigations, Marvin Rudnick was building his case against Sal Pisello.

Since Judge Harry Hupp declared a mistrial in the tax case, Rudnick had been looking into Pisello's past business dealings in Los Angeles. Among other things, he found that Pisello had bilked several investors in the Roma di Notte restaurant—two doctors and a garment company executive—out of several hundred thousand dollars before blowing town in December 1979. Rudnick traced much of the money to three southern California racetracks—Del Mar, Santa Anita, and Hollywood Park. He also discovered that Pisello had ripped off a local nightclub owner named Demetrius Johnson, who'd given Pisello $40,000 to become a partner in converting the restaurant into a nightclub called Jackie O's. The nightclub never got off the ground, however, after the restaurant was firebombed. An arson investigation by the fire department never determined who was responsible for the torching, which conveniently destroyed all the restaurant's financial records, according to Pisello.

Naturally, Pisello never paid taxes on any of the money he received from the investors, nor did he make any attempt to pay them back. One of the investors was a Century City lawyer named Edward Gorman, who had since become a superior court judge and who was, coincidentally, a bridge partner of the cigarette-smoking Judge Hupp.

Armed with the new information about Pisello's finances during 1978 and 1979, Rudnick reindicted Pisello in December 1984, this time on four felony counts of income tax evasion. The two additional counts made it more likely that Big Sal would serve jail time if convicted. Rudnick was determined to "bust this guy's balls," as he put it.

The second Pisello trial began on the last Tuesday in February 1985 and lasted two weeks. In addition to the dry testimony and evidence from the previous trial, Rudnick called the two doctor-investors to the stand—Irving Rubenstein, a West Covina obstetrician, and Raphael Mendoza, a radiologist from nearby Covina. The physicians testified that after handing Pisello several hundred thousand dollars in cash for the purpose of opening and running Roma di Notte, their partner made them pay for their dinner when they went to eat there. The garment executive, Malcolm Sigman, said his aged father became so upset about their being ripped off in the restaurant deal that he pulled a knife on Sal one night when he bumped into him in the Polo Lounge at the Beverly Hills Hotel.

Rudnick effectively portrayed Pisello as a "tax deadbeat" and an unscrupulous businessman who lived off other people's money, routinely lied on financial disclosure documents, casually wrote bad checks in amounts greater than $25,000, and came to the trial owing the IRS $271,000 from a tax court case dating back to 1966—in addition to the more than $100,000 in taxes the government claimed he evaded in the current case.

Usually something of a showman in court, Rudnick was on his best behavior throughout the trial. He avoided clashes with Judge Hupp by refraining from making references to Pisello's Mafia background and made only one arguably inflammatory statement in front of the jury, when he mockingly referred to the Roma di Notte firebombing: "Even my pet Dalmatian at home would probably be able to figure what that was all about."

Judge Hupp also was less hostile toward him than during the previous trial. Rudnick thought that might be because he'd put Hupp's bridge buddy, Judge Gorman, on his list of potential witnesses at the trial. He hadn't really intended to call Gorman, but had put his name down as a subtle warning to Hupp that he suspected the judge might be somehow biased in favor of Pisello, and if that bias showed up in court he might make an issue of it.

On March 6, the jury convicted Pisello on all counts. Following the verdict, Judge Hupp continued Pisello's $15,000 bail until sentencing on April 22. Rudnick argued for a higher bail, but lost. Pisello's attorney, Harland Braun, then asked the court if his client could be allowed to travel to New York City for business purposes.

Mindful of Pisello's history of disappearing when things got hot, Rudnick quickly objected. "What's his business, Your Honor?"

Pisello told the judge that he was employed as the "West Coast representative of Sugar Hill Records," located in New Jersey. Over Rudnick's repeated objection and warning that Pisello was a flight risk, Hupp granted the request to allow him to travel to New York on business.

Rudnick had never heard of Sugar Hill Records. He knew Pisello had some involvement with MCA Records, but he suspected the Sugar Hill story was a con. Sal was just trying to cut himself some slack; he was probably going to try to raise financing from his East Coast Mafia buddies for a permanent relocation to South America. He faced five years in the can—that could be a life sentence for a man his age.

Rudnick theorized that if he could prove that Pisello had lied to Hupp about business dealings with this obscure New Jersey record label, come April 22 he might be able to convince the judge to hand down a stiffer sentence. He decided to "work the lie."

On March 8, two days after the trial, he cut a subpoena for Sugar Hill Records, asking for all documents pertaining to any business dealings the company had with Salvatore James Pisello. Then he waited.

For eleven days, he heard nothing. He was worried because Sugar Hill didn't actually have to respond to the subpoena—either by supplying documents or, as he guessed would happen, saying it had no business dealings with Pisello—until the day of sentencing. If that happened, he wouldn't be able to include the results of the subpoena in his presentencing report to the judge, and Hupp would likely not take it into account when he passed sentence. Rudnick decided to play another card—a very big card, he suspected.

Pisello had claimed during the trial that one of the reasons he didn't pay his back taxes was that he didn't have the money. Rudnick figured that if he could prove that Sal did have funds stashed away, it would be proof of his willfulness in evading and indicate to the judge that no amount of money would have moved him to pay what he owed to the government. Only a stiff prison sentence could do that.

On March 19, without telling anyone in the office what he was doing, Rudnick called the central information phone number at MCA headquarters in Universal City. He asked for the record division. When the receptionist came on the line, he said, "I'm looking for Sal Pisello. Is he there?"

No, the receptionist said. "I haven't seen Mr. Pisello around in a couple of weeks; I don't know where he is."

"Is Sam Passamano there?" he asked.

"I'm sorry, Mr. Passamano is no longer with the company," came the reply.

He was referred to Arnold Stone's office. "Mr. Stone is not in the office today," Stone's secretary said. "May I ask who's calling?"

Rudnick identified himself as an attorney with the Justice Department—he didn't mention the Organized Crime Strike Force, because it sounds so ominous—and said he was looking for information about Sal Pisello. He left a message for Stone to return his call.

The next day he got a call from Zach Horowitz, the vice president of legal affairs at MCA Records brought in by Azoff and Roth.

"Why are you harassing our secretaries?" Horowitz barked.

"I don't know what you are talking about," Rudnick responded, taken aback by both the complaint and Horowitz's angry tone.

Horowitz repeated the accusation: "We understand that you've been harassing our secretaries."

Rudnick explained why he had called. "I just convicted a man named Sal Pisello in federal court and I understand he's had some business dealings with your company. I'm looking for financial transactions on this guy and was hoping you could help me out with some information for my sentencing report."

"How do I know who you really are?" Horowitz shot back.

"You called me," Rudnick said tartly, rallying to the volley.

"We want something in writing, a letter from you or something," Horowitz said.

"Fine," Rudnick said to himself as he hung up. "You want something in writing, you got it." The next day he served MCA with a subpoena for all its records pertaining to Sal Pisello.

A few days later, he found in his office mailbox a copy of a letter that Pisello's attorney had sent to Judge Hupp complaining about the subpoenas: "It is obvious that these actions are designed to harass Mr. Pisello and make it impossible for him to earn a living by poisoning his relationship with Sugar Hill Records and MCA/Universal Studios," Braun wrote. "I think it is a disgrace that acts of harassment should be carried out in the name of the United States District Court.

"Mr. Pisello has asked me what remedy he has against this type of unbelievable government harassment and interference in his personal life. As a lawyer, I know of no remedy other than requesting that Your Honor dismiss the entire criminal prosecution against Mr. Pisello as the only deterrent that could possibly be effective against the Los Angeles Strike Force."

Rudnick chuckled at the letter. He must have really struck a nerve with those subpoenas. He called Zach Horowitz back and asked, "What are you guys going to do about the subpoena, are you going to help me get any business transactions on Sal?"

"We've referred that to our outside counsel, Allen Susman. You should be hearing from him."

Instead, Rudnick heard from Hupp's clerk, who told him, "The judge wants to see you this afternoon." When Rudnick walked into Hupp's courtroom, Pisello and his lawyer were already with the judge at sidebar.

"Mr. Rudnick, why are you serving subpoenas on these companies?" Hupp wanted to know.

"Your Honor, I'm trying to establish facts relating to Mr. Pisello's financial activities. If he had resources to pay his taxes and didn't, then you may find that his failure to do so was willful. At that point, Your Honor, you may decide that he deserves a tougher prison sentence. So what I'm trying to do with these subpoenas is to determine whether he lied to you about his business transactions. So far, I've found that he has some kind of business account at a bank in Queens, New York, and one in Las Vegas. If these monies are hidden from the IRS, it's relevant for sentencing."

"I'm not going to have people come all the way across the country for this case," Hupp said nastily. "The subpoenas are hereby quashed."

Rudnick wasn't ready to give up yet. Back in his office, he called Allen Susman, MCA's longtime outside counsel, and told him that the judge had quashed the subpoenas and MCA didn't have to comply. "But if you still want to cooperate and tell me what happened here, then let me know," he said.

To his surprise, Susman called him back a few days later and said that MCA would cooperate. Susman confirmed that Pisello did have financial transactions with MCA through a company called Consultants for World Records. He said that Rudnick should contact Dan McGill, the chief financial officer for the record company, and McGill would provide the details of the company's transactions with Pisello, right down to the numbers on the checks issued to him in payment.

As promised, McGill was cooperative, passively sketching out a seemingly odd series of business deals the company had conducted with Pisello in 1983 and 1984, including Pisello's role as a middleman in the sale of sixty truckloads of cutout records to a little company in Philadelphia called Out of the Past.

It was the beginning of Marvin Rudnick's education in the record business.

18

"He swindled us"

If Sal Pisello was becoming a headache for MCA, he turned into a full-blown migraine on March 15, 1985. On that day, the *Los Angeles Times* ran a front-page story with the headline, "MCA Uncovers Evidence of Counterfeit Tape Operation." According to the article, the company was the apparent victim of a large-scale, East Coast counterfeiting ring that was distributing illegal copies of older MCA recordings in New York, New Jersey, Connecticut, and California under the guise that they were cutouts.

Although the *Times* article credited MCA with uncovering the counterfeiting scheme, that wasn't exactly correct. A *Times* reporter actually stumbled onto the suspected counterfeit operation while researching a story on the cutout business and, as a practical matter, he went to MCA for help in identifying the apparently illegal product. MCA sent one of its internal auditors, Allen Clement, with the reporter to buy copies of the cassettes at record stores in the New

York–New Jersey area. The pair found apparent counterfeit cassettes of recordings by most of MCA's Platinum Plus artists—Elton John, Neil Diamond, Olivia Newton-John, The Who, Jimmy Buffet, Steely Dan—being sold for $2.99 to $3.99 in the budget bins of nearly every big record store chain. Through sources, the reporter tracked the distribution of the tapes to Golden Circle Marketing in Stamford, Connecticut. Under cover, the reporter and the auditor bought copies of the tapes directly from Golden Circle. Unbeknownst to MCA, the reporter also tracked the tapes, through a confidential source, to John LaMonte's warehouse in Darby, Pennsylvania.

Back in Los Angeles, MCA technicians examined the tapes. It was obvious they weren't manufactured by MCA. The artwork on the packaging was sloppy, with glaring spelling errors. One tape was titled *Elton John's Greatest Hit*. Another misspelled the word *California*. Some were marked "Made in Jamaica." On others you could clearly see that a silver-dollar-size Platinum Plus sticker that had been affixed to an album cover was reproduced on the cover of the cassette box, indicating that whoever made them had simply photographed the cover of an album bought in a record store.

The MCA technicians pronounced the tapes counterfeit, and the company turned the evidence over to the FBI in Newark, New Jersey.

"We have reason to believe that this organization is counterfeiting most of our big midline titles, and the number of units already sold could reach hundreds of thousands to millions, with potential losses in the millions of dollars," said Azoff.

Azoff and his underlings also had reason to believe that the counterfeit operation had something to do with the sale of MCA cutouts through Sal Pisello and Morris Levy. They knew that MCA had shipped more than four million records to John LaMonte, a man with a prison record for counterfeiting cutouts. But in interviews with the newspaper, the executives refused to acknowledge any connection between the two events, nor would they discuss details of the sale or their dealings with Pisello.

Azoff took the opportunity to place blame for the debacle on the retailers for not being more vigilant in their purchasing of budget records and cassettes.

"In all my years in the music business, I've never seen more blatantly obvious counterfeit product and I'm shocked to find it in so many stores in such quantity," the *Times* quoted him as saying.

The story was picked up by the national wire services, Associated Press, and United Press International and was fed to other papers all across the country. TV reporters in other cities did live stand-ups outside local record stores that were combing through their budget inventory pulling out any tapes that looked suspicious. In Los Angeles, TV camera crews descended upon the huge Tower Records store on Sunset Strip, known as the record industry's record store, where the *Times* reported MCA counterfeits had been purchased.

The story was a natural for the media, which historically has understood very little about the inner workings of the record business. But counterfeiting—like payola—didn't need explaining to the public. It was a sexy, easily understood subject, with clearly defined good guys and bad guys. The RIAA had been screaming for years about how counterfeiters stole millions of dollars not only from the pockets of the record companies but also from artists whom the public knew and loved. One RIAA representative once testified colorfully before Congress that a record counterfeiter was "a thief of major proportions, not unlike the gun-wielding stickup man, the bomb-carrying hijacker."

So the story of a big, glamorous record company and its big, glamorous stars being brutalized by an unscrupulous band of music thugs got big play. Lost in most of news reports, however, was any mention of cutout records. The RIAA and its client companies never talked publicly about that aspect of their business, even though the RIAA knew from its many investigations that there was a direct link between cutout sales and counterfeiting and had urged the industry privately to cease selling cutouts because of it.

When John LaMonte read the news reports about the alleged MCA counterfeiting scam, he knew they were talking about him. Obviously, the stuff that MCA was claiming to be counterfeit was his Jamaican "imports." Alvin Ranglin, the MCA licensee in Jamaica, had improvised the artwork on some of the cassettes and had done a crummy job, so they looked like cheap counterfeits. LaMonte knew that because of all the media coverage, the FBI would be contacting him very shortly—it wouldn't take them long to trace the goods to his door. And he learned something new from the *Los Angeles Times* report—that Golden Circle Marketing was knocking off his "imports" and selling them out the back door.

Oddly enough, LaMonte saw a silver lining in all the publicity. Ever since the day Giovanelli, Levy, and Vastola had come to his warehouse to check the inventory, he'd been trying to get MCA to take back the balance of the cutouts and cancel the whole deal. But MCA was stalling. Now, he thought there was a way.

He called Sonny Brocco and told him to warn Vastola that with all the allegations about counterfeiting in the newspapers it was very likely the FBI would raid his warehouse and seize everything—including the cutouts—and hold it until they could determine what was legal and what wasn't, which could take years. "Then we'll all be fucked." The solution, he said, was to put more pressure on MCA to take back the unsold cutouts immediately, credited at the same price they were purchased. He figured that the company had already collected more than $600,000 from Pisello and Levy. If Levy could convince them to accept the balance in unsold goods, they'd all be out of it without losing money. He'd explain to MCA about the Jamaican imports and promise not to do it anymore.

LaMonte's next move was to reach out to the FBI. He called Dick McKean in Miami, one of the agents who'd helped put him in jail in 1979. LaMonte was no great fan of the bureau, but he respected McKean, who had treated him decently during the whole ordeal. The purpose of the call was to head off any action that might be taken against him by the Newark FBI office. Not being experts in copyright law, the Newark agents easily could be manipulated by MCA or the RIAA into charging him with counterfeiting, he explained to McKean. But the records weren't really counterfeits. The nominal manufacturer in Jamaica was a legitimate MCA licensee—he had the contracts to prove it. At worst it was a civil matter between himself and MCA; no federal laws had been broken. "I'm not stupid. You think I want to go back to the joint?" he said.

McKean promised to look into it and do what he could. The two men agreed to meet when LaMonte went to Miami for the annual NARM convention the following week.

LaMonte's plan worked. A few days later, detective Sgt. Bobby Jones overheard Sonny Brocco on the phone telling LaMonte's warehouse manager, Ralph Ford, "We have a solution to our problem with MCA. They want us to repack them; it looks like we're going to ship them back."

Before returning the cutouts, however, Morris Levy wanted one more shot at selling them during the upcoming NARM convention, Brocco said, adding that Vastola needed a list of the inventory to send down to Miami with him.

On March 28, Vastola called Brocco at Video Warehouse.

"They got the list," he said. "Morris called, Sal just called me, everybody called me. There's only two million pieces. Now what are we going to do with this kid?"

There was supposed to be more than four million records on the list. What happened to the other two million? Vastola wanted to know. If LaMonte had sold them, then where was the money?

"Well," Brocco said, "he's going to be down at the convention. I'll waltz him over to Morris and I'll get to the bottom of it face-to-face and he'll explain exactly what's going on."

"I got Rudy [Farone] on the other line," Vastola said. "You don't know what these people are putting me through, you got no idea, no idea, all these phone calls and I have to be put on the defensive like that. Forget about it. After you get done with Morris Levy, tell John to sell his building in Philadelphia, do whatever you gotta do, the money's gotta be paid. They said, 'you gotta have the answer,' meaning me."

When he finished hollering at Brocco, Vastola got on the line with Lew Saka, his sales manager at Video Warehouse and a trusted aide. "You have to stay on top of this," he said. "They think I'm part of a swindle. They feel if John did that [sold two million cutouts] then someone had to allow him to do it. So it had to be me or Sonny. So they says to me in our last meeting, 'There's a nigger in the woodpile,' and I says, 'Fine, then let's toss the nigger out of the woodpile.' So now I know who's going to be tossed out of the woodpile, it's going to be Sonny, you understand.

"Do this favor for me," he went on. "Because I don't want to see anyone get hurt over this, because I don't like what I smell and I don't like what's going to happen, either. Morris called my house last night and says, 'You gotta come down because this is looking bad for you, nobody else. Because if you got people like this around you and they did this here, it's either no respect for you or you're part of it.' This is the way everyone is looking at it. And I just got four phone calls—one from California, one from Rudy, one from this guy, one from that guy, everyone is calling."

"There's going to be a lot of shit down there," Saka put in.

"You wanna know something?" Vastola said. "If Morris punches John right in the mouth, he's going to have a perfect right to do it. Sonny brought this guy. Sonny said push this guy—push, push, push. And now this guy swindled Sonny. And if he swindled Sonny, then I know he swindled us, there's no two ways about it. People who are subnovices in this business are saying he swindled us—Sal is saying he swindled us, Rudy is saying he swindled us, everybody is saying it."

Down in Miami, LaMonte got a call from Brocco saying that Levy wanted to see him in his room at the Hilton—there was a problem with the inventory. LaMonte knew what the problem was. The list he gave Levy contained only the worst titles in the inventory, the bottom of the barrel. He wasn't about to turn over the better stuff to Morris, who'd already ripped him off once. What if Levy sold it and didn't pay MCA? Then MCA would come after him for the money.

LaMonte called agent Dick McKean and the pair met at a restaurant where LaMonte explained again about the Jamaican imports. He then informed McKean about his more immediate problem with Morris Levy over the MCA cutouts.

McKean knew Levy from the days when he worked on the FBI's first big counterfeiting investigation in the late 1970s, code-named "Modsound" because it centered around an FBI-run "front" company called Modular Sounds in Westbury, New York. With undercover agents posing as record counterfeiters, Operation Modsound had uncovered a nationwide ring that included manufacturers, printers, distributors, wholesalers, and retailers of counterfeit records and tapes—among them, John LaMonte. You couldn't poke around in the lower regions of the record business without running into Morris Levy, McKean had learned. Back then, Levy was suspected of distributing counterfeits through Promo Records and selling them through his Strawberries record store chain. The FBI also suspected Levy of demanding "tribute" from some counterfeiters in exchange for letting them operate and strong-arming others who refused to pay for the protection. No charges were ever filed against him, however.

McKean advised LaMonte not to go to Levy's hotel room. He'd checked with the Newark FBI and they said they were aware of LaMonte's problem with Levy. They thought he was in real trouble and might be harmed, McKean said. They wanted to talk to him about it.

LaMonte recoiled at the idea. He wasn't a snitch, he said indignantly. He'd take care of the problem himself, somehow. Nonetheless, he allowed McKean to accompany him to the Hilton Hotel and wait down in the lobby while he went up to Levy's room.

When LaMonte entered the tenth-floor suite, Levy glowered at him. "This list is nothing but shit," he boomed.

"Morris, it's what you guys sold me."

"Where's the rest of the goods, what did you do, sell it?"

"I got it; it's in my warehouse."

"I don't believe you. I oughta throw you right out this window now," Levy said, beckoning to the balcony.

Besides Brocco, there were three other men in the room—thickset, old-fashioned-looking Mafia types, Mustache Petes, well into their sixties or beyond. LaMonte was not introduced to them.

One of the three interrupted Levy and asked casually if LaMonte ever sold cutouts to Strawberries. LaMonte said no, and when asked why, he responded after a moment's hesitation, "Because Strawberries doesn't pay; everybody knows that."

The three old-timers seemed stung by his statement. They immediately turned to Levy and wanted to know why anyone would say that; was that really the reputation Strawberries had? LaMonte's wise-ass remark seemed to have put Levy on the defensive with the odd trio. "The guy doesn't know what he's talking about, he's a bum," said Levy angrily.

From the conversation, LaMonte got the distinct impression that these were the real owners of the record store chain, not Levy. Suddenly, Morris didn't want to talk about the cutouts anymore and LaMonte was dismissed. As he was leaving, Levy fixed him with a malevolent stare and said, "I really hope you don't pay."

Several days after LaMonte returned to Philadelphia, two agents from the Redbank office of the FBI, Jeff Dossett and John Mahoney, showed up unannounced at Out of the Past. They repeated what McKean had told him in Florida, only they were more specific. They'd had a task force on Levy and Vastola for months—wiretaps, surveillance, the works. They felt LaMonte was a victim who was in way over his head with some very bad people. They said they thought he was due to get "whacked," beaten up, or maybe even killed over the debt he owed. They played him a tape recording of a phone conversation between Vastola and Levy in which the two men talked about taking over his business and running it themselves.

The agents wanted LaMonte to become a government witness, maybe wear a wire, a hidden microphone, to help gather incriminating evidence, and ultimately testify in court against the Levy-Vastola group. They would put his entire family in the federal Witness Protection Program, relocate them, give them new identities, and pay them monthly living expenses—a whole new life. It was the only way their safety could be guaranteed.

LaMonte's head spun with the enormity of his predicament. If he was to believe these two government agents, life as he knew it was over for him, and for his family. He could either be killed by the Mafia or become a stool pigeon and spend the rest of his life running, hiding, looking over his shoulder, and taking handouts from the government. Like that Fratianno guy, the one they called "the Weasel."

"I am not a criminal," he protested. "I'm a businessman who made a bad business decision, a mistake. And I'm not a snitch. I can't do what you're asking, no way. You gotta be kiddin' me—put my family through that?"

He told them he thought he could get out of the jam by himself. The record company, MCA, had agreed to take the balance of what was owed—$629,000, they said—in returned goods. He had way more than that right there in this warehouse, enough to satisfy the debt and still have some left to sell and perhaps offset some of his losses on the deal. Levy and the boys will have made some money—not as much as they'd planned, however—and they would be happy. After everything was over, he'd never do business with them again. He hadn't meant to this time; he thought he was buying directly from MCA, through that "piece-of-shit Pisello."

"That's one thing we'd like to know," Mahoney said. "How did the wise guys get into MCA?"

LaMonte said he didn't know. "But if I were you, I'd look into Sal. He's got no business being in the middle of this deal; he doesn't know the first thing about records. MCA's got problems. I've been in this business twenty-five years and I've never seen a major, megabuck company represented by a racketeer before."

Dossett and Mahoney didn't push LaMonte too hard on the

cooperating witness bit. He was in a state of denial, which was not surprising—it wasn't a pretty picture they painted. He needed time for it all to sink in, to talk to his wife perhaps before making a decision.

They weren't trying to scare him, and they couldn't force him to cooperate, they said. It was just that, by law, they were required to warn him of the danger.

They left their cards and told him to call if he changed his mind, or if anything happened. They'd be monitoring the situation and would try to warn him if any action against him seemed imminent. They'd probably be calling him again in any case, just to see how he was doing.

On April 3, investigators monitoring the wiretap on Video Warehouse heard Brocco tell Rocco Musacchia, "I was with our friend last night, the big guy, and he wants to get together Monday. We're going to bring some people down and we're going to count this kid's merchandise, because he claims that most of it is there, including the cassettes. We'll see what he has and go from there; he claims he has more than three million pieces there."

On April 8, investigators overheard Vastola telling Levy, "We're going in Wednesday morning to take over the business."

The investigators had no way of knowing it, but that statement was a lie. Vastola wasn't going to LaMonte's warehouse to take it over. He was going to look at some new documents that LaMonte said would prove once and for all how Levy and Pisello had ripped them off on the MCA cutout deal. LaMonte had taken all the shipping and receiving documents, purchase orders, and billings from the cutout sale, including the paperwork from Scorpio Music, and had it fed into a computer, at a cost of $5,000. What came out of the computer was incontrovertible:

Nearly six hundred thousand units of the best merchandise LaMonte ordered from MCA was diverted through Ranji Bedi's Betaco and shipped instead to Scorpio Music. Scorpio paid sixty-five cents a unit, or a total of about $385,000. Scorpio originally ordered the same cutouts from LaMonte priced at $1.50 per unit, for a total of $900,000. But when Ranji Bedi offered the same goods for less than half the price, Scorpio's John Gervasoni, like any good businessman, took that deal over LaMonte's. As a result, La Monte and his partner, Gaetano Vastola, lost $660,000 in profits, or $330,000 apiece. And the money that Gervasoni paid for the diverted cutouts? It had gone to Sal Pisello and his patron, Morris Levy.

It was all there in black and white.

As he went over the computer printout and the realization began to set in that he'd been cheated by his old friend, Vastola did a slow burn. LaMonte pressed the advantage by reminding him that he'd warned him in the beginning. "Remember that day in the elevator at Morris's office? I told you it looked like Morris and Sal were going to cream our load." He then filled Vastola in on Levy's long history of cheating people in cutout deals. "This is why I would never do business with him before," he said.

Over the next few days, it seemed to investigators monitoring the wiretaps that LaMonte had pulled off a minor miracle. There was no more talk about taking over LaMonte's business. Instead, Vastola was asking his underlings to contact former partners of Levy's in cutout deals to question them on their experience with Morris. "I'm gonna open up a can of worms with this," he told Brocco. "Even Fritzy says the kid was victimized," Brocco said.

At the same time, Vastola kept playing both sides of the fence by lying to Levy that he had gone to LaMonte's warehouse and had "slapped the kid around and got him in line."

On April 16, investigators learned that someone from MCA had shown up at LaMonte's warehouse to look over the inventory prior to it being shipped back to the company. Brocco instructed LaMonte to get the man's business card "to make sure he's from MCA. When the Galoot calls, tell him who this guy is and what he's got in mind."

The MCA representative was Dan Westbrook, the vice president of manufacturing for the record company. LaMonte picked him up at the airport that morning, just as Pisello had instructed him to the day before. "I'm sending one of my guys to see you; you better have all the stuff there," Pisello said on the phone from California.

Westbrook seemed like a nice enough fellow. LaMonte took him down to the basement to see all the MCA cutouts. Westbrook said it appeared that he had plenty of merchandise to send back. He mentioned that he'd talked to Morris Levy and knew that John was in some kind of trouble there. "What went wrong?" he asked.

"Morris creamed my load," LaMonte replied, showing Westbrook the computer printout he'd made for Vastola.

"Now I understand why you didn't pay," Westbrook said.

Sensing he'd found a sympathetic ear in Westbrook, LaMonte

handed him one of the Jamaican cassettes. "You can quit looking for your counterfeiter," he said. "I made this stuff and it's not counterfeit; it's from your Jamaican licensee. If you guys sue me over this we're going to get in a big mess. I'm willing to forget this whole thing. If the guy in Jamaica made a mistake and wasn't supposed to be making The Who, so we stop. I lost money and you lost money. Let me go about my business and leave me the fuck alone. But if you push this, you'll be airing your dirty laundry in public and you'll be opening yourselves up to a wider investigation, number one, for having a hood repping your company."

Westbrook agreed that Pisello was a problem. "We've got to get away from that cancer," he said.

Westbrook called Pisello at MCA headquarters in Los Angeles and told him it appeared that LaMonte had more than enough merchandise to cover the $629,000 balance. After a few moments of saying nothing, Westbrook put Pisello on hold and turned to LaMonte. "He wants you to send back every record you have," he said. "What are you going to do?"

LaMonte got on the phone with Pisello.

"My instructions from Vastola and Levy are to send back only $629,000 worth," he said.

"I want every fucking piece you got sent back or we'll be sending some people to see you and it won't be pretty what happens, you understand?" Pisello shouted.

LaMonte understood that his life was being threatened. "I'll see what I can do," he said, and hung up.

Over the next couple of days, investigators listened as the return shipments to MCA got under way.

"They're going to send it to within fifty miles of here; they're going to scrap it," Brocco told Vastola's aide, Lew Saka. "So the kid says, 'Can I buy it?' Then the other piece of work on the coast calls up and is motherfucking him all over the area and says send it all back. If Sal calls you anymore just refer it to the Galoot."

On April 18, Brocco called Out of the Past and talked to LaMonte's secretary, Mary Ann Laberty. "I just spoke to my board of directors in New York. They would like a list of all monies John has paid in, including the notes, to Worldwide Consultants. Make a note they want a figure on all the trucks, what it cost to ship it."

The investigators shook their heads in amazement. It seemed like LaMonte had really done it—not only talked his way out of the deal, but also sown the seeds of dissension among the bad guys themselves. He had them plotting against each other. It was a helluva performance.

The only problem was that with LaMonte safely out of the jam, they'd probably lost any chance of getting him to cooperate. Where did that leave their investigation?

19

*"You crawl
on your
belly"*

On Friday, April 19, 1985, three days before Sal Pisello's sentencing hearing, Marvin Rudnick filed his sentencing memorandum with the court, requesting "a substantial sentence of incarceration."

Throughout his career, Rudnick had been a firm believer in the public record. His experience as a consumer-interest investigator in Florida had taught him that court documents were a good way of shining the light of public scrutiny on the kind of questionable white-collar conduct that law enforcement officials come upon every day but only occasionally get to pursue toward prosecution, because of either political considerations or funding priorities. He'd learned that public disclosure sometimes generated public outcry, which in turn forced government agencies to further investigate matters they otherwise might have let slide.

Rudnick knew his Pisello memorandum would probably cause

quite a few ripples, since it revealed many details of Pisello's dealings with MCA Records. MCA, after all, was a publicly traded corporation, with many large, institutional stockholders and a board of directors that included the likes of former Democratic Party chairman Robert Strauss, New York investment banker Felix Rohatyn, and former senator Howard Baker, who was thinking of running for president at the time. These people would not be thrilled to learn that their record company executives had handed out corporate funds to an operator of Sal Pisello's ilk.

"Salvatore James Pisello, 61 [sic], was born in Brooklyn, New York," the memo read. "Most of Pisello's adult life has been involved in unscrupulous business dealings which have caught the eye of numerous law enforcement agencies. Only the Internal Revenue Service, in the instant case, has been successful in bringing his substantial illicit activities to a prosecution."

The memo went on to explain how the Los Angeles IRS first learned of Pisello from the federal narcotics task force in 1979. It told about Marty Antoci and Pisello's plan for smuggling heroin in lobster tanks, and it added an ominous footnote: "On September 21, 1983, Antoci died from a heart attack. A few weeks before his death, he told FBI special agent Jack Blair that Pisello had threatened him at a restaurant, saying to Antoci, 'You're dead, I'm going to see to that.'"

The memo observed that despite his tax woes, Pisello's business had thrived in recent years. "In 1983, for instance, Pisello convinced MCA Records of Universal City to distribute the Sugar Hill label. Sugar Hill Records of New Jersey specializes in soul and rock and roll music, including the recordings of Chuck Berry. According to MCA, Pisello put the parties together and received the rights to 3 percent of the net proceeds due Sugar Hill. MCA states that Sugar Hill soon had 'cash flow' problems and remains in arrears to MCA for $1.7 million. Pisello personally received $76,530 from MCA in commissions on the Sugar Hill deal. It remains unknown what Sugar Hill paid Pisello for his efforts.

"Pisello also sold MCA a large quantity of breakdancing mats. After paying Pisello's company, Consultants for World Records Inc., $100,000 for the mats, MCA took a $95,000 loss when they didn't sell. MCA also advanced Pisello $30,000 in 1984 for expenses involving his expertise in delivering a Latin music line, and $50,000 in 1985 for future income on the Sugar Hill deal.

"In the fourth deal, Pisello arranged for MCA to sell two of his clients sixty truckloads of out-of-date record albums (commonly known in the record industry as cutouts) and cassettes worth $1.4 million. Although shipped a year ago, the clients have yet to pay. Most of the trucks left the records and tapes at a company called Out of the Past Ltd., in Darby, Pa., and much of the rest went to Arkansas and South America.

"In total, MCA paid Pisello over $250,000 in the past year for various deals. Yet Pisello told the Probation Office that he has but $2,500 in the bank, has earned but $50,000 and owes MCA and Sugar Hill $330,000."

Although MCA Records executives had been arguably cooperative in giving him information about their dealings with Pisello, Rudnick suspected that he hadn't been told the full story. His instincts and experience told him that someone inside MCA was not a completely innocent victim in the matter. A man with Pisello's background doesn't just walk into a company like MCA, introduce himself, and pull up a chair at the executive conference table. Rudnick believed that Pisello probably had gained entry to the corporation through some illegal act. The only other logical explanation would have been an attack of mass stupidity on the part of MCA Records management—giving Sal $30,000 for his expertise in Latin music, for instance. But these were not stupid men—they were intelligent, clever executives who ate other clever executives for lunch.

The immediate purpose of the sentencing memo, of course, was to tell the judge—and the public—just how bad a guy Sal Pisello was. To that end, Rudnick attached as exhibits dozens of pages of law enforcement intelligence reports describing Pisello as a mobster, drug pusher, swindler, and extortionist. Sal had been preying on citizens and thumbing his nose at the government for years, and Rudnick felt the public should know about his alleged activities.

"Despite his conviction," he wrote in the memo, "Pisello told the probation officer, 'There was never any intent to defraud or deceive the Government . . . those [monies] were loans to me, not income . . . that's the reason they were not reported for taxes.' Pisello explained his source of livelihood as coming from loans from friends, relatives and Lucille Barrie, a woman whom he had lived with for twenty years. Despite Pisello's attempt to provide exculpatory explanations to the Probation Office, he failed to inform that office that he spent Dr. Rubenstein's and Dr. Mendoza's money at the racetrack.

"Pisello also told the Probation Office that he was not a member of organized crime. At no time during the trial did the government state or infer that Pisello was a member of any organized crime group. There is evidence, however, that those crimes for which Pisello was convicted are but part of a lifestyle of wrongful conduct.

"Pisello is a criminal who fears little of the criminal justice system. When faced with such overwhelming evidence, most taxpayers seek reconciliation with the IRS, but not Salvatore Pisello. Pisello knows that his success in the world comes from his cunning ability to scheme and deceive for profit. Any effort by Pisello to file tax returns leaves law enforcement with an audit trail to his victims. Thus, concealing income is but part of his overall criminal plan. The government requests that future victims be protected from him by the maximum period of incarceration and payment of costs of prosecution."

It was colorful stuff, typical of a Rudnick sentencing memo.

At 9:30 in the morning on Monday, April 22, Sal Pisello, accompanied by his attorney, Harland Braun, arrived at U.S. District Court for sentencing. There were no spectators in the courtroom and only a single reporter, who peppered Pisello with questions as he pushed through the double doors to face the judge.

"Who did you deal with at MCA?" the reporter asked. "Who at the company signed off on the Sugar Hill distribution deal and the cutout sales? What's your position with Sugar Hill Records? Did you have any dealings with Irving Azoff or Myron Roth?"

"I got nothing to say," Pisello muttered as he entered the quiet, nearly empty courtroom.

Judge Harry Hupp had plenty to say, however, and most of it was about Rudnick's sentencing memo. He wasn't going to consider the information in the report, Hupp announced, "because it is mostly second-, third-, and fourth-hand hearsay." He complained that the memo had been presented to him on Friday, at the last minute, "and it doesn't have much credibility anyway. There's a lot of wild guessing going on that may or may not have validity. A report of some DEA agent in Italy from twelve years ago is not connected up with anything that has validity in this case, as far as I can see. So I'm setting the sentencing memorandum aside."

Rudnick was out of his chair objecting, defending himself. He explained to the judge that there "were certain standards of reliability in sworn affidavits from federal agents," of which there were three in the exhibits, including one "from an FBI agent taken just a few weeks ago."

The sentencing memo was an attempt to show that Pisello had a long history of "covering up income that was obtained from different sources and converted in part to his own use and spent for his personal enjoyment at such places as the racetrack," he said. "It is meant to show that this is not a new pattern, Your Honor."

Hupp dismissed the intelligence documents as being "without any support."

Then Harland Braun jumped in. "Your Honor, this has been a very personalized case, and I find it untoward that the government seems to be suggesting here that it went after Mr. Pisello simply because his name was Pisello. I think that's why Your Honor quashed those ridiculous subpoenas and has rebuked Mr. Rudnick numerous times for the government's conduct in this case."

Hupp agreed that he "didn't care for the prosecutor's tactics." Referring to the sentencing memo, he said, "The strike force may believe this, but I can't pay any attention to it. Mr. Rudnick thinks he has Mafia number one here and that's nonsense."

"Your Honor," Rudnick protested, "the government believes that Mr. Pisello is a sixty-one-year-old businessman from the streets of New York who . . . "

Hupp cut him off. "Strike that," he told the court reporter. "You believe that, Mr. Rudnick, and that has been apparent from the beginning."

"I believe he is an evil man, Your Honor, and that this case was just one more episode in the life of Sal Pisello, Bad Guy. I'd never heard of this man before I was assigned this case, but he is part of intelligence data for twenty years as being connected to organized crime. He stiffed the DEA in a drug investigation . . . "

"Then you should have charged him with evading taxes on the $15,000," the judge snapped, banging his gavel to indicate that the argument was closed.

Asked if he had anything to say before sentence was passed, Pisello stepped forward to the podium and told Hupp, with somber sincerity, "Your Honor, I never had any intent to evade taxes, there was never no doubt about it. I never had intent to evade taxes from anybody."

Pointing out that he could sentence him to a maximum ten years in prison and a $35,000 fine, Hupp sentenced Pisello to two years and the cost of the prosecution. He also ordered that Pisello become eligible for probation after serving one-third of the sentence, eight months.

As he left the courtroom, Pisello's only comment to the reporter was to say that Rudnick "wants to destroy me so I don't work no more."

Rudnick left the courthouse livid, not because Hupp handed down only two years—that wasn't too bad, actually—but because the judge had scolded him like a naughty schoolboy for doing his job. Hupp had impugned his integrity and questioned his motives as a public servant—the same judge who had smoked a cigarette in the courtroom with a reputed mafioso. He noticed that Hupp's sentence contained no provision for forcing Pisello to pay the $243,000 he owed the government in back taxes.

Back in his office, Rudnick called the collections division of the IRS in Los Angeles. He told them about Pisello's years-old tax debt, gave them the number of the Consultants for World Records account at the Bank of Commerce in Astoria, New York, and suggested they might serve a levy on the account to recover Pisello's back taxes. "Let's see if the system works," he said.

Unhappiest of all about the events of April 22 were the executives of MCA. The following morning, the *Los Angeles Times* carried a story on the front page of its business section headlined, "Figure in Record Deals Tied to Crime Family." The article laid out the information in Rudnick's sentencing memo and pointed out the apparent connection between the Pisello cutout deal and the recent discovery of the East Coast counterfeiting operation. It quoted an unnamed MCA spokesman as saying the company had no prior knowledge of Pisello's criminal background. "Sal Pisello is a representative of Sugar Hill Records, an independent record company that MCA distributes," the company said in a prepared statement. "Additionally, he represented a buyer who purchased records discontinued from the MCA catalog. . . . MCA has been in constant contact with the Justice Department during this investigation and has cooperated fully and will continue to do so."

Inside the company, MCA chairman Lew Wasserman angrily called the *Times* article "the worst publicity this company has had in fifty years." Azoff laid the blame on others, telling people,

"Myron Roth and Dan McGill got conned. They approved five transactions that I didn't know about. We've reprimanded several people." He said that Sam Passamano, who now worked for a budget record distribution company called Viking, was somehow involved in the counterfeiting scheme. "Apparently Passamano was sending these records out; we think he's in over his eyeballs."

The company assigned two executives from its corporate internal audit department, audit director Terry Reagan and his assistant, Allen Clement, to conduct an internal investigation of the counterfeiting scheme and the Pisello deals to determine what went wrong. Their report was to be submitted to the board of directors at the annual stockholders meeting in Chicago. The meeting was set for May 2, so they didn't have much time.

On the day that Pisello was sentenced, Gaetano Vastola and Lew Saka were on the phone to each other, talking about how they'd been screwed on the MCA cutout deal by Morris Levy and Pisello.

"That $385,000 they made at the beginning, where did that go?" Vastola said.

"Did they swallow it?" Saka asked.

"That's what I'm trying to find out."

"I'm sure they didn't turn around and pay MCA because that was at the very beginning of the deal."

"Well, where did it go?"

"They cut it up, I figure," Saka said.

"So now I'm beginning to get to the bottom of it. Is there any way we could find out how much the load originally cost?"

"We could ask MCA," Saka responded.

"How do you ask MCA?" Vastola said. "This is where it starts to smell. Now why do they want the whole load back?"

"Not only do they want the whole load back," said Saka, "but they want to send it to some place within fifty miles of where John is, so that means they are selling it to somebody."

"I'm not going to give them the whole load back," Vastola said. "I'm only going to give them for what we owe."

"You think what I think?" Saka asked. "That MCA wants to chop it up?"

"There's something stinky here," Vastola said. "I'm going to open their asses with this."

Later, investigators overheard Vastola and Brocco on a hidden microphone the FBI had installed in the Video Warehouse office.

"The kid was telling me the truth the whole time," Vastola said. "The stuff was there. I called Sal and said, 'By the way, you got a big write-up in the paper. Now all the dirt is gonna come out.' So I said at the meeting—we were all there—the stuff is all there. I asked why they wanted everything back instead of the 650,000. Why? I want an answer.

"So I called Morris and asked, 'Why do you want all this stuff back?' He said, 'I can't talk to you over the phone; I have to talk to you in person.' I said, 'No, no, no, talk to me now, tell me what it is.' Listen to this off-the-wall reason he gave me: The reason they dropped the price from $1.25 million was because of all the free goods they gave us—does that make sense?"

"There was no free goods," Brocco said. "We were billed $570,000 for everything we got."

"What I'm trying to do is make us come out smelling like a rose and Morris and Sal wrong, one million percent wrong," Vastola said, telling Brocco about the subsequent meeting he had with Levy at "the diner."

"I said, 'Moishe, I'm gonna ask you again, did Sal—forget about you for the moment—did Sal sell any part of this load off any way?' He said, 'Sal didn't do anything wrong.' I said, 'I didn't ask that. I want to know, did Sal sell any part of this load off?' He said yes— that low-life cocksucker. I said, 'I'm surprised at you, you of all people didn't tell me what you were doing. Wasn't I your partner? Am I in this deal or not? Why didn't you tell me that you sold six hundred thousand pieces to that guy in California for $385,000? I asked Sal last night on the phone three times, 'Did you sell to anybody?' and he says no. 'Are you sure?' and he says no.

"So I says to Levy, 'Tell him to come here, cause when he comes in here I'm going to chew his fucking head off.' And when he came, he ran to where he had to run. And when they came, all those people from New York, and I says to Levy, 'Do you know what you are? You're a low-life, rotten, fucking, cocksucking partner; you have no loyalty to nobody. You're a fucking lowlife; you crawl on your belly.' I called him every name on this earth, and then he had the nerve to tell me, when the meeting was over, 'I want to apologize for what I did.'"

Referring to the article that appeared in the *Los Angeles Times*, Brocco said, "The FBI is involved. MCA denies knowing Sal is involved with any organized crime families or anything that he did.

He made $250,000 with them and they are denying any knowledge of knowing what he was."

"He made $250,000; I know he made that," Vastola said, adding, "which nobody saw anything of."

Following the discussion with Vastola, Brocco phoned Out of the Past and spoke to LaMonte. "The Galoot was here today and he says the other guy out there made the papers."

"Yeah, with me," LaMonte said. "It says a sales rep of MCA made $250,000."

"Who's the sales rep?" Brocco asked.

"Salvatore," LaMonte replied.

"I didn't know he was a sales rep. He's on payroll there? On what deal?"

"On our deal."

"Did it spell out the deal?"

"It didn't mention Worldwide Consultants; it said MCA directly to me."

Referring to the mention in the *Times* of Pisello's alleged ties to the Gambino crime family, Brocco chuckled, "Who the hell is Gambino? He sells records, too?"

20

"We accept
the fact
that we
were conned"

On May 10, Sal Pisello made the papers again. The *Los Angeles Times* ran an article on the front page of its business section saying that MCA was "more deeply involved with reputed mobster Salvatore Pisello than was previously revealed in court."

The *Times* article was based largely on information contained in MCA's internal audit report to the board of directors eight days earlier. The newspaper had obtained a copy of the nine-page audit report, which was marked "confidential" and was clearly never intended for public dissemination.

The report was written by Allen Clement, the auditor the company originally assigned to investigate the counterfeit tape scam uncovered by the *Los Angeles Times*, and Clement's boss, Terry Reagan, the director of MCA's corporate internal audit department. Based on information gathered in the course of their week-long investigation, Clement and Reagan gave the record division's explanation of seven business deals involving Sal Pisello. The first deal was the distribution agreement with Sugar Hill Records.

"According to Zach Horowitz, MCA Records senior vice president of business and legal affairs, Joe Zynczak, a reputable New York lawyer who represents entertainment clients, approached MCA in 1983 with the possibility of establishing a distribution deal for Sugar Hill Records. A meeting was held between Sugar Hill representatives, including Pisello, and MCA Records executives, including Irving Azoff, president of MCA Records and Music Group, and Myron Roth, executive vice president of MCA Records and Music Group. (Azoff was present at the meeting for a brief period of time and does not recall meeting Pisello.)"

The auditors noted that "Pisello is not employed by Sugar Hill, as far as MCA Records personnel know. Per Roth, there were no prior dealings between Pisello and MCA Records. According to Horowitz, Pisello has been useful in resolving problems that have arisen during the term of the Sugar Hill agreement."

The report stated that MCA had been paying Sugar Hill 3 percent of the net proceeds due Sugar Hill—adding to a total of $76,530 in 1984—but noted that "there is no mention of Pisello, Consultants for World Records Inc. or a consulting fee in MCA's distribution agreement with Sugar Hill."

According to the auditors, as of March 30, Sugar Hill was in arrears to MCA in the amount of $1.7 million. "This unrecouped balance is secured by MCA's secondary interest in the Sugar Hill catalog masters (including the Chess/Checker masters) subject to Morris Levy's primary interest of $300,000. The balance is also secured by any monies payable to Sugar Hill under the distribution deal as well as the Sugar Hill inventory of records and album jackets in MCA's possession (approximately $385,000). When MCA's hard costs of distribution are deducted from the distribution fee, the cumulative profit, according to McGill, is approximately $1.4 million."

The report went on to describe the payment of $100,000 to Pisello in 1984 for "the purchase of inventory and test marketing services for a breaker mat venture based on Pisello's idea to market breaker mats and related items used for break dancing." MCA took a $95,000 loss on that deal, "and the inventory is not in MCA's possession. Azoff was aware of the breaker mat venture, but was unaware of Pisello's involvement or the amount involved."

Azoff was also unaware, the report said, of the $30,000 advance to Pisello "to investigate the feasibility of establishing a Latin label."

Of a $50,000 payment made to Pisello on January 17, 1985, the report stated that, according to Roth and McGill, "this is an advance against Pisello's 3 percent portion of future proceeds payable to Sugar Hill." However, "It should be noted that Sugar Hill's future is in doubt if the Checker/Chess acquisition is not completed, and therefore it is doubtful that MCA Records would ever owe Pisello his 3 percent portion."

According to the report, the payments to Pisello were "supported only by the payment requests (signed by Dan McGill and Myron Roth) and check stub legends. There are no signed agreements with Pisello or Consultants for World Records Inc., stipulating the terms of the agreement." It said that Pisello guaranteed the deals by giving MCA checks. "In 1984, Pisello initially gave MCA two dated checks totalling $130,000 to cover the breaker mat and Latin label ventures. However, these checks were replaced by Pisello with three undated checks totaling $180,000 (when the January 1985, $50,000 advance was made). This was done because the 1984 checks had become too old to cash. McGill is still in possession of the latter three uncashed checks, which are not negotiable because Pisello does not now have sufficient funds."

The audit report then detailed two cutout record transactions involving Pisello. The first was the sale to John LaMonte through Roulette Records. "Per Myron Roth, subsequent to the Sugar Hill deal in early 1984, Pisello approached MCA about buying cutout records and tapes. In that the Sugar Hill deal had been successful until that point, Roth saw no reason not to deal with Pisello and he referred Pisello to Sam Passamano, Sr., who was in charge of negotiating all cutout sales."

The report stated that Passamano had been "terminated" and now worked for another company. "Since leaving MCA, Passamano is suspected of attempting to market counterfeit MCA cutouts. We attempted to question Passamano about the cutout sale, but he refused to answer any questions."

Once again, "Azoff was unaware of this sale, and has since instructed personnel that his approval is required for all cutout sales." And yet again, "There was no formal written agreement documenting the terms of the Roulette cutout sale, other than the purchase order and the referenced list. . . . Passamano was the highest ranking MCA Records employee copied on the Roulette purchase order and internal MCA correspondence relating to the deal."

The second cutout sale was the one Pisello made through Ranji Bedi's company, Betaco, to Scorpio Music. Here again, "Azoff was not aware of the sale before it was made." Scorpio was not identified as a customer in the report. Rather, "This customer was set up on MCA's books as 'Pisello/Betaco.' On November 7, 1984, Betaco paid MCA Records $200,000 in advance for this sale, and sent a listing of quantities and titles ordered totaling approximately 3 million units. When McGill received this listing, he noticed that the order included several active titles not authorized to be cut out. Apparently, Pisello had been given an incorrect list of cutout titles by Sam Passamano."

MCA ultimately shipped only 140,000 of the cutouts ordered in the second sale. "Because the $200,000 had been paid to MCA for cutouts it could not deliver, to avoid a legal argument that it was in breach of contract, MCA Records agreed to refund the original $200,000 payment, and a check was issued to Betaco for this amount on January 22, 1985. In exchange for the titles shipped, Pisello gave McGill a signed check dated April 17, 1985, for $52,109. Per a McGill discussion with Pisello, there were not sufficient funds in Pisello's account on April 17 to cash the check, and McGill is still in possession of the check."

The final Pisello deal covered the pending purchase of the Checker/Chess catalog of master recordings from Sugar Hill. The catalog contained old recordings by such blues and early rock 'n' roll artists as Muddy Waters, Howlin' Wolf, Bo Diddley, and Chuck Berry, and it was Sugar Hill's single most valuable asset. In the audit report, MCA Records executives valued the catalog at $1.7 million, which was, coincidentally, the exact amount they claimed Sugar Hill was in arrears to MCA.

The acquisition plan laid out in the report called for MCA to purchase the catalog by canceling the $1.7 million Sugar Hill owed and lending the company another $1.3 million to help with the company's "cash flow" problems.

"According to a verbal agreement between Myron Roth and Sal Pisello," the report said, "MCA advances to Pisello/Consultants for World Records Inc. amounting to $130,000 would be forgiven in consideration for Pisello's involvement in arranging the agreement

with Sugar Hill. . . . In the opinion of outside counsel Allen Susman, Justice Department special attorney Marvin Rudnick consid-
ers MCA Records a victim in their dealings with Pisello, and con-
siders the execution of the Chess/Checker deal to be an effective
way of discontinuing the relationship with Pisello."

The audit report was a remarkable document, and its public disclosure clearly embarrassed MCA. The company immediately
began scrambling to implement some sort of damage control.

An indignant-sounding Susman read a statement to the *Times:*
"MCA intends to get to the bottom of the entire matter and take all
appropriate and available legal steps with regard to any matters
involving Mr. Pisello or any other matters that are in any way
improper. And we intend to pursue this as vigorously, emphatically,
and quickly as can be done."

"We can't say we haven't been stupid; we accept the fact that we
were conned," the *Times* quoted one unnamed executive as saying.

"Our guys simply got swindled out of $250,000," said another.
"After the first deal went bad they should have cut it off, but in the
hope that they could eventually salvage things, they threw good
money after bad."

But the spin control didn't work. The public disclosure of the
internal audit report set in motion a chain of events that would
plague MCA for the next four years. The company soon found that
undoing the damage was like trying to put feathers back in a down
pillow on a windy day.

When Gene Froelich read the account in the *Times,* he was sure
that it spelled the end of Irving Azoff at MCA. Never mind that the
audit report said Azoff was unaware of everything that had gone on,
there was enough questionable corporate conduct there to cause
even Sid Sheinberg to lose patience with his fair-haired boy. And if
Sid didn't move, surely Lew Wasserman would. Wasserman was
widely regarded as one of the toughest and most astute chief executives in the country. In Wasserman's more than thirty years of running the company, MCA had earned the reputation as the tightest-
run ship in show business. Now the company was a laughing
stock—corporate officers accepting worthless checks as collateral
from a mobster? The board of directors must have gone crazy.
Froelich had seen Wasserman fire people—sometimes brutally—for
infractions that paled in comparison to what appeared in this

report. Azoff, Roth, and McGill were history. Or so Froelich thought.

Al Bergamo heard about the revelations through the grapevine in Denver, where he'd opened up his own talent consultant business. What a crock, he thought: Azoff didn't remember meeting Pisello; Azoff was unaware of what Roth and McGill were doing. Hell, those two guys would never do these kind of deals on their own. In Bergamo's experience, Roth didn't make a move unless Azoff told him to. And McGill! Bergamo recalled the time that McGill harassed him for two days about a $160 expense voucher he'd turned in when he had to spend the night in Dallas for a deposition in a lawsuit against the company. Now McGill was supposed to have handed out several hundred thousand dollars to Sal Pisello, on his own and without written authorization? The scenario was preposterous; it couldn't have happened that way.

The most suspicious part of the audit report, Bergamo thought, was the explanation about the Sugar Hill transactions. It said that MCA had "advanced" Sugar Hill more than $2 million. Where did that come from? he wondered. There were no provisions for advances in the distribution contract. Not in the one he signed, anyway. And the idea of lending Sugar Hill another $1.3 million when the company was on the verge of going belly-up was just plain crazy. Either that, or it was some kind of disguised payment. It looked like Morris Levy was going to get his $1 million after all.

For Sam Passamano, the internal audit report was the last straw. Those bastards were blaming him for their problems with Pisello. He'd been set up, just as he'd suspected back at the 1984 NARM convention. And now they were slandering him to boot by calling him a counterfeiter, an allegation based on the fact that the company he now worked for had purchased and distributed some of La-Monte's Jamaican imports. He called George Collier's lawyer, Will Dwyer, and said he was ready to sue MCA for wrongful termination and defamation.

Collier's lawsuit against MCA was filed the day after the internal audit story broke in the newspaper. It charged that he was illegally fired because he'd threatened to blow the whistle on improprieties he'd uncovered inside the company—namely, executives sending out huge amounts of free records in violation of artists' contracts and, possibly, in exchange for money or drugs.

(Two months after he filed the lawsuit, Collier received an envelope marked "Personal" in the mail at Capitol Records, where he'd gotten a job following his dismissal from MCA. The envelope contained a photocopied picture of Collier that had appeared in *Billboard* magazine. It showed Collier standing alongside other Capitol executives at a gold-record ceremony for singer Anne Murray. But the anonymous sender had slashed a large "X" across Collier's face with a black magic marker. Collier's lawyer interpreted the anonymous correspondence as a threat against his client's life, and he turned the matter over to the FBI for investigation.)

The same day that Collier's lawsuit was filed, MCA filed one of its own, accusing John LaMonte, Alvin Ranglin (the Jamaican licensee), and Sam Passamano of counterfeiting.

John Gervasoni was already thinking of suing MCA when he saw the story about the audit report. He'd been bugging Ranji Bedi for weeks about the cutouts he had ordered—and had paid $350,000 in advance for—but never received. Since he wired Bedi the money in November, he had received only about 120,000 records—mostly junk titles, none of the desirable double-LP sets that had caused him to put up the money in the first place. Bedi kept assuring him that the records would be shipped, saying at first the problem was that MCA was busy shipping frontline goods for the Christmas selling season and his shipments would have to wait until after the crush. Lately, however, the excuse had been that the record division was having problems with the corporate auditors over the fiasco with Pisello and the LaMonte sale, and they couldn't ship his order until things cooled down. Because of the long delay, Bedi had returned $150,000 to Gervasoni in February. Bedi had assured him time and again that Pisello wasn't involved in his deal, however.

From the newspaper report, Gervasoni learned not only that Pisello was involved—apparently as Bedi's partner—but that MCA was never going to ship the records and had even refunded $200,000 to Betaco back in January.

He immediately called MCA and asked for Allen Clement, the co-author of the internal audit report. Clement seemed genuinely surprised—and concerned—about the story Gervasoni told him. It was the first he'd heard anything about a $350,000 down payment. As far as he knew, MCA had been paid only $200,000 up front for the records, and that money had been returned, which should have squared the deal and zeroed it out on MCA's books. For an auditor to hear, after the fact, that another $150,000 remained unaccounted for was troubling. He said he'd look into it and get right back to Gervasoni.

Ranji Bedi called Gervasoni back within the hour. He was in a phone booth, nearly hysterical.

"What are you doing calling the corporate auditors?" Bedi screamed. "Are you nuts? That's the worst thing you could have done. Zach Horowitz is going crazy. You're not going to get any records or money back. If you don't calm Zach down you're out of business."

"Ranji, where's my money? It says here they gave you back $200,000 and you only sent me $150,000. Where's the rest of it?"

Bedi said that he had to keep $50,000 in his account because that's what he would have to pay MCA when the order was finally shipped.

"But this says they're never going to ship it. And that still leaves $150,000 of my money out there somewhere. I want it back."

"I can't return that to you now because it's been distributed through the system," Bedi said. "Deals of this nature take cash, you know that. I can't give you the rest because it's gone."

"Are you telling me you gave it all to the guys upstairs at MCA? What did they do with it?"

"What they did with it is none of your business."

"Are you saying they used my money to buy coke for rock stars?"

"Don't be naive, John. Cash runs the record business. I had to take care of a lot of people. How do you think I got this deal? Everyone had their hand in there."

"Ranji, I'm out $200,000 and I have $12,000 in goods, maximum. You told me Sal Pisello had nothing to do with this."

Bedi assured him that Sal was not his partner, no matter what the audit report said. The audit report was all bullshit. Gervasoni would eventually get all the records he had coming. "MCA is too big a company to screw you," Bedi said. "If you don't believe me, would you like to talk to Horowitz? He's the vice president of legal affairs."

Later in the day, MCA counsel Horowitz called Gervasoni. "How many other people know about this deal?" were the first words out of Horowitz's mouth.

"A few," said Gervasoni.

Horowitz repeated what Bedi had told him, that the records

would eventually be shipped. They would work something out. But for now, he said, "You have to keep your mouth shut about this deal. We're in a very sensitive situation here. Right now we're having problems with the corporate audit, and the government is asking all kinds of questions."

Gervasoni agreed to be patient for a little while longer. But if he didn't get either his records or his money soon, he told Horowitz, he was going to sue MCA and make the whole mess public.

For Marvin Rudnick, the story about the MCA internal audit report confirmed what he'd suspected all along—MCA had not told him the whole truth. In his conversations with Roth, Horowitz, and McGill, he'd been led to believe that the $50,000 advance to Pisello on his Sugar Hill fee had happened long ago and far away. Actually, it was in January, right when Sal was getting ready to go to trial and would need money to pay his lawyer. Was that what the money was for? he wondered. Was MCA paying his legal bills under the table? If so, why? To keep him quiet?

The MCA executives had also indicated that the pending Checker/Chess acquisition was not really an issue, that Sal wasn't involved financially. Rudnick checked his notes from his last conversation with Horowitz, the day before he filed the sentencing memorandum. Zach had implored him specifically not to mention the Checker/Chess purchase in the memo because "Sal might retaliate and screw the deal up." So Rudnick had left it out as a favor to MCA. After all, they were cooperating to a degree.

Rudnick found it curious that the audit report seemed to go out of its way to implicate Sam Passamano, who was, conveniently, no longer at the company. Early on, Rudnick had suspected that Passamano might be in cahoots with Pisello, primarily because of his Italian surname and the information Rudnick got from Carol Kaplan that Pisello was "working for Sam Passamano" at MCA. Still, he found it odd that MCA executives had determined that Passamano was a bad guy but still maintained they were unaware of Sal's background. How could they determine the one and not the other?

Most suspicious of all were the references in the report to Azoff's supposed lack of knowledge. They seemed to be protesting too much on that point, Rudnick thought, almost as if that were the real purpose of the report. Sort of like when John Dean was sent to

Camp David to write a definitive report on his investigation into the Watergate scandal—just so long as it cleared the president.

Rudnick decided to look into the Pisello-MCA relationship a little further. The whole thing had the smell of a career case, the most significant penetration of a West Coast company by an East Coast mobster that he'd ever seen. He wrote a letter to Ron Saranow, chief of the IRS Criminal Investigation Division in Los Angeles, requesting the agency's help in looking into possible tax fraud in Pisello's dealings at the record company. The first thing he wanted to do was subpoena the bank records of Pisello's company, Consultants for World Records, and track the money from there, to see if Sal was a pocket or a funnel.

Perhaps the person most upset by the *Times* article on the MCA internal audit report was Sal Pisello himself. Two days after the newspaper story appeared, Pisello made his feelings known in a letter he sent to Irving Azoff.

"Dear Irving," it began. "I was very moved when I saw you at the Palm and you told me how everyone felt badly for me at MCA because of my problem with the government. You suggested that I call Myron Roth.

"Irving, all that I'm going through does not hurt as much as the wounds that have been inflicted upon me by MCA with the back stabbing direct statements made to the press. I am furious as to the statements that I have 'conned' and 'swindled' MCA. These comments contributed by MCA executives to the *L.A. Times* article have destroyed me completely. They are absolutely false! Can anyone understand what they have done at the expense of a human being?"

The letter continued on in the same aggrieved tone for six single-spaced pages, under a flowing-script "Salvatore J. Pisello" letterhead, laying the blame for the soured break-dance mat, Latin label, and cutout deals on the ineptitude of MCA personnel.

"It was obvious that when John LaMonte received the first twenty trailers that MCA had shipped all the garbage and he started to complain," Pisello told Azoff. "John LaMonte had a legitimate beef. I then made ten trips to New York to get the money due MCA from Out of the Past. I pressured John LaMonte and he gave me $300,000 that I then gave to MCA.

"It was difficult to pull more money out of John LaMonte,"

Pisello said, "as his answer was that he had to sell the garbage sent by MCA and was still awaiting the good product he ordered from the list that he never received from MCA.

"Now, to add to the problem, about three weeks ago I had lunch with Myron Roth and Dan McGill and they asked me if I could get the records from John LaMonte back. I told them that I would try to convince John LaMonte to send them back. As you know, Irving, this is being done now."

He ended on a plaintive note. "MCA has destroyed me in the record business and any future business dealings. . . . Something must be done about this slanderous injustice to me."

Azoff never responded to the letter, and Pisello never forgot it.

21

*"He picked
you for a
pigeon and
plucked you"*

When John LaMonte pulled out of his driveway in Landsdowne at 11:00 A.M. on Saturday, May 18, he was running late. He was supposed to meet Brocco and Vastola at noon at a motel in Hightstown, New Jersey, better than an hour's drive away.

He hoped it would be the last time he'd ever have to meet with them about the cutout deal. MCA was taking the records back. With the returns and the money and receivables he'd already paid to Levy, he was finally off the hook. Today they were going over all the paperwork—inventory, sales receipts, trucking bills—to tally up the damage and see what, if anything, was left over to split up. Probably nothing. But he really didn't care anymore. He just wanted to be out of this nightmare, far away from Rudy and Fritzy and Sal and Levy. Especially Levy.

After a quick stop at his office in Darby to grab his briefcase, he cut across the Walt Whitman Bridge, over Highway 130, and onto the New Jersey Turnpike, headed north to Hightstown, driving fast.

How did he ever get into this mess? he wondered. It seemed like such a sweet, easy deal in the beginning: no money down, pay only as he sold the goods, three quarters of a million dollars in potential profits, a customer relationship with a major company, legitimacy for himself and his company. It would have worked out, too, if only Morris hadn't gotten greedy. How do you figure a guy like Levy? He was a millionaire many times over. He owned racehorses that cost more than most people earn in a lifetime. He was going to make $250,000 on this deal—a nickel a record—for not lifting a finger. Honest money. Still, he felt the need to cheat his own people for—what? Another two hundred grand after he split with Pisello? That was pocket change for Levy. What could he buy with it that he couldn't already afford? The only explanation LaMonte could come up with was that Levy did it just to fuck with him, to punish him for their past run-ins.

Anyway, now he had the FBI on his back. After Mahoney and Dossett came to his office and scared the shit out of him, Dick McKean sent another agent to him from the Philadelphia office, Tom Cupples, just to keep the lines of communication open. Actually, Cupples was a pretty good guy for a Fed—not one of those American-flag-lapel-pin types, more of a street guy. They had hit it off quite well. It turns out they grew up in the same Philadelphia neighborhoods. Cupples even knew the nuns at the private school LaMonte's daughter April was attending in the fall. The two had played handball together a few times in recent weeks and had talked a lot on the phone about LaMonte's "problem," as Cupples put it.

LaMonte insisted that his troubles on the cutout deal were almost over. Cupples said it made no difference, the investigation of Levy et al. was going ahead anyway, and someday LaMonte would be called as a witness.

"You're working very close to a line that's very gray," Cupples told him. "A day will come when you're going to have to decide to cross over to my side."

LaMonte said he hoped Levy got everything that was coming to him, but he insisted that Sonny Brocco hadn't done anything wrong. Sonny was a victim in the deal, too. They were partners. He'd taught Brocco how to make money legitimately in the record business. Sonny had gone straight since he got out of prison.

Cupples scoffed at the notion. "Just because you've been rehabilitated, don't think that he has," he said. "Sonny is a career criminal who doesn't see past the scam. Who do you think got you into this in the first place? He set you up. He picked you for a pigeon and plucked you. He's not your friend, John. He's one of them. You think they go out and recruit nice guys to join their organization?"

LaMonte was thinking about Brocco, and how Cupples was wrong about him, when he sped past Exit 8 for Hightstown. Damn! He was already fifteen minutes late.

He got off at Exit 8A, a mile down the road, and made a U-turn just past the toll booth. As he merged with the southbound traffic he noticed in his rear-view mirror that another car—a gray sedan with two men inside—had made the same U-turn. He was sure it was the FBI following him, probably Mahoney and Dossett.

Driving up the ramp at Exit 8, he saw a police car parked under the overpass. A uniformed cop was standing next to the car, doing nothing, just looking toward the turnpike. As LaMonte turned into the motel entrance, the gray car drove on past. Pulling into the parking lot he noticed a man high up on a utility pole about one hundred yards away. "Jesus, they got this whole situation wired," he thought.

They were supposed to, but they didn't. Over the previous two days the investigators had learned from the wiretaps that there was a meeting set for Saturday, but they were unable to determine where or for what time. Around 7:30 that morning, agent Mahoney had been on his way to the Redbank office from his home in Colt's Neck, not far from where Gaetano Vastola lived. As he pulled up to a stop sign at the intersection of Lime Road and County Highway 520, Mahoney saw Vastola driving west toward the Freehold/Howell Township area. He got on his car radio and contacted the surveillance team he'd assigned to try to follow Brocco to the meeting. He knew the team was in the Freehold/Howell area. "Vastola is heading your way," he said. "Be alert; something could be moving."

A few minutes later, the team radioed back that they hadn't been able to locate Vastola, nor had they seen Brocco that morning. Both targets were "out of pocket," they said.

So LaMonte was on his own at the motel. Brocco, Vastola, and Lew Saka were waiting for him at a poolside table when he arrived. Vastola was irritated that he was late; he'd suspected that John might not show up at all.

They got right down to business. The way Vastola and Saka had it figured, after everything was taken into account, LaMonte still owed $91,000.

LaMonte blanched. "Where'd you come up with that number?" he asked.

Vastola and Saka went over their computations, factoring in the credit for the returns and what Levy claimed MCA said it all came out to. Vastola said he expected LaMonte to pay $5,000 by June 15, followed by biweekly payments of $5,000 until the balance was paid off. This was on top of the $1,000 a week LaMonte was still paying on the $50,000 loan from 1982.

LaMonte couldn't really argue about the $91,000, since he'd never received a bill from Consultants for World Records, Levy, or MCA. He looked at Brocco, who just shrugged, as if to say, "What can I do?"

"Okay," he said quietly, getting up from his chair. "I guess I gotta pay what you say I owe, and then that'll be it."

He turned and walked quickly away, trying to control himself. He was seething. The bastards were going to keep bleeding him no matter what, he thought. Now they were hitting him up for the profits they lost on the records that were being returned. What was next?

He was halfway across the pool deck when he stopped, turned around and walked back to where Brocco was sitting by himself now. Vastola and Saka were standing about ten feet away, conferring quietly. No longer able to contain his anger, LaMonte hissed at Brocco, "I'm gonna pay every cent, but when this is all over I ain't ever doing business with you people again as long as I live. From the beginning all I've had is problems with you guys!"

As LaMonte was speaking, he didn't notice Vastola walk up beside him. Suddenly, it happened. Vastola hit him with a round-house right, his ham-sized fist slamming squarely against La-Monte's left temple, shattering bone, pulverizing blood vessels. The concussion was tremendous, sending LaMonte reeling in a wide arc, knocked senseless, his legs turned to rubber but somehow managing to keep him upright. Blood spurted from his nose, mouth, ears, and left eye.

Brocco and Saka froze. Vastola was red with rage. His chest heaved, the veins in his neck bulged. All the months of aggravation with Levy and the New York crew had finally erupted in a burst of violence. Just as quickly, it was over. Vastola could see that La-Monte was badly hurt, and they were standing in a public place. No further action was necessary; he'd made his point.

Through the blur of pain and blood, LaMonte stammered out an apology. "I shouldn't have said what I said. I made a mistake. You'll get your money."

In the motel parking lot, LaMonte fell into the front seat of his car, grabbed the steering wheel to right himself, fumbled for his keys and turned the ignition. He drove several hundred yards to the entrance and realized he'd never make it home. He was fighting to keep conscious and could barely see. His whole head felt like it was broken.

Brocco pulled up next to him in his car and stopped. "You okay, kid?"

"I can't see, Broc," LaMonte replied.

"C'mon, I'll drive you home," Brocco said.

Back at LaMonte's house, Brocco helped him inside, telling his frightened family, "He had a little accident."

After Brocco left, LaMonte told his wife to call FBI agent Tom Cupples and tell him what had happened. When Cupples arrived at the house thirty minutes later, LaMonte was lying on the couch in the living room, barely able to speak. His face was discolored and swollen almost beyond recognition.

"You look very bad, John," Cupples said. "You look worse than bad. You've got bones broken in your face and you need to go to the hospital right away. I'll take you."

LaMonte said no, he'd be all right, he just needed to sleep. "John, you definitely have a concussion," Cupples said. "I'm afraid if you go to sleep on that couch you may never wake up."

But LaMonte was adamant: no hospital. In frustration, Cupples turned to the family—John's wife, Andrea, daughters April and Doreen, son John, Jr., and his mother, all of whom were ashen-faced, confused, in shock. Beaten up by the Mafia? An FBI agent standing in their living room? It was more than they could absorb that quickly.

"You've got a very serious injury here," Cupples said. "Please try to talk some sense into him. If he changes his mind, call me. No matter how late it is, I'll drive over and take him in."

Cupples went back home and called John Mahoney in New Jersey to tell him what had happened. "Shit," Mahoney said. "How is he?"

"Not good. His face is pretty messed up. You wouldn't know him if you saw him."

A few minutes after Cupples hung up with Mahoney, LaMonte's wife called and said John was ready to go to the hospital, please hurry.

On his way out the door, Cupples grabbed a camera and some color film. As a human being, he empathized with LaMonte and his family for the ordeal they were going through. As a trained FBI agent, however, he realized that LaMonte's beating represented a fortunate break in the investigation, a turning point. They now had a bona fide extortion victim, and LaMonte's battered face was important evidence. Cupples wanted to get it on film before the doctors cleaned it up.

Over the next few days in the hospital, as a medical team worked on his fractured eye socket, crushed sinus cavities, and splintered jaw, LaMonte made the decision to cross over to Cupples's side of the line. He'd be a witness, he said, he'd cooperate, he'd do anything they wanted him to do.

His motive wasn't fear—that would come later—it was a desire for revenge. "I'm not a crook," he told Cupples, speaking with difficulty through the wires that now held his jaw in place. "But I'm not going to be a victim, either. If I can't kill these guys, I'll get even this way and then just disappear."

22

"That guy's going to die a horrible death"

S lugging John LaMonte turned out to be one of the worst mistakes Gaetano Vastola ever made.

As word of the Hightstown incident flashed back to FBI headquarters in Washington, the East Coast investigations took on a new urgency. For one thing, Vastola's punch provided investigators with a gold mine of probable cause for obtaining additional electronic surveillance. Within weeks, more than a dozen new wiretaps were in place—on the phones in the Roulette Records offices in Manhattan, at Morris Levy's farm in upstate New York, at Fritzy Giovanelli's and Rocco Musacchia's homes in Queens, and at La-Monte's warehouse in Darby, Pennsylvania.

As agents eavesdropped on hundreds of conversations, the list of suspects grew exponentially, as did the litany of suspected crimes—extortion, wire fraud, mail fraud, insurance fraud, labor racketeering, tax evasion, loan-sharking.

Now that LaMonte was cooperating, he became a lynchpin in both the New Jersey and the New York investigations. Through him, prosecutors could connect the Vastola organization, with its roots in the DeCavalcante crime family, to Vincent Gigante and the Genovese crime family. And smack in the middle of it all was Morris Levy and his little record business empire.

The plan was to prosecute the whole bunch under the Racketeer Influenced and Corrupt Organization (RICO) Act. Passed by Congress in 1970, the RICO statute gives prosecutors even broader authority to go after organized crime than the Interstate Transportation and Aid of Racketeering (ITAR) Act, which was pushed through by Attorney General Robert F. Kennedy in 1962, when he was hounding Jimmy Hoffa and the Teamsters Union.

Under RICO, if any members of a racketeering organization commit at least two crimes included on the statute's list of twenty-five "predicate acts," then all members of the enterprise can be prosecuted. It also provides that any business that's used in the furtherance of a racketeering enterprise—such as a company that launders, invests, or hides money for organized crime—can be seized by the government and forfeited.

From the wiretaps it seemed clear that Roulette Records and Video Warehouse had been used in a criminal enterprise. The role of MCA Records was far less certain, however. When Vastola hit LaMonte, he was attempting to collect on a debt that ultimately was owed to MCA. But did MCA executives knowingly participate in a conspiracy to extort LaMonte? If they did, it wouldn't be easy to prove, and even trying to gather evidence presented prosecutors with a number of problems.

As a practical matter, MCA had the ability to use its enormous wealth to marshal an armada of high-powered lawyers that could legally impede the progress of an investigation for months—litigating compliance with subpoenas, delaying testimony of company executives by arguing that their statements were covered by the attorney–client privilege, or counseling them to invoke the Fifth Amendment if called to testify without immunity. A whole battery of delaying tactics.

Overcoming such organized resistance would require a huge commitment of government resources—money and manpower. Which meant that a decision to proceed against the company would have to be made at the highest level. Which meant politics.

It was no secret around the halls of the Justice Department that Lew Wasserman and MCA had long-standing close ties to President Reagan, and that the Justice Department boss, Attorney General Edwin Meese, was a rabid protector of the president. So even if the investigations did turn up evidence of wrongdoing on the part of MCA or its executives, getting the political juice to bring indictments was another matter altogether. Trying and succeeding could make a prosecutor's career; trying and failing could end it.

At one of his early debriefing sessions with FBI agents Mahoney and Dossett, LaMonte said that one night when he and Brocco were out having dinner, he had asked, "How did a stumblebum like Pisello come out of the woodwork and end up representing MCA in this deal?"

LaMonte recalled Brocco's reply, "He did a job for somebody there. He told me that somebody screwed up and Sal later found out who he did the job for. So he went to the boys and said, 'I think I have a hook into MCA. Who do we have in the record business?' They said they had Morris. So that's how they're taking money out of the company; they own somebody there."

LaMonte said Brocco told him who Pisello allegedly did the job for, but he couldn't remember the name.

Despite that anecdote and LaMonte's insistence that someone at MCA had to be in on the scheme to extort him, a decision was made early on in the New Jersey and New York investigations to focus primarily on the activities of the East Coast wise guys. MCA was three thousand miles away, after all, and investigators already had enough evidence of wrongdoing in their own backyard to keep them busy for years.

From the wiretaps, they were picking up indications that the Vastola-Levy-Gigante group was involved in widespread corruption. Genovese capo and Pisello partner Fritzy Giovanelli talked with former Brooklyn Democratic leader Meade Esposito about an insider stock-trading deal they had going involving a company Fritzy controlled that supposedly had developed a new chemical process called K-20 for disposing of toxic substances such as PCBs and asbestos. If Esposito could use his influence to get the legislature to require companies to use the new process on government projects, the price of the stock would go up and they'd make millions.

Vastola discussed a plan with former Maryland senator George

Santoni for obtaining work on government construction projects by using "straw men" minority contractors. "This minority situation is an absolute bonanza; they have to give you between 15 percent and 30 percent of the work," Santoni told him. "Now what I'm doing is going back to all the old contractors, all the Italian guys I did business with when I was in the Senate."

Vastola also talked with a man named Thomas Boland about setting up an appointment with Alfonse D'Amato, the Republican senator from New York, to intercede on behalf of a business associate who owed money to the IRS and was being pressured.

Levy was doing a private placement of his Strawberries record store chain stock through E. F. Hutton, selling $120,000 blocks of shares to several local judges. When one of the judges said he was unable to raise the money, Levy said no problem, he'd lend it to him.

Gigante capo Dominick ("Baldy Dom") Canterino was talking about changing the serial number on a stolen Mercedes Benz 450 SL convertible, and he'd apparently forged a letter that divided the estate of Frank Caggiano, a deceased Genovese family member.

Canterino's boss, Vincent ("the Chin") Gigante, was making phone calls on a credit card registered to Newmont Mining Corporation, a Park Avenue firm that held the largest known gold reserves on the planet.

Rocco Musacchia, the Genovese soldier that Levy had threatened to send to take over LaMonte's business, was busy handling sports bets and placing extras on the set of the Neil Simon movie *Brighton Beach Memoirs*, which was filming in Brooklyn.

From LaMonte, investigators learned that Vastola's right-hand man, Lew Saka, had burned down a New Jersey diaper company he owned called Dispodype to collect on a $495,000 insurance policy.

LaMonte also told FBI agents Mahoney and Dossett that Brocco and Saka were counterfeiting video and audio cassettes out of Video Warehouse and that Nicky Massaro and Brocco were trafficking in narcotics—cocaine, heroin, and P2P, the chemical base for speed—which was strictly against Vastola's orders. Vastola was a member of the old-school Mafia that believed drug dealing was anathema to good business, its potential profits far outweighed by the official heat and prison sentences it could bring.

The agents' strategy was to keep LaMonte in tight with Vastola and Brocco so he could continue providing them with inside information. Toward that end, the government began giving him the cash to pay off his debt to Vastola. LaMonte's instructions were to stay close to Brocco, who obviously suffered from a bad case of loose lips. Keep pumping Sonny, he was told. Be casual about it, but ask questions, find out everything you can about what Vastola and Levy are up to.

For LaMonte's meetings with Brocco and the others, the agents began outfitting him with a tiny recording device, which they strapped to his ankle, concealed in the blousing of the sweat pants he always wore. They also installed an elaborate two-camera video recording system in his office. One camera was hidden behind one-way glass in a closet in his office. The other, impossibly small, was concealed in a briefcase on a shelf behind his desk, like something out of a James Bond movie. Every sound and movement in the room was recorded when LaMonte pushed a button under his desk.

The first thing the agents wanted him to do was arrange to buy some of the counterfeit videocassettes from Video Warehouse. Next they wanted him to begin purchasing drugs from Massaro, starting with small personal amounts so as not to arouse suspicion, then building up to multikilo buys.

LaMonte didn't much like the idea of running a sting operation for the FBI. He complained that telling the agents what he already knew was one thing, but helping to set people up for other crimes was a little more than he bargained for. Besides, his beef wasn't really with Brocco and Massaro, it was with Levy and MCA. That's who he wanted to get. He sort of liked Nicky, who'd been roughed up himself for falling behind on a loan-shark debt to the Vastola group.

That was exactly the point, the agents explained. In order to take down the big guys you first had to convince one or two of the little guys to "roll over" and cooperate. Brocco and Massaro were the perfect candidates. For people in their line of work, shooting your mouth off or dealing drugs on the sly was an automatic death sentence. With the proper kind of persuasion—a reservation in their names for a twenty-year stretch in the joint, for instance, or the threat of an anonymous tip to Vastola about what they were doing—Nicky and Sonny could be flipped. Then they'd be placed in the Witness Protection Program, too. And with their testimony, maybe the prosecutors wouldn't even need LaMonte to take the stand at the trials.

LaMonte knew he was getting a sales job. "They want to use me like a piece of meat," he thought. "They're worried about my safety as long as I help them with their case, and other than that they could care less what happens."

LaMonte also knew he had no choice but to go along. He'd already taken the government's money to pay Vastola and had worn a wire during several conversations with Brocco. That would eventually come out, and if he withdrew from his agreement with the FBI now he'd have no protection from the bad guys later on. He'd be one dead duck.

But since he didn't fully trust the government to keep its word about protecting him and his family for life, LaMonte took out something of an insurance policy. Without telling Mahoney and Dossett, he contacted the *Los Angeles Times* reporter who'd written the stories about MCA and Pisello. At a meeting in his office several days later, LaMonte told the reporter his story and promised to tell him everything he learned about the East Coast investigations, provided that the reporter didn't print anything until he and his family were away and safe.

"You check out everything I tell you, and if you find out I'm lying you go ahead and write whatever you want," he said. "I'm putting my life in your hands and I'm trusting you to do the right thing. When this is all over, I just want you to tell people what really happened."

Reinforcing LaMonte's decision to do what the agents asked was the fact that there were still problems on the MCA cutout deal. He'd returned 1.9 million records for a total of $629,000 in credit, the balance of the deal, he thought. But now MCA was giving him credit for only $479,000 worth. What's more, the company was saying it never agreed to the $1.25 million purchase price. MCA claimed the deal originally was for $1.57 million. So the company either wanted more records returned or more money, $470,000 to be exact. They were pressuring Levy, threatening to sue if the matter wasn't cleared up quickly. Levy, of course, was claiming that LaMonte was the one responsible for making up the difference.

The last-minute snag was adding to the tension between Vastola and Levy. In a July 3 telephone conversation with Lew Saka, Vastola said of Levy, "That guy's going to die a horrible death."

"I hope he goes off in his sleep," Saka put in.

"No," Vastola said, "he'll never go in his sleep."

On July 17, Saka called Vastola in Los Angeles to tell him that Levy was refusing to sit down with the two of them and LaMonte to try to resolve the differences. Instead, Levy said Vastola should "talk to Dom," meaning Dominick Canterino.

"He's a real cocksucker, huh," said Vastola, knowing that meant the final decision on the MCA matter was being kicked upstairs to Vincent Gigante.

Vastola told Saka he wanted to arrange a meeting with both Levy and Canterino to find out why MCA was saying money was still owed. Both Morris and Sal approved the $1.25 million price the day they were "sitting around Morris's office with all those guys . . . and the girl with the candy," he said.

On August 27, investigators manning the listening posts overheard a phone conversation between Levy and MCA's Zach Horowitz.

"Will you accept more records?" Levy asked.

"There's no reason why we wouldn't; they're our records," said Horowitz.

"So I'm going down there tonight and say, 'You either got to come up with the money or the records,'" Levy said. "I did want to check with you first about the records, and I'm sure it was okay anyway because that cleans it up, you know what I'm saying?"

"Are we still going to get the 150 this week?" Horowitz asked.

"They want to give you that in records, too," Levy said. "But I have that, I was sending you money on that, to be honest with you. You ought to send me a letter saying that they sent all the records back. You got no problem with that, Zach, you got my word."

"What I told my people was—because I found out what happened and basically my trust for you goes a lot more than MCA, which doesn't know you; they don't know that much about the record business—and I basically said you've told me this and you've never lied to me and that your reputation is that when you give your word on something it means something," Horowitz said.

"You know, incidentally, that there's a *Los Angeles Times* reporter in New York asking questions," Levy said.

"Is it that Needlestedler guy?" Horowitz asked. And, apparently changing his mind about the records, he said, "The ideal thing would be to get the money so I could at least say it walks."

At 8:48 A.M. on August 29, Rocco Musacchia received a phone call at his home from a man who identified himself only as "Peter" and who told him that, the day before, an IRS agent had come to the bank and attempted to place a levy for $243,000 on Sal Pisello's account.

The levy hadn't been served, however, because Peter had told the agent there was no account under Pisello's name. The account was in the name of Consultants for World Records, so in order to be legal the notice of levy had to be rewritten. The IRS agent left but said he'd be back.

Peter was calling Musacchia because Rocco was one of the partners in Consultants, along with Pisello and Fritzy Giovanelli. Musacchia said he'd come right over to the bank to get a copy of the levy notice.

News of the IRS's interest in the bank account triggered a frantic exchange of phone calls.

At 9:21, Musacchia called Giovanelli's home and left a message that it was important he talk to him as soon as possible.

At 10:42, Musacchia called Levy at Roulette Records and said he'd just seen Giovanelli "and he told me to get a hold of you right away." He said that his "friend from the bank" had told him about the IRS agent's visit.

Levy instructed Musacchia to bring the papers to him "right away, within the next half-hour." He told him to stand under the bank sign by Roulette's offices on Fifty-seventh Street and he'd send someone down to get the documents.

Agents listening in were intrigued. The bank account apparently was very important in the scheme of things. The problem was that they couldn't tell what bank was being discussed. It could be any one of thousands in the New York area. And who was Peter, the banker with a pipeline to the Genovese family? There was no way of telling. All the wiretaps in the world can't confer omniscience.

Several days later, two agents from the Los Angeles FBI office paid a call on Marvin Rudnick at the Organized Crime Strike Force. They showed him a transcript of the August 29 conversations and asked if he knew what bank they were talking about.

"It's the Astoria Bank in Queens," Rudnick replied. "I know that because I'm the guy who sent the IRS there." He couldn't believe it took the IRS four months to act on the tip he'd given them the day of Pisello's sentencing.

Rudnick didn't know who Peter was and had never heard of Musacchia or Giovanelli. Who were they? Genovese family members and apparently Pisello's partners in Consultants for World Records, the agents said, offering no other information. They thanked him and left.

After the agents had gone, Rudnick stewed. Back in May he'd requested and received Justice Department approval to begin an investigation of Pisello's dealings with MCA. But for some reason the Los Angeles IRS Criminal Investigation Division had been dragging its feet, refusing even to serve a subpoena on Pisello's bank account. He had the go-ahead to issue a subpoena, but no agency to serve it. He'd argued with Al Lipkin, who was in charge of the IRS's organized crime section in Los Angeles, about the lack of cooperation. "All I want is a little peek at that account," he pleaded. But Lipkin didn't seem interested. "What do you expect to find?" he asked.

"What kind of question is that?" Rudnick responded, incredulous. "For openers, I want to see if money is being kicked back to any MCA executives. If it is, you can bet they didn't declare it and that's a tax violation." He shouldn't have to explain this to a seasoned IRS investigator.

Now, with the visit from the two FBI agents, Rudnick learned that money had gone from MCA into Pisello's account and back out to members of the Genovese crime family, suggesting that Pisello wasn't acting alone but rather was an operative of a larger criminal organization. If that wasn't worth looking into, he didn't know what was. MCA was in his backyard, and yet the FBI in New York was working on the case while his own people were twiddling their thumbs. It was maddening.

As it turned out, before the IRS got back to Astoria Bank with a new notice of levy, the money in the Consultants for World Records account—$110,000—was withdrawn.

At 3:58 P.M. on September 12, Dominick Canterino called Levy at Levy's farm in Philmont, New York, and told him that LaMonte said he was going to stop shipping records back to MCA, at Vastola's instruction. "And if that's the case we're getting bullshitted," Canterino said.

"I'm getting nervous and I'm not the nervous type," Levy said. "MCA is getting hot. And they have a right to. I don't want them to sue me because they can hurt me with that other thing. If I have to send them money, I will. I have to pacify them now."

Several hours later, Canterino called Vincent Gigante's common-law wife, Olympia Esposito, and told her about his conversation with Levy, saying he'd told him, "It took you two years to do this. When you come home you turn around and take care of it."

To investigators, the two conversations indicated that Vincent Gigante was now taking an active role in settling the dispute over the MCA cutout deal, and that didn't bode well for LaMonte. Gigante wasn't one to listen to excuses. If the Chin decided to move against John they wouldn't have much time. They began making plans to whisk the LaMonte family into hiding at a moment's notice.

Earlier that same day, LaMonte had met with Nicky Massaro at the Mt. Laurel Diner in Mt. Laurel, New Jersey, and had purchased four ounces of cocaine. He wore a hidden microphone to the meeting and handed Massaro $3,000 in government money, with the agreement that he'd pay another $4,500 after he'd sold the coke. Massaro asked if he was interested in buying heroin, too. LaMonte said he'd think about it.

The FBI was really pushing the drug buys, moving much faster than originally planned because agents weren't sure how much longer they could keep LaMonte in place. It was a risky business. LaMonte couldn't appear too eager or Massaro might sense a setup.

LaMonte felt like he was caught in a vise. The meetings for which he had to wear the microphone were terrifying. The fact that agents were stationed nearby, ready to move in at the first sign of trouble, offered little reassurance. He knew from experience how quickly it could happen—boom! Just like that. Only this time it might not be a punch in the face; it could be a bullet through the heart. Before and after the meetings he bolstered his confidence by snorting cocaine. It seemed as if his life were spinning out of control. He was going through the motions of running his business, buying and selling records knowing he probably wouldn't be around to either pay or collect on the bills. For the second time in six years he was losing everything he'd worked to build.

His wife and children were disconsolate. They'd lived their whole lives in the Philadelphia area. Soon they would disappear with him into the black hole of the Witness Protection Program, a family with no past and a dubious future. He felt so guilty, he couldn't even talk to them about it.

He found himself in the evenings wandering the boundaries of his two-acre property, looking back at the rambling white frame house, nearly one hundred years old and surrounded by a stand of oak trees, the leaves just beginning to turn. This was his dream home. He remembered driving by it when he was a kid on Sunday outings with his parents, thinking it was the prettiest house he'd ever seen. He remembered the day he bought it and the day his family moved in. Now, as he watched the dogs romping in the grass and his sixteen-year-old daughter, April, holding hands and nuzzling with her boyfriend as they leaned against the family station wagon in the driveway, he tried to memorize every detail of the picture, knowing that in a matter of days he would go away and never see it again.

On September 16, LaMonte met with Nicky Massaro again at the Mt. Laurel Diner and purchased four more ounces of cocaine. He gave Massaro $7,500 in cash and said that next time he wanted to buy a pound of heroin. Nicky said he'd set it up, but it would take a week, maybe ten days. They agreed to meet again—same time, same place—on September 26.

That evening, a surveillance team of New York police detectives observed Morris Levy, Dominick Canterino, and Vincent Gigante talking animatedly on the street near Gigante's Triangle Social Club.

The meeting that Vastola arranged with Levy and Canterino to resolve the problems with the MCA cutout deal was set for 10:00 A.M. Monday, September 23, in Levy's office. To investigators working the case, it had all the earmarks of a classic mob sit-down. As Vincent Gigante's official representative, Canterino would be cast in the role of Solomon, asked to hear both sides in the dispute and then issue a final ruling. His decision would be law; there would be no appealing it. The presentation of the arguments promised to be interesting. Judging from some of the comments Vastola had made about Levy in recent weeks, there could be fireworks between the two, bitter accusations back and forth, possibly spilling out a wealth of incriminating information.

The investigators were ready. In a risky predawn maneuver several weeks earlier, a "black bag" team of FBI agents had broken into Roulette Records and installed a hidden closed-circuit TV system. Working from a facsimile blueprint of the premises drawn with the help of LaMonte, the agents had removed acoustic ceiling tiles in rooms on either side of Levy's office, reached over the walls, and concealed two video cameras and two room microphones above his desk. On another floor of the building, a monitoring station was set up in an office the FBI had rented under the name of a fictitious company. On the day of the meeting, the monitors included two New York police detectives, Brian Ford and Anthony Venditti, partners who had been working Canterino for years.

Vastola and Lew Saka arrived at the Roulette Records office ahead of Canterino. Brocco wasn't able to come, they told Levy, because he'd been ill for several weeks with some mysterious blood disease. He might even be dying, they said.

Levy was unmoved by that piece of news. "The only difference is, he was a live cocksucker on Monday and now he'll be a dead cocksucker on Tuesday," he said.

The meeting began without Canterino. Levy started by complaining about the pressure MCA was putting on him to pay off the deal. His negotiations with MCA's Zach Horowitz had not gone well. In lieu of LaMonte shipping back additional records, he'd paid MCA "150 Gs," which Horowitz promised to refund when the records arrived. Instead, "MCA served me with a summons," he said. "Of course he wrote me a cockamamie letter, but it didn't say what it was supposed to say. I said the letter's got to say a lot more, it's got to say that the goods were returned.

"I don't know how to handle this," Levy went on, waving Horowitz's letter in the air. "I'm afraid of something else here. If I get a lawsuit while I'm doing this private placement . . . I ain't worried about the lawsuit, I'm worried about the private placement. If that blows up the whole world's going to end," he said. "I don't even think you know what it's going to create. No you don't, you don't have no idea what it's going to create. Because if it hurts a certain thing here that we are talking about, you don't know what can happen."

(From other wiretapped conversations, investigators knew that Levy was selling 25 percent of the Strawberries record store chain to selected investors, trying to raise $8 million to open thirty new stores in the Philadelphia area and at the same time buy out Vincent Gigante's interest in the chain.)

Vastola and Levy then launched into an argument about who was to blame for getting involved in the cutout deal in the first place.

"That guy convinced you, Sal convinced you, and you convinced me," Vastola said.

"No, no, no. You are believing this guy John because you wanted to be against Sal. You hate Sal and that's how Fritzy was being blinded too."

"You feel that Sal was not responsible for this whole thing, truthfully, Moishe?"

"I think that his hands are cleaner, that he's dirty in everything else he did, but in this little thing here I still think his hands are clean. I really do. The truth's the truth."

"Well, the first thing is the $385,000 of stuff he sold off the load," Vastola said.

"That's clean. But then he sold the second load to that guy nobody knows about. That's dirty, that's dirty."

"So we're partners with the losses and not the wins?" Vastola asked.

"You weren't a partner in the first part of the load," Levy said.

"Why not?"

"Because you weren't; you came in with John."

"I was with me, you, and him and your partner before John got in," Vastola said. "Me, you, and him and your partner was in with that six million records. We said we'd cut it up three ways. . . . You said to 'get me John.' But here's what I'm saying, we were partners—me, you, and him. Then he sold $385,000 off the load. What's the matter? We're not partners on that anymore?"

"I didn't think you were in on that, I did not," Levy said.

(Investigators knew from previous wiretapped conversations and from confidential police informants that whenever Levy referred to his "partner" he was talking about Vincent Gigante. Even in the presumed privacy of his own office, he never uttered Gigante's name.)

The two men went back and forth for ten minutes about who was at fault in the LaMonte debacle and who owed who how much money. It was almost funny listening to them, bickering like schoolboys over a baseball card trade gone bad. Suddenly, Levy blurted out something investigators had not heard before: "We've paid more money to Dom to keep the peace with MCA than we collected from LaMonte," he said.

He didn't elaborate or follow up on the statement, and Vastola didn't challenge it. But the implication was that Dominick Canterino himself was not only financially involved in the deal, but also had direct contact with someone at MCA. That was a new twist.

At one point Vastola seemed to indicate he suspected the authorities might be on to them because of the LaMonte beating: "We're going to wind up in the joint here—me, I know, definitely," he said.

"I'm hotter than you, than all of you." Levy responded. "I'm hotter than all of yous. They'd love to get me, you know that. They'd love to get me for twenty-five years."

Halfway through the meeting, Canterino finally arrived and the tenor of the conversation changed immediately. The arguing stopped. Levy handed him Zach Horowitz's letter. "MCA just wrote this to me," he said. "We gotta do something kinda quick."

"This is the figures I got," Canterino said, glancing at the letter as he pulled up a chair.

Levy interrupted. "Here's what he owes—$436,000 in merchandise and money. That's at one mil 250."

Canterino listened impassively as both sides gave a calm explanation of how the cutout deal came about. Lew Saka and Roulette's accountant, Howard Fisher, presented their conflicting figures on the outstanding balance. Canterino nodded occasionally, but said nothing.

Canterino was an odd-looking bird—short, slightly built, bald, with grayish skin and a gaunt face, bad teeth, dressing more like a Manhattan cab driver than a major Mafioso. His appearance that day was in stark contrast to Vastola, who was twice his size and always dressed in the trendy, elegant style of a Hollywood movie producer. Vastola looked as if he might be boss of the mob's Beverly Hills branch.

There was no doubt who was the more powerful of the two, however. As Vincent Gigante's chief confidante and personal emissary, Canterino was one of the most influential—and feared—Mafia figures in New York. Not surprisingly, everyone in the room that day treated him with obsequious respect. Nobody argued with Dom, or raised his voice to him, or contradicted him. When he spoke, they stopped talking and listened.

Despite his mediator role, Canterino was actually there to protect Gigante's interest in the deal. Fritzy Giovanelli, Rocco Musacchia, Rudy Farone, Levy, and, by association, Sal Pisello, were his subordinates, as well as his business partners. Vastola was the outsider in the equation, and he knew he really had no hope of winning his case that day unless Levy agreed that he himself was responsible for making up the balance on the MCA cutouts. But Morris was too smart for that—he knew where the balance of power lay in the room. He held fast to the position that LaMonte had "made a big score" on the cutouts and was just welching on the deal.

After listening to both sides, Canterino asked, "How do we resolve this?"

"We're resolving it this way," Vastola responded quickly. "If it's all right with everybody, we're going over there Friday morning and we're going to make him ship back all the stuff."

After all his tough talk over the previous few weeks, Vastola had backed down completely. "I want this resolved more than you do," he said to Levy. "Because I know what it means. I know the problem you're having right now with MCA and I want it resolved and we're gonna resolve it. One way or the other, John LaMonte will pay this money! I don't care how he's gonna pay!"

So the meeting reached its predetermined conclusion. The shit was going to come down on John LaMonte, the designated patsy from the very beginning.

The investigators reached a conclusion that day, too. It was time for LaMonte and his family to disappear, before the boys showed up at his place on Friday. The government just couldn't risk another physical attack on its witness. The planned September 26 drug buy from Nicky Massaro had to be scrapped.

John Mahoney called agent Tom Cupples in Philadelphia. "The cat's out of the bag," he said. "We're coming down there now to get John out. Get over to the house quick and put together the bare essentials. Everyone who's going has to go now."

No sooner had Cupples gotten off the line with Mahoney than LaMonte called. Brocco had just telephoned LaMonte's secretary Mary Ann to say he was driving from New Jersey to see John. He wanted to be sure John would be at the warehouse. LaMonte was alarmed. He and Brocco had been pretty much on the outs since the beating. "Why's he comin' here?" he asked Cupples. "This meeting ain't scheduled."

"John, it's time for you to leave," Cupples replied. "Go home now and start packing. I'll meet you at your house."

When Cupples arrived at the LaMonte residence, he found a scene of chaos in slow motion. Instead of just throwing the necessities into boxes, LaMonte was agonizing over which running suit he should pack, which sneakers to take and where was his portable radio. LaMonte's teenage daughters were discussing what friends they should call to say they were leaving town for awhile. John Jr.

was trying to round up the family's two dogs. LaMonte's wife Andrea was explaining to his elderly mother that they were all going away on "a little vacation." When the old woman asked where, Andrea couldn't answer because the family didn't know. Their destination was being kept secret for security reasons. "Don't worry, Mom," Andrea said, "you'll love it."

Cupples was concerned that things weren't moving fast enough, that the family didn't seem to grasp the seriousness of the situation. Either that or they were in some sort of collective state of shock. He tried to instill a sense of urgency without causing panic, loading boxes himself and carrying them out to the car.

When John Mahoney and his partner Jeff Dossett arrived they, too, were worried about the slow pace of the packing. The agents didn't know why Brocco was coming to see LaMonte or whether he was alone or with others. But they had to assume the worst—that LaMonte had been found out and he was in jeopardy. Mahoney kept a watch out the front window, wondering if they would face a showdown with LaMonte's pursuers in the driveway.

A phone call from LaMonte's secretary brought the packing to an abrupt halt. Brocco has just left the warehouse on his way to the house, she said. As far as she knew, he was alone. LaMonte's warehouse was just a few miles from the house. Cupples figured it was a seven- to eight-minute drive. The agents told the LaMontes to carry whatever they had in their hands to the car and leave the rest behind. They hustled the six family members and two dogs out of the house and into the five waiting cars and executed a tire-squealing, high-speed escape down the driveway, onto the street, into the evening rush-hour traffic to safety.

Over the next few days, Levy, Canterino, and Vastola talked back and forth on the phone about the disposition of three tractor-trailer loads of cutouts that LaMonte was supposed to send back to MCA.

"Have they shipped?" Canterino asked Levy.

"I don't know, and I'm concerned because these people are gonna get hot out there and I'll be a liar with them."

On October 3, Vastola called Howard Fisher at Roulette and said he couldn't find LaMonte or his family. He asked Fisher to contact MCA and see if the trailers had gone back to the company. Fisher called Mary Ann Laberty, LaMonte's secretary at Out of the Past, and asked her if the trailers had gone out. She said that LaMonte had told her that two were on the way and another was being loaded. He was not around and she didn't know where he was, she lied.

Later that day, MCA's Zach Horowitz called Levy and complained that they'd received no money and no records, and nothing had been shipped. Levy told him he'd send them a check for $125,000—his own money—for Horowitz to hold until the records were received. "We went out on a limb for you," Horowitz said, reminding Levy that MCA's claim was for $350,000.

The phone calls continued for five more days—Vastola to Levy, Howard Fisher to Out of the Past, Canterino to Levy, Fisher back to Vastola—and each time the voices grew more frustrated and concerned. Something was wrong. LaMonte hadn't been seen or heard from in over a week. There was no one at his home. What the hell was going on?

They got their first inkling on the morning of October 8, when teams of FBI agents and police armed with search warrants raided ten locations, including the homes of Vastola, Brocco, and Nicky Massaro and the Video Warehouse offices. At Brocco's house they seized a large cache of arms—an Uzi machine gun with a silencer, three handguns, nine rifles, and a shotgun. At Vastola's they found a stolen television. And at Video Warehouse they confiscated thousands of suspected counterfeit video and audio cassettes. No one was arrested, however.

One place they didn't hit was Roulette Records. Investigators figured that if they left Levy alone for now everything would filter back to him over the phone lines, perhaps revealing further incriminating information. His whole office was wired six ways from Sunday. If they raided it now they might compromise the surveillance.

On October 10, Levy and Howard Fisher were overheard discussing the raid at "Tommy" Vastola's home and the role they now suspected LaMonte had played.

"They just took this guy's word and went in and searched Tommy's place, without a search warrant?" Fisher asked.

"They got a search warrant," Levy said.

"On what grounds?"

"That he's behind the racketeering and they'll make up a story for him. What did Tommy do? Tommy tried to get MCA paid. What did he do? What did he do?"

"We went out on a limb for [LaMonte]," Fisher said.

"He stole all the money, the prick. There's no case here. I don't know if they can make something of that. It's unbelievable."

"Are they going to start searching the joint now?" Fisher asked.

"It's gonna come," Levy replied. "So let 'em come, them cock-suckers."

They would come, all right, but not for nearly a year.

Irving Azoff in the mid-1970s (HITS *magazine*)

The staff of MCA Records in the famous *HITS* magazine ad. Second from left: Myron Roth; third from left: Irving Azoff; fourth from left: Richard Palmese; second from right: Larry Solters

Irving Azoff, c. 1989 (*Los Angeles Times*)

Lew Wasserman (*Peter Borsari*)

Eugene Giaquinto (*Peter Borsari*)

Sidney Sheinberg (*Peter Borsari*)

Al Bergamo (*author's collection*)

Sal Pisello
(*Douglas R. Burrows*)

Federico "Fritzy" Giovanelli
(*Jerry Engel*, New York Post)

Morris Levy and Martin London (*R. J. Capek*)

Marvin Rudnick (*Bill Knoedelseder*)

Bruce Repetto (*author's collection*)

John Newcomer (*author's collection*)

John Dubois (*author's collection*)

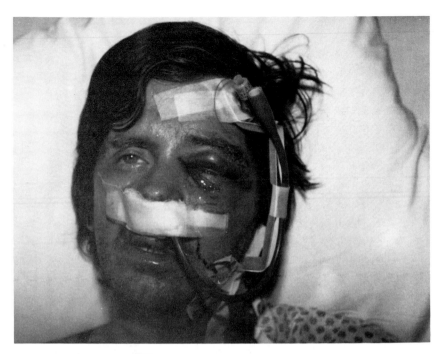

John LaMonte, hospitalized after being punched by Corky Vastola (*FBI*)

Gaetano "Corky" Vastola (*FBI surveillance photo*)

Clockwise, from left: Fritzy Giovanelli, Gaetano Vastola, Sonny Brocco, and Rocco Musacchia, at the LaMonte warehouse (*FBI surveillance photo*)

Morris Levy exiting John LaMonte's warehouse (*FBI surveillance photo*)

Sonny Brocco (*FBI surveillance photo*)

Vincent Gigante,
in trademark bathrobe
and pajamas
(*Michael Schwartz*,
New York Post)

Joseph Isgro
(*AP/World Wide
Photos*)

Part II

MUSCLE

23

The Network

ot every problem at MCA Records in 1985 centered around Sal
Pisello and cutouts.

In the two years after Azoff arrived, promotion expenses at
the company had skyrocketed, shooting up from about $1.5
million a year to more than $6 million, or better than 400 percent.
The main reason was Richard Palmese's stepped-up use of a group
of independent record promoters commonly referred to in the
industry as "the Network."

Members of the Network operated in loose affiliation from mutual-
ly exclusive territories around the country: Fred DiSipio in Cherry
Hill, New Jersey, just outside of Philadelphia; Joe Isgro in Los
Angeles; Jerry Brenner in Boston; Jerry Meyers in Buffalo, New
York; Gary Bird in Cleveland; Ernie Phillips in Dallas; Jim Daven-
port in Atlanta. They'd become increasingly powerful in the 1980s,
as the major companies had cut back their own promotion staffs in

the wake of the business downturn of the late 1970s. In the begin-ning, the independents were a boon to the big companies, allowing them to reduce their cost of operations by trimming their employee rosters. More important perhaps was that the use of independents provided the companies with a buffer against potential payola prob-lems. The industry had been rocked by a federal grand jury investi-gation into alleged nationwide payola practices in the early 1970s. Based in Newark, New Jersey, the two-year probe ultimately yielded more publicity than prosecutions, and the industry had breathed a sigh of relief when the case ended with a single radio programmer convicted of perjury, but with no major record company executives charged. Nonetheless, the lurid headlines the case produced about drugs, prostitutes, and cash given in exchange for radio airplay had painted the entire record industry with the brush of scandal and had badly embarrassed the large publicly held corporations that owned the big record companies.

One idea the record companies subsequently came up with to protect themselves from future charges of corruption was the increased use of independent, nonstaff record promoters to do the dirty work for them. By requiring each independent promoter to sign an affidavit swearing he would refrain from any illegal prac-tices in his pursuit of airplay, record company lawyers figured their own executives would be insulated. They could pressure the inde-pendents to get records added to the stations' playlists—"I don't care how you do it, just get it done"—and at the same time main-tain plausible deniability if some overeager promoter crossed the line into illegality and got caught.

Beginning in 1980, most of the big record companies instituted a pay-for-play policy with independent promoters, meaning they paid them a set fee each time a record was added to a radio station playlist. The companies saw this as both an incentive to the pro-moter and a cost-saving device for themselves, since it also meant they only paid the independent if a record got played. A staff pro-moter, on the other hand, would have to be paid each week no mat-ter what.

The policy soon came back to haunt the industry, however. With fewer record company staffers doing promotion work, members of the Network—the most experienced and influential promoters in their respective regions—gradually became indispensable to the process of making a hit. After a while, the perception grew in the industry that the Network virtually controlled what records were added to the two hundred or so most influential pop music stations around the country.

The general suspicion was that such influence could be gained only through payoffs to radio programmers. But it wasn't so much the possibility of payola or corruption that worried the big companies as it was the rising cost of promotion. With every major record company vying for the services of the same group of independents, fees went up to the point where, by 1983, the price of getting a single record added to a radio station playlist ranged from $500 to $3,000, depending on the size or influence of the station. That pushed the cost of promoting a hit single to more than $150,000. Industrywide, the cost of independent promotion rose to more than $50 million annually at a time when most companies were struggling for profitability. CBS Records alone spent more than $10 million on independent promotion in 1983.

The lion's share of the money went to the Network. Joe Isgro and Fred DiSipio became multimillionaires, with lavish offices and large staffs, chauffeur-driven Rolls-Royces, and even bodyguards. Everywhere, they were referred to as a pair, "Freddy and Joe," as inseparable in people's minds as Abbott and Costello or Mutt and Jeff, except that no one laughed at them to their faces. Isgro and DiSipio scared the hell out of people. To go with their Italian surnames the two men cultivated a tough-guy image that fueled suspicion in the record business that they were somehow connected to the Mafia and therefore were not to be messed with.

It got to the point where the record companies were afraid not to hire them. The fear was that their influence over key radio stations cut two ways—just as it could be used to get records on the air, it could likewise be used to keep them off. The industry had witnessed a chilling example of that power in 1981 when Warner Communications announced publicly that it was discontinuing the use of independent promotion due to its inordinate cost. In the months following the announcement, all the Warner-owned record labels— Warner Brothers, Atlantic, Elektra/Asylum, and Geffen—experienced one of the worst sales slumps in their history as their new releases were virtually boycotted by radio programmers. Warner management tried in vain to get the five other majors to join with them in cutting back on independent promotion, arguing that it was for the overall good of the industry. Instead, its two biggest

competitors, RCA and CBS, poured it on, increasing their independent promotion expenditures and gaining market share at Warner's
expense. After a six-month holdout that coincided with a decline in
the price of the company's stock on the New York Stock Exchange,
a shaken Warner management ordered the resumption of independent promotion at its record labels.

Although some of its competitors took advantage of the situation,
the Warner debacle was profoundly disturbing to the industry at
large. The fact that the second most powerful record operation in
the world could be cowed by a handful of glorified singles salesmen
seemed to prove that the system had gone completely out of whack.
The tail was wagging the dog. With all their billions in revenues
and far-flung manufacturing and distribution operations around
the globe, the six major record companies no longer controlled
their own destinies. They'd given over one vital historical function
of a record company—the promotion of its product—to a group of
outsiders that was exploiting its newly gained power with all the
ruthless zeal of an OPEC. The record companies had created a
monster that they could no longer control and it was threatening to
devour them.

Because of the high cost of independent promotion, records now
had to sell exponentially more copies to turn a profit. A gold or
platinum album wasn't necessarily a financial success anymore.
Well-known and respected artists who traditionally sold in the
range of two hundred thousand to three hundred thousand
copies—Van Morrison, Arlo Guthrie, Bonnie Raitt—were being
dropped from the big companies' rosters because their music was
no longer cost-effective. A number of formerly successful independent labels—notably, Fantasy Records, which produced one of the
biggest-selling rock groups of the 1970s, Creedence Clearwater
Revival—were abandoning the pop field and turning to jazz and
classical music because they could no longer afford the price of promoting a Top 40 hit. By 1984, the majority of record company executives agreed that the most serious problem facing the industry was
what to do about independent promotion.

Then, just when the situation looked the bleakest, Irving Azoff
and his "new MCA Records" came along and made it worse. Having summarily fired most of MCA's field promotion staff in his first
year at the company, Azoff turned to the Network with a vengeance,
routinely paying double and triple the going rate for getting an

MCA record added to a station's playlist. He kicked off an infla-
tionary spiral across the industry, as the other major companies
were forced to follow suit. Soon independent promoters were getting as much as $10,000 every time they got a single record played
on key Top 40 radio stations in Los Angeles, New York, Philadelphia, and other major markets, and the annual cost of independent
promotion was racing toward $80 million with no end in sight.

At the same time he was fanning the flames of inflation, Azoff
was conducting a secret campaign to break the power of the Network, starting with Joe Isgro. Azoff hated Isgro, which was not an
uncommon sentiment in the business. In just three years as head of
his own firm, Joe Isgro Enterprises, the former staff promoter for
Motown Records had become the most conspicuously successful
member of the Network. In his Hollywood office, he conducted
business from behind a huge glass desktop resting on curved legs of
brass elephant tusks, attended by a pair of thick-necked bodyguards
and a fluttering staff of leggy, beautiful young women. Gold-
chained, bejeweled, and always attired in the most outrageously
expensive fashions—"like $14,000 sportcoats made from the throat
of goats that live above the twelve-thousand-foot level in the
Andes," marveled one employee—Isgro owned a yellow Rolls and a
$1.6 million Playboy Mansion–style estate in the Encino Hills that
featured a uniformed butler, an elaborate video camera security system, and a pool that meandered into a rocky Jacuzzi grotto. He'd
reportedly paid cash for the house.

Nearly every night, Isgro held court at Nick's Fish Market, a
restaurant he owned (and later renamed Stefanino's) on Sunset
Boulevard at the entrance to Beverly Hills. With his encouragement, Nick's had become something of a hangout for both local
organized crime figures and visiting Mafia royalty in town on business—Las Vegas mobster Guido Penosi, Philadelphia family boss
Nicodemo ("Little Nicky") Scarfo, New Jersey's Gaetano Vastola,
and Joseph ("Joe Piney") Armone, the underboss of New York's
Gambino family, whom Isgro warmly referred to as "Uncle Joe."

Isgro was a sort of gangster groupie. He'd revered and emulated
them since his boyhood days in Philadelphia, when wise guys were
the most feared and respected men in the neighborhood. His
employees were both unsettled and amused by their boss's
unabashed hero-worship of mobsters, his constant seeking them
out, aping their style with wads of cash and showy $100 tips. Office

rumor had it that Isgro once lost $50,000 on a single roll of the dice at a Las Vegas crap table. Staffers secretly chuckled when Isgro threw a Mafia theme party at his house, insisting that guests come dressed as mobsters.

Isgro's flamboyance didn't sit well with many people in the record business, who were mostly offended that he was pulling down an estimated $5 million a year promoting their records. That was more than any record company president earned, more than Azoff's and Walter Yetnikoff's combined salaries.

One of Azoff's first moves at MCA was to cancel a pressing and distribution (P&D) contract that Al Bergamo had signed with Isgro's label, Larc Records. In closing out the deal, MCA applied the money it owed Isgro on Larc's biggest-selling act, the Chi-Lites, to the losses run up by a number of other records on the label, including one by Joe Armone's nephew that Isgro did as a favor to the old man. As a result of Azoff's move, Isgro figured he lost a couple hundred thousand dollars. Even though he quickly landed another P&D deal with CBS through his friendship with Yetnikoff, Isgro never forgave Azoff. "He's just a punk," he would tell people. "He's like the creepy little kid from the neighborhood who always wanted to be one of the boys but never could be. He's not a man."

Azoff's undoing of Isgro started quietly in mid-1983 when he began putting out the story to his contacts in the news media—not for attribution, of course—that Isgro and the Network had the industry in a stranglehold. According to Azoff, they were, in effect, extorting the record companies through fear and intimidation, and making payoffs to radio stations. It was the record business story of the 1980s, he told reporters. In October of that year, the *Los Angeles Times* was the first major newspaper to identify Isgro and the Network publicly and report the record companies' concern about their growing influence over what music Americans were hearing on the radio.

At the same time he was willingly increasing MCA's—and the entire industry's—independent promotion expenditures by multiples of two or three, Azoff was providing reporters with a list of the Network's members, the Top 40 radio stations they supposedly controlled around the country, and the prices they charged to get a record played on those stations. "I don't know how they do it," he said ominously, raising the specter of another, yet undisclosed, payola scandal. "I just know this is how much we have to pay to get it done." He hinted that there might be some organized crime involvement in the background. Pisello later told several people that as part of his activities at MCA, he'd been asked to dig up dirt on Isgro's alleged Mafia connections.

If the plan had been to make the independent promotion problem so severe and so sensationally publicized that the record companies ultimately would have to seek the government's help to clean up the industry's self-created mess, then it was a perfect example of Azoff's Machiavellian brilliance. "Most people are two-step thinkers," he often said. "I'm a five-step thinker. When other people are planning what will happen two steps down the line, I'm planning five. So I'm always three steps ahead of everyone else."

Such a plan was a risky one for MCA Records, which was well on the way to posting its second straight year of losses and could ill afford Azoff's huge outlays for independent promotion. It was risky for the larger, more profitable companies as well, because any legislative or law enforcement scrutiny of record industry business practices would threaten exposure of a host of corrupt activities by company executives—kickbacks on cutout sales and recording contracts, free goods scams, back-door sales of promotional records, drug dealing, tax evasion, and other indictable offenses—overall, a rather ugly picture, not one the board of directors would like trotted out for shareholders to see on the evening news.

For the plan to work without backfiring, both the press and the government would have to be kept under control. The story would have to be limited to the activities of the Network and kept away from the inner workings of the record companies. Otherwise, the whole thing could blow up in everyone's faces.

24

Rock 'n' roll
rules

During the 1985 Thanksgiving holiday, the record industry had plenty of reasons to be thankful.

Even before the year-end sales figures had been tallied, it was clear the financial recovery that began two years earlier was continuing unabated. Fueled by an overwhelming consumer response to the compact disc and paced by megaplatinum performances by Prince's *Purple Rain*, Bruce Springsteen's *Born in the U.S.A.*, and Madonna's *Like a Virgin*, sales were up 11 percent over 1984, and strong holiday retail orders indicated the trend would continue well into 1986.

Profits were rising even faster than sales, the result of the CD's higher wholesale price—$9 as opposed to $5 for an LP or cassette—and the fact that CD converts were spending heavily on catalog product, replacing their old worn-out vinyl albums with the superior-sounding metallic discs. Catalog sales are pure gravy for the record companies, since they require no additional production costs or promotion expense.

As a completely unexpected side effect to the CD craze, the twenty-five- to forty-year-old audience that the record companies had just about written off as lost forever suddenly was returning to the record stores in droves. The baby boomers, whose music appetites had built the record business into a multibillion-dollar industry ten years earlier, were back, and with more money than ever before. They were lining up to buy jazz and classical CDs along with Sting and Dire Straits, spending $100 at a clip and paying with their American Express cards.

Economics aside, the industry was infused with a sense of noble purpose as Christmas approached. The phenomenal success of the *We Are the World* album, the Band Aid and Live Aid concerts to help the starving millions of Africa, and the Farm Aid concert for the troubled American farmers had rekindled some of the we-can-change-the-world idealism that fired the record business in the late 1960s and early 1970s.

One of the first companies to trumpet its 1985 accomplishments was MCA. In a November 30 *Billboard* magazine article headlined "MCA's Growth Ahead of Schedule," Myron Roth boasted, "What Irving and I thought would take us five years to accomplish, we've achieved in just two years."

Billboard reported that MCA's 13.1 percent share of the albums and singles on the magazine's pop chart for the year placed the Records Group "firmly in fourth place" among the Big Six companies, behind CBS, Warner, and RCA. In 1982, MCA was the seventh-ranked U.S. distributor, *Billboard* said. In a fit of hyperbole, the magazine called MCA's performance "the most dramatic turnaround for a major label in this decade."

As record executives knew, however, the *Billboard* chart was a poor indicator of a company's profitability, since it didn't take into account production costs or promotion expenses, and below the Top 40 it measured mostly radio airplay, not sales.

In reality, MCA achieved very mixed results in 1985.

On the upside, it produced two number one albums during the year, the *Beverly Hills Cop* and *Miami Vice* soundtracks, which sold two million and three million copies, respectively. The Night Ranger's *7 Wishes* album went platinum and New Edition's *All for Love* went gold, as did a debut album by another black group, Ready for the World.

On the downside, MCA's two most expensive and anticipated albums of the year failed. Olivia Newton-John's *Soul Kiss* barely cracked the Top 40 before it sank off the charts like a rock, turning in the worst sales performance of Newton-John's long career. Tom Petty's *Southern Accents,* which was three years in the making, fell far short of the platinum mark.

Even more troubling for the future, in its third year under Azoff, MCA Records once again had failed to break a new pop artist.

Motown—which scored its biggest hit ever in 1984 with Lionel Richie's eight-million-selling *Can't Slow Down* album and had a surprise hit in the double platinum *Big Chill* soundtrack—came up with just one hit album in 1985, Stevie Wonder's *In a Square Circle,* which sold two million copies.

The real bottom line for MCA Records was not reflected in the company's 1985 annual report, which showed the Records Group with operating profits of $25 million for the year, or more than twice the reported profits for 1984. Both those figures included the 20 percent distribution fee from the home video division, which had revenues of nearly $100 million in 1985. When the home video fee and the profits from music publishing—as much as $30 million altogether—were subtracted from the total, MCA Records once again lost money in 1985.

MCA's apparent success as measured by the *Billboard* chart—forty-nine pop albums charted during the year—came at a huge cost. Azoff and company spent nearly $9 million on independent promotion in 1985, including more than $1 million paid out to Joe Isgro. That put MCA second only to CBS in that category, and CBS had ten times the amount of sales. MCA might have turned a profit if it hadn't been for the high price of promotion.

Little wonder then that in the fall of 1985 MCA was at the forefront of an industrywide effort to rein in the growing power of the independent promoters, as well as the runaway costs.

Most of the big companies and all of the little ones wanted to cut back on their use of independent promotion, but no one wanted to act unilaterally, for fear of being placed at a competitive disadvantage. They remembered what happened to Warner Brothers in 1981. The problem was CBS, the company with the most money, the strongest artist roster—Bruce Springsteen, Michael Jackson, Billy Joel—and the biggest independent promotion budget. As long as CBS kept putting out huge sums to the independents, the other companies had to either follow suit or risk the possibility that only CBS records would get played on the radio. Lawyers for Warner in particular were concerned that the inordinate amount of money being paid to the Network was breeding corruption, not only at radio stations but possibly among Warner's own executives, in the form of kickbacks. Warner attorneys had approached CBS several times about instituting a voluntary cutback, but they'd been rebuffed.

At an October 1 RIAA board of directors meeting in the Rainbow Room on the top of Rockefeller Center, two dozen record company presidents and their attorneys discussed the problem at length.

Ever since the *Los Angeles Times* articles two years earlier, the industry had been rife with rumors of payola. Congressman John Dingell's subcommittee conducted an investigation in 1984 but came up with no hard evidence of widespread wrongdoing. Still, the rumors persisted, and now CBS's "60 Minutes" was sniffing around the story.

Arista Records president Clive Davis—in the past a heavy user of independent promotion—worried that the whole thing might blow up into a public scandal that would taint the entire industry. Solar Records president Dick Griffey said he'd met with Congressman William Gray of Pennsylvania and was told there might soon be a federal investigation of independent promoters. Griffey said it would look bad if widespread illegality were eventually uncovered and the RIAA had done nothing about it.

RIAA's general counsel, Joel Schoenfeld, who headed the association's antipiracy efforts for years, suggested that $75,000 to $100,000 be committed to retain a national private investigation firm to look into the independents. The results of the investigation would be funneled back to the RIAA's legal subcommittee, so it would be protected by attorney-client privilege if someone later subpoenaed the investigators' findings.

The only voices raised in opposition to the proposal were from CBS Records. Andy Gerber, a CBS attorney, and Seymour Gartenberg, the company's chief financial officer, argued against an investigation in absence of proof that independents were involved in illegal practices. Without such proof, Gerber said, any group action taken against the promoters by the record companies could violate the antitrust laws. He claimed that a CBS review of its own use of independent promoters had disclosed no impropriety.

Others in the room suspected there was another reason that CBS opposed an investigation. It was widely known in the industry that

CBS Records president Walter Yetnikoff was close friends with Fred DiSipio and—to a lesser degree—Joe Isgro. Yetnikoff once invested $500,000 of CBS's money in a flop Broadway show that DiSipio coproduced called *The History of Rock 'n' Roll.*

Yetnikoff was so sensitive about his association with DiSipio and Isgro that when he learned in early 1984 that the *Los Angeles Times* was looking into the relationship, he canceled all CBS Records advertising in the newspaper for the rest of the year.

Yetnikoff had made it known he had no intention of cutting back his use of independent promotion. Why should he? His company was number one and killing the competition. The $12 million or so that he spent in 1985 was a pittance compared with the profit CBS was making. If the smaller companies couldn't afford to keep pace with CBS's spending, tough. That's the way the capitalist cookie crumbled.

Before Schoenfeld's proposal was put to a vote, RIAA president Stanley Gortikoff suggested that, because of the "sensitivity of the issue," the question of whether to go ahead with an investigation should be decided only by a unanimous vote of the six major companies. Everyone agreed.

When the secret ballots were read, the proposal was rejected by a single vote, with five in favor. Immediately, MCA attorney Charles Morgan proposed a revote under majority rule, with all members present voting. Over CBS's loud objections, the resolution was finally passed by a vote of 9 to 3: "The RIAA should fund and, through its General Counsel, direct a private investigation to determine whether or not the conduct of independent promotion involves or results in criminal violations or other violations of federal regulations or law."

Several weeks after that meeting, MCA president Sid Sheinberg sent a letter to CBS board chairman Thomas Wyman chiding him for his record company's position on independent promotion. The letter was an attempt to take the issue over Walter Yetnikoff's head.

"In our judgment, the questions raised by rumors concerning the practices of independent promoters in the record industry require the attention of corporate management," Sheinberg wrote. Referring to an earlier telephone conversation with Wyman, he added, "It was out of personal friendship to you that I mentioned our concerns and alerted you to a situation which I felt might someday prove embarrassing to you.

"I am told you communicated the thrust of our conversation to Mr. Yetnikoff (by playing a tape recording thereof or otherwise) and I am sure you will do whatever else you feel is indicated in this area."

He ended with a subtle hint that CBS's continued recalcitrance might wind up the focus of an inquiry by the company's own network news correspondents.

"I am sure you understand that I have no axe to grind with CBS Records, Walter Yetnikoff or indeed independent promoters who comply with the law. I am equally sure, based on our conversation, you share our view that it shouldn't take '60 Minutes' to determine what the facts are."

Wyman wrote back on October 31, but didn't give an inch. "Here at CBS, corporate management has long been attentive to those questions [about independent promoters]. Yet, investigations of those 'rumors' in recent years have not uncovered any illegality, and we are a little skeptical about the effectiveness of a further, joint RIAA investigation. If MCA has credible evidence of any illegal practice, I assume you—like we—would already have taken some action on your own.

"For our part," Wyman wrote, "we wish to make sure that any RIAA investigation into independent promoter practices not be used—and not be seen as being used—to injure legitimate promotion activities or to reduce our vigorous competition in the promotion of records.

"Lest it pass without comment," he continued, "I was dismayed that you would give any substance to Walter's intended humor suggesting that I had tape recorded our telephone conversation. Please be 100 percent certain that I have never tape recorded a telephone conversation in my life—nor do I plan to do so."

The testy exchange of letters between the two chief executives was evidence of their growing distraction with what was going on in their record divisions. Despite his statements to Sheinberg, Wyman was deeply concerned about the independent promotion brouhaha and worried about Yetnikoff's reputed relationship with DiSipio and Isgro. CBS owned radio stations, whose valuable licenses could be revoked by the FCC if it were ever established that money from the record company was ending up in the pockets of radio programmers. Yetnikoff wasn't exactly Wyman's cup of tea to begin with. Walter's party-animal reputation and penchant for outrageous public statements—such as continually referring to Wyman as "the goy upstairs"—were a constant source of vexation to CBS corporate management. In truth, the whole record business flat out frightened the CBS brass. It was too volatile, too unpredictable, too much like Walter Yetnikoff. Many in management thought the corporation would be better off selling the record division. If only it didn't make so damned much money.

Sheinberg had his own problems. The *Los Angeles Times* stories about Sal Pisello's dealings with the record company had caused an angry split on the MCA board of directors. Two members of the board, former senator Howard Baker and investment banker Felix Rohatyn, argued forcefully that the record company executives responsible should be fired. Baker felt the explanations given in the May 2 internal audit report to the board stunk to high heaven. The rest of the board, however, had gone along with Wasserman and Sheinberg, who argued that no action should be taken and that the storm of controversy would soon blow over.

But it didn't. On July 8, there had been an opening delay in the trading of MCA stock on the New York Stock Exchange due to an order imbalance, meaning far more investors were selling than buying. The imbalance was caused by a report from influential Merrill Lynch analyst Harold Vogel alerting his investor clients to the *Los Angeles Times* stories. The price of MCA stock dropped 2¾ points the day of Vogel's report.

The show business trade papers, meanwhile, were reporting rumors of merger talks between MCA and RCA. Industry scuttlebutt had it that MCA chairman Wasserman was fed up and wanted out but wasn't confident that his heir apparent, Sheinberg, could run the company effectively without him—as evidenced by the internal problems in the record division. So Wasserman was looking for a soundly managed buyer. Speculation was that if RCA bought MCA it would immediately put the record company on the sales block.

Surprisingly, Irving Azoff seemed to have emerged from all the hubbub relatively unscathed. In April, Sheinberg had extended Azoff's employment contract and increased his base salary from $400,000 to $550,000 a year—the same amount that Wasserman, Sheinberg, and Universal Pictures president Frank Price earned. In addition, Azoff had received MCA stock worth $726,000 and another

$130,000 in unspecified "royalties from MCA subsidiaries," according to the company's annual report. Despite all of MCA's growing problems, Azoff was ending 1985 on a series of personal high notes.

On December 22, Azoff announced that MCA Records had signed a three-year contract to finance and distribute a new jazz label called Cranberry Records in partnership with Los Angeles Lakers center Kareem Abdul-Jabbar. A longtime jazz buff, Abdul-Jabbar thus became the tallest record company president in history—reporting to perhaps the shortest ever. "I've been working with Irving Azoff directly and he's given me a lot of encouragement," the athlete said in a *Hits* magazine interview. "They're going to pay me money to go around the world and listen to music and promote jazz and do wonderful things like that. I couldn't be more thrilled."

Nor could Azoff. A rabid Lakers fan, he had held $50,000 worth of Lakers season tickets for years—floor seating, right down there with Jack Nicholson, Dyan Cannon, and Rob Lowe. Azoff once even scored for the Lakers, sort of. During a 1980 playoff game with the Philadelphia 76ers, he got into a shouting match with Darryl Dawkins, the Sixers' six-foot-eleven, 260-pound center. When Dawkins gave Azoff the finger, he was charged with a technical foul and the Lakers sank the free throw. (Abdul-Jabbar no doubt felt like flipping the bird to Azoff in the summer of 1988 when, two years into his Cranberry Records deal with MCA, he abruptly closed down the company, claiming that Azoff had not lived up to his commitments.)

On December 30, 1985, Azoff sold his old house at 708 North Elm Drive to *Big Chill* writer-director Lawrence Kasdan for $2.8 million. The same day, he bought a new home in the even more fashionable area of nearby Holmby Hills—a 9,600-square-foot English Tudor with twenty-three rooms—including eight bathrooms—a pool, tennis court, and city view. Price tag: $6.3 million.

The Azoffs would not be missed in the old neighborhood. Residents there had come to dread the couple's frequent parties. It wasn't so much the noise and valet-parking bustle they created on the usually quiet street. What disturbed people the most were the teams of security guards and attack dogs that Azoff hired to patrol the perimeter of his property during the festivities.

Perhaps no one was happier to see the Azoffs go than their next-door neighbor, cable TV entrepreneur Marc Nathanson. In March 1980, shortly after Azoff moved into the neighborhood, he asked Nathanson for permission to tear down a wall on Nathanson's property that separated the two homes. Azoff said he wanted to build a tennis court and the wall would interfere with the construction crew's access. He allegedly promised to have the wall rebuilt at his own expense after the tennis court was completed and pay for any damage that might occur to the six-foot-high hedge that ran alongside the wall.

But after ten months of noisy construction the tennis court was finished, the crews had departed without rebuilding the wall and the hedge was dying. When Nathanson called to ask about it, Azoff replied, "Oh, I thought you were going to do that and send me a bill."

So Nathanson paid $11,000 to rebuild the wall and replace the hedge and he sent a copy of the bill to Azoff's office. After weeks of hearing nothing, he finally accosted Azoff on the sidewalk in front of their houses as Azoff was returning from a jog around the neighborhood. "What's the deal?" Nathanson asked. "Why don't you return my phone calls?"

"Have you ever heard of rock 'n' roll rules?" Azoff replied. Nathanson admitted that he had not. "Those are the rules I play by and they mean I can change my mind any time I want," Azoff said, adding that he'd decided not to pay for the wall after all. He then turned his back on Nathanson and trotted into his house.

Incensed, Nathanson sued both Azoff and his wife, Shelli. On his way out to work a few days after the lawsuit was filed, Nathanson found that neither of his family cars would start. It turned out that sugar had been poured into both gas tanks. Though he had no proof, Nathanson suspected the vandalism was related to the suit. He had his lawyer press the issue with Azoff's lawyer, but Azoff denied it. Azoff's insurance company eventually settled the suit out of court for $15,000.

The final high note for Azoff at year's end was his being named as the keynote speaker for the 1986 NARM convention, to be held in Los Angeles in March. According to *Billboard* magazine, the topic of Azoff's address would be the "dramatic turnaround" he'd engineered at MCA Records.

But unbeknownst to Azoff, things were about to get a lot more dramatic for himself and MCA. On November 26, the tax division of the Justice Department authorized Marvin Rudnick to conduct a grand jury investigation "of potential criminal tax and other related violations." The prime focus of the investigation, indeed the man identified in IRS and Strike Force documents as the "target"* of the grand jury probe, was Irving Lee Azoff of Beverly Hills, California.

On the East Coast, meanwhile, powerful forces were at work that would plunge the record business into the worst scandal in its history. And Azoff would be right in the middle of it.

---

*Investigators were using the dictionary definition of the word "target" rather than the definition contained in the U.S. Attorney's Manual. According to the manual, in order for a person to be officially designated a "target," the government must possess "substantial evidence linking him/her to the commission of a crime and who, in the judgment of the prosecutor, is a putative defendant." It is clear, however, that investigators considered Azoff the prime focus of their efforts. His name is listed at the top of the Strike Force's Case Initiation Report dated May 1985. The CIR states that "We have this date opened an investigation of the above subject [Azoff]" and lists as possible criminal violations conspiracy, mail fraud, and tax evasion. An IRS document dated October 15, 1986, specifically describes Azoff as the "target" of the grand jury investigation.

25

"Those aren't
my cameras"

On Tuesday evening, January 21, 1986, New York police detectives Anthony Venditti and Kathleen Burke were pulling surveillance duty for the joint task force investigating the Genovese family. (Venditti was one of the officers who had monitored the electronic surveillance of Morris Levy's Roulette Records office the day of the big sit-down with Vastola and Dominick Canterino in September.)

Dressed in plain clothes and driving an unmarked, brown Lincoln sedan, Venditti and Burke were following Genovese capo and Pisello business partner Fritzy Giovanelli through Queens, where, according to wiretap information, he was supposed to meet with Rocco Musacchia. Venditti and Burke's assignment was to observe that meeting, but at about 8 P.M. they lost sight of Fritzy's silver BMW in traffic.

They drove around trying to pick up his trail again, cruising by several of the clubs where he carried on his gambling business, including Vincent Gigante's Triangle Social Club down on Sullivan Street. But after about half an hour with no luck, they gave up and decided to go back to the strike force office in Brooklyn to do some paperwork.

At 8:25, as they approached a commercial stretch of Myrtle Avenue in the Ridgewood section of Queens, where Myrtle opens into a triangled intersection with Woodbine Street and St. Nicholas Avenue, Venditti asked Burke to stop so he could use the restroom. Burke parked across the street from Castillo's Mexican Diner and watched as her partner went inside. As she waited in the car, she saw in her rear-view mirror that Giovanelli's BMW had come up quietly behind her with its headlights off. Apparently, Fritzy had picked up their tail and turned the tables on them.

Burke pulled away from the curb, made a left on Woodbine and two more quick lefts to bring her back around on Myrtle. She parked the Lincoln behind a dumpster half a block from where Fritzy's car now sat empty. She got out of the car and walked toward Castillo's. The diner had an odd entrance, with two separate stairways leading up to a vestibule. As Burke trotted up the stairway closest to her, she spotted her partner heading down the other one on his way back to the street. She went back down the stairs and turned up the sidewalk to intercept him.

Exactly what happened next remains in dispute. According to the police report of the incident, Burke saw Venditti being accosted by three men at the foot of the other stairway. Two of the men muscled him up against the building, while the third drew a pistol.

"Look out, Tony. He's got a gun!" Burke shouted, drawing her own weapon. "Police, freeze!"

At the sound of her voice, all hell broke loose. As Venditti tried to push his way out of their grasp, one of the men drew a gun and shot him twice in the back. Burke opened fire. Giovanelli wheeled around and shot back, hitting her in the chest. The bullet struck the plastic clip on her bra strap and went clean through her body, collapsing her lung. She went down firing, emptying her .38 police special before she hit the pavement. As Venditti slumped to the sidewalk, one of the other men—later identified by a witness as Carmine Gaultiere, a gambling associate of Fritzy's—leaned over and shot him twice more in the face at point-blank range.

The three men then took off in different directions on foot.

Leaving his car behind, Giovanelli ran two blocks down Palmetto Street under the el, where he was apprehended by officers responding to an all-cars radio call, code 10-13, officer in trouble.

Burke was rushed to Bellevue Hospital in serious condition. She later received a consoling visit from New York mayor Ed Koch. Venditti, a thirty-four-year-old father of two, died on the operating table at Wyckoff Heights Hospital in Brooklyn.

Giovanelli was taken to the 104th precinct and booked for second-degree murder, attempted murder, and aggravated assault. He complained of dizziness and chest pains during questioning and was transferred to the County Hospital under heavy guard.

The next day, Gaultiere and the third man, Stephen Maltese, turned themselves in and were booked on the same charges. All three were held without bail.

News of the shooting shocked the other members of the strike force and the law enforcement community at large. Mafia attacks on peace officers are extremely rare. It's happened only three or four times this century, the last time in 1963, when six members of the Lombardozzi family beat up an FBI agent who was conducting surveillance during a Mafia funeral at a Catholic church in Brooklyn. The agent was hospitalized with a fractured skull.

During questioning after the shooting, Giovanelli and the two others claimed that Burke had not identified herself as a police officer. They said they were gamblers who usually carried large amounts of cash, and they thought the two detectives were actually criminals who were planning to rob them. Giovanelli claimed he had been held up at gunpoint in front of the diner several weeks before. Burke fired first, they said, and they only fired back in self-defense.

Oddly enough, that scenario sounded plausible to some investigators. It didn't make sense that Giovanelli, a seasoned Mafia soldier, would knowingly shoot a cop, especially over something as unthreatening as a routine surveillance. Guys like Fritzy were used to being followed by the police; it was all part of the game.

The investigators speculated that Giovanelli may have thought he was about to be hit by members of a rival crime group, possibly the Gambino family. It was a time of general upheaval in the New York Mafia world. Five weeks earlier, on December 16, Gambino boss Paul Castellano and his bodyguard, Thomas Bilotti, were gunned down as they stepped out of their limousine in front of

Sparks Steak House on Manhattan's East Side. Three men in trench coats pumped six bullets into their heads at close range and then disappeared into the 5:00 P.M. sidewalk crowd.

At the time of his murder, Castellano was on trial, along with the heads of the other four New York Mafia families, charged in a seventy-eight-count indictment with running a racketeering enterprise involving murder, bribery, extortion, car theft, and prostitution. "Big Paul" was accused of being the head of the Mafia's ruling commission, the "boss of bosses." His death—and that of his longtime underboss, Aniello Dellacroce, from cancer two weeks earlier—created a power vacuum in the Mafia hierarchy and fueled tension between the Gambino and Genovese families.

Castellano was succeeded as head of the Gambino family by forty-five-year-old John Gotti, formerly an obscure middle-echelon capo in Dellacroce's crew. As a Mafia boss, Gotti stood in marked contrast to Castellano, who had risen to power by marrying Vito Genovese's sister and had managed the family's assets and criminal operations in the conservative manner of a commercial banker. Said one New York police investigator of Castellano, "If you handed him a gun, he'd probably jump out a window."

Gotti, on the other hand, rose up through the ranks on the strength of his hair-trigger temper and penchant for violence. In 1973, he was convicted of manslaughter for his role in the killing of a Gambino soldier who was suspected of turning informant. The murder earned him a promotion in the family and only two years in prison. A few years later, Gotti's eleven-year-old son was killed when he rode his bicycle into the path of a neighbor's car. Shortly thereafter, the neighbor disappeared and was never seen again.

Because Gotti was the primary beneficiary of Castellano's death, New York authorities believed he was the architect of Big Paul's murder. In the weeks following the killing, the new boss seemed to revel in the spotlight of the New York media, quickly becoming a fixture on the evening news—always decked out in flashy $1,800 designer suits with a silk handkerchief protruding from the breast pocket, sporting a diamond pinky ring, his steel-gray hair elegantly coiffed into a pompadour. New York newspaper writers dubbed him the "dapper don."

The Genovese family had a new boss, too. With Anthony ("Fat Tony") Salerno in failing health at age seventy-five and faced with a string of indictments that could send him to jail for a lot longer than he had left on this earth, Vincent Gigante had taken over running things. Some Mafia experts predicted that the simultaneous ascension of two new bosses to head the two most powerful crime families had set the stage for an all-out war for control of the New York rackets.

The day after the Venditti-Burke shooting, investigators for the New York State Organized Crime Task Force, headquartered forty-five minutes outside Manhattan in White Plains, received information that John Gotti and several of his top aides were going to attend a meeting the next evening at the posh Helmsley Palace Hotel on Fifth Avenue. The information came from a bug the task force had placed in Gotti's favorite hangout, the Bergin Hunt and Fish Club on 101st Avenue in Ozone Park.

According to snippets of conversations overheard by investigators, the meeting had something to do with the record business. Over the previous few days, in fact, agents monitoring the hidden microphone noticed that there was suddenly an unusual amount of talk among the wise guys at the club about the music business. They overheard someone talking about "Joe Piney's man in the record business, the kid from California." Joe Piney, they knew, was seventy-year-old Joseph Armone, a convicted heroin trafficker and longtime Gambino capo.

On Thursday, January 23, the task force received information from other sources that Vincent Gigante was also going to attend the Helmsley Palace meeting that evening. Presented with a rare opportunity to eavesdrop on a summit meeting between two Mafia bosses, the task force immediately assigned a team of undercover investigators to stake out the hotel to try to find out what Gotti and Gigante were up to and what connection it had to the record business.

As it turned out, the Helmsley and most of Manhattan's best hotels were booked solid that week with record industry professionals in town to attend the First Annual Rock and Roll Hall of Fame Awards dinner Thursday night at the Waldorf-Astoria Hotel. About one thousand recording artists, producers, and record company executives were gathering to honor the pioneers of rock 'n' roll—Elvis Presley, Chuck Berry, Buddy Holly, Jerry Lee Lewis, the Everly Brothers, Little Richard, Ray Charles, James Brown, Fats Domino, and Sam Cooke—at the glamour event of the year for the industry. Tickets to the affair cost between $300 and $1,000 a pop.

Among those in town for the dinner—and staying at the Helmsley Palace—were independent promoters Joe Isgro and Fred DiSipio.

About 3:30 Thursday afternoon, Brian Ross, an investigative reporter for NBC News, was hanging around the lobby of the Helmsley hoping to catch a glimpse of Isgro and DiSipio. Ross and his longtime producer, Ira Silverman, were working on a planned report about independent record promotion and the so-called Network. They'd heard from sources that Isgro and DiSipio had Mafia connections and were the architects of a "new payola" scheme that virtually controlled which records did and didn't get played on the radio around the country. The information was sketchy, especially the part about the Mafia connections—Isgro supposedly was linked to some guy named Joe Piney. But Ross and Silverman knew that if they could get the story, it would make for a sexy, sensational Special Segment report on the "NBC Nightly News." They knew Isgro and DiSipio were staying at the hotel and they hoped to get some videotape footage of them to use in the piece.

At approximately 4:45, as he made his third or fourth casual stroll around the perimeter of the Helmsley's palatial first floor, Ross stopped short. He saw John Gotti stride into the lobby from the parking garage, flanked by his underboss, Frank DeCicco, and Gambino family consiglieri Joseph N. Gallo. Transfixed, Ross watched the trio walk up to an older man sitting on a tufted leather banquette near the center of the room and begin talking. Ross bolted for the house phone and dialed up Silverman, who was staying at the hotel. "Ira, get down here quick. You won't believe who just walked in—John Gotti."

He then called the NBC New York bureau to order up another camera crew—two were already heading for the Waldorf to catch Isgro and DiSipio when they arrived for the awards dinner. Ross watched from the phone as Gotti, DeCicco, and Gallo left the old man and got into an elevator—just as Silverman got out.

Moments later, Ross and Silverman were huddled by the phone, going over the logistics of filming both the record promoters and the Mafia boss that evening, when Isgro emerged from the elevator followed by his bodyguards, Bruce Pond and David Michael Smith. The record promoter walked directly over to the old man who'd been talking with John Gotti just moments before and greeted him with an affectionate embrace.

The two newsmen were stunned. Until that moment they had

not made the connection between Isgro and the Mafiosi in the lobby.

As Isgro and the old man talked animatedly, a limousine pulled up at the front entrance of the hotel and disgorged Fred DiSipio and an entourage—his bodyguard Mike Santacapito, business associates Ronnie Kyle and Matty Singer, and several flashy young women. The men wore tuxedos, the women were swaddled in sequins and furs, obviously dressed for the awards dinner. They swept into the lobby and were greeted by Isgro, who introduced them to the old man. They immediately split into two groups—the bodyguards and the women to one side, the promoters and the old man to the other—and talked for about ten minutes.

Suddenly, Frank DeCicco reappeared, gathered the two groups together, and shepherded them all toward the elevators, right past where the two newsmen stood trying to will themselves into invisibility. "Joe's got a room upstairs we're using," they heard Armone say as the group crammed into a single elevator car.

Ross and Silverman were seized with the heart-quickening elation that investigative reporters live to experience. Working from tips, vague hints, and educated hunches, they'd just seen their story come together in an instant before their eyes: the most powerful and famous Mafia boss in the country apparently meeting with the two men who supposedly dictated what music the young people of America heard on the radio. This was a slam dunk.

There was just one problem. They had nothing on tape, no pictures to show. It's the television news version of a tree falling in the forest—since there were no cameras around to capture the event, it might as well not have happened.

Roth was back on the phone to the NBC bureau. Where was that third camera crew? There was still a chance to catch the entire bunch when they left the hotel—they had to come back down the elevator at some time. When they did, Ross wanted to have a camera outside every entrance. The two crews at the Waldorf were to be sent over to the Helmsley as soon as they could be contacted.

The calls made, Ross and Silverman paced the lobby nervously, waiting for the cameras to arrive. After about fifteen minutes, Isgro, dressed casually in one of his trademark $500 sweaters, came back to the lobby, found an empty easy chair and sat down. About this time, Ross and Silverman noticed they weren't the only ones closely observing the action. Stationed around the lobby were a handful of trench-coated men who looked suspiciously like undercover cops. Ross recognized one of them as an agent from the U.S. attorney's office in Manhattan. They nodded to one another, exchanging knowing looks.

Actually, there were two separate surveillance teams in the lobby, one from the state task force and one from the federal strike force, each surprised and a little annoyed to find the other there. But as the agents recognized one another, and Brian Ross as well, they had to chuckle. This might have been the least secret Mafia rendezvous since Appalachia, when New York State troopers stumbled onto a national conference of Mafia kingpins gathered for a barbecue at the upstate New York home of mob boss Joe Barbara. (That incident, in 1957, sent the heads of the U.S. underworld scrambling through the woods to avoid arrest and opened the eyes of law enforcement authorities to the fact that the Mafia was indeed organized and national in scope.)

In the Helmsley lobby, Isgro kept checking his watch and fidgeting. At one point he got up and used the house phone, then went to the front desk and asked for a package from the hotel safe. He came back and sat down with a thick envelope in his lap. After a few minutes, the promoter arose and went back upstairs.

Next, the DiSipio entourage emerged from the elevator, sashayed across the lobby, and climbed back into the limo for the block-and-a-half ride to the Waldorf. Waiting outside, an NBC camera crew filmed their exit.

Shortly thereafter, Isgro and his bodyguards emerged from the elevator, this time dressed in their tuxedos. They, too, were caught by the news camera as they left the hotel and walked to the Waldorf.

Gotti, Gallo, DeCicco, and Armone—the Gambino family's board of directors—followed about half an hour later. As they stood talking just inside the hotel entrance, waiting for their car to be brought around, DeCicco apparently "made" the surveillance. He walked up to one of the task force agents and asked politely, "Are you following us?"

"No, I'm just waiting for someone," the agent replied nonchalantly. DeCicco walked back to where Gotti and Gallo stood. That's when he spotted the NBC camera outside the hotel, apparently filming him through the glass door. He strode over to the agent again and said, annoyed this time, "What? Are you bullshitting me? You've got cameras outside."

"Those aren't my cameras; they're from the media," the agent said, watching as the lights began to go on in DeCicco's head.

Alarmed, DeCicco hurried back to Gotti and whispered the situation into his boss's ear. The four mobsters then walked quickly out the door and split into twos, with Armone and Gallo getting into one car and Gotti and DeCicco into another, while the NBC camera rolled. Meanwhile, the agents in the lobby bailed out through the hotel's rear entrances. The surveillance was over, their covers were blown, and it would hardly enhance their careers to have their faces show up on the evening news. There was a Keystone Cops quality to the scene as the good guys and bad guys simultaneously scurried to opposite exits.

A second team of task force agents picked up Gotti's and De-Cicco's car as it pulled away from the hotel and followed the pair to P. J. Clark's Restaurant, where they later terminated the surveillance.

The state agents were angry with the FBI. If they'd known the "feebies" were going to be at the Helmsley, they wouldn't have shown up themselves. The lack of coordination between the two agencies had produced a situation that was at best clumsy and confused, at worst dangerously volatile. The task force blamed the FBI for the presence of Brian Ross, whom they knew had close ties to the U.S. attorney's office in Manhattan.

They also blamed the FBI for Vincent Gigante's not showing up for the meeting. The night before, teams of FBI agents and New York police officers had gone to a number of the Genovese family's social clubs, including Gigante's Triangle, and questioned people about the murder of detective Anthony Venditti. They acted more out of frustration and anger over the killing of one of their own than out of solid law enforcement strategy. The show of force yielded nothing in the way of evidence or information, and it may have blown a terrific opportunity for New York authorities. The task force agents figured that Gigante had passed up the Helmsley meeting because of the heat the night before.

Still, the incident at the Helmsley had provided some interesting leads. From a brief conversation one of the agents had with reporter Ross outside the hotel, they learned who Joe Isgro and Fred Di-

Sipio were. In return, the agent told Ross that the old man Isgro had embraced in the lobby, the man who appeared to be the connection between the promoter and John Gotti, was Joseph ("Joe Piney") Armone.

In the grand ballroom of the Waldorf-Astoria later that night, the record industry put on the show that few in the crowd would ever forget. People stood on tables and chairs, stomped their feet, and whooped it up as an all-star band for the ages—Chuck Berry, John Fogerty, Jerry Lee Lewis, Neil Young, Billy Joel, Steve Winwood, Chubby Checker, and Keith Richards and Ron Wood of the Rolling Stones—performed a medley of rock 'n' roll's greatest hits.

Throughout the evening, Isgro and DiSipio worked the room like visiting diplomats. A few people at the dinner noticed that despite the presence in the ballroom of some of the biggest names in the record business, an NBC camera crew spent an unusual amount of time focused on the two promoters.

The evening closed out with John Fogerty leading the house through a euphoric rendition of Creedence Clearwater Revival's biggest hit, "Proud Mary": "Big wheel keep on turnin', Proud Mary keep on churnin', Rollin', rollin', rollin' on the river," they all sang together.

The wheels were turning elsewhere for Fred DiSipio and Joe Isgro, however. Already, the FBI and the New York State Organized Crime Task Force had entered their names into the computer as suspected organized crime associates and had begun making calls to find out more about their businesses.

26

Muscle ...
Nuts and Bolts ...
The Snowman

Several days after the Helmsley Palace incident, Marvin Rudnick received a phone call from Neil Kreitz, a detective with the Los Angeles Police Department's Organized Crime Intelligence Division (OCID).

"Marvin, you're the record business expert; we think we've got something the strike force might be interested in," Kreitz said. "It involves the Mafia and payola."

Rudnick was swamped with work. He was writing the appellate court brief responding to Sal Pisello's appeal of his tax evasion conviction. He'd just indicted a land-fraud case in Phoenix that was requiring him to fly back and forth all the time. He also had an extortion case and a loan-sharking case, and he'd just gotten department approval to begin issuing subpoenas to MCA for all documents pertaining to the company's business dealings with Pisello.

Still, Mafia and payola were tantalizing, a connection he'd never thought of before. It wouldn't hurt to listen.

"I've got a pretty full plate right now, Neil," he said, "but come on over and tell me what you've got."

They met later that afternoon in the strike force library, where Kreitz and another detective, Herm Kaskowitz, briefly laid out the story: The OCID had reason to believe that a local independent record promoter named Joe Isgro, another promoter named Fred DiSipio, of Cherry Hill, New Jersey, and others were operating a nationwide payola ring that was providing radio programmers with cash, drugs, and women in exchange for playing records. The record companies were paying these guys millions and millions of dollars a year, partly out of fear of reprisal if they didn't.

Rudnick listened, intrigued. The intelligence division had been keeping an eye on Isgro for some time, the detectives said. They believed he had contacts with the Los Angeles family and with East Coast kingpin John Gotti.

The cops had a hard-on for Isgro, that was clear. Kreitz and Kaskowitz went on about his extravagant life-style—his Rolls-Royce, his bodyguards, the flamboyant way he carried himself—ticking off the points as if reading from a rap sheet.

Rudnick had to smile at their naiveté. His wife covered the entertainment industry for the *Los Angeles Times* financial section, so he knew something about show business types. And if inordinate income and conspicuous consumption were criteria for criminal indictment, then half the people in Hollywood would be in jail.

What they didn't have yet, the detectives admitted, was any hard evidence that crimes had been committed—no one saying they'd given or received payoffs, nobody claiming they'd witnessed payoffs, no insider providing information on the details of Isgro's operation.

Nonetheless, it sounded to Rudnick like something worth looking into. Illegal payments, by their nature, breed tax fraud. An organized system of such payments could make for a good RICO case. And the fact that the OCID was so hot to go after Isgro was a bonus. Usually, half the battle in a strike force case was enlisting an investigative agency—the police, FBI, IRS, or DEA—to do the actual legwork.

He suggested they make their pitch directly to the new strike force chief, Ted Gale. "It sounds good to me, guys," he said. "I'd love to work on it with you."

Privately, Rudnick had mixed feelings about what the detectives had told him. For one thing, the timing was curious. They'd never had a Mafia-in-the-record-business case in the office before. Suddenly, it appeared they had two. "Why haven't we heard about Isgro before?" he wondered.

Part of his concern was selfish. He'd had a helluva time getting the IRS interested in the MCA-Pisello investigation. It had taken almost a year to get approval for the MCA subpoenas, and the criminal division so far had assigned him only one agent to work on the case. When he wrote up the case initiation report back in May, he'd called the Los Angeles FBI office to see if they had any organized crime background on the major players in his investigation—Sal, Azoff, Morris Levy. The FBI gave him information about Levy and Pisello, but said they had nothing on Azoff. They expressed no interest in joining in on the case. He hadn't heard from them since.

Rudnick could see the obvious headline value in a big payola bust linked to the Mafia, and he knew that Ted Gale would see it, too. The media would call it a scandal and play it up big. Attorney General Meese could tout it at a Capitol Building press conference as another example of the Reagan administration cracking down on organized crime and striking a blow for the little guy. All of which would reflect glory on the Los Angeles strike force. Careers would be enhanced.

He knew that decisions to launch—or not to launch—an investigation oftentimes turned on just such considerations. And he feared that, given a choice between MCA-Pisello and the sexier-sounding, more grandiose payola case, the powers that be would choose the latter, leaving his investigation to die on the vine.

He didn't want that to happen.

A week later, Kreitz, Kaskowitz, and a handful of other OCID detectives were back for an official meeting with Ted Gale in the strike force conference room. Rudnick didn't attend the meeting because Gale hadn't invited him. Instead, Gale asked John Dubois, the newest attorney in the office, to sit in. Gale didn't intend it as a slight to Rudnick, he just wanted to start getting Dubois's feet wet. He figured if there was something in what the OCID had to say, he'd put Dubois in charge of the investigation and Rudnick could back him up. Al Lipkin, who headed the IRS Organized Crime

Section, and several IRS agents also attended the meeting.

This time, the detectives brought visual aids with them—a chart showing Isgro's suspected connections to organized crime figures on both coasts and another linking him to the other members of the independent promotion Network and their various companies around the country. Beneath Isgro's name on the Network chart, the word *muscle* was written. Beneath DiSipio's name were the words *nuts and bolts*. Another Network member was dubbed *the snow man*, indicating he was considered a source of cocaine.

The detectives went through their spiel, focusing on Isgro. They told about his recent apparent meeting with John Gotti at the Helmsley and his meeting with Nicky Scarfo at his restaurant on Sunset Strip. They said that, based on intelligence gathered from several police informants in the Hollywood vice division, they believed Isgro was providing radio programmers with prostitutes. He was using the services of one "very high-class" call girl whose name they didn't mention.

Gale, Dubois, and the IRS men were impressed. Obviously, the OCID had done a lot of preliminary work. With the added subpoena power and wiretap authority of a federal investigation, it might turn out to be a helluva case. The IRS was enthusiastic.

After the meeting, Gale and Dubois talked strategy. They were looking at a potentially huge undertaking, one that could consume an enormous amount of manpower. Perhaps the best thing to do was go slow until they started seeing some results in terms of hard evidence. Rather than initiate an entirely new grand jury investigation, it might be easier to start out under the umbrella of Rudnick's MCA-Pisello investigation—first find out about MCA's relationship with the independent promoters before subpoenaing the other record companies.

So on February 6, as Rudnick sat at the office computer writing up the subpoena for MCA's documents regarding the Sal Pisello business transactions, he added a single sentence at the bottom asking for "any and all documents pertaining to the company's use of independent promoters." It was a shot in the dark.

The subpoenas were answerable within twenty days. About a week before the documents were due, Ted Gale called Rudnick into his office for a meeting with MCA's outside counsels, Allen Susman and Bill Billick. The two lawyers were already sitting across the desk from Gale when Rudnick arrived, and Rudnick was already bristling. He didn't like the idea that they'd gone directly to his boss, or that Ted had allowed them to do it. That was a mistake, he thought. It undercut his authority. Now MCA knew from the outset it really didn't have to deal with the prosecutor in charge of the case.

The meeting began cordially enough, with Billick saying—pointedly, Rudnick thought—"I've talked to your wife at the *Los Angeles Times* before."

They wanted to "fully cooperate," the attorneys said. The problem was that the subpoena was very broad, requiring the production of thousands of documents, which was a hardship and would require a lot of time and great expense.

"If we just knew where you guys were going on this case, we might be able to simplify things and just supply what you're looking for," Billick said. He suggested that rather than turning over everything at once and burying the government in possibly unneeded documentation, the company could deliver the records in stages, thereby giving the investigators time to digest the information as they went. He even offered to allow an IRS agent to come to MCA's offices and go through the financial files to find whatever the government was after. It would save everyone a lot of time and effort.

"After all, if there is something wrong, we want to get to the bottom of it just as much as you do," Susman said.

Rudnick recognized the seemingly reasonable proposal as a standard defense attorney ploy—find out everything you can about the government's case, buy time, and try to confuse. It was good, sound defense strategy.

He was hoping Ted wouldn't swallow it. One underlying purpose of a subpoena is to establish the government's authority, to assert the primacy of a federal agency's reasoned need to know over a company's, or individual's, desire to protect confidential information. Outside the courtroom, that was the real battle.

If you gave MCA the wiggle room to dole out the information in dribs and drabs, you allowed the company to control the pace of the investigation. Plus, you handed the MCA lawyers a road map with the progress of your investigation practically marked for them in red. Tactically, it could be a disastrous move.

However, Susman and Billick were impressive men—smart, articulate, tough, sophisticated, manicured, and tailored in Brooks

Brothers' best. Not some oily mob lawyers or moussed-up mouth-pieces for a Medellín cocaine trafficker. Rudnick could see that Gale was leaning toward allowing MCA to answer the subpoena in stages.

"I got a better idea," Rudnick said, getting up from his chair and starting to pace around the room the way he always did in court. "We just want to get at the truth about the relationship between the record company and Pisello. We could cut this whole process down quite a bit and save a lot of time, if you would give us the notes from your interviews with the record executives about their deal-ings with Pisello. You give us those and we'll be the judge of whether any more investigation is needed. Hey, maybe your guys explained it all away and we can stop right here."

Billick looked at him with cold eyes. "That's privileged," he said, flatly.

"Then waive the privilege." Rudnick responded. "You can't be claiming cooperation on the one hand and not give us what we need on the other."

"The company will not give that up," Billick said.

"Well, can you tell me off the record what they say? Do you believe these guys?"

Billick stared at Rudnick for what seemed like a full minute and then said quietly. "The story is hard to believe."

Rudnick stared back, stunned by the statement. "He's saying he doesn't believe his own people," he thought to himself.

Before Rudnick could follow up on the remark, however, Billick asked, "Why aren't you going after the real problem in the indus-try? Independent promotion. That's what you should be looking at instead of raking us over the coals." He launched into a discourse about how independent promoters were controlling what records got played on the radio, demanding extortionate fees that were threatening the record companies' profits and possibly corrupting some record executives with kickbacks on promotion contracts. He indicated that MCA was prepared to help the government rid the industry of this scourge.

Rudnick continued to be surprised. MCA apparently was ready to snitch off the entire industry if the government let the Pisello matter drop. That seemed to be the unspoken quid pro quo.

"They're not afraid to let us into the stadium," he thought. "They just want us to look over here and not over there."

It was starting to get dark outside and Susman said he had to leave to attend an Israeli Bond banquet that evening, so the meeting broke up with Ted agreeing to let the company answer the subpoenas in stages.

Rudnick didn't like it, but he didn't argue with Gale's decision. He knew that the MCA-Pisello investigation would require spending quite a bit of political capital and he wasn't sure how much of that he had saved up. He needed Ted's backing. He didn't want to be out there on his own.

Before Gale left the office that night, he wrote up a letter to MCA officially confirming the agreement on the subpoena compliance.

The government had given MCA a big break, the first of many to come.

27

"An industry
under siege"

For weeks, the record business had been buzzing about NBC's upcoming report on independent promotion. Brian Ross and Ira Silverman had talked to a lot of people and attempted to interview many more. The word had gotten around fast, and some people were worried. What did the network have? Did it tie any company promotion executives to payola?

On the evening of February 24, the other shoe finally dropped. Much of the industry was huddled around office TV sets at 7:18 P.M. as "NBC Nightly News" finished up a story on the investigation into the space shuttle disaster.

"On Special Segment tonight," Tom Brokaw intoned, "the new payola, a sour note that is tainting the rock music business again. . . . It was back in the 1950s that payola became a way of life in this industry. Record companies and promoters paying off disc jockeys to plug new releases and to boost sales. Today, the practice appears to be back, with a group of independent promoters playing a major role, and several authorities are investigating a Mafia connection. NBC's investigative reporter Brian Ross has additional details."

The TV screen showed several old men talking on the sidewalk on a busy city street. In a voice-over, Ross explained: "This block on First Avenue on the Lower East Side of New York is a stronghold of the Gambino Mafia family. According to the FBI and New York police, the Mafia capo who runs things on this block, and in places far from this block, is Joseph Armone, the man with the glasses, a convicted heroin trafficker who on most days can be found conducting mob business at a back table in this pastry shop."

"For months now," Ross said, "the activities of Armone and others have been watched closely by the FBI and police as far away as Los Angeles, as part of an investigation of corrupt practices in the rock music business, and what appears to be the reemergence of payola at rock music radio stations."

The scene then switched to the Rock and Roll Hall of Fame dinner at the Waldorf-Astoria that was held the previous month.

"Among the guests, two of the most powerful and feared men in the rock music business: Joseph Isgro, who authorities say has described Mafia capo Armone as his partner; and Isgro's close associate, Fred DiSipio, who rarely does business without his associate, Mike, by his side.

"DiSipio and Isgro, each with his own company, are top men in what is called the Network, about thirty men, many at this dinner, all known as independent record promoters, who industry executives say are getting millions of dollars a year from record companies to make sure that certain new songs become hits on certain rock music radio stations. And how some independent promoters go about their business, how they get records on the air, is now the scandal of the industry."

The story went on to allege payoffs and threats to program directors from independent promoters. It showed Isgro and his bodyguard driving around Los Angeles in his yellow Rolls. Ross noted that both Isgro and DiSipio had refused to speak with the reporters. In addition, he said, "Of ten record company presidents contacted by NBC News—including the heads of such major labels as CBS, Warner, RCA, and MCA—none would agree to talk on camera about Isgro or DiSipio or the Network of independent promoters—some saying they feared repercussions."

Then came the kicker, the part that nearly everyone in the record business suspected about Isgro and DiSipio but no one knew for sure: "Just how important the rock music business is to the Mafia became clear last month at this New York City hotel," Ross said, as the screen filled with pictures of Armone talking with several men in the lobby of the Helmsley.

"Joseph Armone, the man from the pastry shop, arranged an unusual meeting with the top three men in the Gambino Mafia family, including Gambino family boss John Gotti—in the view of the FBI, a mob summit meeting.

"Also observed here: Joseph Isgro, who authorities say meets frequently with Armone and other gangsters, and Fred DiSipio," Ross said, over videotape footage of the two promoters, dressed in tuxedos, leaving the Helmsley for the awards banquet.

"One hour after meeting the top people in the American Mafia, Isgro and DiSipio were at the Waldorf-Astoria, taking their place among the top people in the American music business. Brian Ross, NBC News, New York."

As the network segued into a report on the postelection state of emergency in the Philippines, the top people in the music business already were assessing the damage.

At a party at the Beverly Hills home of entertainment mogul Jerry Weintraub, Walter Yetnikoff scoffed at the report. "It's all bullshit; there's nothing there," he told the gathering of record executives.

Others weren't so sure. After the *Los Angeles Times* article on the Network two years earlier, there'd been a short-lived and unproductive congressional investigation into payola. But this was national television, seen by tens of millions of people, including the record companies' own board members and shareholders, who'd just been told that their executives were handing out $80 million a year to men who did business with the Mafia—with John Gotti himself, for God's sake! The pictures were devastating. There would be hell to pay for this, they predicted.

The reaction to the NBC report was swift. The next day, Capitol Records and MCA Records announced they were ceasing immediately the use of all independent promotion. MCA promotion vice president Richard Palmese argued with Azoff about the decision, claiming it would put the company at a competitive disadvantage. But Azoff argued back that with all the recent publicity about Sal

Pisello, the company could not afford to be seen doing any more business with people connected to the Mafia. Besides, he said, all the other major labels were sure to follow suit.

He was right on both counts.

On February 26, NBC came back with another report by Ross, this time focusing in part on the Pisello affair at MCA and the New York and New Jersey grand jury investigations into the extortion of John LaMonte over the MCA cutout deal. Ross named Sal Pisello, Morris Levy, and Gaetano Vastola as the targets of the investigations and juxtaposed their pictures with those of Azoff and MCA's corporate headquarters in Universal City.

The second NBC report also reiterated the new payola and Mafia allegations and said that the two grand juries, along with a third in Los Angeles, were investigating payola and its suspected links to the Mafia. That wasn't exactly true. At the time, only the Los Angeles grand jury, through Rudnick's subpoena of MCA, had made any move to investigate payola.

It hardly mattered, though, in the rush of news stories and government and record company posturing that followed the NBC report. The next day, February 27, U.S. Attorney Rudolph Giuliani in Manhattan issued subpoenas to all the major record companies, asking for "any and all reports, summaries, memoranda of interviews, notes, documents and records, video and audio recordings and other material reflecting or relating to or generated, compiled or obtained in connection with an investigation into the role of independent promoters in the record industry and/or related topics."

A consummate media manipulator, Giuliani subpoenaed literally a warehouseful of documents on the basis of little more than what was contained in the NBC reports.

The same day, the RIAA—which only weeks earlier had been ready to spend $100,000 on a private investigation of independent promoters—issued this indignant statement: "We have no knowledge that any firm or individual with which our companies do business is engaged in any illegal activity, contrary to reports in recent televised network broadcasts. If law enforcement agents were to inform us that such individuals or firms are engaged in any illegal activities, we would take immediate and decisive corrective action. Until such time, we find it unjustified and distressing that the recording industry is so indiscriminately maligned by insidious innuendo. Such broad and unspecific allegations unfairly taint the innocent. They also detract from the monumental contributions of the industry to American and international humanitarian charitable causes."

Insidious innuendo or no, one by one the major record companies announced their decisions to stop using independent promotion. Even CBS went along, albeit reluctantly, saying it was "substantially reducing" its use of independent promoters.

Within a week of the initial NBC report, Joe Isgro and Fred DiSipio were virtually out of business. So were scores of other promoters around the country, many of them middle-aged music pros who'd been earning a middle-class living and had never seen a mobster except in the movies. "I feel like a Japanese-American in World War II being placed in an internment camp," one promoter told the *Hollywood Reporter.* "There's no one to complain to."

If anyone in the industry felt remorse over the indiscriminate punishment of an entire profession for the alleged business practices of a few, they kept it to themselves. When CBS announced it was cutting back on independent promotion, the heads of the other companies were elated. With the help of NBC and the Justice Department, they'd finally found a solution to the problem of skyrocketing promotion costs. Now that CBS was getting out of the game, nobody else had to play. Ding dong, the wicked witch was dead.

MCA Records, however, had bigger problems than independent promotion.

On March 3, the *Los Angeles Times* published an article headlined, "Probe Points to Mob Role in Record Deal." Using information gathered from LaMonte, who was now in hiding, the *Times* reported that members of three crime families—Gambino, Genovese, and DeCavalcante—had been involved in the 1984 MCA cutout sale and that one principal in the sale, Fritzy Giovanelli, had recently been arrested for the murder of New York police detective Anthony Venditti.

The *Times* story was followed by articles in the *Philadelphia Inquirer* ("Mob Is Trying to Call the Tune for the Record Industry"), the *Washington Post* ("Probes Seek Mob Links to Record-Sale Business"), *Rolling Stone* ("Feds probing Mob involvement in record business"), and the Knight Ridder papers ("Unraveling Mob's Ties to Music").

Publicly, MCA's position was that its executives merely sold the cutouts to Roulette Records—they had no prior knowledge of Sal Pisello's alleged Mafia ties and were not responsible for what happened after the records left the company's warehouse. "We're a victim of counterfeiting," MCA vice president and Azoff mouthpiece Larry Solters told *Rolling Stone.* "We conducted an internal investigation and we found all of our employees innocent of any wrongdoing."

But under the heat of the news stories and countless inquiries from reporters around the country, a bunker mentality was developing at the record company. The pressure could be clearly seen in an incident that took place on Saturday, March 8, during the 1986 NARM convention at the Century Plaza Hotel in Los Angeles.

Azoff was the convention's keynote speaker. Just moments before his speech was set to begin, at approximately 9:30 A.M., he arrived at the hotel surrounded by a phalanx of bodyguards. As the group swept through the lobby, they encountered an NBC camera crew that was stationed in the hallway just outside the entrance to the auditorium, where the conventioneers were being entertained by a group of gospel singers. When the news crew attempted to film Azoff, who was hidden behind a wedge of bodies as he entered the auditorium, a scuffle broke out, sending both the cameraman and Azoff's factotum, Larry Solters, sprawling on the carpet. During the brief melee, Azoff managed to slip into the auditorium without being filmed, but the camera caught Solters lying on his back on the floor, shouting, shaking his fist, and looking like an ineffectual thug.

Inside, Azoff launched into a spirited speech titled, "An Industry under Siege."

"Good morning, distinguished members of NARM, fellow record company executives, any artists or store managers who are still up from last night, Washington wives, future legislators, would-be censors, process servers, hidden cameras, members of the media, God, and Walter Yetnikoff," he began.

The speech was pure Azoff—combative, humorous, arrogant, intelligent, and outrageous. He called the RIAA "the laughing stock of the entertainment business." He attacked the Grammy Awards show, the trade magazine *Radio and Records,* Tipper Gore's lyric-censoring organization (the PMRC—Parents' Music Resource Center), and NARM itself. *Billboard* magazine called it "the most hard-hitting keynote speech in memory."

Azoff called for the industry to band together against its "mutual enemies," which he identified as "do-gooders, legislators, and certain members of the media."

"There are certain bad apples in every basket. But are we really the villain we are now being painted to be? And in the year of such widespread industry giving, how can we get so demolished?" he asked. "The attacks and witch hunts have become too intensified to laugh off . . . the media thirsts for any news of our industry and roots for our demise."

Though he never directly mentioned the problems at MCA Records, he alluded to them in an anecdote that was intended to be funny but came off strained and angry: "Many of you know that in my earlier career I was in the personal management business. The first time I spoke at this hotel, some idiot served me with a subpoena because I wouldn't let the Eagles play at his stupid rock festival. I've finally figured out the difference between being a manager and a record company president: as a record company president, you can get served subpoenas every day just by showing up for work."

"So you see, we are an industry under siege," he said in closing. "I love this business, I love its artists and its people. I think we are good people, with good intentions, and that our industry deserves an important place in society for all the good influence it has. We're not perfect, but who is?

"I know I've brought up some volatile points of view. I've done so in the hope that it will challenge you to think about our industry, because in the end we are one industry.

"According to *Rock & Roll Confidential*, what rock now faces is a series of brushfire wars, local smear campaigns coordinated nationally in the face of zero opposition. That publication says the music industry has become an ostrich, with his head in the sand and a firecracker in the strategic place. If performers, retailers, and executives don't take immediate steps to mobilize the audience to fight for its rights, a loud and painful bang is guaranteed."

For MCA, the firecracker was already lit. In addition to dealing with Marvin Rudnick and his investigation into the Pisello affair, the company was trying to mollify John Gervasoni of Scorpio Music, who was threatening to go public with his complaints about his aborted cutout purchase through Pisello and Ranji Bedi. Gervasoni wanted MCA to fulfill his cutout order or pay him the $200,000 he was still owed on the deal.

The record company was in a bind. With MCA's internal auditors nosing around all over the place, there was no way to fill Gervasoni's original order, since many of the records weren't actually cutouts—they were still in the company's active sales catalog. The company argued that it had all been a mistake, that Sam Passamano had given Bedi the wrong list. MCA attorneys had offered Scorpio another batch of cutouts, but Gervasoni had rejected it as "garbage."

At the same time, MCA could not refund the money, its attorneys said, since the company had no contract with Scorpio, and it hadn't received the money in the first place. The cutouts had been sold to Ranji Bedi and Betaco, they said. So Gervasoni should look to Bedi for satisfaction. As far as MCA was concerned, Scorpio could take the replacement cutouts or nothing.

As part of a proposed settlement, MCA attorneys had drawn up a complicated dual agreement they wanted Gervasoni to sign with both MCA and Betaco promising never to divulge the content or even existence of the settlement. Betaco's lawyer, Sam Galici, told Gervasoni the agreement meant he couldn't even talk to the FBI about the cutout deal if agents ever came around asking questions. Gervasoni refused to sign.

The week after the NARM convention, Scorpio's attorney, Dennis Eisman, presented MCA with a draft of a $45 million fraud and racketeering lawsuit he said he intended to file if the company didn't settle with his client immediately.

The proposed lawsuit charged that MCA Records executives—including Azoff, Myron Roth, and Zach Horowitz—had conspired with Pisello to entice Scorpio into advancing $350,000 for the cutouts and then wrongfully converted the money to their own use, thereby defrauding not only Scorpio, but MCA stockholders as well. In one of its more colorful passages, the suit alleged that the "co-conspirators" had used the beating of John LaMonte "as an example to keep victims such as Scorpio from going to authorities." As it turned out, Eisman was also John LaMonte's attorney.

Eisman figured that, faced with such embarrassing public charges, MCA would capitulate and settle with Scorpio. He figured wrong, however.

On March 18, MCA answered Scorpio's threatened lawsuit by filing a preemptive suit of its own, charging that Scorpio had counter-
feited millions of dollars' worth of MCA recordings. MCA's suit
also denied in advance the charges in Scorpio's impending action,
dismissing them as "totally baseless and without merit." Among
other things, MCA claimed that Sal Pisello had never acted as an
agent of the company in selling cutout records. Larry Solters told
reporters that Scorpio had "maliciously threatened us with a
frivolous lawsuit," and that the company had a history of dealing in
counterfeit goods.

If anything, it was MCA's lawsuit that was frivolous. The only
evidence the company had that Scorpio was involved in counterfeiting was Gervasoni's own admission that he'd purchased several
thousand of LaMonte's questionable Jamaican imports. When the
story first broke in the *Los Angeles Times* about the suspected counterfeiting operation, Gervasoni had called MCA internal auditor
Allen Clement and said he was concerned about the authenticity of
the goods. At Clement's request, he sent samples of the tapes to
MCA. But he'd never heard back.

As in the case of the Sam Passamano lawsuit, the counterfeiting
charges against Scorpio were an attempt by MCA attorneys to
counter negative publicity by positioning the company as a victim.
Having lost the high ground in the fight, Scorpio went ahead and
filed its lawsuit in federal court in Philadelphia on March 20.

A grandstander of the first order, Scorpio attorney Dennis Eisman had learned the art of media management in the late 1970s as a
member of a team of lawyers representing Jeffrey MacDonald, the
former Green Beret doctor convicted of brutally murdering his wife
and two daughters in the case made famous by the book *Fatal Vision*
and the TV miniseries of the same title.

On March 25, Eisman filed a motion in federal court in Philadelphia asking for the expedited depositions of Irving Azoff and Sam
Passamano on the grounds that they were potential victims of mob
violence because they could "provide essential information linking
organized crime" to MCA. Citing the beating of John LaMonte,
Eisman contended that there had been "a pattern of violence
already inflicted upon potential witnesses" in several grand jury
investigations into the MCA cutout deals, and he argued that the
Mafia "might attempt to eliminate further witnesses because of
their knowledge of this conspiracy."

In other words, Eisman was saying he wanted to get Azoff and Passamano under oath before the Mafia killed them.

"MCA Head in Danger, Court Told," read the headline in the *Philadelphia Inquirer.*

MCA counsel Allen Susman called Eisman's allegations "ridiculous. He's making a claim that Azoff has ties to organized crime and there's no basis to that, no truth to it. The premise and the conclusion are simply wrong."

Nonetheless, MCA quickly assigned Azoff two full-time bodyguards who stood outside his office door during the day, accompanied him to business lunches, and guarded his home at night.

The brushfires kept flaring up.

On March 31, the *Los Angeles Times* reported that Sugar Hill Records had become the subject of both the Los Angeles and Newark, New Jersey, grand jury investigations because of the company's connections to Pisello. Citing information contained in MCA's internal audit report, the *Times* said that two deals arranged by Pisello on Sugar Hill's behalf had resulted in loans and advances to the company of more than $3.5 million from MCA in 1984 and 1985. "Investigators are trying to determine where the money from MCA went," the *Times* said.

The same day, however, the *Wall Street Journal* ran a surprisingly positive front-page feature on Irving Azoff that pretty much breezed over what it termed "the Pisello affair." "MCA Records' Chief Turns the Firm Around by Being Aggressive," read the headline. In a passage that might well have been written by Larry Solters himself, the *Journal* reported that "at the age of thirty-eight, Mr. Azoff . . . has emerged as one of the most successful executives in the record industry. In just three years, the longtime manager of rock bands has reversed a string of losses at MCA Records and turned that once-sleepy operation into an aggressive competitor against much larger record companies owned by CBS Inc. and Warner Communications Inc."

The *Journal* article was an effective piece of counterprogramming. At a time when the rest of the media sharks were circling, the *Journal* was granted broad access to MCA's embattled record company president. Starting with a morning ride to the MCA offices in Azoff's new black Mercedes coupe—with Azoff showily talking on the phone most of the way—the paper's reporter was allowed to witness Azoff presiding over a staff meeting (a rare event) and attend a negotiating session between Azoff and John Branca, Michael Jackson's attorney.

The result was a portrait of a brash, talented young record company president "racing through his business day at the pace of a rock video," apparently unconcerned with the controversy that swirled around him. The article noted that Azoff claimed he wasn't directly involved in any of the Pisello deals, but only MCA president Sid Sheinberg addressed the issue directly. "You have to ask yourself if [the record company executives] were as smart as they should have been in all this," the *Journal* quoted Sheinberg as saying. "The answer has to be: they were not."

There it was. Disguised as a mild criticism of its executives, the company's bottom-line legal position, one familiar to defense attorneys everywhere, was: "My client is not a criminal, Your Honor, he just made a stupid mistake."

The same day the *Journal* article appeared, "NBC Nightly News" came back with an update on "The New Payola," this time suggesting a link among independent promoters, top industry executives, and drug trafficking. Leonard Marks, a New York entertainment lawyer whose clients included the surviving Beatles and Yoko Ono, was shown in an interview saying that it was "no secret in the industry" that several independent promoters were close friends with record company heads who had drug habits. An instant after the attorney's remark, Walter Yetnikoff's picture came on the screen in close-up, as Ross reported that Yetnikoff had put the kabosh on the proposed RIAA investigation into the independents a few months back, and that CBS had been "by far the heaviest user" of independent promotion.

Few in the record industry who saw the NBC report failed to miss the implication. Reporter Ross and producer Ira Silverman were hinting that Walter Yetnikoff had a drug habit. Yetnikoff was so enraged by the report that he went to CBS chairman Tom Wyman and demanded he do something about it. Wyman complied. The next day, April 1, he issued a statement commending Yetnikoff's "distinguished career," saying "You may be sure he has our 100 percent confidence, admiration and support." He called the NBC report a "second-class example of broadcast journalism." NBC chairman Grant Tinker shot back in his own statement: "Tom Wyman's comments were unfortunate and his words ill-chosen. NBC News does not do second-class work."

On the same day, April 1, Senator Albert Gore, Jr., from Tennessee announced at a press conference on the steps of the Capitol that his Permanent Subcommittee on Investigations would begin immediately looking into alleged illicit practices used to promote records. Claiming that "payola is alive and well and worse than ever," Gore said that "the cumulative evidence is overwhelming that this practice has gotten out of hand and has come to dominate some portions of the industry in their decisions as to what records got on the air and which ones didn't. . . . Recent disclosures in the public media, as well as the announcements by the Justice Department that grand juries have been convened to investigate this matter, make it clear that something is wrong."

According to Gore, the new payola was "much more extensive, involving much larger sums of money" than in the old days, with promoters dividing regions of the country into "fiefdoms." He said that he and subcommittee staffers would begin nationwide interviews that week with promoters, disc jockeys, record executives, and "other individuals who wish to step forward with information."

When pressed by reporters about any new evidence uncovered by his staff, Gore was evasive, saying only that "some people in the industry are now more willing to speak up."

Asked if he'd been approached by record industry executives to launch an investigation, he sidestepped again, responding that "the record companies are the ones, I would say, who are most anxious about stamping this out."

He referred to a "conspiracy of silence" that had prevented investigators for his congressional subcommittee from coming up with any credible evidence of payola in 1984. "I think the tide has changed," he said. "Some people didn't come forward then, in some cases because of threats of being physically hurt."

The subcommittee would hold public hearings after the investigation, Gore said, adding, "our goal is not to establish the basis for criminal prosecution, but to determine whether or not current laws are working and whether changes are necessary."

Gore's press conference was a bombshell for the media. The story immediately went national, being picked up by the wire services, *Time, Newsweek, Business Week*, all the major networks, CNN, and local TV stations in most major cities. It leaped onto page one of the *Los Angeles Times*, which had been running the MCA-Pisello story inside in the financial section.

It didn't matter that there was really little new evidence of widespread payola, as subcommittee staffers privately confided to reporters, or that federal agents working the grand jury investigations in Los Angeles, New York, and Newark said they didn't know what Gore was talking about—for one thing, contrary to what the senator claimed, the Justice Department never announces the launching of grand jury investigations. The payola story was one that served everyone's needs, starting with the handsome young senator from Tennessee with presidential ambitions and a vivacious wife who'd recently become a household name for battling the record industry over the issue of explicit lyrics in pop recordings. And it was good for the record companies because it portrayed them as victims who were joining forces with the government to rid their industry of a scourge. It was also great fodder for the media, which could fill its yawning news holes with reports on the history of payola without having to waste time checking the current facts. The senator had said it and that was all that mattered.

In Los Angeles, Marvin Rudnick marveled at the impact of the NBC News reports. Responding to the barrage of publicity, the IRS criminal division had assigned eight agents to work the payola investigation. The IRS team had actually moved into the strike force offices, which was highly unusual—representatives from other agencies had a right to use offices in the strike force, but they rarely took advantage of the privilege.

The LAPD's Organized Crime Intelligence Division detectives seemed to be all over the place, too. Detective John St. John, the division's top intelligence analyst and an expert on the Gambino family, was really pushing the investigation, and someone at the department seemed to have a pipeline to NBC News, judging by the way the detectives were able to predict the content of the NBC News reports. The California Department of Justice had gotten into the act, and both the New York State Organized Crime Task Force and the Manhattan U.S. attorney's office were cooperating by providing information.

The thing had taken off like a horse race. The only problem was that as far as Rudnick could see, there was no finish line. Other than the fact that Joe Isgro was stinking rich and MCA claimed there was something criminal going on, there was still no hard evidence of wrongdoing to justify the tremendous amount of resources the government was committing to the case.

At the same time, Rudnick still had only one investigator assigned to the Pisello case, IRS agent John Anderson. And MCA was not making it easy on Rudnick and Anderson. In answer to the subpoenas, the company had turned over a mere handful of black three-ring binders marked according to subject matter—Sal Pisello, the Checker/Chess deal, the cutout deals, the Sugar Hill distribution deal, and so on. It was all slickly packaged, almost like a sales presentation introducing a new product line. Clearly, the company had given the strike force a carefully culled selection of documents from its files, one that, like the internal auditors' report, offered its executive version of events.

But that was not what Rudnick wanted, or for that matter what the subpoenas demanded. For investigative purposes, prosecutors want documents in their raw form, the way they occur in their natural state at the company, so they can determine for themselves what took place.

The collection of documents turned over was notable mostly for what it didn't contain. The was no memo traffic between executives explaining who Sal Pisello was or where he came from. Was he somebody's friend? A friend of a friend? Who introduced him? Who recommended him as an agent for cutout sales? It was as if he'd materialized out of thin air.

There was no file on Pisello's company, Consultants for World Records; no evidence of a background check or even a cursory credit check on an entity to which MCA had paid hundreds of thousands of dollars.

Likewise, there was no background information on Sugar Hill Records—no analysis of its viability, past sales performance, no assessment of the worth of the Checker/Chess catalog, for which MCA ultimately paid an equivalent of $3.5 million. MCA was going to invest millions more distributing Sugar Hill's product, but there was no indication that anyone did any research to determine if the investment was sound. Why did they want to take on Sugar Hill distribution? What was the overall business plan?

In short, there was none of the normal internal documentation you'd expect from a legitimate, supposedly well-run company like MCA.

Rudnick complained to Bill Billick, telling him that MCA's answer to the subpoena was unacceptable. There had to be more files than what was given to him.

"You don't understand the record business, Marvin," Billick responded. "This industry just doesn't use a lot of memoranda in making deals. A lot of it is done on gut feeling and on handshakes."

One thing the MCA documents did provide, however, was a dead-bang tax evasion case against Pisello. MCA turned over canceled checks that had been paid to Pisello and Consultants for World Records totaling more than $300,000 for the years 1983 to 1985, and Sal had not reported that money on his tax returns for those years.

Rudnick immediately asked for permission from Washington to prosecute Pisello on a second set of tax charges. He really wasn't interested in going after Pisello again, but he knew he needed to make some kind of case quickly or his Justice Department superiors would likely tell him to fold up the investigation and get on with something else.

Given that he wasn't getting compliance on his subpoenas from MCA, Rudnick's fallback plan was to bring new charges against Pisello in hopes of getting him to talk about what went on inside the company. Then, if it looked like the executives were lying about the nature of the payments, he would immunize Sal and use him as a witness against them. But he needed an indictment in his hip pocket if he were going to keep the investigation going until he uncovered the truth. He was relieved when, around the beginning of April, he received written permission from the strike force director in Washington, Michael Defeo—Iron Mike, as he was called—to proceed against Pisello.

Rudnick had been spending most of his time in March writing his brief responding to Pisello's appeal of his conviction. Sal's attorney was arguing that the conviction should be overturned because of prosecutorial misconduct. Among other things, Harland Braun claimed that Rudnick had prejudiced the jury at the trial with his comment about his pet dalmation being able to figure out the fire in Pisello's restaurant. Rudnick thought the appeal was laughably weak, but he put a lot of hours into his brief anyway. He didn't want to take any chances at this stage of the game.

Oral arguments before the Ninth Circuit Court of Appeals were set for April 10 at the Pasadena Court House. John Dubois and John Anderson went along with Rudnick that morning to watch him perform.

In the empty courtroom, the three federal judges listened impassively as Pisello's attorney made his pitch. Then it was Rudnick's turn. As he walked to the podium, before he even had time to say "May it please the court," Senior Justice William Wright leaned forward in his chair and said, "Mr. Rudnick, what was the tone of this case?"

Surprised at being questioned before he'd uttered a word, Rudnick paused for a moment, then said, "Your Honor, in order to answer that question I'd have to go off the record." Hearing no objection from the justices, he went on. "The tone of this case was not very happy. This was a case in which the presiding judge at one point smoked a cigarette with the defendant in the middle of the courtroom."

Judge Wright sat back in his chair, sighed, and exchanged what Rudnick thought was a knowing glance with the two other justices.

Rudnick then launched into his planned argument. At one point, Wright interrupted to ask him about the dog. Rudnick chuckled. "There really is a dog, Your Honor, a Dalmatian who lives just down the arroyo from me here in Pasadena, and he comes by our house every day." The judges chuckled, too.

When he was done, Rudnick thanked the court and turned to leave, figuring it would be weeks or months before the justices issued their written opinion. But as he pushed through the swinging gate leading to the gallery of the courtroom, Judge Wright said, "Mr. Rudnick, stop; we have an announcement to make. We are hereby ordering that this conviction has been confirmed."

Rudnick stood speechless. Dubois leaped up from his seat to congratulate him. "Marvin, that was amazing," he said, slapping him on the back. "I just attended two weeks of appellate advocacy school and this broke all the rules. You won it from the bench. That never happens."

Back at the strike force office, another surprise was waiting for them. Joe Isgro was coming in the next day for an interview. Voluntarily. And he was bringing all his corporate financial records with him—again, voluntarily.

Isgro's arrival the afternoon of April 11 caused something of a sensation at the strike force office. After all, he was supposed to be a bad guy, an acquaintance of major organized-crime figures and one of the kingpins of payola in the country. Bad guys usually don't come in to talk to prosecutors without being subpoenaed.

Isgro showed up accompanied by his so-called tax lawyer, Dennis

DiRicco, a former IRS attorney. The record promoter looked the part: black hair slicked back, pencil-thin black moustache, expensive black silk suit. But once the meeting got under way in the strike force conference room, he came across as surprisingly forthright, intelligent, calm, and very, very respectful.

He asked for no immunity or any other kind of consideration. He simply wanted the opportunity to tell the authorities what he knew and answer any questions they had, he said.

Rudnick and Dubois had expected him to come in whining and complaining about the unfairness of their investigation and how it violated his constitutional rights. But they heard none of that.

Right off the bat, Isgro admitted that he'd known Joe Armone for years, that he'd been his uncle's best friend and he considered him family. "I call him Uncle Joe and I have a linguine dinner with him every time I go to New York," he said.

But he said he'd never met John Gotti in his life and had never done business with any members of the Mafia, including Joe Armone.

He told them that he'd been destroyed by the NBC News reports; they had killed his business. He said the payola allegations were nonsense. Sure, the record companies paid him a lot of money—in some cases a ridiculous amount. But he didn't have to pay anyone to play the records. Before the news reports, he was hired to promote virtually every pop single put out by the major companies, so he had nothing to gain by violating the law to get one record played over another. The record companies paid him because he'd built relationships with program directors over many years. He was an expert, he had his ear to the street, and the program directors trusted his judgment about what records would help them build their listener audience.

For two hours, Isgro answered any and all questions, only occasionally deferring to DiRicco on specific queries about items on his federal tax returns, which the strike force had subpoenaed.

His demeanor was off-putting to Rudnick and Dubois. Either this guy was a great actor or somebody was trying to do him in, they thought. Isgro told them he'd learned through his own sources that NBC's Brian Ross was a longtime close friend of the RIAA's general counsel, Joel Schoenfeld. The record companies were just trying to force down the price of promotion, he said, so they sent Ross after him to try to put him out of business.

He said he thought that Irving Azoff was one of the driving forces behind the move against him. He told them of an incident he'd heard about involving Azoff. Several weeks before the NBC stories came out, Azoff was being interviewed by Rona Barrett for a segment on "Entertainment Tonight" about Tipper Gore and the PMRC. During a break in filming, while the camera was turned off, Barret asked him what was going on at MCA with all the Pisello allegations. Azoff told her it was nothing, just the media exaggerating a minor screw-up by his underlings. He then tried to get Barrett interested in looking at independent promotion and payola, telling her that it was the real story of the record business in the 1980s.

He couldn't prove it, Isgro said, but he believed that Azoff was using the independent promotion issue to try to deflect the spotlight away from himself and MCA.

A few minutes after the meeting broke up, Rudnick was on his way to the restroom when he ran into Isgro standing alone in the hallway, apparently waiting for DiRicco. Rudnick usually made it a point to never talk to a potential investigation target outside the presence of a witness. But this time, for some reason, he did.

"What do you know about Sal Pisello?" he asked as casually as he could. "Only what I've read in the newspapers," the promoter replied, just as casually.

As he walked away, Rudnick wasn't sure what he'd expected from the question. If the two men were both connected to the Gambino family, as people seemed to believe, chances were they knew each other. But it was highly unlikely that Isgro would have spilled his guts to a prosecutor standing outside the men's room in a federal office building.

Oddly enough, however, Rudnick believed Isgro. His gut feeling was that for all his money, perceived power, and wise guy connections, Isgro was a fall guy, a victim in the larger scheme of things. Not a very sympathetic victim, perhaps, but a victim nonetheless.

28

*"... because
I thought
there might
be a gun
in there"*

Marvin Rudnick was up at five the morning of April 29, 1986, shaving and putting on his best government-lawyer gray suit. It was going to be a big day, one he'd been eagerly anticipating.

He was meeting IRS agent John Anderson at Los Angeles International Airport to catch the Delta Airlines seven o'clock flight to Atlanta. From there they would hop a puddle-jumper commuter to Montgomery, Alabama, where they would be met by FBI agents John Mahoney and Jeff Dossett and be taken to an undisclosed location for an interview with John LaMonte.

The LaMonte meeting was Rudnick's idea. He'd pushed it with Ted Gale and had gotten him to call Assistant U.S. Attorney Bruce Repetto, the prosecutor in the New Jersey investigation, and ask for a sit-down. Convincing Repetto hadn't been easy. He was naturally protective of his star witness and his case, and after a year of hard work he didn't want anything to happen that could screw things up.

But Rudnick argued effectively through Gale that LaMonte's knowledge of Sal Pisello's activities was critical to both the tax evasion case and the broader investigation into what happened inside MCA, and Repetto reluctantly agreed to allow the interview.

From studying the documents he'd subpoenaed, Rudnick was convinced that the cutout deal Pisello brokered through Roulette Records was the key. Of all the MCA-Pisello transactions, the cutout sale involved—potentially, at least—the most money to Pisello. But since Pisello hadn't been paid directly by MCA on the deal, there was no way of telling how much money he'd pocketed, or exactly what he did to earn it.

The cutout deal was also the link between Pisello and MCA in California and Levy, Vastola, and their mob henchmen on the East Coast. What had really gone on between the two groups? Rudnick was hoping that LaMonte held the missing pieces of the puzzle. "If LaMonte can give us a clear picture of what went down at the other end of the deal, it will help us understand what took place at our end," he told Gale.

Rudnick knew the most difficult part of investigating a sophisticated white-collar scam was determining exactly what crime had been committed. How did it work? Who were the victims? Who earned money and didn't pay taxes on it? Who were the witnesses?

All the strike force had at this point was MCA's version of events, which Rudnick didn't believe for a minute. Why should he? MCA's own board of directors didn't buy the record executives' story. The minutes of a February 5, 1985, MCA board meeting, which Bill Billick had turned over to the strike force in response to Rudnick's subpoenas, showed that members of the board's audit committee had raised serious questions about the internal audit report.

In a discussion of the Pisello affair, Felix Rohatyn had recommended that management make some "personnel changes" at the record company. Another board member, Mary Gardiner Jones, had agreed, saying pointedly that Irving Azoff was responsible for the people he'd brought into the company. Howard Baker said bluntly that he didn't believe the board had been told all the facts and that the matter required "further investigation."

"Well that's what I'm here for, Senator Baker, Sir," Rudnick joked to himself as he sat next to John Anderson on the plane that morning. "I'm just trying to find out what the record executives knew and when they knew it."

One thing Rudnick couldn't figure was why, given the board's reaction, nobody at the record company had been fired for the Pisello fiasco. Not only that, but according to his information, the company had recently extended Azoff's and Myron Roth's employment contracts—for more money! Roth—the man identified in the internal audit report as the executive who approved the dealings with Pisello—was rewarded with a new three-year contract at $400,000 a year.

What was that all about? Rudnick wondered. It was almost as if they were being paid to keep quiet. Hush money. What if this thing, whatever it was, went up higher in the company than Azoff?

Rudnick caught himself doing it again. His colleagues in the office called it "what if-ing." Marvin was great at it—coming up with plausible scenarios that could explain how a certain scheme worked, the underlying motivation, what the real purpose of it was. John Dubois in particular was impressed with the way Rudnick's mind operated. In sessions with agents, he'd seen Marvin sift through a set of seemingly unrelated facts and come up with connections that no one else saw. Sometimes he was so far ahead of the others in his theorizing that they couldn't quite grasp what he was saying. Dubois thought Rudnick was brilliant, the best prosecutor he'd ever known. "Every U.S. attorney's office in the country should have a Marvin Rudnick. But just one," he joked.

Watching out the window of the commuter plane as it began its descent into Montgomery, Rudnick stared down at the deep spring-green patchwork of the southeastern United States, criss-crossed by the silver threads of the Chattahoochee River flowing along the border of Georgia and Alabama. It was a world away from the sprawling steel-and-concrete grids of Los Angeles, New York, and Philadelphia. But somewhere down there was a frightened man on the run who might hold the answers to the mystery, who could possibly connect MCA, Morris Levy, Gaetano Vastola, and God knows who else in a criminal conspiracy that turned on a shipment of thirty-five-cent record albums. Who would have thought?

John Mahoney was waiting for them as they got off the plane, a jowly, ruddy-faced Irishman with eyes that twinkled with wry humor and a paunch that poured over his belt. Mahoney drove them directly to a commercial strip on the outskirts of Montgomery where the U.S. Marshals Service had stashed LaMonte in a Holiday Inn. As a protected witness, LaMonte was officially in the custody of the Marshals Service, not the FBI. In fact, although Mahoney and Dossett were the case agents on the New Jersey investigation, they were not supposed to know LaMonte's whereabouts, for security reasons. If they needed to meet with him, they contacted the Marshals Service, which set up a rendezvous. It was the service that had picked Montgomery as a sight for the meeting with Rudnick and Anderson.

In the motel room, Rudnick and Anderson shook hands with LaMonte. He was younger, more boyish, than Rudnick had pictured. Like the two FBI agents, he was dressed casually in slacks and a sport shirt. He seemed genuinely glad to meet them and eager to talk.

They got right down to business. LaMonte and Anderson sat on the couch. Rudnick pulled up a chair facing them across a small coffee table and took out his pen and note pad.

"Sorry, no notes," Mahoney said from the position he'd taken, propped up on one of the room's double beds.

"What?" Rudnick responded.

Mahoney shrugged. "Repetto's orders. He said no notes."

Rudnick looked at Anderson, who was equally surprised by the new wrinkle in the situation. Repetto's edict meant they wouldn't be able to use anything they learned from LaMonte as evidence in the event of a trial in their case. Not unless LaMonte testified.

The New Jersey prosecutor was playing it very close to the vest, making sure he remained in control of the situation. Rudnick didn't like it, but he recognized the move as a smart one on Repetto's part. He put away his note pad and started questioning LaMonte, carefully and chronologically, cross-examining every step of the way and trying to memorize what was said.

From the outset he was impressed. LaMonte was a good, credible witness, answering questions forthrightly and in vivid detail. The story poured out of him as if it had been bottled up for too long.

LaMonte told about how he'd first met Pisello at the 1984 NARM convention and assumed he was an employee of MCA because he was carrying around an official computer printout of the company's cutout inventory that was marked "Property of Sal Pisello." He told about meeting Morris Levy at the hotel and how Levy had rejected his first offer for the cutouts.

That made sense, Rudnick thought. He'd wondered how Pisello, who knew nothing about the cutout business, could have negotiated with an experienced professional like LaMonte without getting taken to the cleaners on the transaction. Clearly this was a Levy deal from the start, and Sal was just a middleman installed by Levy. But why?

LaMonte described the meeting at the Palm restaurant in Los Angeles with Brocco and Pisello. That's where he met Azoff and a bunch of other MCA executives whose names he didn't recall, he said. Actually, he didn't realize he'd met Azoff until later when he saw his picture in *Billboard* magazine, he said. "He was the little guy, wearing a white suit."

LaMonte explained how he'd learned for sure that his load of cutouts had been creamed when Sam Passamano called him on the phone and confirmed it from MCA's internal shipping documents. Brocco was in his office at the time and overheard the conversation, he said. Later, when he learned that Sam had been fired, he assumed it was because Brocco had told Vastola about the call and word had gotten back to MCA that Passamano had given him this information.

He told about the meeting at Roulette Records when he gave the $30,000 in cash to Levy, Vastola, and Giovanelli. He described how they'd played with a wad of cash bound up with a rubber band, tossing it around the office like a football, and how Levy had sent his secretary off with $300 to buy chocolate.

The scene struck Rudnick as just the sort of thing that juries often seize on as evidence of guilt in the midst of a complicated white-collar conspiracy trial: the defendants spending the proceeds of their illegal activities on gluttony. LaMonte would be terrific on the witness stand, he thought.

LaMonte wasn't finished. He told about how, at the same meeting in Levy's office, the three men had seemed to know in advance that Pisello was going to be sentenced to two years in prison on the tax charges Rudnick prosecuted. He recalled that when he asked them what Sal's share of the thirty grand was going to be, they'd joked that Sal wasn't going to need his cut because he was "going on an expense-paid two-year vacation."

LaMonte went on to describe the day of his beating, recalling that as he sat slumped in the front seat of Brocco's car on the drive back to his home that afternoon he'd kept one foot propped against the glove compartment "because I thought there might be a gun in there and was afraid I was being driven to a hit."

Rudnick kept steering the narration back to what LaMonte knew about MCA and Pisello. The other information was provocative, but it didn't help the West Coast investigation.

"Any idea of how Sal got into MCA in the first place?" he asked.

"Just what Brocco told me," LaMonte replied almost casually, as if Rudnick had already heard the story. When the prosecutor's blank look indicated he hadn't, LaMonte recounted the evening in 1985 when he'd put the same question to Brocco.

Rudnick and Anderson listened to the reconstructed conversation about Pisello "doing a job" for an unknown MCA executive. According to Brocco, Pisello wasn't supposed to know who he did the job for but he somehow found out. That's when he went to Levy and they concocted a plan for taking money out of MCA. "So they own somebody there," LaMonte quoted Brocco as saying.

Rudnick looked at Mahoney, who was leaning back against the headboard of the double bed, smiling broadly at his witness's bombshell. "How about that one?" he seemed to say.

Damn! Rudnick thought. Could that be it? Could all these shenanigans with cutout records and break-dance mats and Latin music labels be a payoff for a crime, an act committed years ago and having nothing to do with the business of MCA? Was that the real motive behind the transactions?

As wild as it sounded, there was a certain logic to the scenario. If you were a high-level MCA executive being extorted by the mob, what better way to funnel money out of the company than through the record division, with all its Byzantine bookkeeping practices and murky contracts and payment procedures? It made sense. But how to prove it? He had no mandate for launching a wider investigation. Certainly not based on this kind of second-hand hearsay.

He asked about Consultants for World Records. "All I know is that's the phony-ass company of Sal's that I was supposed to pay the money for the cutouts to," LaMonte said. He hadn't known that Fritzy Giovanelli and Rocco Musacchia were partners with Pisello in Consultants. He knew Rocco as "an enforcer," he said. "He was the guy they kept threatening to send down on me if I didn't pay."

LaMonte likewise knew very little about Pisello's connection to Sugar Hill Records. From conversations he'd overheard in Levy's office, however, he'd gotten the impression that "wise guys owned a piece of Sugar Hill. Morris controlled Joe Robinson. They all called him 'Morris's nigger.'" "They" in this case were Levy, Giovanelli, Pisello, and probably Vastola. LaMonte recalled going to Sugar Hill's New Jersey offices with Sonny Brocco one day. "And Brocco walked around like he owned the place. I heard him call Robinson a nigger to his face, and Robinson took it."

He said he understood that the same group was part owner of a New Jersey company that manufactured album jackets and cassette insert cards for a number of major record companies. He explained the significance: "You gotta understand, the key to counterfeiting is the graphics, the artwork. It's the hardest thing to get. The music and plastic parts are easy. So here you have major companies handing over their plates, their camera-ready art, to this company."

It was getting dark outside. They'd been talking for nearly three hours. LaMonte was growing tired and so were Rudnick and Anderson. They'd been on the go since before dawn and hadn't even checked into their hotel yet. They thanked LaMonte for his help and said good-bye. Mahoney and Dossett drove them to the hotel where the two agents were also staying and suggested they all go out to dinner later. That sounded good; it had been a long day.

They ate at P. J. Tripps, a crowded, touristy restaurant located in a remodeled old factory overlooking the state's capitol building in downtown Montgomery. Mostly they talked shop, swapping war stories about their respective run-ins with Mafia soldiers and government bureaucrats. They talked about Rocco and Fritzy, Levy and Vastola, with Mahoney providing most of the play-by-play.

Rudnick liked Mahoney. He was street-smart, confident, and very proud of the Levy-Vastola investigation. He didn't know much about the MCA end of things, but he had his side of the case down pat and wasn't about to get fooled on the facts. Mahoney encouraged Rudnick and Anderson to "go after MCA." Repetto was being too cautious, he said, sticking too closely to what occurred with the East Coast wise guys and not looking at the bigger picture. Rudnick would have liked to have had Mahoney working with him in Los Angeles. He was aggressive and extremely inquisitive.

By the time the evening ended—after a drive around the Capitol area looking for some sort of landmark statue to the Confederacy that they never found—the four government men were in agreement that between their two investigations they were on to something very big, possibly the most far-reaching cases of their careers.

They promised they'd continue to communicate and exchange information.

On the flight back home the next morning, Rudnick felt satisfied with the results of the twenty-four-hour excursion. Although La-Monte couldn't provide much information on what happened inside MCA, his testimony would sink Pisello. LaMonte could place Sal in the middle of the cutout deal, thereby shooting down his likely defense that the money he received from MCA was merely a loan. That was Sal's longtime M.O., disguising business transactions as unpaid loans so he wouldn't have to pay taxes.

With LaMonte, Rudnick knew he could convict Pisello a second time for tax evasion. Which meant Sal might be forced to make a deal. He was already going to prison on the first conviction. He'd get even more time on a second. At his age, he might be willing to do anything to avoid going to jail twice, maybe even roll over and talk, give up his benefactor inside MCA.

It wasn't going to be a piece of cake, though, especially if there really was some illegal act in the background. Plus, there could be political problems with New Jersey. LaMonte, after all, was their guy. They controlled access to him.

Still, based on his dinner discussion with Mahoney and Dossett and their pledge of future cooperation, Rudnick felt confident that he would eventually get to the bottom of what had transpired in the MCA-Pisello affair.

He didn't know that his visit to Montgomery would be the last time he'd ever talk to the New Jersey investigators or LaMonte about the case.

29

"1000 percent legitimate"

When Rudnick got back to his office on the morning of May 1, John Dubois greeted him with some surprising news: Joe Isgro had just filed a $25 million antitrust lawsuit against twelve major record companies (every one except CBS, in fact) and the RIAA. The promoter claimed the companies and their trade association had illegally conspired to put him out of business in order to cut the cost of promotion.

"That doesn't sound like a mob guy to me," Rudnick said. "He's opening himself up to testifying under oath. They usually avoid that like the plague."

Dubois agreed. Isgro's action was a puzzlement to the entire payola investigation team, which now numbered eleven—eight IRS agents, two LAPD detectives, and Dubois. They had to hand it to Isgro, he had balls. Even if it wasn't such a smart move on his part.

The way Dubois saw it, Isgro's lawsuit would be a boon to the payola investigation. It would bring out a lot of information in depositions concerning both Isgro's operation and the record promotion practices of the entire industry. Dubois could simply subpoena the court records in the civil case, thereby cutting down on his agents' legwork. The strike force would be in the enviable position of having the person they were targeting putting himself on a stage and educating them about his activities. "Isgro will be doing our discovery for us," he thought.

Early on, Dubois and his team had decided they'd focus primarily on Isgro and seek the cooperation of their sister strike force offices on the promoters in other cities. The Philadelphia strike force was contacted about Fred DiSipio, and Ted Gale had arranged to meet in New York later that week with Barbara Jones, who was chief of the Brooklyn strike force and was heading up the grand jury investigation launched by Rudy Giuliani.

One thing Dubois was learning was that, contrary to popular belief, the government was not monolithic in its war on crime. There was a surprising amount of jealousy, competition, and secrecy among federal and local law enforcement agencies. Even different offices of the same agency often held back on one another, afraid that if they revealed too much information about their investigation to their counterparts, the case might be stolen away from them. The Los Angeles investigators were very concerned about sharing information with New York, primarily because of Giuliani, a renowned grabber of cases and credit. Since the payola investigation was national in scope, New York could take their information and indict Isgro themselves, Dubois's investigators warned.

New York, of course, had the same fears about Los Angeles. As a result, "Tell them as little as possible but get as much as you can" became the operative slogan for cooperation—on both sides.

It was a problem for Dubois and his team. Giuliani had beaten them to the punch with his blunderbuss subpoena of all the record companies' promotion documents, so every place they went they heard the same thing from record company lawyers: "We already gave you that." They'd have to explain, sheepishly, that things didn't work that way. Los Angeles needed its own copies of the documents. It quickly became evident to people in the record business that the government's left hand didn't know what its right was doing.

The record industry itself was another problem. While the company presidents all agreed to talk to investigators, Dubois quickly got the impression they did so primarily to find out what the investigators knew. The executives weren't uncooperative in their interviews, but they weren't exactly helpful either. Some adopted a smug, disdainful attitude, rolling their eyes toward the ceiling if an agent misused record business terminology or displayed ignorance of some arcane industry practice. At times, Dubois and his investigators suspected the industry was laughing at them, that the executives called each other on the phone after the agents left their offices and hooted at their ignorance. They felt like they were being outmaneuvered in a foreign territory.

The agents began compiling glossaries of record business jargon: an "add" is a record added to a radio station playlist; a "breaker" is a record that just entered *Radio & Records*'s weekly Top 40 chart; "CHR" stands for contemporary hit radio, a fancy name for Top 40. They were knocking themselves out trying to learn the ways of the record business so they could ask the right questions, and the industry was playing it cool. It was worse than stonewalling, in a way.

Dubois didn't get it. If these companies were being forced by the independent promoters to spend extra millions to get their music played on the radio, then why weren't they helping the investigation? The record executives impressed Dubois as a group of overpaid men living in a fantasy world where appearances were everything and there was very little to do except gossip. He was amazed at the nasty things they said about each other to the agents. And he heard nothing good about Irving Azoff. Practically every company president they talked to had his own Azoff anecdote, usually ending with, "And then he just said, 'So I lied.'" One even claimed that Randy Newman wrote his song "Short People" with Azoff in mind.

As it turned out, there was no consensus among record executives about the existence of payola. Some said yes, widespread payoffs were taking place; they knew it but just couldn't prove it. Others said no, the idea of an organized, national payola scheme controlled by the Mafia was a ludicrous notion, and the government was naive to believe it. Dubois wondered. If payola really were going on, then how come nobody could point to a specific instance? How could something so pervasive be so hidden? At times he felt like he was chasing a ghost.

This sort of investigation was new to Dubois. A thirty-one-year-old native of Albuquerque, New Mexico, he'd graduated Phi Beta Kappa from Vanderbilt in 1976 and earned his law degree at the University of New Mexico in 1980. His job history included a stint in the felony trial division of the Albuquerque D.A.'s office, where he'd specialized in violent crimes, mostly murder cases. He'd been a trial attorney for the Office of Special Prosecutions in Santa Fe, a unit created specially to prosecute crimes arising from the New Mexico penitentiary riot of 1980. And he'd served for a year as chief counsel to the New Mexico Organized Crime Commission. But when he joined the Los Angeles strike force in October 1985, Dubois had little experience with white-collar crime.

Which is why he came to rely on Rudnick for help and advice. Dubois had liked Rudnick from the moment he met him. On his first morning on the job at the strike force, he walked into the office and there was Rudnick, sitting at one of the secretaries' word processors, sleeves rolled up, tie loosened, pounding away on some motion. "You the new guy?" he said, getting up and offering his hand and an impish smile. "Welcome to the strike force. We don't take prisoners."

Dubois loved sitting around in Rudnick's big corner office, bull-shitting and exchanging investigative theories. Rudnick had a tenacious curiosity and was famous around the office for spinning new cases out of old ones. He was fascinated by the questions that inevitably were left unanswered by any organized crime or white-collar prosecution. He had a theory that by pursuing all the unanswered questions in individual cases you could eventually connect all the bad guys. "If organized crime is ubiquitous, then shouldn't we be ubiquitous, too?" he argued.

Most prosecutors didn't think that way. They took a case brought to them by an investigative agency, zeroed in on the target, got an indictment, prosecuted, and moved on to the next case. But Rudnick was a digger who loved getting his hands dirty unearthing evidence. "An indictment is just a search warrant," he liked to say. Or, "You don't know how good evidence is until someone tries to destroy it." Dubois often thought about putting together a little red book of Rudnick quotations.

Rudnick's views marked him as something of an oddball at the strike force. Jim Henderson, Ted Gale's predecessor as chief, once warned Dubois, "Don't let this guy influence you too much; he's sort of a wild man."

But Dubois found that Rudnick was tremendously successful in his methodology. In bull sessions on cases, he'd hypothesize out loud, "If this exists, then what else has to logically exist? If this guy created this phony document to disguise income, what other documents did he have to create?" And inevitably, it seemed to Dubois, investigators would eventually find the other documents that Rudnick had concluded must exist.

Rudnick also seemed to have a real handhold on human nature. He was like a walking lie detector. Whenever a witness told a story that didn't jibe, he would pick it up immediately. "Sometimes people give you more information by lying to you than by telling you the truth," he'd say.

That sort of guidance proved immensely helpful to Dubois in the payola investigation. This wasn't like a robbery or a murder case, where it was easy to tell the victim from the perpetrator. Violent crime had that kind of purity to it. But with the payola investigation, Dubois was never sure whom he was talking to. The record companies supposedly were the victims, but it was their money that was fueling the alleged payola scheme. Isgro supposedly was the bad guy, but he claimed the record companies were out to get him. Which side was telling the truth? Who was the victim and who was the victimizer?

The investigation of Isgro turned into a heavy-duty paper chase as the IRS began pulling together his tax returns, bank records, and telephone logs. Using a California Department of Justice computer system and three full-time operators, they analyzed Isgro's phone calls going back half a dozen years, a tremendously time-consuming job. They researched the history of his various companies and checked into his employment record, looking for blank spaces in his past, trying to determine how this former marine and Vietnam veteran from Mafia central casting was able to rise so far and so fast in the record business.

They chased a number of leads down blind alleys. In one such instance, an LAPD surveillance team turned up an acquaintance of Isgro's, a student-actress who was maintaining an extravagant lifestyle—Mercedes convertible, fancy clothes, expensive apartment—with no visible source of income. The immediate suspicion—fueled by Brian Ross's NBC News report—was that the woman was a call girl employed by the promoter to provide sex in exchange for airplay. Investigators ran down every aspect of the woman's life, even checked her parents' finances to see if that might be where her money was coming from. It wasn't. After weeks of work, one of the LAPD detectives came into Dubois's office downcast, with some documents in his hand. It turned out that the woman had recently been awarded a six-figure insurance settlement from an automobile accident caused by another driver. She wasn't a prostitute; she was a victim. All that work had been for nothing.

Rudnick, meanwhile, was having his own problems. In addition to the Pisello-MCA investigation and assisting Dubois on payola, he had three other cases in the works and he was frustrated that he had so little time to devote to the one he believed in most. The Pisello-MCA investigation excited him like nothing had since his days as a public-interest prosecutor in Florida. Back there he was still remembered as the ballsy kid who once convicted two accused Cuban marijuana smugglers by using spy satellite photographs and a coast guard expert in ocean currents to prove that the pair's boat, though seized outside U.S. territorial waters west of Cuba, nonetheless had been on its way to Florida.

The Pisello-MCA case made Rudnick feel that way again—passionate about being a prosecutor. No matter what else he was doing, the investigation pulled at him.

He was anxious about going off to Phoenix for six or seven weeks and leaving the investigation in the hands of John Anderson. He was an honest, intelligent agent. But he wasn't as aggressive as Rudnick would have liked. Anderson thought they had a good second tax case against Pisello, but beyond that he showed little enthusiasm for pursuing the case deeper into MCA. He hadn't even opened the boxes of subpoenaed MCA documents and read them. Without his daily prodding, Rudnick feared the investigation might lie fallow the whole summer and wind up being killed by Washington for lack of results. He felt helpless.

Rudnick was back in court with Pisello again the morning of May 3, standing in front of Harry Hupp to hear the judge set a date for Sal to start his prison sentence. Rudnick, of course, made a motion to have Pisello jailed immediately. "There is substantial new evidence linking him to criminal activities in the record business," he told Hupp. Specifically, Pisello had "received approximately $700,000 in income involving record industry business transactions for tax years more recent than those for which he was convicted," he said, adding that "Pisello did not report such income on his pertinent tax returns." Rudnick argued that, because of possible new charges that might be brought against Pisello, "we believe there is good cause for him to flee, Your Honor."

Not surprisingly, Hupp denied the motion and set May 23 as the date for Pisello to voluntarily surrender himself to begin serving his prison sentence. In the meantime, he was to remain free on $15,000 bail.

On his way out of the Federal Court Building that day, Pisello gave an impromptu, ten-minute interview to a small group of reporters who'd turned up for the hearing. It was the first time he'd talked publicly about the events that had befallen him, and he apparently had a lot he wanted to get off his chest.

"I'm not a member of organized crime and never have been; I'll go to prison for twenty years if anyone can prove that," he said. "I live in a two-room flat. I can't even pay my doctors for the aneurysm I just had. I go to church every Sunday and the only organization I belong to is the Holy Name Society."

When one reporter asked what church he attended, Pisello fixed him with a long, cold stare. Coke-bottle-thick glasses magnified his blind right eye. "St. Anthony's," he said, flatly.

He denied any wrongdoing in connection with the MCA transactions, which he characterized as "1000 percent legitimate."

"I been in the record industry one year and I'm supposed to have destroyed the industry? They are ruining the entire record industry over me—one man? What did I do? I ask you, what did I do? Mr. Rudnick has got me painted as the reincarnation of Al Capone, and, believe me, I don't know what the hell it's all about."

Asked how he ended up working out of MCA Records headquarters, Pisello said, "I just went in off the street. All I did was walk up to MCA and make an appointment with Myron Roth. I said I represented Sugar Hill Records. I was a friendly guy who could talk. I was trying to get involved in selling records."

He defended MCA as "the nicest corporation in the world. There was nothing wrong in this on MCA's part." He met Irving Azoff several times but exchanged "just ten words with him in the year that I was there," he said.

Who was Rocco Musacchia? he was asked. "My business partner," he shot back. "I've known him since we were kids." And

Fritzy Giovanelli? "A friend of Rocco's that he wanted to sell 25 percent of the company [Consultants for World Records] to. I met the man once and I thought he was a gentleman."

And yes, he knew Gaetano Vastola, "but I never seen him in twenty-five years." Morris Levy, too, was an old friend from New York whom he hadn't seen for years prior to the cutout deal. "They used to come in my restaurant in 1962, the Red Sauce. I been in the food business all my life, forty-three years. I suppose every restaurant owner in the world oughta be in jail."

Pisello said he'd bumped into Levy by chance walking along the beach in Santa Monica in 1984, and he'd gotten him interested in buying the cutouts. "He's a gentleman, as far as I'm concerned."

He wanted to cooperate with the grand jury investigation, Pisello said. "I got nothin' to hide. All this organized crime stuff started with that guy [LaMonte] back in Pennsylvania, and the guy's a crook himself. I'm a victim. Mr. Rudnick has made me a victim. Me, MCA, Roulette, and Levy—we're the victims here."

"Mr. Rudnick has called me everything under the sun. I'm sixty-three years old. Am I so clever that all these people couldn't put me in court before? Mr. Rudnick says I'm organized crime. I don't know what it's all about to this day. I look in the mirror in the morning and say, 'Who the hell am I?'"

Pisello was starting to ramble. His attorney, Harland Braun, who had been standing a discreet three feet behind him all during the dialogue, suddenly cut in. "Do you think a member of organized crime would give you an interview in the court hallway?" he asked the reporters.

It was an ironic comment for Braun to make. For months previous he'd been distancing himself from Pisello in interviews, pointing out to reporters that he was "just hired to represent him in this tax case, that's all." Braun had a number of prominent clients at the time, including film director John Landis, who was charged with (and ultimately acquitted of) manslaughter in the death of Vic Morrow and two child actors on the set of the movie *The Twilight Zone*. "I don't want people to get the impression I'm a mob lawyer," Braun said to one reporter.

As Braun tugged at Pisello's elbow to signal the end of the interview, Pisello turned to the reporter who had questioned him about his church attendance. Cocking his head to focus with his good eye and smiling slightly, he said. "You asked me about my church like you didn't believe me. Well, I used to be an altar boy."

In the strike force office the following Monday, Rudnick and Dubois read Pisello's comments in a *Daily Variety* article and howled. "Can you believe such nonsense?" Rudnick laughed.

The next day, May 6, they read in the *Los Angeles Times* that MCA was going to buy Irving Azoff's three outside companies—Front Line Management, Full Moon Records, and Facilities Merchandising, a company that sold T-shirts and souvenirs at rock concerts. The acquisition plan was announced at the company's annual shareholders meeting in Chicago. A press release stated that "Irving Azoff, president of MCA Records and Music Group, and one of the principals of the acquired companies, will enter into a new long-term pact with MCA Inc. and will oversee the new acquisitions."

The price MCA paid for the companies was not disclosed at the time, but it was later revealed to be five hundred thousand shares of MCA stock, worth about $30 million at the time. The acquisition surprised and angered many in the record business. For one thing, although the Azoff companies were private and therefore did not report earnings, industry estimates of their combined worth ranged from $3 million to $5 million. Front Line's artist roster had grayed a bit in recent years. Most of its big names—Don Henley, Heart, Chicago, Dan Fogelberg, Stevie Nicks, Jimmy Buffett, Michael McDonald, and Boz Scaggs—were now middle-aged and wealthy, so they didn't record or tour as much as they used to. The Eagles and Steely Dan had disbanded. Consequently, Front Line was not as big a money-maker as it once was. Full Moon's only assets were a handful of recording contracts, notably Fogelberg and Chicago. There was no Full Moon building, and the label's records were manufactured, marketed, and distributed by Warner Brothers. According to MCA proxy statements, Azoff received a little over $200,000 annually from his 25 percent stake in Facilities Merchandising, meaning the company earned profits of less than $1 million a year.

Unless MCA knew something the rest of the record industry didn't, the acquisitions appeared to be MCA's way of giving Azoff a fat bonus while minimizing his tax bite. Sheinberg made the deal without consulting MCA's corporate finance department, which no doubt would have pointed out that a cash purchase would have allowed the company to take about a $12 million tax write-off on the deal. Instead, Azoff got the tax break.

The most controversial part of the acquisition involved MCA Records taking over the management company. "You cannot be in the record business and manage artists on your own label—it's a conflict of interest," groused David Geffen, echoing the sentiments of many label executives and artist managers. "How can a manager get the best deal for his client if the manager also works for the record company? It's very disturbing. If it's legal, it shouldn't be."

It is ironic that, twenty-four years earlier, Robert Kennedy's Justice Department took a similar view of MCA's acquiring Decca Records and Universal Studios. At the time, MCA Artists was the largest talent agency in Hollywood. MCA also owned a company called Revue Productions, which was then the most prolific producer of television programming. Claiming it was a conflict of interest and anticompetitive for MCA to both represent performers and control companies that employed them, the Justice Department's antitrust division filed a criminal complaint against the company on July 18, 1962, charging violations of the Sherman Antitrust Act. The government also obtained a temporary restraining order barring MCA's purchase of Decca and Universal. Rather than stand trial on the charges and hold up the acquisition, MCA eventually signed a consent decree with the government agreeing to divest itself of its talent agency and refrain from representing performers in the future.

At the time of the divestiture, MCA's lead counsel in the negotiations with the Justice Department was Allen Susman. Among the clients of MCA Artists was an actor by the name of Ronald Reagan. In 1986, with Ronald Reagan in the White House, the Justice Department apparently saw no problem with MCA reentering the same business it was forced out of in 1963. In announcing the Front Line acquisition, MCA attorneys said the company had sought and obtained Justice Department approval for the deal.

Rudnick wasn't thinking about antitrust, however, when he read about the Front Line acquisition in the newspaper. "MCA is buying up the evidence," he thought. "They're circling the wagons to control the information. They can't afford to leave Front Line out there and possibly expose MCA to inconsistent evidence." Rudnick checked himself. No, he wasn't being paranoid; he was just being logically suspicious, like he was paid to be.

Several months earlier, two investigators from the district attorney's office had come to the strike force looking for information about the management company. It seems one of their surveillance teams had observed a Front Line employee meeting with a suspected Mafia hitman. It could have been nothing, of course. Rudnick never heard anything more from the D.A.'s office. But juxtaposed with Pisello, the story Rudnick had just heard from LaMonte, and all that was going on with Morris Levy back in New Jersey, the fact that a Front Line employee may have met with a hired killer seemed awfully suspicious. For him to think otherwise would be irresponsible, Rudnick thought. He wouldn't be doing his job.

The acquisition placed Front Line under the wing of MCA. Now any law enforcement agency seeking information from the management company would have to subpoena the parent corporation, whose lawyers had already demonstrated an ability to schmooze the Justice Department into allowing them to pick and choose what they turned over. Very neat.

On the morning of May 8, the week before he was to leave for Phoenix, Rudnick found an envelope from Judge Hupp's clerk in his office mail slot. Inside was a copy of a letter Hupp had sent to the Bureau of Prisons on Pisello's behalf: "I am attaching two medical reports received by me in connection with the proceeding at which the date for Mr. Pisello's surrender is to occur," Hupp wrote. "They show that Mr. Pisello had, in October 1985, an operation for an abdominal aortic aneurysm. He apparently also suffers from hypertension. The selection of the appropriate facility for Mr. Pisello may, therefore, need to consider the availability of medical resources for any post-operative care necessary, and the availability of medicine for hypertension.

"I continue to believe that a low-security institution is appropriate for Mr. Pisello. The Strike Force attorney who prosecuted the instant case states that there may be further legal proceedings involving Mr. Pisello, presumably in the Central District. If so, and if otherwise suitable, placement at the Boron or Lompoc camps might be appropriate. Very truly yours, Harry L. Hupp."

Rudnick resisted the temptation to crumple up the letter and throw it across the room. Boron and Lompoc were country clubs.

There were no bars or high walls there. Inmates were housed in dorms. They had tennis courts. Thanks to Hupp, Sal was going to do soft time, thereby lessening his incentive to cooperate with the continuing investigation.

There was nothing Rudnick could do about it now, however. Hupp had already taken a bite out of him in court. To protest the recommendation would just look like sour grapes. Besides, it wasn't a prosecutor's place to publicly criticize a judge's decision. He would have liked to know why Hupp cared so much about Pisello's welfare, but he knew he wasn't going to find that out by yelling about it. The case was closed and he had another one to put on in Phoenix.

30

"Now you have two of them"

Throughout the summer of 1986, with the Pisello-MCA investigation all but idled by Rudnick's preoccupation with his other cases, MCA fought back against what the company saw as its other enemy: the news media, in particular the *Los Angeles Times*.

By the time Pisello entered the federal prison camp in Lompoc, California, the *Times* had published more than a dozen articles that focused on Pisello's dealings with MCA, the New Jersey investigation of Levy and Vastola, the cutout record trade, and questionable practices in the record business in general.

Other publications had reported the Pisello-MCA story, but it was the *Times*'s coverage that most upset MCA. The newspaper had broken the story about Pisello's mob ties and his role in the cutout sale, and later compounded the offense by publishing the contents of the company's internal audit report. All the other news coverage had flowed from that. In MCA's view, it was the *Los Angeles Times* that first threw the shit at the fan.

Allen Susman was particularly indignant at the newspaper's revelation of the audit report, going so far as to accuse the reporter of committing a "morally questionable act" in obtaining the confidential company document.

At one point, Susman refused to speak to the reporter on the telephone unless a *Times* editor monitored the conversation. "I desire anyone in a position of authority to be on the line because this company is really outraged at what's happening, what the *L.A. Times* is doing," he shouted into the receiver. "The complete redoing of these kind of articles oblivious to the facts that exist is something that is beyond the purview of what responsible journalism should be. Look at the corporate internal audit report that you managed to get out of the files of my company and you'll find that this company was unaware of Mr. Pisello's alleged background. We were completely cooperative with the Department of Justice and Mr. Rudnick. Somehow, it seems the more the company tries to be cooperative the more it's tied to the Mafia without just cause. This is an ethical company."

As far as Susman knew, prior to the *Times*'s revelation of Pisello's organized crime connections, "No one at this company thought there was anything remarkable or unusual about him."

Following a May article that detailed Pisello's almost daily presence at MCA Records from late 1983 to early 1985, Susman's office fired off an impassioned letter to the *Times*'s executive editor, Bill Thomas, charging that the newspaper's coverage of the Pisello affair was "unfair and unbalanced" and accusing the reporter of maliciously engaging in "a personal vendetta to harm our reputation. . . . The reporter has crossed the line from objective reporting to a preoccupation with proving a thesis—that MCA Records is inextricably linked with organized crime and is engaged in a continuous series of questionable practices. . . . In a year of articles making this 'connection,' there has not been one shred of evidence to contradict the truth of the matter—that no MCA employee had knowledge of Pisello's alleged ties to organized crime; that, if anything, MCA was a victim.

"The constant repetition of the so-called ties between MCA and suspected underworld figures inevitably leaves the distinct impression that MCA was intimately involved with these acts. We know that this impression was in fact created since we received countless phone calls from people who advised us that this was the clear implication of the story. The harm of such innuendo to the personal and business reputation of MCA executives and the pain and sufferings occasioned thereby are severe and continuing."

Actually, the media coverage had had no apparent impact on MCA's image in the financial world. Except for the one day after Harold Vogel's newsletter recommendation in 1985, the price of the company's stock did not go down as a result of the *Times* articles. That was partly because Wall Street viewed MCA's record division as insignificant to the overall value of the parent corporation—estimated at $5.2 billion, or $72 a share, at the time—and partly because the *Los Angeles Times* is not widely read in the East Coast investment community. The *New York Times* ignored the story. The *Wall Street Journal* had presented it in the best possible light—an unfortunate and embarrassing screw-up by naive executives who were conned by a reputed Mafia swindler. The *Washington Post* did a broad-stroke once-over on the various investigations into the record industry, but buried it in the back pages of its style section. Nothing had appeared on the CBS or ABC network newscasts, and NBC didn't follow up its original report, preferring to focus on the payola investigation instead.

For the most part, the story of Sal Pisello and MCA Records remained relegated to the entertainment-oriented publications— *Variety, Billboard, Rolling Stone, Radio & Records*, the *Hollywood Reporter*.

MCA had its own way of dealing with the trade papers. After *Radio & Records* ran a May 17 article about the Pisello affair that was based largely on a *Los Angeles Times* story the week before, Azoff reportedly canceled all MCA Records advertising in the publication, which depends heavily on record company ads for its income. On another occasion, Azoff and Larry Solters met with *Daily Variety*'s editor in chief, Tom Pryor, to complain about the publication's coverage. When Pryor made it clear that they weren't going to score any points by attacking the credibility of his reporter, Henry Schipper, Azoff invoked Lew Wasserman's name, saying the MCA chairman was extremely upset with the *Variety* articles. "Lew Wasserman and I have been friends for years," Pryor responded. "If he ever had a problem with our coverage, I'm sure he would call me himself; he knows where I am." The visit did nothing to chill *Variety*'s coverage. If anything, Schipper's reporting subsequently became more aggressive.

MCA waged a media battle on another front in the summer of 1986 by issuing a continuous stream of press releases about changes at the record company, changes that reinforced the impression that Irving Azoff was fully in charge and had the backing of the corporation.

"Sid Sheinberg, president and chief operating officer of MCA Inc., announced today that MCA Records and Publishing Group will now be known as the MCA Music Entertainment Group," said a May 22 press release. "Irving Azoff, MCA Inc. vice president, is president of the group. As part of the restructuring, the Universal Amphitheater will now be part of the newly formed MCA Music Entertainment Group." (The Universal Amphitheater is a 6,250-seat year-round concert venue situated in the center of MCA's Universal City complex. It is one of Los Angeles's finest concert halls, attracting the biggest names in the recording industry.)

The release quoted Sheinberg as saying, "The new Group name reflects not only the broadened scope of MCA's current music entertainment activities, but also signals an increasing commitment to the entertainment field, which is MCA's original heritage, namely music."

Azoff now had six different MCA operations reporting to him—records, record distribution, music publishing, talent management, concert promotion, and merchandising. And, come fiscal year's end, the earnings of MCA Records would be further obfuscated in the corporation's annual report.

In addition to the official announcements, a number of MCA-related items popped up in the music industry gossip columns. According to *Hits* magazine, for example, "Irving Azoff and Larry Solters, MCA Sr. VP of Artist Development, are flying east shortly for a double-header industry happening: first, the second annual Hall of Fame Induction Dinner at the Waldorf, and the next afternoon, the kick-off lunch at the Pierre for this year's T. J. Martell dinner, of which Azoff is the honoree, to be held in April." (The T. J. Martell Foundation for Leukemia and Cancer Research is the music industry's premiere charity. It was founded in the mid-1970s by CBS Records executive Tony Martell after his son, T. J., died of leukemia. The Martell foundation was naming Azoff as its 1987 Humanitarian of the Year, an honor that carried with it the responsibility of serving as the dinner's chief fund-raiser. Walter Yetnikoff was the honoree in 1984.)

On August 13, the *Hollywood Reporter* noted in its widely read "Rambling Reporter" column that "the hottest Hollywood chatter these days revolves around expected executive chair changes at Universal Studios." And according to the *Reporter*, "While the major buzz centers around NBC chief Grant Tinker and MGM's head man Alan Ladd, Jr. as the leading possibilities for the choicest available spaces in the Universal parking lot, there also appears to be a wild card in the deck who wouldn't have far to travel, namely MCA Records' topper Irving Azoff.... Azoff, who turned the record division of MCA into a major music force over the past few years, is not only close with Sid Sheinberg, but also has had experience producing movies. But don't go hunting for Azoff. He's currently on vacation until early September."

The presidents of the other major record companies no doubt were amused to read once again that Azoff had turned MCA Records into a powerhouse. In truth, the label barely turned a profit in 1986. Its one Top 10 album that year, Boston's long-awaited *Third Stage,* sold three million copies, according to the RIAA, but returns were heavy—about a million copies came back. Motown's Lionel Richie had a triple platinum follow-up to his 1984 *Can't Slow Down* album, but MCA netted only 8 percent on Motown product. MCA's country music and jazz division performed well, but on *Billboard*'s year-end list of top-selling pop artists, MCA's first entry, Patti LaBelle, appeared at number 35. A rundown of other MCA artists who released albums in 1986—New Edition, Charlie Sexton, the Alarm, Ready for the World, Stephanie Mills, Alice Cooper—was not one to make any competitor nervous.

When the 1986 results were published later in MCA's annual report, they showed that Azoff's new Music Entertainment Group had operating profits of $33 million that year, $8 million more than in 1985. But if Motown, Home Video, Music Publishing, Front Line Management, Facilities Merchandising, and the Universal Amphitheater had been subtracted from the equation, it would have shown that MCA Records earned approximately $3 million, with a profit margin of approximately 1.1 percent. Which meant that for every dollar MCA spent operating its record company, the company earned back about a penny.

There was one colorful incident in Irving Azoff's personal life that didn't get a mention in the Hollywood gossip columns that summer. He had been feuding for some time with Michael Lippman, a former friend who managed a number of big-name acts, notably George Michael. In the midst of a fortieth birthday party thrown for Lippman by his wife at the couple's Benedict Canyon home, a messenger showed up at the front door bearing a gift-wrapped box for Lippman from Azoff. As many of the party's two hundred-plus guests looked on, Lippman opened the box to find a large, coiled boa constrictor and a note insulting his wife: "Happy Birthday, Michael," it read. "Now you have two of them."

31

"Somebody very big and important liked him a lot"

Newark, New Jersey, is a grimy, decomposing city of 330,000 at the northern end of the state, just ten miles west of New York City—close enough for Newark International Airport to serve as a dropping-off point for Manhattan-bound travelers.

Between the airport and the government center at the edge of downtown Newark lies a vast expanse of rundown buildings, littered, crumbling streets, and smoldering chemical plants that have leaked a half-century's worth of industrial sludge into the lifeless swampland bordering the Passaic River. If not for the presence of late-model automobiles, it could be a scene straight out of the Great Depression, populated entirely by abject welfare families, swaggering street criminals, and case-hardened cops.

"If New Jersey is the Garden State, then Newark isn't the rose, it's more like the compost heap," said one federal agent who works there.

On the morning of September 24, 1986, a large contingent of the
national news media invaded Newark and gathered outside the federal building across the square from the old courthouse. Government employees were used to seeing crime-beat reporters from the
Newark Star-Ledger and the *Philadelphia Inquirer* working the halls
of the courthouse, covering the seemingly endless string of Mafia
trials that go on there. But this was a different, more exotic group—
Rolling Stone; *Billboard*; *Variety*; Washington-based correspondents
from ABC, NBC, and CBS; and camera crews from CNN and the
Canadian Broadcasting Company.

The occasion was a press conference called by Thomas R. Greelish, the U.S. attorney for the District of New Jersey, to announce a
117-count grand jury indictment against members of the so-called
Vastola Organization. Just after dawn that morning, a force of sixty
FBI agents had fanned out across metropolitan New York and New
Jersey and had rounded up and arrested seventeen men allegedly
connected with Gaetano Vastola's illegal business empire, including
Sonny Brocco, Lew Saka, Dominick Canterino, and Nicky Massaro. Vastola and Rudy Farone were charged in the indictment but
managed to elude arrest, authorities believed, because they were
tipped off to the government's planned move. Morris Levy was
arrested around 7:00 A.M. at the Ritz Carlton Hotel in Boston,
where an NBC camera crew taped him being escorted out of the
lobby in handcuffs and put in a car by a pair of federal agents. Obviously, NBC, too, had been tipped to the action.

In fact, when the nearly one hundred newspeople were ushered
into a stuffy, sterile-looking room on the fifth floor of the Newark
Federal Building at 11:00 A.M. that day, most of them knew the gist
of the charges—if not the exact details—before Greelish stepped to
the microphone to make the announcement. So much for the supposed secrecy of sealed grand jury indictments. Clearly the government wanted this story out.

On either side of Greelish stood John C. McGinley, special agent
in charge of the FBI's Newark office, and John Stamler, the Union
County prosecutor. Behind them were Bruce Repetto and FBI
agents Mahoney and Dossett. It was dark suits, club ties, and black
wingtips all around for the G-men, with Mahoney managing to
look rumpled and informal nonetheless.

The Vastola Organization, headed by Gaetano Vastola, had "carried out a pattern of racketeering activity," Greelish said, "involving

heroin and cocaine trafficking, loan-sharking, use of threats and violence in the collection of debts and the takeover of businesses indebted
to the Organization, operation of 'bust-out' businesses organized to
defraud suppliers of merchandise to those businesses, a scheme
to defraud the Western Union Telephone Company, a scheme to
defraud the owners of copyrighted motion pictures, a fraudulent
insurance scheme, bankruptcy fraud and gambling."

If convicted on all counts, Vastola faced 286 years in prison.
Sonny Brocco was looking at 539 years; Lew Saka, 447 years; Nicky
Massaro, 430 years; and Rudy Farone, 160 years.

Morris Levy was charged in only three counts of the thirty-page
indictment, but they were the charges that most of the reporters
had come to hear. *Rolling Stone* and *Billboard* had little interest in a
racketeering case brought against a bunch of New Jersey hoods.
They were there for the far sexier story of the Mafia in the music
business, the MCA Records-Sal Pisello angle.

Levy, Vastola, Dominick Canterino, and Roulette Records controller Howard Fisher each faced sixty years in prison for their participation in what the indictment called "the MCA extortion."
According to Greelish, Vastola and Levy had guaranteed to MCA
the payment of $1.25 million for approximately five million cutout
records that were purchased by John LaMonte and his company,
Out of the Past. "But when the records arrived at his place of business—sixty tractor-trailer loads—LaMonte determined that they
had been 'creamed,' meaning the choicest items had been
removed," Greelish said. When LaMonte refused to pay for the
cutouts, the alleged conspirators used "extortionate means, which
resulted in the beating of LaMonte, requiring his hospitalization
for a broken jaw, in an attempt to collect the debt that was owed
to MCA."

The reporters pressed with the obvious question: What, if anything, did MCA know about the alleged extortion conspiracy?
Greelish sidestepped. "I'm sure MCA knew they shipped out four
to five million records, and that they went to Out of the Past," he
said. "But the billing went to Morris Levy at Roulette Records."

Even reporters with no background on the MCA-Pisello story
sensed there was something missing in Greelish's explanation. Why
were Mafia thugs used to collect a debt owed to a legitimate record
company?

"This indictment charges that there was a loan-sharking

arrangement between LaMonte and the Vastola Organization which led to the MCA transaction," Greelish said. "Vastola was considered by Mr. Levy to be responsible for LaMonte and it was Vastola and Levy who guaranteed payment to MCA."

Greelish continued, "There is no charge in the indictment that MCA was involved in collecting the debt that was owed to it." He refused to comment further on the role of the record company "because I understand that is the subject of a lawsuit between La-Monte and the company." Actually, there was no lawsuit.

The most surprising aspect of the indictment was that it did not mention Sal Pisello. "There are no charges against Mr. Pisello at this time," was all Greelish would say about the omission.

What the reporters were not told was that the New Jersey authorities had originally planned to indict Pisello in the extortion conspiracy but they were kept from doing so on orders from Washington. Fearful that the New Jersey action would interfere with their tax case against Pisello, as well as the attendant investigation of MCA, Marvin Rudnick and Ted Gale had lobbied their strike force superiors in Washington to have Sal cut out of the indictment. They played to the ego of their bosses, arguing that it was a question of whether the supposedly independent strike force was going to back its own case in California.

New Jersey, of course, saw it differently. Bruce Repetto felt that Rudnick had double-crossed him. Though the record business angle was downplayed at the press conference that day, neither Greelish nor Repetto were convinced that MCA was an innocent victim in the whole cutout caper. Greelish was aware of how the record business operated. As an assistant U.S. attorney in Newark back in the early 1970s, he'd spearheaded a three-year federal grand jury investigation into payola. What he'd found were widespread questionable business practices, wise guys all over the place, and an industry that was either afraid or just plain unwilling to aid the government in investigating itself.

The investigation, code-named Project Sound, had cost the government millions of dollars and produced precious little in the way of results. One disc jockey was convicted of evading taxes on income earned from payoffs, but only one major record company executive was ever charged. Columbia Records president Clive Davis eventually pleaded no contest to tax charges unrelated to payola and was given probation. Davis was fired from Columbia but quickly reemerged as the president of Arista Records. He later wrote an autobiography—titled simply *Clive*—that detailed what he characterized as his unfair persecution by the government.

The lesson of the previous investigation was not lost on Greelish. Back then, the Justice Department had been investigating the record business and ran into organized crime. This time out, the Feds were looking at organized crime and stumbled onto the record business. Common sense said the two were inextricably linked. Greelish knew from experience, however, that making a case against a financially powerful industry—one known for closing ranks under scrutiny and calling in favors from its friends in high places—was infinitely more difficult than taking down a group of local mobsters.

Besides, in Greelish's world, Vastola was a big prize. The Vastola Organization was the largest and most successful organized crime operation in the New Jersey district. New York authorities were following up the Roulette Records–Genovese family angle and the Los Angeles strike force was apparently on MCA's case. So Greelish had decided to pursue the Mafia prosecution first and see what developed on the record business front later. It was the prudent thing to do. He didn't want to overreach, to risk losing the bird in his hand while aiming for a bigger one in the bush.

Two days after the indictments were announced, Vastola and Rudy Farone turned themselves in and were booked on the charges. The government asked that Vastola be denied bail pending trial— not as a flight risk but as a danger to the community, particularly to the government's protected witness, John LaMonte. At a bail hearing before Federal Magistrate Serena Peretti, Bruce Repetto presented a strong case for keeping the reputed mob chieftain off the streets.

The judge was shown blown-up color photographs of LaMonte's face—the ones taken by agent Tom Cupples—before and after his reconstructive surgery. Peretti winced at the gruesome photos and quickly put them aside. Transcripts of the wiretapped phone conversations between Brocco and Vastola were read—Vastola calling LaMonte a "dirty motherfucker" and vowing to "put him in a bucket," threatening to "tell Rudy, Sal, to go over there and do whatever you have to do," shouting that "you are going to witness such a beating I'm going to give this kid when this thing is over." The judge was informed of Vastola's two previous extortion charges.

As he sat listening in the courtroom that day, Vastola looked nothing like the traditional New Jersey mobster. He was dressed casually but elegantly, in impeccably tailored mauve-tone slacks and matching waist-length jacket, an off-white silk shirt open at the collar, and soft leather loafers. His stylish black metal-rimmed glasses were the kind favored by Hollywood film directors. Seated just behind him in the courtroom pews, Vastola's wife, Dorothy, likewise was resplendent in Rodeo Drive couture, right down to the large Louis Vuitton bag she cradled in the crook of her arm. Vastola's lawyer, Michael Rosen, resembled a fifty-year-old Richard Widmark—handsome and deeply tanned, with pearly gray hair curling slightly over the collar of his charcoal pinstripe suit. Vastola's twenty-five-year-old daughter, Joy, a recent law school graduate employed by Rosen, was acting as cocounsel. She, too, looked smashing—man-tailored dark pinstripe jacket and skirt, set off by a bright-green knit tie and a mass of crimped reddish-blond hair. Annie Hall as a lawyer.

In arguing against the government's no-bail motion, Rosen described his client as a family man, "married to the same woman for twenty-six years," the loving father of a daughter—"an officer of this court who lives with him"—and a twenty-three-year-old son who, at that very moment, was lying in a coma in the intensive-care ward of a hospital, the victim of a horrible automobile accident. (Guy Vastola had been in the midst of recording an album for RCA Records when the accident occurred. At the time, the doctors were not sure whether he'd sustained severe brain damage.)

Rosen pleaded with the judge to grant Vastola "reasonable" bail so that he could continue to take care of his family and business obligations while awaiting trial. The community had nothing to fear from Vastola, Rosen said. Nor had LaMonte, who would be "legally destroyed on the witness stand, not physically harmed by Mr. Vastola."

If anything, his client was a victim of LaMonte, the lawyer said. "Mr. Vastola got MCA to give LaMonte this large number of records.... The facts of this case suggest that LaMonte is a total con man and swindler who was injured in his warehouse when a crate fell on his face. That's the statement he made that night at the hospital. My client never laid a hand on him."

In the end, the judge denied the government's motion and granted

Vastola bail, but with severe restrictions. He would have to put up his million-dollar house in Colt's Neck as security, and he could not leave his home except to travel to his attorney's office in New York City. In effect, he would remain under house arrest until his trial.

Morris Levy was out on $500,000 bail less than twenty-four hours after his arrest. Almost immediately, he went public with his side of the story, appearing live on NBC's "Today" show and sitting for a two-and-a-half-hour interview with the *Los Angeles Times*. He denied all the charges and claimed he was a victim of government misconduct and harassment. Levy's lawyer, Leon Borstein, told the *Times* that when he first learned of Levy's indictment and impending arrest from a writer for the *Hollywood Reporter*, he called the U.S. attorney's office in Newark and offered to have his client surrender. "But they preferred to embarrass Morris by having him arrested on national TV." Referring to the camera crew outside the Ritz Carlton that day, Borstein said, "Somebody had to tell them when to be there."

Howard Fisher complained that, two months earlier, an FBI agent and a New York police detective had kidnapped him off the street and held him for four hours in a Manhattan hotel room. He said they tried to frighten him into joining the Witness Protection Program and gathering incriminating evidence against Levy, for whom he'd worked for twenty-seven years. "They told me Morris was going away for twenty years, that they had him cold," Fisher said. "They said I was the weak link in the operation and that Morris and his Mafia friends were going to kill me. They said if I didn't cooperate, I would be indicted and arrested at my home in front of my family and neighbors, which they eventually did."

Levy said the same agent and detective came to his office and told him that unless he joined the Witness Protection Program, he, too, would be killed. "I said, 'By who? You?' I think they want me to say a lot of things about people I know," Levy said.

Borstein put in that the government specifically wanted Levy to tell what he knew about Vincent Gigante and the Genovese crime family.

"I have nothing to say on that crap, but the government thinks I know something," Levy said. "I honestly believe that if I'd joined the Witness Protection Program I would not have been indicted.

The only thing I know about organized crime is my five ex-wives," he laughed. "Right now, I don't think I'm in danger from anyone, except maybe the FBI."

The government believed that Levy's statements to the *Los Angeles Times* and to NBC's Brian Ross on the "Today" show were aimed not so much at telling his side of the story to the public as they were at assuring Vincent Gigante that he was not cooperating with the FBI. Gigante now knew that he was the target of the New York grand jury investigation, so he was bound to be nervous. And when mob bosses get nervous they tend to want to eliminate potential witnesses against them. The FBI pegged Levy as a prime candidate for a pair of cement shoes: he was nearly sixty years old, accustomed to the life of a millionaire, had never spent more than a day in jail, and knew a lot about Gigante's operation. It was a profile of a man likely to roll over and talk rather than live out his golden years behind bars. That's how Gigante might view the situation anyway. And the FBI figured Levy knew it.

With his comments to the press in the days immediately following his arrest, however, Levy was announcing that he was going to be a stand-up guy and fight the charges—for now at least. But while he was close-mouthed about the Chin, in his interview with the *Los Angeles Times* Levy went out of his way to point the finger of suspicion at MCA and Sal Pisello: "Who gave directions for the shipment of the records? I never spoke to anyone at MCA. The only person who ever gave instructions was Sal Pisello. Sal was in complete control of the cutouts. They sold me a load of records and then took instructions from him. I lost 120 Gs on the deal; I got fucked by MCA and Pisello.... There's no question that Pisello had the door at MCA. Somebody big loved him. Somebody very big and important liked him a lot. If you wanted to reach Sal you called him there. And now they're denying they even know him. They washed it up beautifully."

Levy accused MCA and Pisello of concocting a scheme to fraudulently take over ownership of Sugar Hill Records. "The distribution deal they cut was for MCA to take no returns on old Sugar Hill product. Joe Robinson was a fucking independent and still they took $1.7 million worth of returns. The bulk of the returns came from the Philly area. Somebody got money to do that."

According to Levy, MCA charged Sugar Hill full wholesale price—$5—for each returned record, thereby running up what the company claimed was a $1.7 million debt owed by Sugar Hill. "Now here's how cute they are at MCA," he said. "They then agree to buy the company for $1.7 million to eliminate the debt." He suggested that MCA paid Pisello, who supposedly was Sugar Hill's representative, to look the other way.

"Sal knew how to dance," he sighed. "He danced at all the weddings."

Several days after the Newark indictments, the *Los Angeles Times* and the Los Angeles strike force received a duplicate of an anonymous letter postmarked September 24, the day of the indictments, from New York City. Addressed "To whom it may concern," the letter reiterated the LaMonte-Brocco story about Pisello doing a job for someone at MCA, only in more detail.

The letter was only five sentences long, but the added specifics made everything else that happened seem logical. No scenario Rudnick had come up with tied up all the loose ends so neatly, down to the question of why MCA had not filed a lawsuit against Pisello, who, the company's executives claimed, had swindled them out of at least $250,000. MCA sued practically everyone else—LaMonte, Scorpio, Sam Passamano. Why not Sal?

Rudnick was curious about who would send such a letter. Not LaMonte. He swore up and down he didn't know any more than what Brocco had told him. Rudnick imagined that LaMonte would tell if he knew, since he had nothing to lose; he was already a protected witness.

Who then? Some crackpot with a vivid imagination? A disgruntled former or present MCA employee? Or was it someone who really knew what he was talking about? Was this the mob striking back at a corporate executive who'd done business with them and was now trying to back out of his devil's bargain?

Whatever the truth, Rudnick knew he didn't have the political juice at that point to investigate the matter. He called up Neil Kreitz and Herm Kaskowitz, the two LAPD detectives attached to the strike force for the payola investigation, and turned the letter over to them.

"Maybe you guys can do something with this," he said, "but I sure can't."

It was the last he'd ever hear about the anonymous letter.

In the days following the Newark indictments, Rudnick finally found time to begin work in earnest on the Pisello-MCA investigation. The Newark indictments had energized him. He interpreted the Justice Department's agreement to drop Pisello from the Newark case as support for what he was doing in California—Washington was backing his investigative theory. But he knew the support wouldn't continue indefinitely unless he came up with new evidence of wrongdoing at the record company. He had to keep his iron hot.

On October 8, the government had to respond to a motion filed by Pisello's lawyer, Harland Braun, to have Sal's prison sentence reduced from two years to one. Pisello claimed that the U.S. Parole Commission had denied him parole in September based on "unreliable information" about his alleged Mafia background that Rudnick had put into the court record.

Rudnick had a dictum that had served him well as a prosecutor: whenever a defendant files a motion, respond with everything you've got, blast him with both barrels, make him sorry he filed the motion and reluctant to do it again. He responded to Pisello's motion accordingly, managing to get in a few subtle shots at Judge Harry Hupp in the bargain: "Pisello's attack comes after he convinced the Court on March 29, 1986, to quash a subpoena served upon MCA Records Inc. and Sugar Hill Records Inc. Pisello had claimed to the Court that the subpoenas were 'designed to harass (Pisello) and make it impossible for him to earn a living by poisoning his relationship with Sugar Hill and MCA.' Pisello characterized government counsel's actions as a 'disgrace.'"

In a tone dripping with indignation, Rudnick wrote: "Pisello's purpose in deceiving the Court was to protect his scheme to sell Sugar Hill's Chess-Checker record label to MCA for $8 million. Pisello had been promised a 15 percent finder's fee for putting the two record companies together. Even though Pisello received a substantial amount of his fee, he did not pay the IRS any portion of the nearly $200,000 he then owed from a 1979 judgment against him in the U.S. Tax Court. Why should he be given favorable treatment by a Court which convicted him of tax crimes?

"Pisello also received substantial monies from Sugar Hill's distribution deal with MCA, and a cutout record deal involving millions of records that were sold through Morris Levy's Roulette Records. Levy was recently indicted in New Jersey for extorting one of the buyers of those records. Some of the monies coming from Pisello's record deals were laundered through a Queens, New York, bank account which he shared with another East Coast mobster. How Pisello was able to get into the record business remains under investigation."

Referring to the cutout sale from Ranji Bedi to Scorpio Music, Rudnick said: "One of the cutout buyers claims he lost $200,000 after being assured that Roulette was not involved. Pisello disguised his role in the deal by placing another as a seller of MCA product, collecting his profit through a cash payment in a Santa Monica parking lot and a wire transfer to a secret bank account in Las Vegas. This transaction occurred the same week Pisello was tried before the court in 1984. Pisello chose not to pay his IRS debt with the funds."

Rudnick knew that Pisello recently had given an on-camera interview to "Entertainment Tonight" up at Lompoc. He couldn't resist getting that in: "Pisello refuses to tell the government how he became successful in the record business. Perhaps any disclosures would further incriminate him and others. He has been interviewed by 'Entertainment Tonight,' a nationally syndicated television program that specializes in news of the celebrity community. So far the government has been unsuccessful in securing tapes of the interview. If Pisello wants the court to give him the keys to his cell, maybe he can first promise that he will give the same courtesy to the government as he gave to the TV show."

"Before any reduction of sentence," Rudnick wrote in closing, "the Court should require Pisello to explain his deals with MCA— transactions Pisello was directing outside the courtroom while he was on trial. Those who pay taxes should be told that a reduction of sentence for tax evasion should come at a cost. Pisello chooses not to cooperate, not to pay his taxes, not to file truthful tax returns. Instead he chooses to associate with known Mafia members and engage in fraudulent business activities."

Pisello's sentence was not reduced.

Throughout October and November, Rudnick spent every available moment interviewing potential witnesses. He started with former MCA executives—Sam Passamano, George Collier, Gene Froelich, Kent Crawford, Al Bergamo, and Arnold Stone, who was still employed at MCA but due to retire in a few months. Some he merely talked to over the phone; others he brought into the strike force office to speak to the IRS investigators; a few he put before the grand jury.

Stone told Rudnick that, sometime in 1984, Myron Roth ordered him to switch part of MCA's record jacket manufacturing over to a New Jersey–based company with whom MCA had never done business before and whose reputation for quality was not the best. Stone said the order was given at a meeting in Roth's office that was attended by Pisello. He said he'd gotten the impression that Pisello was part owner of the company. Rudnick remembered LaMonte's comment that "the wise guys owned a piece" of this particular company. The jacket manufacturing deal had not been mentioned in the internal audit report.

Rudnick felt that Al Bergamo was a particularly effective witness. His story of Pisello's alleged bribe attempt was devastating to MCA's position that its executives suspected nothing about Pisello's activities until Rudnick informed them of his Mafia background in the spring of 1985. According to Bergamo, Myron Roth knew Pisello had attempted to engage the company in a questionable business deal as early as the fall of 1983. And yet MCA continued doing business with him. What's more, the numbers added up. Bergamo said Pisello asked for $1 million under the table for Morris Levy. As it turned out, MCA paid Levy $300,000 directly for his security interest in the Checker/Chess catalog and entered business deals with Pisello that resulted in approximately $700,000 in income to Consultants for World Records, whose bank account Levy controlled.

The problem was that all the former MCA executives had their various axes to grind with the company—a fact the defense would play up in any trial, attacking their credibility as "disgruntled ex-employees."

From the former executives, Rudnick moved to the outside players in the other Pisello transactions—Ranji Bedi, John Gervasoni of Scorpio, Sugar Hill Records president Joe Robinson, and Robinson's partner Milton Malden. They, too, had their credibility problems.

Bedi said that when he called MCA to inquire about buying cutouts in 1984, it was Sal Pisello who called him back. But then Bedi admitted that he had paid Pisello part of his commission on the cutout sale in crisp new hundred-dollar bills handed over in the parking lot of a Santa Monica bank. That might not play too well with a jury—legitimate businessmen usually pay by check.

Gervasoni came across as sincere, smart, and credible, but he was suing MCA and its top executives for racketeering, so his testimony at a trial would seem self-serving.

Robinson and Malden likewise were furious with MCA, claiming they'd been smeared in the press by MCA's claim that Pisello had been introduced to the company through Sugar Hill. Actually, it was the other way around. "They sent him to me," Robinson said. The Sugar Hill president was eager to join in the trashing of MCA and Pisello, but he was reluctant to discuss his relationship with Morris Levy. He gave evasive answers to questions about Rocco Musacchia, who he admitted was a friend of his and who had been present at Robinson's first meeting with MCA executives in Irving Azoff's office in the fall of 1983. Rudnick's impression was that Robinson feared for his life if he talked about the East Coast wise guys.

Malden, however, seemed more concerned about MCA. In the midst of his questioning before the grand jury, he blurted out to Rudnick, "You're never going to find out the truth, you know."

"Why is that?" Rudnick asked reflexively.

"Because of this," Malden said. He reached down into a shopping bag he'd placed on the floor between his feet and pulled out a book, which he held up for the grand jurors to see—*Dark Victory: Ronald Reagan, MCA and the Mob*. Written by investigative reporter Dan E. Moldea and published just a few months earlier, *Dark Victory* was the hottest read in Hollywood at the time. It traced Reagan's connections to MCA and MCA's connections to organized crime going back many years. The gist of the book—and Malden's reference to it—was that MCA was a corporation so powerful that it literally owned the president of the United States.

Nonetheless, on November 20, Sugar Hill filed an $80 million lawsuit against MCA, charging that it was defrauded and brought to the verge of bankruptcy in a racketeering scheme engineered by MCA Records executives and Sal Pisello. According to the suit, MCA and Pisello created "fraudulent transactions which could then be charged against income otherwise due and payable to Sugar Hill." The transactions included the false returns scheme previously alluded to by Levy, the preparation and mailing of "fraudulent accounting reports" to Sugar Hill, and the unauthorized "secret sale" of Sugar Hill's inventory as cutouts.

As a result of the transactions, the suit claimed, Sugar Hill was placed in a financial crisis, was compelled to sell to MCA its principal asset, the Checker/Chess catalog, for less than its fair market value, and was ultimately forced to seek relief under Chapter 11 of the Bankruptcy Code. Sugar Hill claimed that "due to manipulation of Sugar Hill's account," the company received only $481,000 for the Checker/Chess catalog.

In a tearful interview with the *Los Angeles Times,* Joe Robinson complained that "nobody in the record business will deal with us because they think we are connected to the Mafia. This has hurt my business to the point that my family and myself are looking for some bread to put on the table."

Although Pisello was named as a defendant in the Sugar Hill lawsuit, he told the *Times* in a telephone interview from Lompoc that Robinson's accusations were accurate, except that he himself had nothing to do with it. A couple of months in prison had apparently altered Pisello's perception that MCA was the "nicest corporation in the world."

"I caught MCA executives with their hand in the cookie jar," he said over the phone from prison. "They were stealing money from Sugar Hill."

According to Pisello, he discovered that MCA had billed Sugar Hill more than $300,000 for record promotion services at a time when Sugar Hill had no records in the marketplace to promote. When he confronted MCA executives about the promotion charges, he was told the money had been paid to Joe Isgro. He'd wanted to complain to Isgro about the bogus charges but was dissuaded by MCA executives, who asked that he instead dig up dirt for them on Isgro's alleged organized crime ties. Pisello said he didn't follow through on that request and later discovered that Isgro had never worked at Sugar Hill records and had never billed MCA for $300,000.

MCA reacted to the lawsuit in typical fashion by releasing an angry statement to the press accusing Sugar Hill of fraud. "MCA is outraged by the news that Sugar Hill is accusing it of violating the RICO act. Considering that over the past several weeks MCA has confronted Sugar Hill with extensive evidence indicating Sugar Hill's apparent massive fraud and material breaches in its dealings with MCA Records, it is obvious that this lawsuit is a bad faith effort to try to avoid MCA Records' claims and obscure the real issues. MCA Records intends to vigorously defend against this frivolous lawsuit and aggressively pursue its legitimate claims against Sugar Hill."

Things were getting very interesting, Rudnick thought. Scorpio, Isgro, and now Sugar Hill—the lawsuits were flying like fur in a cat fight. That could only help the government in its investigation.

Rudnick noticed that the Sugar Hill suit made no mention of Morris Levy or Roulette Records. That was hardly surprising, considering Robinson's relationship with Levy. Rudnick surmised that Levy was behind the Sugar Hill suit. Morris and the boys were striking back at MCA.

32

"Fruit of a poisoned tree"

By December, Rudnick had worked his way up the chain of potential witnesses and was ready to start calling on current MCA Records executives. He would begin testing in earnest the power of the corporation and its vaunted political connections.

The list of people to be questioned included Irving Azoff, Myron Roth, Zach Horowitz, Dan McGill, and John Burns—the "big five," as Rudnick called them, the highest-ranking executives who had face-to-face dealings with Sal Pisello.

As a result of being named in either the Scorpio or Sugar Hill lawsuit, each of the executives had obtained outside legal counsel—on the advice of MCA and with the understanding that the company would pay the cost of their defense, unless they were found guilty of wrongdoing.

Azoff had hired Howard Weitzman, one of the best-known and

highest-paid criminal defense attorneys in Los Angeles. A partner in the high-powered law firm of Wyman Bautzer, Weitzman gained national exposure in 1985 with his successful defense of former automobile magnate John DeLorean on cocaine-smuggling charges. He managed to win an acquittal despite the prosecution's videotape of DeLorean fondly patting a two-pound brick of cocaine and saying, "This stuff is better than gold."

Shortly after Azoff hired him, Weitzman called the strike force and said his client was eager to come down and talk to the investigators. But Rudnick was in Phoenix at the time, and Dubois and Gale decided that he should be present for any questioning of the MCA Records president. Dubois also wanted to make sure that the strike force had as much information as possible before they sat down with Azoff. He guessed that Azoff's real motive in seeking the meeting was to find out what the strike force had, where the investigation was going. If that were the case, Dubois wanted to impress Azoff with their knowledge, not their ignorance.

Another reason they put off interviewing Azoff was that at one point he was the jfocus of the investigation. For lack of an official code-name, like Brilab or Miporn, the case became known in the office as "the Azoff investigation," which applied to both the Pisello-MCA and the payola probes. Rudnick intended to question Azoff last.

MCA Records president Myron Roth's lawyers also made overtures to the strike force over the summer. In a meeting in Ted Gale's office, Michael J. Lightfoot and John D. Vandevelde said their client was willing to cooperate if the government granted him immunity first. Rudnick was adamantly opposed to it. He was irritated that the attorneys had gone over his head to Gale to set up the meeting and even more irritated that Gale had agreed to it. "Well, what's your guy got to tell us? I can't give a witness immunity before I know what he has to say," Rudnick said. "We haven't finished examining all the documents yet, so we don't know what to ask him. How will we know he's telling us the truth? "

Vandevelde seemed offended. "Are you suggesting our client is a liar?" He turned to Gale. "We'd like to move on this. We don't think it's fair of you to put our client in the position of being under suspicion for so long. We'd like to clear this up."

"Well, I don't like you coming in this office and trying to push us around," Rudnick said, his voice rising.

At that, Vandevelde got up from his seat. "This is ridiculous," he said, and stomped out of the office. The meeting was over. Lightfoot was embarrassed and Gale was furious at Rudnick for his rudeness and "unprofessional behavior." But Rudnick didn't care. He had effectively scuttled the discussions and avoided what he considered to be a serious mistake. It was too early to be talking about immunity for Roth, who, he knew, was scheduled for a deposition in the Scorpio racketeering lawsuit the following week. Roth was either going to have to take the Fifth in his sworn deposition, thereby hurting his company, or talk and run the risk of having his statement used against him. If he talked, he waived any claim to immunity. Rudnick suspected that Roth's lawyers were attempting to snooker Gale into granting their client immunity prior to the Scorpio deposition.

Rudnick knew from years of experience that immunity negotiations were a delicate dance that required careful choreography, especially in white-collar cases, where the identity or roles of the key players is not always clear. If you moved too quickly, you could inadvertently immunize a trigger man. Or you could jeopardize critical outside evidence by giving the defense an opening to argue that it was developed directly from the witness's immunized statement, the "fruit of a poisoned tree." Plus, the minute you immunize a witness, especially in a Mafia-related case, the value of his testimony drops like a rock because the defense can be counted on to argue to the jury that his statements are tainted by the promise of favor from the government.

As Rudnick argued to Gale after the aborted meeting with Lightfoot and Vandevelde, there were serious questions about Roth's role in the Pisello affair that had to be explored further before they could even think about granting him any kind of immunity. For starters, in his first telephone conversation with Rudnick in 1985, Roth had laid responsibility for the cutout sale on Passamano and McGill. Then came the internal audit report saying, in effect, that the whole thing was all a big mistake by Myron, that he was the highest-ranking executive responsible for what had happened.

"What if," Rudnick said to Gale, "the whole plan is for Myron to act as the fall guy? What if we give him immunity and he comes in and tells us a bullshit story that it was all his doing and that no one else at the company knew anything about it? He takes the rap for someone else higher up? Then we're left with nothing but a Pisello tax case."

Rudnick was also curious about why Roth's office appointment logs for 1983 were missing from the documents that MCA had turned over. The subpoena had specifically asked for those logs, since they represented a critical time period for determining whom Pisello met with first at the company. The strike force had asked for the documents a second time and still had not heard back. "We need to reconstruct what took place through documents that don't lie before we question the key players," he said.

After the Roth episode, Rudnick wasn't surprised when lawyers for Zach Horowitz and Dan McGill also sought immunity in exchange for their clients' cooperation. What they requested was known as "informal" immunity, meaning that any statements the executives made to investigators could not be used as evidence against them in a later trial, although evidence developed from their statements could be used. Also called handshake immunity or gentleman's immunity, informal immunity does not require an order from a court; it's up to the discretion of the prosecutor. Over at the U.S. attorney's office, granting gentleman's immunity was a common practice, especially when the defense lawyer was a former assistant U.S. attorney. That's one reason former Justice Department lawyers command such big fees in Los Angeles—they can practically guarantee a client will be treated with deference.

Getting informal immunity at the strike force was a little more difficult, however, and getting it from Rudnick was damn near impossible. His standard position was, "If your client didn't do anything wrong, then he doesn't need it. He's going to have to tell us the truth and trust us. He's either on our side of the law or the other side." One former assistant U.S. attorney once got so angry at having his request for informal immunity turned down by the strike force that he called Rudnick a "motherfucker" over the phone and hung up on him.

For the MCA executives, Rudnick decided he was going to play it by the book. According to the U.S. Attorney's Manual, a witness can be given formal immunity only if he first asserts—either in writing or before a grand jury—that without immunity he intends to invoke his Fifth Amendment privilege against self-incrimination. "Tell them to put it in writing and then give me a proffer, and

we'll go from there," he told lawyers for the two executives. (A proffer is the statement a witness is prepared to give if he is granted
immunity. If, after evaluating the proffer, the prosecutor chooses
not to grant immunity, the proffer is withdrawn and the statement
cannot be used against the witness. It can, however, be used to
impeach his testimony if he changes his story at a later trial.)

Rudnick's strategy was to lock each of the executives into a position on Pisello that they couldn't back out of later.

Horowitz, McGill, and Roth responded in writing that they
intended to invoke the Fifth Amendment if called to testify without
a grant of immunity.

John Burns and his lawyer, Janet Levine, waited until the morning Burns was scheduled to testify before requesting immunity.
Rudnick put Burns on the witness stand and the executive promptly
took the Fifth, refusing to answer questions. After his testimony,
Burns gave an oral proffer to Rudnick in a cordial meeting in the
strike force conference room. Burns recalled that at one point Pisello
explained to him that his primary responsibility at Sugar Hill was
"keeping the niggers in line."

Rudnick took a written statement from McGill. Horowitz and
Roth were interviewed at the strike force offices for several hours
each. After evaluating the proffers, Rudnick decided to offer immunity only to McGill. As the record company's chief legal officer,
Horowitz was able to make frequent claims of attorney-client privilege, which rendered his statement virtually useless.

Roth's proffer was exactly what Rudnick had expected—it stuck
closely to the scenario laid out in the internal audit report and was
rife with I-don't-recalls on important questions concerning Azoff's
role in the Pisello transactions. He said he didn't remember much
about how Pisello got into the company or why the company decided
to do business with him. Rudnick just didn't believe Roth's story; it
sounded too rehearsed.

The decision to grant McGill immunity wasn't based on any
explosive evidence he provided about wrongdoing by higher-ups at
the company. Rudnick needed at least one company executive to
testify at Pisello's trial that the money paid to Consultants for
World Records was for services performed and was not a loan, as
Pisello no doubt would claim. As the record company's chief financial officer, McGill could testify to that directly.

Rudnick wasn't giving up much in return for immunizing

McGill. The executive acknowledged participating in several questionable financial maneuvers. He testified, for example, that he'd kept the undated worthless checks from Pisello in his desk drawer in order to convince MCA's outside auditors from Price Waterhouse into thinking the company was making some effort to collect on the $180,000 in advances to Sal. Still, it seemed obvious that McGill was acting on instructions from Roth, his superior, and was not the architect of whatever took place.

McGill did provide one chink in MCA's armor, Rudnick thought. When asked the purpose of a January 1985 payment of $50,000 to Pisello, he said he was told it was to enlist Pisello's help in taking possession of the Checker/Chess master tapes from Sugar Hill. That conflicted with the internal audit report, which said the $50,000 was an "advance against future royalties"—a statement even the auditors questioned when they pointed out that at the time the payment was made it was unlikely the royalties would ever be due Pisello. Why the discrepancy? McGill said he didn't know.

John Anderson couldn't understand why Rudnick was so excited about the conflicting versions of the $50,000 payment. "Trust me, it's important," Rudnick said.

With McGill's grand jury testimony and the other proffers in hand, Rudnick now had four of the "big five" locked into a story on Pisello. The only one left was Azoff.

33

"Either tonight
I'm a hit
or tomorrow
morning
I get hit"

I n the weeks leading up to the 1987 T. J. Martell Foundation dinner, a series of full-page color ads appeared in the record industry
trade publications featuring pictures of historical figures and the
famous wrong-headed statements they uttered:

"Heavier-than-air flying machines are impossible."—Lord Kelvin,
President, Royal Society, 1895.

"Sensible and responsible women do not want to vote."—Grover
Cleveland, 1905.

"Who the hell wants to hear actors talk?"—Harry M. Warner,
Warner Brothers Pictures, 1927.

And last, "Nobody will pay $3,000 a table to honor Irving Azoff."
Tony Martell, 1987.

Put together by MCA's Creative Services Department, the ads
were intended to play off humorously on Azoff's reputation as one
of the least-liked people in the record business, and they were inter-

preted by some in the industry as a subtle dig at Tony Martell, who was known to harbor misgivings about Azoff serving as chief fundraiser for the charity named in honor of his son.

In the previous ten years, the foundation had raised more than $19 million, at least 95 percent of which went directly to funding cancer research and aiding record industry victims of the disease. The foundation's remarkably low 5 percent administration cost—20 percent is considered excellent for a charity—is accomplished with the help of a largely volunteer staff and the tireless efforts of Tony Martell himself, who made a promise on his son's deathbed that he would raise money to find a cure for the disease that killed the boy.

The annual Humanitarian Award dinner—held each year in the ballroom of the Sheraton Centre in New York City and attended by fifteen hundred contributors—is the Martell Foundation's primary fund-raising event, accounting for 85–90 percent of the charity's income.

As the honoree, Azoff was expected to solicit outright contributions, line up paid attendance at the dinner, and sell advertising in the evening's printed program. He was also expected to pick up about $75,000 worth of expenses for the event. In addition, MCA was committed to release a commemorative album compiled from previously recorded performances by well-known artists. Martell Foundation volunteers had worked for months convincing artists to donate cuts from their hit albums, and the CBS Records legal staff had obtained all the necessary legal clearances from the artists' record labels.

"You can help in the fight against leukemia and cancer," the trade paper ads said. "Please join Irving Azoff in supporting the T. J. Martell Foundation."

Naturally, Azoff put his right-hand man, Larry Solters, in charge of the evening, naming him chairman of the event. One of Solters's goals for the dinner was to raise more money than CBS Records president Walter Yetnikoff had raised three years earlier.

A week before the dinner, *Hits* magazine, an extremely Azoff-friendly publication, ran a photo of the MCA Records chief and his wife, along with a laudatory editorial note: "We've shared a lot of laughs with Irving Azoff's MCA. Without a doubt, he has brought the company back to the forefront of the industry with an aggressive, colorful style. This time, however, we want to seriously congratulate Irving and Shelli Azoff on helping raise over $3 million for the T. J. Martell Foundation for Leukemia and Cancer Research. The label topper is being honored at the annual dinner in New York on Saturday, and it's testimony to the man that such a large sum was donated to this great charity."

Dinner chairman Solters used the *Hits* editorial as a forum for some petulant carping: "I'm very proud of the industry for the job it has done," he was quoted as saying. "With all the cheap shots taken at the music industry, and all the bad press we get, it's funny how you never see us getting any recognition for things like the Martell Foundation."

Tony Martell must have gagged when he read those comments. At the time, he and his staff were tearing their hair out over Azoff's and Solters's self-aggrandizing antics. The week before the dinner, Azoff threatened to pull out as the honoree unless the foundation acceded to a number of demands. For starters, Shelli Azoff didn't like the napkins and tablecloths that had been ordered for the dinner and wanted them changed to a color and style of her own design. She also wanted to be in charge of seating at the dinner. And Azoff wanted to do away with the tradition of having a head table at the event, primarily because he didn't want to have to individually introduce the approximately one hundred people that were to be seated there. If the charity didn't make the changes he wanted, the Humanitarian of the Year wasn't going to show up.

The foundation staff was stunned and outraged at the demands. Changing the tablecloths and napkins would cost thousands of dollars, they explained. Seating at the head table—and near the head table—was a matter of extremely delicate diplomacy. The places were reserved for individuals who had contributed either a tremendous amount of time or at least $25,000 to the cause over the course of the year. They were not to be handed out to Shelli Azoff's social friends who had nothing to do with the charity.

After much agonizing—during which Tony Martell put his fist through a wall at his home and injured his hand—the foundation decided to call Azoff's bluff. The record company president apparently wanted his night in the philanthropic spotlight, since he backed down immediately on the napkin and tablecloth issue, as well as on the seating arrangements. He did make one more demand, however: He would show up for the dinner if Capitol

Records president Joe Smith was brought in to introduce the people at the head table.

Known for his rapier wit, Smith had long been the industry's toastmaster general, renowned for turning introductory speeches into fall-down-funny roasts of his colleague-honorees. His most celebrated emcee performance was at a 1973 United Jewish Appeal dinner honoring Morris Levy as a "pioneer of the record industry." Stepping to the microphone that night, Smith commented, "With this group of cutthroats on this dais, every one of you would be safer in Central Park tonight. . . . Either tonight I'm a hit or tomorrow morning I get hit, one or the other." He closed his speech by telling the audience, "I've just gotten word from two of [Levy's] friends on the West Coast that my wife and two children have been released." Fourteen years later, Levy was still handing out taped copies of Smith's speech to friends.

Tony Martell called Smith at home the Saturday afternoon before the 1987 dinner and pleaded with him to come in and save the day. Though he was no big fan of Azoff's, Smith agreed. The crisis was averted, but Martell was so upset by all the demeaning haggling that up until the night before the dinner he was threatening not to attend.

Irving and Shelli Azoff got what one observer called "a sitting ovation" that night. But Smith brought the house down when he introduced the couple as "Hans Brinker and Snow White." Describing Azoff as a "little bundle of hate," Smith said that "naming Irving Azoff Humanitarian of the Year gives new meaning to the term. Actually, it was a close call. The finalists for the honor came down to Irving and Abu Nidal. Nidal couldn't make it, however. He had to be in Paris to bomb an orphanage."

Throughout the evening, Azoff seemed to revel in his bad-boy image. As part of his speech, he showed a videotape—put together by Larry Solters—that featured clips from the old "Dragnet" TV show intercut with interviews of some of his colleagues, including Yetnikoff, talking about his character. The running joke was that Sgt. Joe Friday and his partner were trying to track down this near-mythical liar and goniff named Irving Azoff.

"All in all, it was not a dignified evening," one Martell staffer said later.

A week after the dinner, Joe Smith received a thank-you note from the Azoffs, along with a framed photograph of the couple that was signed, "From Hans and Snow."

The Martell Foundation didn't fare nearly as well. Following the event, it never received money pledged by Azoff nor did it receive MCA's payment for the company's table at the dinner. However, MCA eventually did release the promised commemorative album.

34

"We're not here to maximize somebody's civil rights"

W e're on the air. 2:00 P.M. post time, February 25, 1987."
Rudnick checked the tape recorder and looked across the strike force conference table at Irving Azoff, sitting in the same seat Joe Isgro had occupied a year earlier.

Next to Azoff, on Rudnick's right, was Azoff's attorney, Howard Weitzman. To Rudnick's left were IRS agents John Anderson and Chuck McCalmont.

"You understand that the circumstance of our meeting today is that we are making tapes," Rudnick began. "But it is essentially a statement which you are just making, giving us any information concerning the questions we have about Sal Pisello. There is no immunity being granted. You're not seeking immunity. You're not taking the Fifth Amendment. You do understand that you are making a statement to an agency of the United States government and that the statute relating to obstruction of justice, Title 18, 1623, doesn't apply because we are not in grand jury. But 1503 and 1512 probably do."

He was referring to sections of the penal code that make it a crime to "impede the due administration of justice" by intentionally misleading a federal investigator. "Are you familiar with those sections of the law? The obstruction of justice statute?"

"Mr. Azoff probably is not; I am," Weitzman replied. "We're here ready, willing, and able."

Rudnick turned to Azoff. "How did you meet Sal Pisello?"

"Sal Pisello, to the best of my recollection, I met through our dealings with him as an agent for Sugar Hill, Chess/Checker in an early October 1983 or 1984 meeting at which my colleagues tell me all of us first met him. So I guess that's the first time I met him."

"I don't understand. What do you mean by that?"

Azoff explained that he only recalled the meeting from "looking at the appointment sheet and talking to others. . . . I honestly don't remember Pisello being there. . . . What I think happened here was Myron asked me to make an appearance, a sort of bless-the-deal appearance. What I remember doing is coming into this meeting—initially I didn't remember the meeting at all, but my guys said I was there, so I believe them—and what they say happened is I came in, listened to a little music, said, 'It's wonderful, we're doing business,' and that was it."

Rudnick produced a copy of Azoff's 1983 appointment calendar that the strike force had subpoenaed. It showed that a "Mr. Musaki" also attended the meeting in Azoff's conference room that day.

"I'm assuming Myron Roth set the meeting up with my office," Azoff said. "He called my office . . . said we're going to have this meeting and his assistant probably rattled off names. . . . I've never seen that name."

"But who is Musaki?" Rudnick asked.

"Don't have a clue."

"Who is the best person to testify as to who the parties were that were there that day?"

"Either Myron or Bergamo."

"Even though Bergamo wasn't there?"

"Bergamo wasn't there? I don't know; I thought Bergamo was there."

Rudnick pressed. "Have you ever heard of a person named Rocco Musacchia?"

"No."

"M-u-s-a-c-c-h-i-a?"

"Never," Azoff said. "The instigating MCA party that scheduled this meeting, his name doesn't appear here."

"And that's . . . ?

". . . Myron Roth."

Azoff went on to explain that at the time of the meeting he knew very little about the operational side of the record business. "I get to the company and as much as I know about the record business at this point is that a record is round. Okay? I take this job; I walk . . . I didn't know anything. I really didn't understand the retail, distributing, return privileges. If you asked me what a P&D was, I didn't know what the word P&D meant."

It was an astounding statement for someone who'd been in the record business for eighteen years and who had owned a record company, Full Moon, that had a pressing and distribution deal with Warner Brothers.

Azoff was some piece of work, Rudnick thought. Not at all what he expected from the way others had described him. Rather than combative and abrasive, he came on soft-spoken, charming, and, above all, cool—as he laid off all the blame on his subordinates.

"I have an expertise in spotting and dealing with creative talent," Azoff went on. "So I immediately took the creative side of the company and gave Myron what I call the administrative business. Myron then and probably now knows many more people and has touched many more people in the music business than me."

Azoff said that he was initially against the Sugar Hill distribution deal but was talked into it by his underlings, principally Bergamo and Roth. "My original instincts were 'This is not a deal we want.' . . . My instincts were right, but when you put together a team of people and other people want to do something, you know. I make many decisions where I say, 'All right, I don't really like this, but if you can get X, Y, and Z, go ahead.' Sheinberg does that to me and I do it to people below me.

"I will tell you my instincts about this whole [Pisello] thing were terrible from the start," Azoff said. "My instincts from the three chance meetings, I'll call them, that I had with Pisello were terrible from the start. It's created a lot of stress and pain in all of our lives over the past couple of years. I understand exactly why you guys are looking into this stuff."

"And you understand, we have no axe to grind," Rudnick said.

"I understand that."

"We have to understand why a person I convicted in court with the assistance of the IRS for failure to pay taxes . . . "

". . . ends up at the most conservative, supposedly well-run entertainment company in the business," Azoff put it.

"That's right," Rudnick said. "And a person, Sal Pisello, that opened the door on October 3 in a meeting with Joe Robinson and a person that we believe is Mr. Musacchia."

"You think? Was he there?"

"Well, let's put it this way. [The name *Musaki* is] on your list of people that were supposed to be there and it's a phonetic spelling but it's close enough to a person who ended up sharing much of the money that MCA paid on the Sugar Hill deal. Because Mr. Musacchia is a partner in Consultants for World Records. And that's very important to us."

"Well, I'm glad my appointment sheets provided that to you," Azoff said, "and I wish we would've been down here many months ago."

"I wish so, too."

"As we tried to talk about it . . . "

"Well, I'm not sure that's correct, Mr. Azoff. I'm not sure you made the kind of effort you're implying to come down here. You've known about this investigation for a long time."

"Is Rocco not a nice guy, Marvin?" Weitzman interjected.

"Rocco Musacchia is a person who is associated with, as we understand it, the Genoveses. Now, I need to tell you that so you can understand . . . "

". . . why you're looking at this," said Weitzman.

"I don't have to defend why we're looking at this," Rudnick said. "I mean, we already had Sal Pisello, a Gambino soldier. Now we've got a Genovese soldier and we've got them both sharing money that came from MCA."

"Are you aware of Myron, of his personal crisis during this time?" Azoff asked. "I have rationalized in my mind . . . that maybe Myron didn't have both eyes on the job, which is real understandable at this point in time. . . . Why didn't I fire Myron over all this shit? Because I believe that Myron's wife was dying at the time. That his intentions were good, that after what he's been through with this, between his wife dying and what we've put him through,

I believe that the guy's probably the most careful guy that exists in the record business after going through all this. He and I are kind of a Mutt and Jeff team. I get mad and yell and scream at people and he's good with people and the younger staff likes him. This was bad judgment, okay?"

Azoff also unloaded on McGill: "He was part of the old system— Bergamo, Passamano, McGill. All the old team that was there and, one by one, Myron and I fired everybody. I think at this point McGill is just happy he had a job."

"But why would he go along with a guy like Pisello?"

"Bad judgment."

The two cutout sales he blamed on Passamano: "Look, we could do thirty minutes on Passamano. He's senile, he's bitter, he's lying."

Bergamo, too, was lying, he said, and so was the *L.A. Times*. "The *Times* is on notice. I can't wait to file that lawsuit."

Rudnick asked about the January 1985 payment of $50,000 to Pisello. Why were there two stories on that? Why did the internal audit report say it was an advance on future royalties, while one MCA executive said in a statement that it was for Sal's help in getting the Checker/Chess tapes?

"All I can tell you is that I was not consulted about it," Azoff said. "To the best of my recollection, I did not approve it. They definitely had the authority to do that. The biggest question in my mind all along has been—we have a very sophisticated system of deal memos—why Zach Horowitz never signed off on that. . . . I have no knowledge of any collaboration that I participated in, or any other MCA group participated in, to provide funds to Sal Pisello, to do what you describe here. I guess what you're talking about is a bribe to Sal: 'You deliver Chess/Checker and we'll give you $50,000.'

"There are people who do not like to be yelled and screamed at who are afraid of me in the halls of MCA," Azoff continued. "There is a theory that I do not dispute to you that some people said, 'Uh oh, this deal's going sour. It wasn't a deal Irving liked in the beginning. If we can buy Chess/Checker the whole deal will look good.'

"And I have had to wrestle with the decision of should I fire people. But, you know, whether there is gross negligent conduct by people or whatever, I'm referring to words like cover-up, okay? And I can't tell you what was going through people's minds. I could tell you that there are a lot of people that probably figured their jobs were a lot safer if they could deliver the Chess/Checker catalog to me. But I never gave anybody express instructions. No marching orders that 'You better get me the Chess/Checker catalog or your ass is gone,' you know. I'm loud, I yell, I terrorize people. I was pissed off that these things were going bad.

"My answer is: I was not involved in the decision to give him the fifty. I don't know why they gave him the fifty. I think a lot of people were scared shitless of me in the halls at that point."

Azoff seemed eager to relate "three specific instances" when he had conversations with Pisello after the initial meeting in his office. "I always had a bad feeling about the guy," he said. The first instance was at the 1984 NARM convention. He was walking through the lobby of the Diplomat Hotel.

"I'm grabbed by a guy, a black gentleman by the name of Reverend Sharpton, who is best described in our business as a mini Jesse Jackson. He has some claim to be a reverend. I've now come to know he's mostly hot air. He'd organize black promoters, black promotion men, and do crack benefits. He was boycotting, trying to get black people to boycott the Lionel Richie tour because he wasn't using black promoters, or boycott the Michael Jackson tour. I was involved in starting to plan the Jackson tour at the time. One of our other businesses is concerts, so I had always been told, 'Listen, Sharpton can cause trouble. Just shake his hand and be nice to him.'

"So Sharpton walks up to me and he's just talking to me. Okay, I guess Pisello saw me talking to Sharpton. No sooner did Sharpton turn away and I go into the coffee shop to sit down and talk to one of the big retailers and Sal is all over me like a glove and he says something to the effect that—he did use the word *nigger*, because I remember it very precisely—'If that guy ever gives you any trouble, for $1,500 I can take care of that nigger. You call me. I got friends in New York. I got this, I got that.' Okay, I immediately go to Myron.

"I said, 'What is this?' He said, 'You don't understand Sal. He's just trying to be . . . Mr. Warmth, Mr. Big . . . He's full of shit. . . . I assure you that Sal is just blowing off hot air, just ignore it.'

"Another time I remember somehow the guy gets in the door of my office. No appointment, nothing. Got a tape in his hand. 'I got this great girl; you got to hear this girl.' I said, 'Fine, Sal, give me the tape. I'll send it to A&R, whatever.'

"I go to Myron and say, 'What's this guy doing walking in my office handing me a tape?' I put a plant, a huge four-foot-round plant right outside my door because he'd gone around the back side and avoided the secretary. I blocked it off. That's not going to happen again.

"Another time at the Palm, which is the record business lunchtime hangout. I can walk through there and have twenty-two meetings in ten minutes. I took Howard to lunch there today on the way down here, so he could get the flavor of it. You walk in, you turn left and there's a stool at the end of the bar. You cannot enter that restaurant and not come face-to-face with the guy sitting on that stool. Okay, now I would be there two days a week maybe for lunch. And the guy is there! You're not going to get by him. One day . . . "

"He sits on that same stool all the time?" Rudnick asked.

"Oh yeah. I don't think he eats lunch. I think he just sits on the stool so he can harass people. So I'm there; I'm having lunch. Gigi, who I guess is the maitre d'—I don't think he's an owner, he started out as a waiter, whatever—comes over to me. I'm having a business meeting. I don't remember with who. I don't remember when. He says, 'Sal Pisello, the owner of Sugar Hill, would like to pick up your lunch check. Would you like a drink or dessert or something?' I said, 'Gigi'—I very nicely explain to him—'I'm here on MCA business. I have a very nice expense account. Thank you very much, but nobody picks up my check.'

"Gigi comes back over and says, 'You're making Sal angry.' Okay. I said, 'Tell him no.' He says, 'Can he buy you a drink?' No. I go to walk out of the place, you know, and [Pisello] says, 'You insult me.' I mean, you just try and get by the guy. . . "

"He said that to you? Was he threatening?"

"Unfortunately, no, though I'd like to help you," Azoff laughed.

"But after the, I'll call it the trouble starter, after our note or public notification from you of him being a bad guy or whatever, he's on that stool and there are several instances when, man, I can't get in that restaurant without getting him right in my face. You know, what can you say to the guy other than, 'Gee, Sal, I'm sorry you're in trouble.'

"I mean, you know, he got me a couple of times. He would like almost push me in the corner to try and talk to me. After one of these instances I would say anything I could to not have to talk to the guy. I would try and sneak in between people, and I burrow pretty good and all that. After one of these instances where he says, 'I hope you know I never did anything to hurt MCA. I consider it like my company.' Yeah, that's all I need to hear, Sal. The next day I get that letter that I'm sure you're going to ask me about."

Rudnick couldn't suppress a smile. So that's what this long, breathless monologue was leading up to—the May 13 letter. "Dear Irving, I was very moved when I saw you at the Palm and you told me how everyone felt badly for me at MCA ...," Rudnick could practically recite it from memory.

Azoff knew the government had the letter and he knew the contents made it look like he had something more than a nodding acquaintance with Pisello. So he was explaining it away in advance, at the same time answering any witnesses the government might produce later saying they saw Azoff and Pisello meeting at the Palm. Azoff's version of the event may have been true, but it certainly seemed rehearsed to Rudnick. In fact, Azoff went to the Palm with his lawyer just before the interview, perhaps to go over the choreography one last time.

Azoff was similarly specific in describing his dealings with Morris Levy over the years: "When I was about eighteen, nineteen, or twenty years old, going to school at the University of Illinois, I had a band and we made a record independently. The record ended up on a big Chicago radio station. Through a friend of a friend of a friend, we ended up in Morris Levy's office. He picks up the record nationally. So that's the first and last time I ever recall meeting with Morris Levy. The record stiffed. It was a bar band from Illinois. It's been fifteen, sixteen, eighteen years ago. I think I might have been at a table with him once at a T. J. Martell Foundation dinner.

"I remember once or twice on the New Edition thing he did call me. Then he called one time to say, 'I'm gonna pay you for those cutouts; I'm having trouble collecting. We sold them to someone else. ... Don't worry, I'm gonna pay you.' I said, 'I don't know what you are talking about, Morris.' I mean, I didn't even know he was in the cutout deal. I switched him to McGill. My relationship with Levy is zip, okay? Zero. Zip."

He recalled one meeting with Joe Robinson and Milton Malden when Robinson came to MCA to complain about the terms of the Sugar Hill distribution agreement: "Bruce Resnikoff comes to me and says, 'Joe Robinson is camped out in the reception room. He says he's going to come every day from ten to six until you see him.

He's crying; the man is visibly shaking. What do you want to do?' I got Zach on the phone. Zach and I and maybe others—I don't think Myron was present—met with Malden and Joe. The first thing that Joe said to me was, 'We made our deal with Pisello because he told us he was paying off the number one or two guy in the Tower [MCA's corporate headquarters building]. That's the only way we could deal with MCA.'

"I mean, that was the point at which, in my mind, the words 'Sal the Swindler' really crystallized. You know, because when I heard that he told Joe Robinson he was paying off someone in the Tower. It wasn't even 'I'm paying off Myron; I'm paying off Irving; I'm paying off this guy.' But he said he was paying off Sheinberg or Werthheimer or one of those guys! It became very obvious how out-to-lunch or wacko this guy was."

Rudnick told him that the strike force had received an anonymous letter and had a statement from a witness making a similar allegation, saying that Pisello "had done a job for someone at MCA."

"I can't believe it," Azoff said.

"It's hard to believe that Sal Pisello would even know somebody in the Tower, much less be paying somebody off," Rudnick agreed.

"I mean," Azoff said, "if you would have told me when I took the MCA job, 'Take choice A or choice B: someone is going to come interview you from the government because they think you're an operative for Muammar Qaddafi, or B, you are going to be interviewed by the government for supposed Mafia involvement,' I would have picked choice A. This whole thing has been in the Twilight Zone.

"I don't believe he extorted anybody; I believe he defrauded us," Azoff said. "I'm not ruling out your theory that some people did some things with Mr. Pisello out of the ordinary in hopes that the ends would justify the means, thinking maybe Irving won't find out or maybe Irving won't be mad at me . . . but in my heart's heart I don't believe anybody at my place was threatened. I don't believe they were extorted. I don't believe they were paid off. I do believe they were swindled."

When the questions turned to independent promotion, payola, and Joe Isgro, Azoff instantly warmed to the subject, saying, "Isgro is another guy I always had a bad gut feeling about."

He said he was convinced there was a national racketeering conspiracy going on among independent record promoters. "I can't pinpoint the date, but there was a point in time when Isgro, Di-Sipio, Brenner, and Bird all sat down and said, 'This is my territory, that's your territory, that's my territory. And any other guys who want to break into the indie [independent] business will have to work for us and split when they get a city or a station.'

"I always contended that if you sat down and were given the names of the top twenty-five stations and the guys picking the music for those twenty-five stations and the proper IRS examination of those twenty-five guys, in this era of drugs and carelessness and everything else, that with a good portion of those twenty-five there would be something off-kilter in their IRS records that could then lead up the ladder."

He pointed out that MCA was a driving force behind the exposure of the independent promotion problem. "We were the company that gave the *Wall Street Journal* the list of who had what station. . . . We spoke to [Congressman] Dingell. I talked to [Senator] Gore. We gotta do something about this independent thing. . . . I think that if I spent a couple of days with you guys—it should have been a year ago—digging out the research of some places to go . . . There are guys around the country, you know. I'm sort of above it, but I think I can find out, first of all how these guys split up the country. . . . I mean you could track certain stations where they went through four program directors, but yet Joe Isgro kept the station for seven years."

He complained that eighteen months after all the record companies cut back on independent promotion, the pressure was growing to resume using it. "We can't afford it and we're not doing it. But these guys would punish us. Yetnikoff said a couple of times, 'I'm gonna make a call to Freddie DiSipio and then none of your records are going to get played' and stuff. I mean, these guys, you know, CBS. . . . Nobody was happier than us to see the plug pulled. It's a shame that the Pisello stuff came along and it's created a great pain for everybody. People's children, school. I've been turned down for a house loan by Prudential Life Insurance because they think I'm with the Mafia. It's not been pleasant. But this indie [independent promotion] thing is coming back. And it's coming back because nothing has happened.

"Isgro is out to get me, you know. My security guys tell me Isgro is, that I should be careful because he's going to kill me. . . . In the Isgro lawsuit, if we knew there was going to be some heat on him we might stand a little stronger on our lawsuit. We can't get any-body to join with us in a countersuit against him."

"Why is it so quiet?" Azoff asked of the payola investigation.

"While we're doing our job we don't have press conferences on the steps of the courthouse," Rudnick replied.

"I know there are only a few of you, but, Marvin, you know what I mean. If people were coming down and being interviewed or sub-poenaed, the word spreads. Right? The reason the independent thing is creeping back in is nobody's calling up saying they're being interviewed by anybody. . . . Right now is the turning point for it to come back. If you guys would turn the screws a little bit . . . "

"We're not here to maximize somebody's civil rights," Rudnick said coolly. Azoff was making a naked request for the government to help MCA defend itself against Isgro's lawsuit. And he apparently was offering to snitch off the entire industry, including several of his reputed friends—Gary Bird, Walter Yetnikoff—to get the gov-ernment off MCA's back and onto payola.

"How close are you and Yetnikoff?" Rudnick asked.

"We have a love-hate relationship."

"We heard both. . . . Do you eat dinner with him?"

"Not recently. He was civil to me at this luncheon the other day. The big rift between he and I, he told my wife the other day at this luncheon he showed up for—which is all these people from this charity. It's a big CBS thing. Tony Martell works at CBS. It's a won-derful charity. Anyway, he told my wife the other day that he's mad at me because . . . I told the government that CBS was the leader of independent promotion. And what I've been mad at Walter for was when MCA acquired my management company he was raising a big stink about it."

"Was he jealous or what?"

"Just jealous that I made the hit and he didn't. I shouldn't use that word here," he laughed. "I mean *score* . . . You guys know Wal-ter is a little crazy. "

"Let me ask you another question," agent McCalmont piped up. "Do you think people from the record companies—vice presi-dents—are getting kickbacks also?"

"Yes," said Azoff. "I think some have major drug habits. I think if you carefully looked through bank records and see which ones ended up in drug rehab programs, you can start there. If I were run-ning this thing . . . "

"Do you have any idea who the source of supply is?" Rudnick asked.

Azoff laughed. "Irving," Weitzman cut in, "my advice is that . . . "

". . . I shut up," Azoff said, finishing the sentence amid general laughter in the room.

The interview had been going on for better than two hours and Weitzman was getting impatient. "I have a five o'clock meeting and you're asking him questions about things he doesn't remember," he said to Rudnick. "And he's guessing, and I don't want to sit here and listen to Irving guess for an hour."

Before wrapping things up, however, Rudnick decided to take one more shot at obtaining the results of MCA lawyers' interviews with the record company executive.

"We are interested in your cooperation. What I want to know is, will you give us the Upjohn materials?"

"What's Upjohn?" Azoff asked.

Rudnick explained that it was the material he'd requested from Bill Billick and Allen Susman at their first meeting in Ted Gale's office. "They were here in their pin-striped suits. . . . I said, 'Well, if you're here to help me, give me the Upjohn material.' Which means all their attorney-client stuff. 'If you've done an investigation internally, give me what you've got so I won't have to have the agents do all the work over again.'

"And what did they tell me? And what did they tell me? They told me, 'We won't give you the Upjohn material.' And he [Billick] and I looked at each other like we were about ready to tear each other's eyes out. And we didn't talk for a long time thereafter."

"Well, why did he do that?" Azoff responded. "Because he wanted to make sure that MCA Records was never going to get . . . "

"I don't know why he did that," Rudnick interrupted. "If he claims that MCA is a victim of this entire Pisello episode and the strike force and everything that's gone on in the last year and a half . . . then he should have no reason not to give us what we want."

"Marvin, that was his job," Azoff soothed. "He didn't want to have to someday go to Sid Sheinberg and say, 'Joe Blow and XYZ were indicted today for blah, blah, blah; and, by the way, MCA Records was indicted and now you have stockholder lawsuits.' Okay, so that's all he's looking for. He wants you to write him a letter that says, 'MCA Records will not be indicted in this matter.'"

As the meeting was breaking up, Azoff posed a final series of questions to the prosecutor.

"Marvin, what if there really is no one explanation? What if different people really thought different things about the $50,000? That it was a conglomeration of people and that there was no one person that made that decision, and that different people had different perceptions?"

"Roshomon," Rudnick thought. He knew it was a possibility that the whole Pisello episode was merely a series of miscues and faulty communications among the management team that Sal exploited, and that no one really held the answer to what had gone on. But he didn't think it was likely.

"We've got all the symptoms of a diseased animal here," he said to himself after Azoff and Weitzman had gone. "We've got people taking five and making inconsistent statements, former employees saying the Mafia came into the company and they were thrown out after thirty years of work. And we've got money going out of a public company into the hands of hoods—with no good explanation as to why."

That didn't solve his problem, however. The interviews with the record executives had produced nothing in the way of hard evidence that a crime had been committed inside the company. The executives appeared to have adopted what prosecutors call a "lock-step defense" that hewed closely to the company line laid out in the internal audit report. McGill took orders from Roth, Azoff wasn't aware of those orders, and Roth couldn't remember why he gave them.

Rudnick was disappointed. He'd hoped the executives would turn on one another in the interviews, that someone would break from the herd and make a run for it on his own. But it hadn't happened, so he wouldn't be able to make a case based on the testimony of the executives.

He still had the Pisello card to play, however. As long as he had Sal as a defendant in a tax case involving the same money, there was a chance that Sal would decide to cooperate to avoid going to jail again. If that happened, and if Pisello's testimony could be corroborated—he couldn't simply use Pisello's word against the company—he had them.

Of course, that was a very big if.

Part III

JUDGMENT DAYS

35

Odds &
Sods

After months of depositions and bitter accusations, lawyers for MCA and John Gervasoni's Scorpio Music finally brought their battle to federal court in Los Angeles on March 10, 1987, almost a year to the day after their lawsuits were filed.

The case was to be heard in a nonjury trial before U.S. District Judge Stephan B. Wilson. Appointed to the bench by Ronald Reagan in 1985, Wilson was the former chief of special prosecutions in the Los Angeles U.S. attorney's office and had a reputation as a highly intelligent, tough, cut-to-the-chase jurist.

During pretrial conferences, Wilson ruled that he would hear the case in four phases, starting with MCA's claim that Scorpio was involved in massive counterfeiting of recordings by such MCA artists as The Who, Jimmy Buffet, and Tom Petty. The second phase would be Scorpio's breach of contract claim against MCA. If Scorpio won that phase, he would hear Scorpio's fraud claim. But only if Scorpio "won all the way down the line" would he consider Scorpio's racketeering complaint, Wilson said.

The morning the trial opened, MCA counsel Bill Billick was quoted in a *Hollywood Reporter* article as saying the counterfeiting phase of the case would not take long because of a "paucity of evidence." In an unusual admission by an attorney for a plaintiff in a $10 million lawsuit, Billick told the *Reporter,* "We don't have that much."

As it turned out, Billick may have overstated the case. MCA's "evidence" against Scorpio quickly boiled down to just three cassettes—one copy of The Who's *Odds & Sods* album purchased by MCA internal auditor Allen Clement at a Los Angeles record store, and two other The Who cassettes supposedly purchased by a former RIAA investigator at a flea market in New York.

The testimony produced moments of absurdist comedy, as when Judge Wilson, a lover of Jewish cantor music, asked MCA counsel Fred Shreyer what "The Who" was and what "Odds & Sods" meant. Shreyer explained that The Who was an English rock band, but he was at a loss to define the meaning of the album title.

Early on, Wilson set a tone that would continue throughout the trial when he interrupted Clement's testimony to ask why the executive had purchased just one copy of the allegedly counterfeit cassette when supposedly hundreds of thousands of them were in the marketplace. Clement responded that he was "trying to spend as little as possible" on the counterfeiting investigation. Wilson stared at him in disbelief. "You work for MCA and you're not interested in spending another $1.75 for a tape?" he said. When the judge inquired about the cost of the investigation, Clement replied that the entertainment conglomerate had spent a total of $300.

Things went straight downhill from there for MCA. Michael Ostroff, a staff lawyer for the record company, was called to the stand for what was supposed to be perfunctory testimony establishing MCA's claim to the copyright on the *Odds & Sods* recording. But what MCA presented to the court was a certified copy of a claim to the copyright by a European company called Track Records. Though he admittedly had no knowledge of record industry business practices and little experience in copyright law, Wilson immediately questioned the document. "All I see here is something in the files of MCA that is not self-authenticating. There is no stamp of registration of copyright," he said.

Scorpio attorney Raphael Chodos quickly chimed in that among "twelve thousand documents in eight boxes" that MCA had turned over to the defense in discovery, "there is no document linking MCA to Track Records."

Wilson responded that MCA seemed "woefully unprepared to prove their hold on the copyright. The first applicant for registration is Track Records; MCA doesn't have diddley poo."

Turning to a visibly uncomfortable Shreyer, the judge said sternly, "You're supposed to be ready to prove these things; you're the plaintiff. This shouldn't have happened, and I'm being rather generous with you. As of now you have no claim; maybe you're the wrong plaintiff."

The first day of testimony ended with MCA lawyers promising to produce proof that MCA held the copyright to the recording.

On the second day of the trial, MCA put its key witness on the stand, Rick Kauffman, a former RIAA counterfeiting investigator turned free-lance sleuth. Kauffman testified that he had purchased two cassettes—*Odds & Sods* and *Who's Next*—from a New York flea market vendor named Tony Dibichi, aka Tony Dee, in March 1985. After determining that the cassettes were counterfeit, Kauffman said he asked Dibichi where he'd gotten the cassettes and was told they were from Scorpio. Kauffman testified that "during the third week of March" he accompanied Dibichi to Scorpio's New Jersey warehouse, where he saw thousands more counterfeit cassettes of albums by The Who stacked up in "one-hundred-count boxes."

Kauffman had told a similar story to the *Los Angeles Times* in 1986, except he said the warehouse he visited was that of another budget record distributor.

MCA backed up Kauffman's testimony with a sworn deposition from Dibichi, who, the lawyers explained, was afraid to testify in person because he said his life had been threatened.

Wilson was clearly suspicious of Kauffman's testimony and immediately began a rapid-fire cross-examination of the witness, asking him why he waited more than a year after buying the cassettes before bringing them to the attention of the company and what prompted him to do so. "Are you just a good Samaritan?" the judge asked.

By the end of the second day of testimony, MCA had still not presented documents proving it held the copyright to *Odds & Sods*, and Wilson was going into a slow burn. When Bill Billick asked for more time to conduct discovery on Scorpio's business records and complained that the government had denied MCA access to a key witness in their case, namely John LaMonte, the judge erupted.

"My initial view is that this case is not nearly as straightforward as the plaintiff thinks it is," he said. "And I'm surprised at the cavalier approach of MCA. You're alleging that Scorpio violated copyright laws. The instances you know of are before the court or others would be here. All you know is that Clement by happenstance walked into a store and bought one tape that the retailer traced back to Mr. Gervasoni. That's all you've produced so far. Now you are saying 'Give me access to all his business records so I can rummage around and see if I can find something.' What I see is, you started out with a thread that's now down to a hair, and based on that I don't think it's the role of the court to give you full opportunity to do an investigation of Mr. Gervasoni."

Wilson asked Bill Billick when the company had served notice to depose LaMonte. They had never done so, Billick replied, but had taken the word of prosecutor Bruce Repetto that LaMonte would not be produced for the civil case.

"You should have noticed the deposition by sending a letter to the Department of Justice or the U.S. attorney in Newark," Wilson said. "They have a mechanism whereby they have to respond and say whether or not they'll produce him. . . . You didn't even try."

Billick did not show up for the next two days, leaving the case in the hands of Shreyer. At the end of the fourth day of waiting for the promised copyright registration for *Odds & Sods,* Wilson's patience had run out. He gave MCA its "last chance" to get the proof of copyright to the court.

"I'm not impressed with your case," he told Shreyer. "I may rule tomorrow from the bench. I could have cut your legs out from under you two days ago. I find it curious that Mr. Billick has dumped this off on you. I want to see Mr. Billick here tomorrow morning."

Billick was in court the next morning, along with Shreyer, Ostroff, and five other staffers from Allen Susman's law firm, Rosenfeld, Meyer and Susman—eight lawyers, all with long faces.

Gervasoni was the last defense witness. At the conclusion of his testimony just before noon, Billick told the judge that MCA was still working on producing proof of its copyright on *Odds & Sods* and asked that the court record remain open to receive the document when it came. Wilson cut him off. "My patience is wearing out," he said. "The bulk of this case is one tape out of millions. The copyright registration is a necessary ingredient of the case. You could lose on those grounds, and you may. The record will not be open. You've had more chances than you deserve." He banged his gavel and adjourned for lunch.

During the lunch recess, Billick made a last-ditch attempt to settle with Scorpio—for no money. "Let's just forget this ever happened," he told Chodos, who not only rejected the idea but angrily threatened to sue Billick and his law firm for malicious prosecution.

Following the recess, Wilson wasted little time. "It appears to me that this is a case juxtaposed," he said. "In most cases you look at a set of facts and then try to determine who is culpable. In this case, the plaintiff determined who was culpable and then looked for a set of facts."

"I have a very sour view of this presentation," Wilson said, addressing Billick. "For a firm that undoubtedly makes a good part of its living from these type of cases, this has been a very, very weak showing."

He called into question the testimony of MCA's key witness, saying, "The court views Mr. Kauffman as something analogous to what is termed in criminal law as an informant or a snitch, and they're always to be viewed with great suspicion."

In ruling in Scorpio's favor, Wilson seemed to go out of his way to exonerate Gervasoni, saying that even if the tape were counterfeit and traceable to Scorpio, "such an event could only have occurred through happenstance." He set July 14 as the trial date for the second phase of the case.

The outcome of the case created bad feelings between the Rosenfeld, Meyer and Susman firm and MCA Records executives. The attorneys would have preferred that the counterfeiting claim be dropped for lack of evidence and they were angered that the record executives had insisted it go forward. The executives, in turn, blamed the lawyers for the loss in court, and that view apparently carried the day at the corporation.

MCA issued no official statement following the trial, but *Billboard* later quoted a "spokesman from the company"—usually a euphemism for Larry Solters—as saying, "The case against Scorpio established that there was massive counterfeiting of over 300,000

MCA tapes. Unfortunately, we were unable to succeed in our counterfeiting case against Scorpio. Our case was made more difficult by the government's refusal to make available a key witness and Scorpio's scarcity of business records."

Shortly after the trial, MCA hired another Los Angeles law firm—Munger, Tolles and Olson, known for its hardball litigation—to take over the remainder of the Scorpio case, as well as to handle the company's ongoing problems with the Justice Department. The change was big news in the Los Angeles legal community and an apparent slap in the face to Allen Susman, who had labored for nearly forty years as Lew Wasserman's chief outside counsel. It was also a sign that despite the problems his record division had brought upon the parent corporation, Irving Azoff's star was still in ascendancy at MCA.

Marvin Rudnick stopped by Judge Wilson's courtroom several times during the Scorpio trial, hoping to glean some little piece of information that would prove helpful to his own investigations. He got nothing, however, except the impression that John Gervasoni would make a fairly good witness if he needed him at Pisello's trial.

The MCA-Pisello investigation had been on the back burner since the Azoff interview. John Anderson was pulled off the investigation and put on another IRS case. Rudnick found out about it only after the fact—Anderson left without even saying good-bye. John Dubois was leaving the Los Angeles strike force, too. He was going to Washington to join Attorney General Meese's pornography task force. So Rudnick was now fully in charge of the payola investigation, on top of everything else. Ted Gale was arguing that he should forget about MCA, indict Pisello, and concentrate on the payola investigation. "Marvin, what have you got on MCA?" he said. "Where's the crime?"

Maybe Ted was right, Rudnick thought. For now at least he was swimming against the current with MCA, while the payola investigation finally seemed to be producing results. There'd been a series of intriguing developments in the case.

One of the first things Rudnick did after taking over the investigation was subpoena Joe Isgro's bodyguard, David Michael Smith, to testify before the grand jury. By all accounts, Smith spent more time with Isgro than any of the promoter's other employees. So it stood to reason that he would know something about Isgro's alleged dealings with organized crime figures. Rudnick got the Immigration and Naturalization Service to deliver the subpoena to Smith, a British citizen, as he was eating breakfast at a Denny's restaurant in the San Fernando Valley. But Smith never showed up to testify and word was that he'd fled the country.

From studying the federal payola statute, Rudnick had come to the conclusion that trying to pursue a payola case against Isgro would be futile. For one thing, payola was a misdemeanor, punishable by a maximum one year in prison and a $10,000 fine. Even if the government could prove multiple counts of payola, a misdemeanor couldn't be used as one of the "predicate acts" in a racketeering case.

The thirty-year-old payola law was poorly written, taking into account primarily money or "valuable consideration" given to a radio station employee in a direct exchange for playing a specific record, the old "hundred-dollar handshake," as it was known in the business. But record promotion practices had become increasingly sophisticated in the years since the law was passed. What about expense-paid vacations and prizes awarded to radio programmers as part of record-company-sponsored "contests"? Or the common record company practice of paying radio programmers large fees to introduce a performer at a concert—"Ladies and gentleman, please welcome . . . "—the same week that that performer's new record was being released? Such gimmicks made the radio programmer beholden to the record company and, therefore, predisposed to playing that company's records. They could accomplish the same thing as handing over a bag full of cash or an ounce of cocaine. But were they payola? Probably not, since the law did not take such practices into account.

Moreover, according to the statute, it wasn't the payment that was illegal, but rather the failure to disclose the payment to the public. However, the law didn't specify who was required to disclose the payment—the promoter? the employee? the station management? If it was the promoter, then how was he supposed to make the disclosure—call a press conference? take out an ad in the newspaper? All of these arguments would probably be raised by the defense in any payola prosecution.

On top of all that, Rudnick discovered that in 1979 the Federal Communications Commission held in an administrative ruling that "social exchanges between friends are not payola." Which meant if the payer and payee could establish that they were social friends, they had a solid defense for any gifts or money exchanged. The FCC's so-called friendship exception carved a gaping loophole in an already weak law. Little wonder that there had never been a successful prosecution under the payola statute.

Rudnick determined that the best way to pursue the independent promotion investigation was to look for tax fraud. If illegal payments were being made, then the money had to be buried somewhere in the promoters' books and records, disguised as something else. Payola then would be the motive for more serious crimes.

From going over Isgro's financial records, investigators found that hundreds of thousands of dollars were going out each year to a San Mateo–based record promoter named Ralph Tashjian, whom Isgro claimed was a "subcontractor" of his. Prior to 1985, however, Tashjian had been Isgro's partner and operated out of his Los Angeles office.

Rudnick subpoenaed Tashjian's financial records to see what he did with all the money from Isgro. "Look for a 'bubble' in his books," he told the IRS agents, "any unusually large expense items he might be using to soak up the money as a cover for payola payments."

They quickly found what appeared to be inflated entertainment receipts, lunch and dinner checks for amounts that seemed systematically too high. They picked out the worst examples, subpoenaed the restaurants for their copies of the bills, and began the painstaking process of comparing them with Tashjian's receipts. Bingo! They got hits all over the place. Tashjian's copies invariably showed amounts larger than those of the restaurants. Rudnick was elated. If Tashjian had turned over phony records to the strike force, they had a solid obstruction of justice case against him.

Then, during a routine background interview with a former employee of Tashjian, an IRS investigator was told that from 1983 to 1985 the promoter made regular payments of cash and cocaine to a group of radio programmers. The payments were hidden in cassettes and record album sleeves and shipped via Federal Express, the employee said. Rudnick subpoenaed Fed Ex's main office in Memphis for the records of deliveries from Tashjian's office. This was potentially a tremendous break. While the receipts themselves wouldn't prove anything, they might be a Rosetta stone showing which program directors received payola. The investigators knew that Isgro billed the record companies by radio station, date, and record added. If they could match up Isgro's invoices for the records with Tashjian's Federal Express deliveries to program directors who added those records, they would have broken the case.

A further look into Isgro's books revealed several suspicious-looking tax shelters that had been set up by his attorney, Dennis DiRicco. The shelters allowed Isgro to claim losses of several million dollars over a two-year period, about three times what he supposedly invested.

Investigators also found payments of nearly $600,000 to Star Promotions, a company that no one in the record business seemed to have heard of. A quick check revealed that Star was owned by a twenty-nine-year-old San Fernando Valley man named Jeffrey Monka who had pleaded guilty in 1985 to possessing six and a half ounces of cocaine with intent to sell. Monka turned out to be the son-in-law of Isgro's accountant.

Rudnick also found that Isgro had claimed as a business expense tens of thousands of dollars' worth of clothing that was purchased from Mark Michaels, an exclusive men's store in Marina Del Rey, and delivered to a New York City apartment. Rudnick checked New York real estate records and discovered that the apartment was owned by Ray Anderson, the vice president of promotion for CBS's Epic Records, Michael Jackson's label.

On the face of it, the expensive clothing looked like a kickback. Anderson, after all, was the executive charged with hiring independent promoters at Epic. Rudnick knew that Epic had paid Isgro and other members of the Network a fortune to promote Michael Jackson's *Thriller*, an album that even Isgro admitted needed no added promotion. It was also curious that CBS was the only major record company not named in Isgro's lawsuit.

The discovery of the clothing receipts tracked with Rudnick's belief that some people at the record companies had to be involved if there was a widespread payola scheme going on. From the beginning, he suspected the record companies' motives in steering the government onto the independent promoters. It never made sense to him that these big, cutthroat corporations would meekly turn over $50 million to $80 million a year to a group of outsiders without some guarantee that they would get what they were paying for. All along he had the feeling that the government was galloping off in the wrong direction as the record companies stood by the side of the road pointing their fingers and shouting, "They went that-a-way!"

Rudnick intended to double back and follow the investigation up the ladder as well as down. He started by subpoenaing CBS for any records it had regarding Ray Anderson's dealings with Isgro.

36

"I'm getting tense"

In early June, after listening to two thousand hours of wiretapped phone conversations and poring over thirty thousand pages of transcripts and FBI affidavits that had been turned over by the prosecution, Morris Levy's attorneys came up with a novel idea.

In a motion before U.S. District Judge Stanley Brotman in Camden, New Jersey, they argued that, according to the government's own documents and confidential informants, Levy was actually the "victim" of a long-running extortion conspiracy by Vincent Gigante and the Genovese family. They submitted as proof pages of previously sealed government documents alleging that the Genoveses had developed a "stranglehold" on Levy's music operation, that they used the Roulette Records president as a "lucrative source of cash and property," and that Gigante had even threatened to kill Levy if the record executive didn't continue buying real estate for the crime group.

If all this were true, the lawyers reasoned, then their man was obviously acting under duress if he took part in the alleged extortion conspiracy against John LaMonte. (Duress is a defense in a criminal case.)

Levy's lawyers were walking a fine line. They were not admitting that their client was controlled by organized crime. "That's not what we are saying," Leon Borstein told Judge Brotman in a June 12 hearing. "It's what we're saying the FBI is saying." And since the FBI was saying it based largely on the say-so of thirteen confidential informants, Levy's lawyers were asking the judge to compel the government to reveal the identities of those informants and make them available to the defense so they could be questioned about any "exculpable" evidence they might have that would be helpful to Levy's case.

The lawyers knew they stood a snowball's chance in hell of getting to the government's informants. As expected, prosecutor Bruce Repetto vehemently objected to the motion, arguing that since some of the informants were mob insiders, revealing their names to Levy—hence, possibly Gigante—was tantamount to a death sentence.

Levy's attorneys were simply trying to throw a wrench into the government's case, hoping against hope that the judge would rule that Levy needed access to the informants in order to properly defend himself. Which would place the government in an untenable position and—just maybe—force Repetto to drop the charges rather than risk the lives of thirteen cooperating witnesses.

It was a shot in the dark, and it backfired. Brotman denied the motion, saying he would take the government's word that the informants had no exculpable evidence other than what was stated in the documents the government had already turned over to the defense. At the same time, the confidential law enforcement intelligence documents that Levy's lawyers put into the public record proved great fodder for the media. "Extortion case ties music-industry executive with mob," read the banner headline in the *Philadelphia Inquirer.*

The lawyers chalked up one small victory, however, when Judge Brotman agreed to separate the extortion trial of Levy, Howard Fisher, and Dominick Canterino from the racketeering trial of the Vastola Organization. At least Levy would not have to sit in court next to Vastola, the man accused of actually beating LaMonte. That would help distance him from the crime in the minds of the jury.

Another of Levy's planned defenses in the extortion case was entrapment. As he told reporters shortly after his indictment, "I think the government told LaMonte not to pay for the records, so I'd get mad and punch him in the nose." Borstein said they had information that LaMonte actually began cooperating with the government long before he ran afoul of Corky Vastola, perhaps as early as 1979.

Their strategy was to portray the man they expected to be the government's star witness as a snitch, a coke-head, and an incorrigible counterfeiter who continued to ply his illegal trade even while under the protection of the federal government. Levy's investigators had learned that LaMonte was still operating his budget and oldies record business via telephone calls to his former employees. He was contacting customers and making deals, collecting money. They knew all this because they were interviewing those customers and attempting to talk to LaMonte's employees. It was all part of a perfectly legitimate investigation in the service of a client. And it turned LaMonte's life into a hell on the run.

LaMonte had managed to keep his business operating in some fashion through daily phone contact with his loyal and gutsy secretary, Mary Ann Laberty, now the president of a company called Satellite Sounds, which was in her name but really belonged to LaMonte. He knew he was taking a terrible chance with his life in trying to stay in the record business. Levy's private detectives had been to his warehouse. They were visiting his customers, scaring them with questions about counterfeiting. Bogus telephone repairmen had tried to gain access to the Satellite Sounds offices. After that, the office was destroyed by a suspicious fire that started in the space next to it. Mary Ann was forced to move to another rented space.

There was no doubt in LaMonte's mind that he was being tracked. He believed that at least one of his longtime customers was working for the other side. The red flag went up the day the customer tried to get him into a conversation about Levy. "You had some sort of vendetta against Morris, didn't you?" he asked. "By the way, Levy's lawyers want to talk to you." Then he added, "How's your mother and brother?"

LaMonte's family was not in good shape. In 1986, on the Wednesday before Thanksgiving the FBI had scooped them up from their new location and moved them overnight to another city. Investigators had picked up intelligence information that the bad guys had located them. After that, the marshals moved LaMonte around several times by himself. His mother back in Philadelphia was gravely ill. His daughter April needed surgery to correct a congenital deformity of her foot and he was without medical insurance. He had no car and was forced to hitchhike around the cities that the marshals left him in for weeks at a time, unguarded.

"I'm hanging out like a time bomb," he told a *Los Angeles Times* reporter in a late-night phone call from "somewhere out in God's land."

"I can't live in this program," he said. "Nine out of ten people in the program go back to prison because they can't live in the system. A legit guy cannot survive under these circumstances. If I bite the bullet, you have to blast them. They did not give me enough money to survive. I have five people. I have medical bills of over $10,000 because when I left they told me to stop my insurance. They said, 'Don't worry, we'll pay for everything.'"

The government was upset with him for trying to carry on his record business, he said. But the monthly subsistence checks were not enough, and they often arrived late. "So I'm under pressure to expose myself by making a living. Maybe it's better for them if I get whacked. I thought I was not just a witness; I thought they felt I was a human being, too. At ten o'clock last night I was watching television and I saw on the news that some guy got killed by the mob. I think I should have someone from the government outside my door. I'm getting tense."

It had been nineteen months since he left his other life behind. "I'm the victim and I'm the one in jail," he said, "while Morris and the boys are free to walk the streets. I can't believe nothing is happening."

Actually, Levy et al. were not having as good a time as LaMonte imagined. In March, authorities in Philadelphia broke up what they called the longest-operating and most profitable drug network in the city's history when they arrested a man named Roland "Pops" Bartlett and thirty-four of his employees on a variety of charges, including murder. In the course of investigating Bartlett's drug empire, the FBI found that much of the money from the operation was laundered through a New York company called Domino Records, which operated out of the Roulette Records office at 1790

Broadway. Wiretaps in the New York grand jury investigation indicated that Levy had access to the Domino Records bank account, which linked him to a far more serious racketeering conspiracy than the LaMonte case. This one could send him to prison for life.

Fritzy Giovanelli, meanwhile, was on trial in Queens for the murder of detective Anthony Venditti. During tear-choked testimony on June 15, Venditti's partner, Kathleen Burke, told the jury, "I will never forget that night as long as I live." She told how Giovanelli fired at her as she approached the three men who had pinned her partner against the wall of the diner. "After Mr. Giovanelli fired a second shot at me, he turned and fired on Tony, and the other two defendants were also firing in my partner's direction."

"I was hit in the chest and I fell to the ground," Burke said, biting her lip and trying to keep her composure as Venditti's widow, Patti, listened from the front row of the spectator seats in the courtroom. "I remember seeing Tony bend over and then his body just gave a jerk."

After more than seven weeks of testimony and eight days of deliberation, the jury reported it was hopelessly deadlocked nine to three in favor of convicting Giovanelli and the others. A mistrial was declared, but Giovanelli remained in custody without bail.

On July 6, the *Los Angeles Times* published an article revealing that Rocco Musacchia, business partner of Pisello and Levy, had worked as a "technical adviser" on a number of big-budget Hollywood movies that were filmed in New York City, including Neil Simon's *Brighton Beach Memoirs, A Chorus Line,* and, ironically, two Mafia-themed pictures, *The Pope of Greenwich Village* and *Prizzi's Honor.* The latter film starred Jack Nicholson and Kathleen Turner as a husband-and-wife hit team for the mob.

The *Times* reported that while Musacchia was working on *Brighton Beach Memoirs* in the summer of 1985, his telephone conversations were intercepted by the FBI and he was overheard on several occasions handing out jobs on the movie set. In one intercepted call, he was overheard talking to Morris Levy and promising to find a job on the film for one of Levy's former wives.

According to sworn FBI affidavits obtained by the *Times,* "Electronic surveillance to date has continued to illustrate the illegal control exercised by the Genovese family, through Vincent Gigante, over a variety of activities, including the movie industry."

Gaetano Vastola was still confined to his home, and Bruce Repetto was being hard-nosed about letting him leave for any reason. Repetto rejected out-of-hand a request from Vastola's lawyer that the mobster be allowed to travel to Florida, where his now-recovered son, Guy, was making a record with the Pointer Sisters.

Sonny Brocco had been in jail since his arrest in September 1986, unable to post $500,000 bail and probably safer where he was, considering that his cousin, the Galoot, blamed him for much of what had happened.

On July 9, the federal grand jury in Los Angeles handed up an indictment of Sal Pisello on three counts of income tax evasion. He was charged with evading taxes on nearly $600,000 in unreported income for the years 1983 to 1985, most of which was earned in MCA-related business transactions. He faced a maximum fifteen years in prison and a $600,000 fine.

When Marvin Rudnick returned to his office from the grand jury room that day, he was told by Rick Small, another strike force lawyer, that U.S. Attorney Robert Bonner's office wanted him to write up a press release on the Pisello indictment. It was an odd request, Rudnick thought, since the strike force as a rule did not issue press releases on its cases. He'd never done one before.

But Rudnick was getting used to unusual things happening around the office, starting with Ted Gale's abrupt departure on June 1. That shocked everyone. Gale had called all the staff lawyers into his office on a Wednesday and told them he was leaving to join the U.S. attorney's staff back in Rhode Island. His last day at the strike force would be the following Friday, he said.

The lawyers were so stunned at the news that no one ever asked Gale why he was leaving, or why on such short notice. Did something happen? Ted had warned them a few months earlier that there was a movement afoot in Washington to merge all the strike force offices in the country into their local U.S. attorneys' offices. If that happened, he told them, they should all be concerned about their future in the Justice Department, since it would be up to each U.S. attorney to decide which strike force personnel he retained on his staff. Maybe that's why Gale left—he didn't want to have to report to Bonner. Or perhaps it was for some secret personal reason; he never said.

Following Gale's departure, Rick Small was named acting chief of the Los Angeles office. A new chief had been appointed—John

Newcomer, from the Detroit strike force—but he wasn't expected to report for full-time duty until October.

Rudnick sat down at the word processor that afternoon and typed up a press release as his new boss had ordered. "Central Figure in MCA Records Probe Indicted," the headline read.

The release detailed the MCA transactions through which Pisello earned the unreported income—the Sugar Hill distribution deal, the Latin label deal, the break-dance mat venture, and the cutout sale to LaMonte. It was practically boilerplate stuff by now. But Rudnick added a few colorful flourishes of his own. He noted that much of the money was passed through Consultants for World Records, "a company that Pisello shared with New York movie production assistant Rocco 'the Butcher' Musacchia and Genovese crime figure Frederick [sic] 'Fritz' [sic] Giovanelli, who is currently awaiting trial for the murder of a New York police detective."

Pisello, the release said, was "the first person indicted in Los Angeles in a continuing investigation of payola and organized crime influence in the recording industry."

At Pisello's arraignment the following Monday, July 13, Rudnick asked U.S. District Judge William Rea to set a "high, reasonable bail" for the defendant, whom he described as "a threat to the safety of others." He backed up his request by disclosing a series of strong-arm incidents that Pisello had been involved in over the years. In 1983, for example, Pisello threatened to kill a government witness, he said. In 1985, Pisello made an "offer" to unnamed MCA Records executives to "shake down" record promoter Joe Isgro for "nonpayment of a $300,000 debt to Sugar Hill Records." And according to a statement from another unnamed MCA executive, Pisello once offered to "take care of" Reverend Al Sharpton.

"Most damning of all," Rudnick continued, was Pisello's relationship with "a group of Mafia figures" who face racketeering charges in New Jersey stemming from the sale of MCA cutout records that Pisello set up."

Rudnick knew he risked being accused of engaging in overkill. Pisello, after all, was still in federal custody on his previous conviction. After serving a year in Lompoc, he'd been transferred to a halfway house in Los Angeles to serve out the balance of his sentence. The assignment to the halfway house indicated that the Bureau of Prisons didn't consider him a problem.

Rudnick's motive in making the disclosures was twofold. First of all, he wanted to send a message to Pisello that he had serious problems that he should deal with right away and not wait for the outcome of the trial. He was hoping that Pisello would agree to talk. Second, he was trying to educate Judge Rea that this was not going to be a typical tax evasion case. MCA, the company that provided the unreported income to Pisello, was not exactly a willing witness. He felt it was important for the judge to know there might be some larger scheme in the background, just in case MCA executives back-pedaled later in their testimony and raised reasonable doubts about the nature of the income items.

Pisello's new lawyer, David Hinden, argued vociferously that his client was not a bail risk, that he had shown up for all previous court appearances and had voluntarily surrendered to begin serving his prison sentence on the previous conviction.

Rudnick rebutted that Pisello's own life might be in danger if he were to be released from custody. "He may be a man who knows too much," he said. "I believe he could be hounded to his worst detriment by MCA on one side and organized crime on the other."

In a sidebar discussion, he informed the judge that, according to the FBI, Vincent Gigante had put a contract out on Pisello's life—at the request of Morris Levy. The FBI had gone to Pisello in prison and told him about the alleged murder contract.

In the end, however, Judge Rea said he was not convinced that Pisello posed a danger to the community and he set bail at $50,000.

The next day, Rudnick got a call from Dennis Kinnaird, who introduced himself as MCA's new lead counsel from Munger, Tolles and Olson. "We're taking over from the Susman firm on the Scorpio case and the grand jury matter," he said.

"Welcome to the case," Rudnick replied.

Kinnaird suggested they sit down together to discuss where the investigation was going. He was in a cooperative mode. "We want to get to the bottom of this thing, too," he said.

"Lookit," Rudnick said, "we've got this Upjohn problem. I've asked Bill Billick for the statements your guys made to the company lawyers, and I also asked Irving Azoff and Howard Weitzman for them. We need those statements before I can put your MCA employees on the stand."

Kinnaird said he'd see what he could do and get back to him. It was all very cordial.

Privately, however, MCA lawyers were livid about Rudnick's

press release and his remarks at the Pisello arraignment, particularly the part about Pisello's life being in danger. The way they saw it, the prosecutor was using a simple tax case to smear the company in an irresponsible campaign of innuendo. The marching orders from MCA management were to do something about the pesky prosecutor. This had to stop.

And MCA figured Dennis Kinnaird was just the man for the job. He was a former chief of the special prosecutions unit in the Los Angeles U.S. attorney's office, a position that U.S. District Judge Stephan Wilson held before him. Rudnick learned later that Kinnaird was also a close friend of Robert Brosio, the longtime chief of criminal prosecutions in the U.S. attorney's office. In short, Kinnaird had all the right connections for going over Rudnick's head—if that became necessary.

Rudnick had a similar situation with the payola investigation. CBS Records had been slow in complying with his subpoena for documents regarding Ray Anderson's dealings with Joe Isgro. Shortly after he served the subpoena, Rudnick received a call from a CBS outside counsel, Richard Kuh, who told him—pointedly, Rudnick thought—that he'd contacted a local judge about the prosecutor and had asked the judge to make an introduction for him to U.S. Attorney Bonner. It was a not-too-subtle way of saying the record company was prepared to go over Rudnick's head on the matter.

The day the story of Pisello's arraignment hit the entertainment industry trade papers, Rudnick received a phone call from a federal agent in New York. The agent said he was the "handler" of the Reverend Al Sharpton, an FBI informant who was cooperating with the government in an undercover investigation of boxing promoter Don King. Sharpton also knew a lot about the record business, the agent said. He was a friend of Joe Robinson's and he knew Irving Azoff. "Sharpton would like to cooperate in your investigation, too," he told Rudnick.

"Have him call me; I'll be glad to talk to him about whatever he knows," Rudnick said, trying to mask his amazement at this new twist.

Oftentimes, prosecutors don't fully realize the impact their words can have far beyond the courtroom. This was one of those times. Rudnick's statement to Judge Rea about Sharpton had rustled the bushes back in New York and flushed out yet another investigation.

It seemed like every time he turned around, the story got more bizarre.

Rudnick didn't know it then, but there was one other statement he made in court that day—the one about Pisello being caught in the middle between the mob and MCA—that was already having far more impact that he ever imagined.

37

"Being verbally frisked"

On July 21, Scorpio Music lost the second round of its battle with MCA on a technicality. The jury found that the New Jersey cutout distributor had no valid contract with the record company and, without a contract to breach, MCA had no liability for Scorpio's losses on the 1984 cutout sale. Case dismissed.

MCA was elated. "I'm not at all surprised by the verdict," Azoff told *Daily Variety.* "The case was a witch hunt from the start. I hope this puts an end to a lot of unfair finger-pointing against MCA." But though the case was decided in MCA's favor, testimony during the week-long trial raised a number of questions about the company's sale of cutouts in 1984 and 1985.

For the first time, MCA counsel Dennis Kinnaird conceded that Pisello had acted as the "apparent agent" of the company in the cutout deals, meaning he held himself out to be MCA's agent and the company had acted in such a way as to reinforce that impression among outsiders, including Scorpio.

Ranji Bedi testified that when he first called Sam Passamano about buying MCA cutouts, Passamano told him he was no longer in charge but would have the new man call him. It was Pisello who called back, Bedi said, and arranged to meet him at a restaurant, where "he presented me with a list [of records] and gave me the rules of the game."

Bedi said the rules according to Pisello called for him to pay sixty cents a record, of which fifty cents would go to MCA and ten cents would go to Sal. MCA was allowing him to make whatever he could on the side, Pisello said. Since Bedi was selling the records to Scorpio at seventy cents each, he would also make a profit of ten cents a record, or $100,000 on a million units.

Even Judge Wilson thought the whole arrangement sounded suspect. Noting that MCA had sold cutouts to Scorpio directly on a number of occasions in 1982 and 1983, Wilson said at one point, "I'm finding this case very curious. Something about it doesn't sit right with me. Why is there a Ranji Bedi in the deal? Passamano knows the business; Bedi doesn't know the business, he's operating out of his home."

Other questions raised in the course of the trial included why MCA's Dan McGill refunded $200,000 on the Scorpio deal at a time when Pisello supposedly owed the company more than $500,000 on the LaMonte sale. McGill said he was following orders, but he couldn't remember who gave them.

All the questions became moot, however, once the jury decided that whatever contract existed was between Scorpio and Bedi, not Scorpio and MCA.

The day after the Scorpio trial ended, Rudnick received his first phone call from the Reverend Al Sharpton. Since being contacted earlier by Sharpton's FBI handler, he'd done some checking on the thirty-three-year-old Pentecostal minister. Sharpton had no church, but as president of the Brooklyn-based National Youth Movement, he'd become an increasingly visible and controversial leader in a variety of civil rights protests in New York. He'd recently earned the enmity of millions of Manhattan commuters by leading his followers in a three-day pedestrian blockage of the Brooklyn Bridge, protesting an ugly racial incident in which several black youths were attacked—and one killed—by a white mob in Howard Beach.

The flamboyant, pompadoured preacher-without-portfolio was well known in the record business, where he was viewed as something of a civil rights shake-down artist. Sharpton's modus operandi was to target a company that he claimed wasn't employing enough blacks and then either throw up a picket line or threaten a boycott. He was considered no more than a minor irritation, however, since a cash contribution to his National Youth Movement was usually all it took to make him go away. As he told one company president, "This really isn't about black and white; it's about green."

Rudnick found that Sharpton was widely regarded as a flake, if not an outright crook. Still, he figured he had nothing to lose by listening to what the reverend had to say.

"The FBI has authorized me to talk to you," Sharpton announced. "I know Joe Robinson; he and I have a close mutual friend."

"How do you feel about telling me what he knows?" Rudnick asked.

"I'll tell you anything you want to know." Sharpton said he'd just received a call from Irving Azoff, who wanted him to intercede with Robinson to "help settle the Sugar Hill lawsuit and the criminal matter."

Rudnick didn't like the sound of that. The "criminal matter" had to be the Pisello case. He wondered how Azoff intended to settle that by talking to Robinson.

"Here's what I need," Rudnick said. "One of the mysteries in our case is the relationship between Sal Pisello and MCA. For some reason both MCA and Joe Robinson were paying Sal money. Any leads you can give me that those payments were for something other than legitimate business purposes would be helpful."

"I'll help you any way I can," Sharpton said. He promised to call back when he found something out.

Several days later, he did. There'd been a meeting between MCA lawyers and Robinson, he said. He didn't know what happened at the meeting, however, or whether there had been a settlement.

Rudnick was immediately on the phone to Sugar Hill's attorney, Paul Hollander, in New Jersey. Yes, the two sides had met, Hollander said, but there had been no settlement of the lawsuit and no discussion of the criminal case. "I told them up front we wouldn't talk about that," Hollander said nervously.

"Well how did the criminal case even come up?" Rudnick

inquired. His antennae were tingling. Robinson was going to be a key witness in the upcoming Pisello trial. His testimony, as it stood, would be damaging to Pisello and, consequently, to MCA. But Robinson was a real Nervous Nellie and was desperately in need of money. It wouldn't take much for him to start forgetting things. All MCA had to do was dangle a fat settlement proposal in front of him. It could all be accomplished with a wink and a nod, under the cover of a legitimate civil settlement.

There was little Rudnick could do about the situation, however, except fret and wait to see if Robinson's memory suddenly began to fail. The proof would be in his trial testimony.

Another problem was the IRS. Since Dubois left, some of the agents had been chafing under Rudnick's more authoritarian role. He liked to run his own investigations and he expected the agents to follow his directions. As he told Dubois on several occasions, "Once the agents start directing the investigation, you're in trouble."

One agent in particular, Kemp Schiffer, was giving him fits. Schiffer had a reputation around the strike force for being something of a right-wing zealot. While all IRS CID agents were cleared to carry firearms, Kemp was the only one who regularly packed a pistol to work. Rudnick had received several complaints from potential witnesses in the case claiming that Schiffer had tried to intimidate them into cooperating.

Schiffer appeared to be a hard worker, but Rudnick never knew exactly what he was doing. That made him nervous. But what made him mad was when Schiffer failed to show up on two occasions for scheduled testimony before the grand jury. Once he went to the firing range instead. After that, Rudnick complained to Schiffer's IRS superiors about his comportment, which precipitated a shouting match between Kemp and himself in front of the secretaries in the middle of the strike force outer office. Later, Chuck McCalmont warned him, "Be careful; Kemp's got friends upstairs."

One of Schiffer's friends upstairs turned out to be Rick Spiers, the number three man in the IRS's Criminal Intelligence Division. Shortly after the shouting incident with Schiffer, Spiers called Rudnick into a meeting with a number of IRS agents and dressed him down. "We can't work with you, Marvin," he said. "My agents have been complaining that you're too involved in investigation; you're calling too many shots."

"That's my job," Rudnick fired back. He in turn criticized Spiers for failing to control Schiffer. "He's running around intimidating witnesses; we can't have that."

The meeting was a standoff. Afterwards, several agents who were present approached Rudnick and apologized for Spiers's behavior. Rudnick didn't believe the majority of the agents were against him, as Spiers said. More likely, this attack on him was coming from higher up. And Rudnick thought he knew why.

Back in the early spring of 1986, shortly after the first subpoena went out in the payola case, Rudnick had been called to the office of Ron Saranow, the chief of the IRS criminal division in Los Angeles. At the time, Rudnick was preparing to indict a sitting IRS agent for helping a convicted fraud artist named Danny Mondavano prepare a phony tax return. The strike force was investigating Mondavano, who was on parole, for his involvement in another fraud scheme in the San Fernando Valley. Nonetheless, at the meeting with Rudnick, Saranow asked Rudnick to go easy on the agent and indict him on misdemeanor charges instead. He said he was a friend of the agent's lawyer.

Shocked at what he considered an improper attempt to interfere with an investigation, Rudnick refused and later reported the incident to Ted Gale. He never knew what Gale did with the information, however. The agent eventually pleaded guilty to the felony charge.

That's what this was all about, Rudnick thought. He was getting paid back. It was all politics.

The third week of August, on his first day back in the office following a badly needed two-week vacation with his family at Yosemite National Park, Rudnick was told by Rick Small that Michael Defeo, deputy chief of the Justice Department's organized crime and racketeering section, would be in town the next week to meet with him about the payola investigation.

"Uh oh," Rudnick thought. Defeo was in charge of all strike force offices west of the Mississippi. A forbidding figure with brush-cut hair and a brusque military manner, he was the quintessential Fed. They didn't call him Iron Mike for nothing. John Dubois likened his first interview with Defeo to "being verbally frisked." Rudnick knew Defeo didn't just drop in to chew the fat and kick around investigative theories with his staff lawyers. This visit meant somebody was in trouble. He hoped it wasn't him.

But it was. The meeting with Defeo in Ted Gale's old office the following Monday was also attended by Rick Small and incoming chief John Newcomer. It was Rudnick's first meeting with his new boss.

"We've got a problem with the IRS," Defeo said. "We've had a complaint against you from the IRS district director, in writing."

"About what?"

"Your inability to get along with agents."

"That's not true. It's only one agent and he wasn't doing his job right," Rudnick said. He went on to explain about his troubles with Schiffer. "Rick knows all about this guy," he said. He asked to see a copy of the letter from the IRS district director, but Defeo refused to show it to him. (Rudnick later checked the file but the letter was not there.)

"To calm things down between you and the IRS, we're going to have you and Rick work together on this," Defeo said. "Rick will be in charge for the next forty days, a sort of cooling-off period. Until Newcomer arrives in October, you are not to do any work on the investigation other than with him. . . . We are going to give you a full-time agent on the MCA matter," Defeo added. "The IRS has agreed to that. From now on you can spend all your time on it."

Six months earlier, Rudnick would have been glad to be rid of payola. But now they were finally making major strides in the investigation. They had tracked down a number of radio program directors who had received Federal Express packages regularly from Ralph Tashjian. He'd subpoenaed them to testify before the grand jury starting next week. Small couldn't possibly be brought up to speed in time to question them effectively.

"Rick will take care of it," Defeo said, ending the discussion with a curt, "That's all."

Rudnick left the meeting as angry as he was disappointed. He felt like he'd been bushwhacked by his own bosses. Small and Newcomer said nothing at the meeting. Defeo had apparently made his decision before he heard Rudnick's side of the story.

And to put Small in charge! He specialized in credit-card fraud and Treasury Department cases. Office rumor had it that he was leaving the strike force in a few months to take a job with Treasury in Washington. What kind of a way was this to run an investigation?

Later that afternoon, Small told Rudnick he was canceling the grand jury session on Thursday. "You can't do that," Rudnick practically shouted. "We can't lose our momentum on this case. I can question these witnesses; their testimony has nothing to do with me supposedly not getting along with the IRS."

But Small was adamant. There would be no grand jury session on Thursday. He was in charge now.

Rudnick realized at that moment there would be no "working together" with Small, as Defeo had said. It was over. He was off the case.

38

"We can
make life
very difficult
for you"

One day during the first week of September, Rudnick returned from lunch and found a message in his mail slot saying that Allen Susman had phoned and wanted him to return the call.

He hadn't heard from Susman in months, not since MCA replaced his firm with Munger, Tolles. But the seventy-year-old lawyer quickly made it clear that he still spoke on behalf of the corporation.

"Mr. Rudnick, we want you to know that we are not happy with the way you're handling the Pisello case," he said coldly.

"Oh yeah?" Rudnick replied. Something in the deadly serious tone of Susman's voice warned him not to say more but instead to listen very carefully. He'd been standing at his desk when he dialed the phone. Now he sat down and waited for the lawyer to go on.

"We have friends in the courthouse, too, you know," Susman said. "We can make life very difficult for you."

Rudnick said nothing. There was dead air for what seemed like minutes.

"Well, I don't know what to tell you," he started in. But before he could finish, Susman said good-bye and hung up.

Rudnick sat motionless in his chair. His mind raced to access the situation. He'd suspected all along that if he kept pressing, the company would eventually retaliate somehow. Still, he was stunned by Susman's call, at the nakedness of threat.

Sitting in the silence of his office, he thought he heard the sound of the other shoe finally dropping. MCA apparently was prepared to spend all its political fuel to keep him from going any further. It was an unnerving thought. This was a company of enormous power, with tentacles that supposedly reached all the way to the White House. Looked at from that perspective, he was no more than a gnat. He could be easily squashed.

He decided not to report Susman's call to anyone. Who would he tell? Small? Newcomer? Certainly not Mike Defeo, who'd just canned him from the payola investigation as a matter of political expediency. He knew Defeo wouldn't back him. More likely, he'd pull him off the Pisello case, too. In the past, he would have gone to Ted Gale. Despite his differences with his former chief, Rudnick always trusted Gale to do the right thing, or at least to not do the wrong thing. But with Ted now gone, there was no one he could count on to be in his corner. It was a lonely feeling, and a little scary.

"Well," he said to himself, "let's just see who their friends are and where the next shots come from."

On Monday, September 15, he filed a response to Pisello's motion asking for a list of the prosecution's witnesses in the upcoming trial. In an eight-page brief, he argued that Pisello should not be given the list until the eve of the trial because "he may retaliate" against the witnesses, which included a number of MCA executives. "The MCA witnesses are important to the government's case, so their identities should remain secret," Rudnick wrote. He buttressed his argument by stating that Pisello had recently told one federally protected witness that he would "do whatever he had to do to not go back to prison" and is "capable of having witnesses intimidated or even killed."

The brief revealed that "one ex-MCA official corroborated another MCA executive's 'proffer' that Pisello's job at Sugar Hill Records was to 'keep the niggers in line.'"

"Since Pisello had no previous experience in the record business," Rudnick continued, "his role as an enforcer seems to be more the nature of his business." He also revealed that the unnamed MCA executive's statement about Pisello would not be admissible as evidence in the trial because the executive "has asserted the Fifth Amendment privilege against self-incrimination."

Rudnick attached to his brief a copy of a confidential internal memo written by a CBS Records executive in 1983, when CBS was considering acquiring the distribution of Sugar Hill Records. According to the CBS memo, which Rudnick had obtained through a subpoena, Sugar Hill was "the Black Mafia" and it "mistreated its artists." In recommending against taking on Sugar Hill's distribution, the CBS executive wrote that the Checker/Chess catalog was "not worth a damn" and valued it at "about $500,000 longterm, not $5 million."

The next day—Tuesday, September 16—MCA chairman Lew Wasserman played host to fifteen hundred of the country's most prominent entertainment and media leaders at the Registry Hotel in Universal City. The occasion was a reception for Pope John Paul II, whose two-day visit to Los Angeles had shut down traffic around the downtown civic center as hundreds of thousands of people lined the streets to see the pontiff pass by in his famed bubble-topped Popemobile.

The reception at the Registry turned out to be Hollywood's hottest ticket in years. Stars and studio heads alike inundated Wasserman's office with calls, begging for an invitation to the comparatively intimate gathering. Being granted an invite became an instant arbitrament of show biz social status—if you weren't going, you simply didn't count.

Every Los Angeles TV station and all three networks broadcast live as John Paul stood on the podium in the Registry ballroom—flanked on his left by Wasserman and on his right by Archbishop Roger Mahoney—and told the extraordinarily wealthy crowd that they were a "force for great good or great evil" and must therefore choose to produce works that are "noble and uplifting" rather than appeal to "what is debased in people."

Following the pontiff's address, Wasserman led him gently around the room to shake hands with some of America's biggest celebrities, who pressed forward like awestruck schoolchildren meeting their first movie star. One by one, they took his hand and

mumbled their admiration: Bob Hope, Charlton Heston, Phil Don-
ahue, Merv Griffin, Ed Asner, Barbara Walters, Columbia Pictures
president David Puttnam, film director Peter Bogdanovich, Walt
Disney Studios chairman Michael Eisner, and, yes, MCA Music
Entertainment Group chairman Irving Azoff.

"Talk about having friends in high places," Marvin Rudnick said
to himself as he watched the event on the news that evening.

On Thursday morning, *Daily Variety* published a front-page article on Rudnick's latest court filing in the Pisello case. "Documents
Describe Pisello as Sugar Hill's Enforcer," the headline read. With
Hollywood still basking in the glow of the Pope's visit, MCA found
itself once again publicly linked to a Mafia soldier whose job,
according to the article, was "to keep the niggers in line." KCBS-
TV in Los Angeles led its evening newscast with a five-minute
report titled, "Mafia Connections in the Recording Industry,"
which ended with reporter Chris Blachford saying, "The question
is, was MCA using mob muscle to watch over a black record company?"

At 4:20 Friday afternoon, Rudnick got a message in his mail slot
to call Bob Brosio, the chief of the Justice Department's criminal
division in Los Angeles. "Here it comes," he thought, "MCA's
friend in the courthouse." He waited until Monday morning to
return the call.

"Marvin," Brosio said, "I know that technically this is not our
jurisdiction, but Dennis Kinnaird and I go back a while, and he's
been complaining about how you're handling the Pisello case. So
I'd like to get a meeting together with you two, and I want to do it
by Wednesday, before Rob [U.S. Attorney Robert Bonner] gets back
from out of town."

"I'll have to check with my superiors and get back to you," Rudnick said. "This is it," he thought, "the big fix." He called Newcomer in Detroit and told him what Brosio had said.

"Don't go to that meeting," Newcomer told him. "Brosio is no
friend of ours."

Rudnick was due in Judge Rea's courtroom at three o'clock that
afternoon, September 21, for a hearing on Pisello's motion seeking
the list of witnesses. He arrived early. The courtroom was empty
except for Pisello, who was sitting in one of the pews, staring
straight ahead. For five or six minutes, the two men who'd been
locked in a bitter legal battle for three years shared the room alone

without saying a word. Neither acknowledged the other's presence.

Pisello's lawyer, David Hinden, opened the hearing by attacking Rudnick's brief: "Your Honor, I'm faced with the same tactic Mr. Rudnick used in the previous case against Mr. Pisello before Judge Hupp. That is, trying to turn a tax case into a Mafia case. And I find myself compelled to attempt to respond to anonymous charges. In a sense it's like trying to grab smoke.

"Mr. Pisello is not charged with being a Mafia member. That issue has no place in this case. Because the government says it's so doesn't mean that it's so, especially when there has not been offered one single piece of competent evidence or proof.

"I also want to comment on some of the allegations that are contained in the pleading itself. The allegations, which in some instances deal with proffers of testimony which couldn't be completed because witnesses for a large corporation have invoked the Fifth Amendment, seem to me, Your Honor, to be absolutely irrelevant to any conceivable issue in this case, and the only reason that I could imagine they would be in the pleading would be so they would show up on the newscast at night.

"And indeed, when I came home on Friday night from the movies and turned on the local news, I saw pictures of the pleading, which I had not yet received, quoting some of these charges, which are absolutely unprovable. And I think it's absolutely improper for Mr. Pisello and for MCA to be faced with charges like this which are completely anonymous and to which there can be no response other than a denial.

"I'm not interested in the addresses of the witnesses. What we need in this case, and we need it desperately, are the statements of the witnesses," Hinden said, noting that he'd already obtained the names of the MCA witnesses from IRS agents' memos that had been turned over to the defense. "And to my knowledge no harm has befallen any of these individuals."

Rudnick stood up and drew a breath. He was faced with a tricky legal problem with the record company executives and he wanted to be sure the judge understood it. He explained that it wasn't so much a case of not wanting to give Pisello the witness statements as it was being unable to do so.

"For example, we've now made reference to one witness at the record company who gave us a statement that was part of a proffer. That witness may be called to testify in this court. But unless he gets immunity, I can't call him because he's asserted the Fifth. Now, until I can be sure what he's going to say, I can't represent to the court that he will indeed be a witness.

"The witnesses at the record company are very important," he said, as was the $50,000 payment to Pisello, "which is going to become very important as an income item in front of this court. To get that evidence into testimony clearly and fairly and truthfully, I have to put MCA witnesses on the stand. But I can't do that without knowing what they are going to say, and I can't do that without giving them immunity because several of them have taken the Fifth Amendment.

"Now, if you take the two key people who approved the $50,000 payment, Mr. Roth and Mr. McGill, both have asserted the Fifth Amendment privilege. . . . The problem I have is we have not gotten the bottom line from these two witnesses as to what happened in the MCA deals."

Hinden came up out of his chair so fast that his feet almost left the ground. "Excuse me, Your Honor, I'm going to do something I don't often do," he said. "I want to interrupt because Mr. Rudnick is about to make statements that are absolutely irrelevant. He's making them for the gentlemen that are sitting back there," Hinden said, gesturing toward a handful of reporters who'd suddenly become riveted by the dialogue.

"I'm not asking for proffers of testimony. What Mr. Rudnick is doing is a violation of the reason we have a grand jury in this country, and that's to protect people who go into that body, to be able to testify in secrecy and invoke their rights in secrecy. And what Mr. Rudnick has just done is a gratuitous act, in part because one of those individual's attorney is in this room." He was referring to Myron Roth's attorney, Michael Lightfoot, who was sitting in the back of the courtroom and not looking very happy.

"To spill out their names on the record, to say that individuals working for a large corporation in this country have invoked the Fifth Amendment in the grand jury . . . he can say it because he's in the courtroom, but it's wrong for him to say it."

Rudnick was surprised at the vehemence of Hinden's objection. So were the reporters present. Hinden, after all, was representing Pisello, not the MCA executives, who might turn out to be his client's adversaries at the trial. Why did he care whether the prosecutor identified them, fairly or unfairly?

"We don't have the real statements, Your Honor," Rudnick said. "That's the problem. He's asking for something that's a proffer and I can't turn that over. The law, Your Honor, says that there is no legal basis to turn over the statements until after the witness testifies. And the court knows that.

"I don't know Mr. Hinden's problem about these reporters. I thought we still have an open court here. None of these things I'm saying, Your Honor, is being said for any other reason than to explain it to the court truthfully and honestly. And if Mr. Hinden has a problem . . . I don't know who he's trying to help out with this little outburst of his, but all I want the court to know is we're going to try and have an honest, fair, reasonable, and professional trial. And if Mr. Hinden has some other agenda, I think we ought to get that straightened out right now as we sit here before the court without the pressure of trial over our heads."

"I resent the gratuitous references to innocent individuals invoking the Fifth Amendment in the grand jury," Hinden said. "I think it's wrong and that was the source of my objection. I have no other axes to grind."

Judge Rea had listened impassively throughout the attorneys' heated exchange. He was clearly not as upset by Rudnick's Fifth Amendment disclosures as Hinden was, though he did say at one point that it was not necessary to reveal the executives' names. In the end, he ruled that the prosecution should turn over whatever bona fide witness statements it had, but not until two weeks before the trial, which had been rescheduled for January 12.

When Rudnick walked out of the courtroom that day, he knew that he'd rung a bell that could never be unrung. He had used the legal proceeding—properly and appropriately, he believed—to inform the judge and the public that MCA and its executives were not "cooperating fully" with the government in the Pisello case, contrary to what they had been claiming constantly for the last two years. Whatever else happened, he'd managed to get that little piece of truth into the public record.

He was not prepared for the firestorm of controversy that erupted in the wake of the hearing, however.

"Pisello Case Drops Bombshells on MCA," blared the banner headline in *Variety*. "MCA Executives Take the Fifth in Grand Jury Probe," said the *Los Angeles Herald Examiner*. "Attorney Claims Roth Cites Fifth," said the *Hollywood Reporter*. Even the usually timid *Radio & Records* went with the story, proclaiming, "Explosive Charges at Pisello Hearing." In every story, lawyers for MCA and its executives were quoted as denying categorically that anyone at the company had asserted his Fifth Amendment privilege.

"Myron Roth has never been before the grand jury and has never invoked the Fifth," Dennis Kinnaird told *Variety.* "He did meet with Rudnick and he basically answered all of his questions in the presence of his counsel." Kinnaird said further that no MCA Records employee had taken the Fifth before the grand jury.

Lawyers for McGill and Roth claimed that their clients had been given informal immunity and a promise from Rudnick that their statements would not be used against them. But they had not asserted the Fifth, ever.

Howard Weitzman chimed in that his client had rejected an offer of immunity. "I was contacted by Mr. Rudnick regarding Mr. Azoff's cooperation," he told *Variety.* "Mr. Rudnick did offer to consider immunity for Mr. Azoff. My reply was, 'Mr. Azoff did not do anything wrong. We do not request or need immunity, and we will be glad to cooperate.'"

In effect, all the attorneys said that Rudnick was lying. Dennis Kinnaird went so far as to accuse the prosecutor of violating the law in revealing secret grand jury matters. He characterized Rudnick as "a loose cannon on the decks" whose allegations were "not appropriate or right."

Rudnick was not surprised the MCA lawyers were upset about his revelations, but he was puzzled by their flat-out denials. What confidence did they have that they could get away with accusing a government prosecutor of lying and violating the law? He was glad he'd gotten it all in writing. It was right there in the files, "This is to advise you that Myron Roth would assert his Fifth Amendment privilege against self-incrimination if called to testify or be interviewed with respect to Salvatore Pisello's dealing at MCA Records," dated February 5, 1987, and signed by Roth's attorney, Michael Lightfoot.

Where did these guys get off calling him a liar? he wondered. What gall! Surely the Justice Department would have some sort of response to their allegations of prosecutorial misconduct on his part. Unless, of course, they knew something he didn't.

It appears they did.

On Wednesday morning, September 23, MCA's top legal advisers gathered for a meeting at the U.S. attorney's office. Present were Allen Susman and another member of his firm, Gail Title; Robert Hadl, general counsel for MCA; MCA outside counsels Dennis Kinnaird and Ronald Olson from the Munger, Tolles and Olson firm; Rick Small from the strike force; Richard Drooyan, chief assistant U.S. attorney in Los Angeles; and Kinnaird's old friend Robert Brosio, the chief of the U.S. attorney's criminal division.

The MCA lawyers were there to "lodge a formal complaint," based on what they believed to be "the continuing unfair and improper treatment of MCA by special attorney Marvin Rudnick," according to a memo written later by Small. The attorneys said that "their client MCA is extremely sensitive to adverse press" and that Rudnick was "taking advantage of the situation."

They complained about the press release on the Pisello indictment, saying it was "unethical" for it to have included references to Rocco "the Butcher" Musacchia and accused cop-killer Fritzy Giovanelli—"information not relevant or pertinent" to the "simple tax counts."

They were angry about the "keeping the niggers in line" statement that Rudnick had put in his motion, saying they "did not believe that a statement such as this would have emanated from any employee of MCA, and to include it was detrimental to MCA and outrageous conduct" on the part of Rudnick.

They said that Rudnick's Fifth Amendment statements in court "were completely erroneous and constituted a clear violation of rule 6(e) of the Federal Rules of Criminal Procedure." And they said that because of Rudnick's statement they believed "that Roth's and McGill's jobs were in jeopardy and that their lives may also be in jeopardy."

Rudnick had "an obsession with the persecution of MCA," the lawyers claimed, and was "attempting to do in the press what he could not otherwise accomplish."

The attorneys had one final complaint, according to Small's memo: "Approximately two weeks ago, a Pacific Bell employee was discovered in the basement of a building housing MCA offices, working with wires in the telephone box. When questioned by building security, the Pacific Bell employee stated that he had a work order to perform such activities. Since MCA has a contract with AT&T to handle all phone lines within this particular office building, the Pacific Bell employee was escorted to the security area at which time a Pacific Bell supervisor was contacted. The supervisor stated that the employee had been sent to [the] building by mistake. Upon further investigation by MCA attorneys, it was discovered that the Pacific Bell employee who had been in the basement was headquartered in San Francisco. The Pacific Bell employee's supervisor was contacted, at which time he stated that Pacific Bell had been attempting to install a wiretap at the direction of the Federal Bureau of Investigation."

Noting that the building—identified as number 508 on MCA's Universal City lot—housed both MCA Records and MCA Home Entertainment, the lawyers said they were "outraged that if, in fact, a wiretap had been attempted, then government attorneys would have had to submit false statement to the issuing judge—based on their belief that MCA is not the subject or target of any investigation. The attorneys insinuated that any misinformation provided to the issuing judge would have most likely come from Special Attorney Rudnick."

Small wrote up the memo immediately after returning to the strike force office from the meeting. As a courtesy, he let Rudnick read it when it was done. "You're creating waves, Marvin," he said.

Rudnick wasn't particularly upset by what he read. After eleven years as a prosecutor, personal attacks from defendants rolled right off his back. They came with the territory. There wasn't a single allegation in the memo that couldn't be explained, he thought. Sure there'd been a lot of publicity surrounding the Pisello case. What did they expect? That the media wouldn't be all over a story about a Mafia figure operating out of MCA's corporate headquarters? They were giving him too much credit and the press not enough. It wasn't as if he'd been calling reporters and leaking information about the investigation. He'd done all his talking in the bright light of a public courtroom.

The Fifth Amendment stuff was nonsense. He knew rule 6(e) by heart, and it specifically allowed for the revelation of grand jury matters to a judge in the course of a legal proceeding. He hadn't divulged any secret grand jury testimony.

As for the wiretap attempt, he had nothing to do with that, and his people knew it. That was part of an FBI investigation that Rich Stavin was handling for the strike force. All Rudnick knew about it was that it had something to do with labor racketeering in Hollywood, that there was at least one wiretap in place and it somehow involved MCA. He recalled Ted Gale coming to him before he left the strike force and saying something to the effect that, "Boy, those guys at MCA are really dirty." He was glad to hear that someone besides himself thought so. Right after the flap about the "niggers in line" statement, Rudnick had seen the FBI agent in charge of the other investigation, Tom Gates, in the hallway. "Is what I'm doing in the Pisello case hurting you guys in any way?" he asked. "Not at all," Gates replied. "Pour it on."

When he stopped by Small's office to return the memo that day, Rudnick asked, "What's the story on the wiretap?"

Small made a face. "I told them they shouldn't go into MCA; they'd get caught."

On Tuesday, September 29, Rudnick was working at a word processor in the outer office when he noticed one of the secretaries stuffing a large envelope with newspaper articles about the Pisello case.

"What's going on?" he asked. "Are they sending that back to Washington?" Looking uncomfortable, the secretary nodded affirmation. "Is that Rick's memo?" he asked.

Again, she nodded. "Have they said anything to you about me putting my side of the story in?" She shook her head no. "Can I see that?" he asked.

"I don't think so," she replied.

"Damn it," he said. He couldn't believe they were going to forward MCA's complaints to Defeo without getting his response, too. He sat back down at the computer and angrily pounded out his own memo, addressed to John Newcomer: "I was disappointed to learn that Rick Small's memo was forwarded to Mike Defeo before I had a chance to respond to the MCA allegations," he wrote. "As you may or may not know, MCA has been feigning cooperation since they were served with their first subpoena in February, 1986."

In answer to the subpoenas, "rather than [provide] memos describing Pisello's business at MCA, we were encouraged to look into independent promotion and the activities of Joe Isgro," he said. "To this day MCA has not produced documents that support their executives' memories of the transactions. If anything, there appears to have been some efforts to cover up the matter."

He complained that the Pisello-MCA investigation "has been in limbo" since Ted Gale left, and that the new IRS agent who'd been assigned to assist him "has a conflict, since one of his closest friends is an MCA executive, though not in the record division.

"If one believes the proffers of the MCA witnesses seeking immunity," he went on, "their testimony remains in conflict with the overall facts of the case. Most important, it remains a mystery how Pisello entered the company. When I considered these facts in 1985, I believed that I was helping a local company to learn about a Mafia figure that had somehow infiltrated it. At this stage, I believe that he must have been helped. I believe that MCA's stand against my litigation against Pisello is [meant] to probably assist Pisello. When I first began asking questions at MCA about Pisello, rather than a friendly reception, I found myself before Judge Hupp responding to attacks on my integrity for interfering with Pisello's business at MCA. This latest barrage of criticism comes from the same group that has been trying to suppress whatever be the truth."

He printed out the memo and handed it to the secretary. "Make sure this gets to them, too," he said.

The package went back to Washington without Rudnick's memo. But it did contain a six-page letter from Dennis Kinnaird laying out MCA's case against Rudnick. "Given the lack of evidence against MCA and its executives and employees, the government's use of its powerful position and the media to taint the corporation and its executives constitutes prosecutorial misconduct," it said.

"MCA takes pride in the ethical and fair-minded manner in which it conducts its business," Kinnaird's letter continued, "and values highly its longstanding reputation for integrity among those with whom it transacts business, and among the general public. The government's actions have not only caused MCA, its executives and employees and related entities extreme prejudice in their business dealings and damage to their public image (so essential to the success of those in the highly visible entertainment industry), it has also caused irreparable and totally unjustified harm to the personal lives and professional careers and reputations of those involved.

"Such government conduct is intolerable. We urge you to take steps to ensure that it ceases immediately. We request that in view of the foregoing you consider the propriety of having Mr. Rudnick continue to conduct the pending investigation."

Rudnick was not told of Kinnaird's letter. Nor was he aware of a response letter that U.S. Attorney Bonner sent to MCA a few days later: "This refers to your October 2nd letter concerning statements by Strike Force personnel regarding MCA Records and its executives and employees," Bonner wrote. "I have reviewed the materials you submitted with your letter and I want to assure you that I take very seriously your charges of improper conduct on the part of Department of Justice representatives.

"I have asked Mr. Newcomer to take whatever action is necessary and appropriate to ensure that the case is handled in accordance with the highest standards of the Department of Justice. I also asked Mr. Newcomer to respond to your letter. I am confident that Mr. Newcomer will take the necessary steps to insure that the Pisello case will be properly and appropriately handled by his office."

At 9:30 in the morning on October 6, his first official day as chief of the Los Angeles strike force, John Newcomer buzzed Rudnick on the office intercom. "I'd like to see you in my office immediately," he said.

Ever since he wrote his rebuttal memo to MCA's complaint, Rudnick had been uneasy. Things just didn't feel right. He'd heard nothing back from Newcomer on the memo. In fact, he hadn't spoken to him since the Brosio call. He imagined that Defeo was not going to be pleased by MCA's complaint. That's probably what Newcomer wanted to discuss, he thought. It was a helluva way to start off with a new boss.

He walked into Newcomer's office and offered his hand. "Welcome to the strike force," he said.

Newcomer looked at him icily and said, "Sit down."

Rudnick took the chair he'd occupied a hundred times before in conversations with previous chiefs—Jim Henderson, Bruce Kelton, Ted Gale.

"I want you to know that you're under investigation," Newcomer said.

Rudnick's mouth dropped open. It was one thing he never expected to hear in his life.

"For what?"

"For this," Newcomer said, tossing Kinnaird's six-page complaint letter across the desk. Rudnick leafed through it quickly. It looked pretty much like the same stuff he'd read in Small's memo.

"There's nothing to this," he said.

"Well, we're taking it very seriously; we're referring it to OPR in Washington." The Office of Professional Responsibility was charged with looking into allegations of serious misconduct by Justice Department employees.

"What about my memo?" Rudnick asked. Newcomer stared back at him and said nothing.

Rudnick felt his blood starting to rise. He couldn't believe the way he was being treated, as if he were corrupt.

"Listen," he said, getting up from the chair, "you tell OPR to give me a call right away and I'll tell them the whole story." Then he turned and left the room before his anger got the best of him.

Back in his own office, he sank down into a chair and sat there dazed. The department was not going to back him. If his superiors were going to take MCA's word without even hearing his explanation, that meant they'd already made the decision. He knew that an OPR investigation was a death knell for a career. Even if you ultimately were cleared, you were forever tainted in the Justice Department. There would be no more promotions or raises, no more good cases. It was finished.

At his home that evening, he stared at the framed letter from the Justice Department on his office wall, welcoming two-year-old Lipe Mendel Rudnicki, a displaced person, to America. April 13, 1949. That was the happiest day of his parents' life. This was the saddest of his.

39

"They
stiffed us"

Back in New Jersey, Detective Sergeant Bobby Jones had reached some conclusions from listening to the hundreds of hours of wiretaps in the Levy case. A fourteen-year veteran of organized crime investigation, Jones knew a mob scam when he heard one, and the sale of MCA cutouts had all the earmarks.

"Why does MCA have to sell its cutouts through a paper company, Consultants for Records, the principals of which—Sal Pisello, Fritzy Giovanelli, and Rocco Musacchia—can't put three words together?" Jones had asked himself over and over. "Why was La-Monte supposed to pay Levy and not MCA? Why would MCA practically give away six million records to this motley group of wiseguys?"

Jones couldn't come up with a satisfactory answer. It appeared to him that MCA didn't intend to make any money on the deal until the whole thing became public. Only then did the company start scrambling to collect. Jones's conclusion—based on his knowledge of hundreds of instances of mob infiltration of legitimate business—was that someone at MCA was making good on some past favor performed by Levy, Sal, or Vastola. Either that or someone at the company was being extorted. Jones just didn't know why.

"We're just dealing with the tip of the iceberg," he said of the New Jersey indictments. He thought that the scope of the investigation should be expanded to include MCA and its record executives. His boss, Union County prosecutor John Stamler, agreed with him. But they weren't running the investigation, the Justice Department was, and assistant U.S. attorney Bruce Repetto wasn't interested in taking the case wider at this point.

In late September, Jones had received an unexpected call from Marvin Rudnick. "I hear you know a lot about Sal Pisello and Morris Levy and that you're someone I can trust," Rudnick said by way of introduction. "I could use your help on my case."

When Rudnick explained the theory behind his prosecution of Pisello, Jones wanted to reach through the phone and kiss him. Jones had been saying all the same things at his end for more than a year and nobody seemed to hear. Finally, he was talking to someone who saw it the same way he did.

"I may need an expert witness to testify about Sal's organized crime affiliations back there," Rudnick said.

"I'm your man," Jones replied. "You and I are on the same page as far as MCA goes."

Jones went to John Stamler and asked for permission to go to California to testify. "Rudnick's an honest guy trying to do a good job and I want to help him," he said. Stamler agreed immediately, saying, "Go on out there, take as much time as you need."

Just to make things official, Rudnick issued a subpoena for Jones to testify at the Pisello trial on January 12, 1988. Jones excitedly began making plans to travel to the West Coast.

He never got there. Shortly after Rudnick's subpoena was served, Jones's chief of detectives, Patrick Maloney, walked into his office and told him, "Forget about California; the Justice Department killed the subpoena."

Jones was flabbergasted. He'd never heard of a law enforcement agency quashing the subpoena of one of its own prosecutors. Maloney then handed him a memo he was sending to all Union County investigators working on the Levy and Vastola cases. It read:

"As per assistant United States attorney Bruce Repetto, any inquiries regarding the investigation from assistant United States attorney Marvin Rudnick in California are to be referred to Mr. Repetto.

"Under no circumstances are any participants in this investigation to have conversation with Rudnick.

"If any member is contacted by Mr. Rudnick regarding information concerning this investigation, a written report will be submitted with details."

Jones didn't believe for a minute that an assistant U.S. attorney on his own had the clout to issue such a directive. Clearly, this had been approved by higher-ups in Washington. Rudnick's Justice Department superiors were hanging their own man out to dry. And just as clearly, to Jones's mind, they were doing it in response to pressure from MCA. Jones wanted to go over Maloney's head and appeal to John Stamler, but he couldn't. Stamler was at home, dying from complications of a recent heart transplant. So Maloney was the final word.

Jones felt badly for Rudnick, whom he'd never met but whom he liked a lot from their half-dozen phone conversations. Having his bosses aligned against him didn't bode well for Rudnick's career. But Jones didn't have much time to feel sorry for Rudnick. Maloney next informed him he was being transferred out of the organized crime section to the trial division. Instead of working on the street, he was being given a suit-and-tie desk job helping assistant prosecutors prepare for trial. Jones had been expecting a promotion to lieutenant for the work he did on the Levy and Vastola cases. Instead, he got a slap in the face.

Jones called Rudnick in California to warn him. "It's all going down the drain, buddy," he said. "They stiffed us."

40

*"I think
the fix
is in"*

In the weeks following his meeting with John Newcomer, Rudnick began to feel more and more like a bystander to a bizarre drama. As far as he could tell, not much was going on in the payola case. Small had called no one before the grand jury.

No sooner had depositions begun in Joe Isgro's antitrust suit against the major record labels than the big companies began settling out of court. Capitol, Motown, Polygram, RCA, and Arista all bowed out, each reportedly paying Isgro a six-figure sum.

Lawyers for MCA—along with Warner one of the remaining two major distributors left defending against Isgro's $25 million claim—suddenly seemed positively chummy with Rudnick's bosses. The secretaries in the office told him the company attorneys were in constant telephone contact with Newcomer and Rick Small.

One day, Newcomer came to Rudnick with a formal request from Bill Billick for MCA to inspect and copy Ralph Tashjian's financial records, which had been subpoenaed by the strike force. MCA wanted the documents to help defend against the Isgro lawsuit, but Tashjian's attorneys had refused to turn them over to the company, citing the Fifth Amendment. So MCA wanted the strike force to provide them.

"How should we handle this?" Newcomer asked.

Since the documents MCA wanted were part of a grand jury investigation, they were technically secret, covered by rule 6(e). The general policy of the strike force was not to give civil litigants access to documents in matters pending before a grand jury, even if the owner of the documents consented to their release. But it was not a hard-and-fast rule; it was negotiable, provided it didn't go against the government's interests.

Rudnick's natural instinct was to say, "Tell them to take a hike." But considering his position, he didn't want to seem unnecessarily confrontational. So he tempered his response.

"I don't think we ought to give this stuff out without a court order, to protect ourselves," he said. Otherwise, Tashjian's lawyers could claim the strike force had violated the grand jury secrecy law.

"I'll call Bob Brosio and see what he thinks," Newcomer said, and walked away.

That was quite a change, Rudnick thought. In a matter of weeks, Newcomer had gone from saying, "Brosio is no friend of ours," to asking Brosio's advice and approval on strike force matters.

MCA later obtained a court order for production of the documents, in part by telling the judge that Newcomer and Rick Small had no objection to turning them over. It is doubtful a judge would have issued such an order against the wishes of the prosecutors, since the courts generally give precedence to criminal cases over civil matters.

Shortly thereafter, Rudnick bumped into Bill Billick by the office Xerox machine, where he and several other MCA lawyers were running off copies of Tashjian's financial records.

After exchanging pleasantries, Rudnick said to Billick, "Boy, your guys certainly gave me a shot."

Glancing to make sure the other lawyer couldn't hear, Billick replied, "I have never seen so much political action on anything in all my years working with MCA."

Later, Rudnick saw the MCA lawyers on several occasions going over documents in the IRS records room—unattended. He couldn't believe it. They could have been looking at anything, including documents gathered in the Pisello-MCA investigation.

Around the end of October, Newcomer's secretary, Pam Thomas, told Rudnick that MCA had a new attorney—"some guy named Bill Hundley from Washington"—who had stopped by to see the boss. Hundley, as Rudnick would learn, was a former chief of the Justice Department's Organized Crime and Racketeering Section under Attorney General Robert F. Kennedy. After that, he'd served as chief of security for the National Football League, where he reportedly was instrumental in getting the U.S. attorney's office in Alexandria, Virginia, to scuttle an ongoing grand jury investigation into gambling among the players of the Washington Redskins.

As a criminal attorney in private practice, Hundley had earned a reputation—and a lot of money—representing well-heeled defendants in high-profile cases. A "champion of the upperdog" was how one publication described him. Hundley was the lawyer you hired when you had serious problems with the Justice Department, where his many contacts and years of insider experience could provide clients with "the best mercy money can buy," according to the *Philadelphia Inquirer. Washingtonian* magazine called him the man "to turn to when you're really scared." Among those who turned to him over the years were former U.S. attorney John Mitchell, the Reverend Sun Myung Moon, South Korean lobbyist Tongsun Park, Louisiana governor Edwin Edwards, and United Mine Workers president Tony Boyle.

By 1987, at age sixty-two, Bill Hundley had become known around the nation's capital as the consummate fixer. As he told the *Washingtonian* in a 1985 article, he had a 90 percent success rate in either keeping clients from being indicted or working out a plea that made a trial unnecessary. "To a certain extent, from this side of the fence, when you end up in court you've already lost," he said.

Just prior to being hired by MCA in late September 1987, Hundley was invited to become a partner in the prestigious Washington law firm of Akin, Gump, Strauss, Hauer & Feld. The surname *Strauss* belongs to MCA board member and former Democratic Party chairman Robert S. Strauss, reputedly one of the most influential behind-the-scenes power brokers in Washington.

One of the first things Hundley did in MCA's employ was to have lunch with strike force chief David Margolis and the force's deputy chief, Mike Defeo, in Washington.

On November 9, *Forbes* magazine published an article revealing that Ron Saranow, the chief of the IRS's Criminal Investigation Division in Los Angeles, was under investigation by the agency's Internal Security Division for possible corruption. According to the article—headlined, "Does Guess Have a Friend in the IRS"—the owners of Guess Jeans apparently had used their influence with Saranow to launch a harassing series of IRS actions against their archcompetitor, Jordache, as well as to shut down several criminal investigations of Guess. All of this happened while Saranow reportedly was mulling over a job offer from Guess.

Rudnick wondered if Saranow might also have entertained a job offer from MCA.

By mid-November, the media had sniffed out the fact that Rudnick had been removed from the payola investigation. It wasn't difficult to learn, since a number of recent court filings in Isgro's lawsuit indicated that Rick Small was now in charge of the case.

At the same time, MCA attorneys began attempting to dissuade reporters from continuing to chase the MCA-Pisello story by showing them a letter the company received from John Newcomer, dated October 14. "Ladies and gentlemen," it read. "References made to your letter dated October 2, 1987, in which you identified alleged misconduct on part of Special Attorney Marvin Rudnick. . . . Allegations against an attorney in the Department of Justice are a matter of the highest priority, and the allegations set forth in your letter are a cause of great concern to us.

"We have carefully reviewed the material you have provided. Without comment on whether Mr. Rudnick's conduct violated the rules of professional conduct or Rule 6(e) of the Federal Rules of Criminal Procedure, we have taken the necessary steps to insure that only relevant statements that are factually accurate will appear in pleadings, oral arguments and press releases.

"We do reaffirm Mr. Rudnick's statement to counsel during the investigation and pretrial proceedings related to *U.S. v. Pisello*, CR. 87-553-WJR, that neither MCA nor any of its executives or employees are targets of that case or its attendant investigation. However, we respectfully decline to issue any press release confirming this statement, because we believe it would be inappropriate under the circumstances, potentially prejudicial to Mr. Pisello, and would generate additional publicity, which is not necessary. If you have additional questions please call me. Very truly yours, John L. Newcomer."

"You see, there is no story; the case is over," Dennis Kinnaird said in showing the letter to a reporter.

If he were attempting to end news coverage of the MCA-Pisello affair, Kinnaird badly misjudged the media. Coupled with Rudnick's removal from the payola investigation, Newcomer's letter apparently exonerating MCA added new fuel to the fire.

A day after being shown the letter, KCBS-TV's Chris Blachford went on the air with a report that featured Will Dwyer—the lawyer for Sam Passamano, George Collier, and Al Bergamo—decrying the apparent muzzling of Rudnick and saying, "I think the fix is in."

Blachford ended his report by saying, "Serious questions have been raised about mobster Pisello and MCA, questions that haven't been answered. But it appears, on the surface at least, that this investigation has stopped. And we don't know why. The Justice Department, at the same time, has a big 'no comment.'"

The entertainment industry trade papers followed. "L.A. Strike Force Says MCA Not a Payola Target," said the slightly inaccurate headline in *Billboard*. The article quoted Kinnaird as saying, "We considered that Rudnick was not conducting himself according to the law and the rules, and we brought it to the attention of the Justice Department. We also asked for confirmation that MCA was not a target of their investigation, and they gave us a letter of confirmation."

Variety ran an article headlined, "Lame Duck Goes in For Attorney Pulled Off Industry Payola Case," pointing out that Rick Small, the new man in charge of the case, was leaving the strike force in a month. That called into question the government's management of the payola investigation. The article also included Dwyer's "the fix is in" allegation about the MCA-Pisello investigation. "There is something strangely suspicious about the way in which a renowned federal prosecutor is suddenly being as constrained as one might imagine the defendants most deeply desire," Dwyer was quoted as saying.

Dennis Kinnaird issued an angry statement in response to Dwyer's comments: "Mr. Dwyer's allegations concerning MCA and the Justice Department are untrue, reckless and totally irresponsible. They should be recognized as self-serving statements by an attorney representing clients who were fired by MCA and who have unfounded claims against the company.

"It is outrageous that Mr. Dwyer would distort the government's finding of no evidence of wrongdoing by MCA into a media circus to attempt to benefit his clients. Accusing the Department of Justice and MCA of this type of impropriety is merely a smokescreen and a feeble negotiating tactic to attempt to enhance the position of Mr. Dwyer's clients."

Kinnaird argued that "there is nothing extraordinary about asking the government for and receiving reassurances" that MCA was not a target of the investigation.

Getting such reassurance in writing was extraordinary, however, as most government officials knew. Privately, Justice Department officials were furious that MCA had released Newcomer's letter to reporters, thereby creating what the department apparently feared most—more publicity on the case. In their view, the government got snookered. Now the media's angle on the story had changed from focusing on potential wrongdoing inside MCA to focusing on possible scandal inside the Justice Department.

Whoever ordered and approved the Newcomer letter apparently misjudged MCA's motive in asking for it. Since there was no legal basis for MCA to require the statement in writing—wouldn't private assurances have satisfied?—the only other explanation was that the company intended to use it in countering the bad press it had been getting. The government should have realized that. And MCA should have known the press wouldn't buy it.

Rudnick was appalled by Newcomer's letter, which he learned about only when reporters began calling him for a comment. It seemed obvious to him that the department had taken MCA's complaint and swallowed it whole. They passed Kinnaird's letter on to OPR for investigation, knowing that at least one allegation—that he had attempted an illegal wiretap of MCA offices—was absolutely false. In a sense, they had presented a misleading record. What kind of investigation was it when no one—not his chief, his superiors in Washington, not even OPR—ever asked him if any of MCA's allegations were true? Apparently, the Department of Justice was going to let him twist slowly in the wind.

Rudnick wanted to say all this to the reporters who called him about Newcomer's letter. But he held his tongue, knowing that any comment he made would only buttress MCA's position that he was using the press to taint the company.

As it turned out, he got blamed for the news stories anyway. On the Monday morning following Thanksgiving, he returned to the office from a short vacation to see his mother and father in Glens Falls, New York. Newcomer came into his office and told him he was being called back to Washington. Mike Defeo and David Margolis wanted to talk to him. "It's a command performance," he said.

"Do I need a lawyer?" Rudnick asked.

Newcomer laughed, the first time Rudnick had ever seen that from him. "Of course not," he said. "You're going to get chewed out. They think you're becoming too high-profile in this case. You'd better be respectful," he warned.

Rudnick flew to Washington on Thursday, December 3. He checked into the Inn at the Foggy Bottom, a small European-style hotel just around the corner from the Watergate complex, and later went to dinner with some old friends.

The next morning it was cold and raining—appropriately, he thought. He took the subway from his hotel to the federal triangle at Tenth and Pennsylvania Avenues and walked into the main Justice Department building—flanked on one side by the J. Edgar Hoover Building, the FBI headquarters, and on the other by IRS. Three huge edifices that symbolize the enormous investigative power of the federal government.

He arrived at Mike Defeo's office at the appointed hour, 9:00 A.M. sharp, and was told by the secretary that there was going to be a delay. He should come back at 12:30.

He called up John Dubois and the two of them went for coffee in the basement cafeteria. He filled Dubois in on his situation. Dubois was astonished at the turn of events since he left Los Angeles. "Marvin, I don't even know what to tell you," he said, shaking his head in disbelief.

At 12:30, Defeo emerged from his office and led Rudnick in a silent march down the long corridor to Margolis's office. Margolis was sitting at the far end of a large conference table—slouched in a chair, with one foot propped up on the table. They were an odd pair: Defeo with his Republican dark suits and boot-camp white-sidewall haircut, Margolis with his long hair and penchant for showing up at the office wearing a Mickey Mouse watch, jeans, and cowboy boots.

Today, however, Margolis was wearing a white shirt and tie. Rudnick opened the conversation by noting a copy of James B. Stewart's book, *The Prosecutors*, laying on Margolis's desk. "Inside the offices of the Government's most powerful lawyers ... " the dust jacket said.

"Is that any good?" he asked

"I haven't read it yet," Margolis replied, smiling and offering his hand.

"You ought to read *Presumed Innocent*," Rudnick said, referring to former prosecutor Scott Turow's best-selling novel about a prosecutor who winds up unjustly accused of a murder he was investigating. He hadn't intended to be ironic. He was just trying to cut the tension.

Truth be known, Rudnick was plain scared, for the first time in his professional life. The fact of the meeting was totally out of character with how things usually worked in the strike force. Normally, all directives from Washington were effected through the district chiefs. If they were going to pull him off the Pisello case, that's how it would have been done, through the chain of command. Newcomer would have broken the news to him. But being called back to headquarters for a personal audience with Margolis was unprecedented in Rudnick's experience. So it had to be something else they were going to tell him, some other message they wanted to impart. He wasn't going to get a pat on the back and an "atta boy," that was certain.

His plan going in was to be conciliatory, not confrontational. He knew that fighting and arguing weren't going to do any good. He was obviously in serious enough trouble as it was. He didn't want to appear unmanageable, a loose cannon, as Kinnaird called him. But he wanted to make sure they had all the facts. He didn't want there to be any gaps in their knowledge of what had happened out in California. Maybe Newcomer hadn't told them everything, for whatever reason.

"Marvin, we have a problem," Margolis started in. "You've got to be less controversial. So we're going to have to warehouse you for a while. You can try the Pisello case, but we can't have you on a high profile."

"You're not Rudy Giuliani," Defeo interjected.

"I understand," Rudnick said.

"Newcomer will sit with you at the trial," Margolis said.

"Good, I could use the help."

"He won't try the case with you, but you must run everything through him."

"Okay," Rudnick said. He was relieved—at least he still had his trial.

"Bonner is upset about all the controversy," Margolis said, without elaborating.

"You know that Dennis Kinnaird is a friend of Brosio's," Rudnick put it.

Margolis ignored the remark. "Bob Strauss represents MCA here, and his law partner, Bill Hundley, has been by to see me," he said. He pointed to a framed picture of Hundley that was hanging on his office wall. "He's a reasonable person, and if he starts complaining about you then you're in trouble."

Rudnick felt like asking, "Who are you working for, Hundley or the government?" Instead, he told them about Allen Susman's phone call and warning that "we have friends in the courthouse, too."

Again, Margolis ignored what Rudnick said. It was as if they were having two separate conversations.

"You may have to be transferred to another city," he said.

"That would be a tragedy, devastating to my family," Rudnick replied. "We moved to Los Angeles because it was a large enough city for two careers."

"You just try the case and then we'll deal with your career in the long run," Margolis said.

It was all over in less than fifteen minutes and Rudnick was back having coffee with Dubois. "I finally hit that big stone wall in the sky," he joked sadly. "They didn't ask me anything about the case. They didn't want to know what happened. They didn't care about the Brosio call, or Susman's threat. It's all about politics."

He knew his career in the Justice Department was over. "The only way I can salvage anything out of this is to win the Pisello case and then get out," he said.

Dubois walked him outside to the subway stop and said goodbye. It was still gray and raining. By 3:30 he was on a flight home.

Back in Los Angeles, Rudnick quickly discovered how short a leash he was on. Newcomer turned down his request to draw up subpoenas and immunity requests for the executives he expected to call as witnesses, most importantly Myron Roth and Al Bergamo. Newcomer said he didn't need them; McGill would suffice. Newcomer also rejected his request to fly back to New Jersey to interview Joe Robinson and prepare his testimony for trial. "It's a simple tax case, Marvin," he said.

Newcomer was crippling him, Rudnick thought. It was clear what was going on. The government had made an agreement to make sure MCA wouldn't be embarrassed at the trial. And it was going to be difficult to do that and put on an effective case at the same time. Sure, it was easy to establish that Pisello didn't pay taxes on the money he took in from the MCA transactions. But Rudnick had to be able to prove beyond a reasonable doubt that the money was income and not a loan or a gift, as the defense would probably claim. "Income" is a term of art in a tax case. He had to show that Pisello received the money as a result of a business transaction. And that was not going to be easy without Bergamo or Roth on the stand.

The problem was that at the MCA end, Pisello got his money under the heading of "advances" and there were no memos saying otherwise. At the Sugar Hill end, it was carried on the books as loans—at Pisello's request, according to Robinson. That left Sal enough room to raise a reasonable doubt in the jury's mind as to whether this was in fact income.

McGill was a weak witness for the prosecution since he wasn't in the middle of the deal; he just prepared documents on orders of higher-ups. But Roth could drive a stake through the heart of Pisello's defense. In legal parlance, he was a percipient witness, a witness to the event that was the subject of the case, one who had perception of the event. Having actually dealt with Sal, Roth was perhaps the best person in America to tell what the deal was.

Bergamo, too, could hurt Pisello. If he told his attempted bribe story on the stand, it would put Sal in the middle of a business deal, not a loan. His testimony would also be very damaging to MCA.

But Newcomer wouldn't let Rudnick call either man as a witness. "It's irrelevant," he said. "It's cumulative."

Since Bruce Repetto in Newark was refusing to let LaMonte testify at the trial, that left Rudnick with Joe Robinson and Ranji Bedi as witnesses to the transactions. Both of them were a little flaky and neither was directly connected to MCA.

Either his superiors didn't understand the intricacies of a tax prosecution or they were willing to risk losing the case rather than put anyone from MCA on the witness stand. Rudnick believed the latter was the case. To him, a trial was a truth-finding exercise. As a prosecutor, his job was to write the facts on the blackboard, where they couldn't be erased or covered up. But the powers that were

MCA couldn't take the chance of letting him write those facts on the blackboard where the students could see them. So they were taking away his chalk. And the government was helping them do it.

"Don't tilt at windmills," Newcomer told him. "Didn't they tell you in Washington? It's over."

41

"What a Year!"

The record business closed out 1987 with the stunning news that CBS was selling its record division to Japanese electronics giant Sony for $2 billion, by far the highest price ever paid for a record company.

The sale marked a major payday for Walter Yetnikoff, who had initiated the talks between the two companies and tirelessly pushed the deal through months of on-again off-again negotiations. For his efforts, Yetnikoff was to receive a reported $20 million bonus from Sony when the sale was finalized and remain on as chairman of the company at a salary of $2.5 million a year. He would be making more money than Irving Azoff, and he wouldn't have to answer anymore to CBS president Laurence Tisch, whom he discovered he disliked almost as much as former CBS chairman Tom Wyman, even if Tisch was Jewish.

But Yetnikoff's big coup was viewed with mixed feelings in the industry at large. Many were appalled that the oldest record company in America—the dominant worldwide distributor, the jewel of the music business—was going to the Japanese. Now only two of the six major record distributors would be American-owned: Warner and MCA. Capitol-EMI was a British company, Polygram was Dutch, and RCA had recently been bought out by the West German publishing conglomerate Bertelsmann. Experts bemoaned the fact that the record business—an industry born and raised in America and one of the few bright spots in the U.S. balance of trade—was passing into the hands of foreigners.

Relations between the American record companies and the Japanese in particular had been strained for some time over the issue of digital audio tape, or DAT. Developed by Sony, DAT was a new technology designed to replace traditional magnetic-tape cassettes with metallic, "digitally recorded" tape capable of reproducing the near-perfect sound quality of the compact disc. The Japanese electronics manufacturers wanted to introduce DAT machines into the U.S. market; the American companies were fighting to keep them out, fearing the new product would result in untold millions in losses from counterfeiting and home taping. The RIAA was lobbying Congress to require that an anticopying chip be put in all DAT machines sold in this country and to levy a prohibitive royalty on the sale of blank DAT cassettes. In addition, the record companies were refusing to license their music for use on prerecorded DAT cassettes, figuring that if consumers couldn't buy Michael Jackson's new album on DAT, then they probably wouldn't buy an expensive DAT player either. Leading the fight to keep DAT out of America was CBS Records; spearheading the Japanese attack was Sony.

It was not surprising that the general suspicion in the record industry was that Sony's purchase of CBS was a back-door maneuver to introduce DAT into the U.S. market. A Sony-owned CBS could be expected to quickly license its huge music catalog for use on prerecorded DAT cassettes, thereby forcing the other companies to go along and collapsing one line of defense against the dreaded product.

Some in the record industry saw a silver lining in the CBS-Sony sale, however. The fact that CBS Records could fetch such a huge sum meant that the record business—long considered the poor step-sister of the entertainment industry—was finally getting some respect from the investment community. The $2 billion value that Sony placed on CBS Records instantly increased the worth of every other record label. David Geffen, for instance, immediately calculated that his relatively small Geffen Records was now worth "at least half a billion." The heads of other independently owned labels—Herb Alpert and Jerry Moss of A&M Records, Chris Blackwell of Island Records, and Richard Branson of Virgin Records—suddenly had dollar signs dancing in their heads as cash-rich entertainment conglomerates like Paramount and Disney, along with some of Sony's powerful Japanese competitors, began looking for record companies to buy.

Forgotten were the dark days following the crash of 1979, when blue chip media and entertainment companies scrambled out of the record business like rats from a sinking ship. Now the rats were trying to climb back aboard, and they were willing to pay unprecedented prices to book passage.

The reason for the new respectability could be read right there on the industry's bottom line. For the third year in a row, record sales had increased nearly 20 percent, stopping just short of the all-time high set in 1978. Both CBS and Warner ran up historic profits—$200 million for CBS and just pocket-change less for Warner. Polygram and RCA were resurgent. Capitol-EMI was still struggling for profitability, but its parent company, Thorn-EMI of England, was continuing to pump millions into the operation, confident of a turnaround.

MCA's Music Entertainment Group also posted record profits—$40.8 million, with the usual asterisk that the reported amount included a lot more than records. If home video distribution, talent management, and concert revenues were taken out, MCA Records earned more in the area of $8 million in 1987. Still, it managed that figure with almost no help from Motown, which had only two modest hits during the year, Stevie Wonder's *Characters* album and Smokey Robinson's *One Heartbeat*.

At year's end, MCA had four albums in *Billboard*'s Top 40, including the self-titled debut by sixteen-year-old shopping-mall sensation Tiffany, which was bulleting up the chart to number one and eventual sales of more than four million copies. Tiffany was something of a breakthrough for MCA—the first new white pop artist the company had launched since Azoff took over.

In addition to Tiffany, MCA had gold albums in 1987 from newcomer Jody Watley, Stephanie Mills, former Go-Go's lead singer Belinda Carlisle, the rock group R.E.M., and a revitalized Elton John, who had re-signed with the label after several disappointing years with Geffen Records. MCA dominated both the black and country music charts during the year.

Azoff had become increasingly involved in directing MCA's growing concert business. In September, he negotiated a five-year agreement giving MCA's music division the right to manage the Los Angeles Coliseum and the Los Angeles Sports Arena, the homes of the Raiders football team and the Clippers basketball team, respectively.

Under the agreement, MCA and its partner in the venture, Spectacor Management, would receive a $300,000 annual management fee, plus a percentage of the revenue. The plan was to book concerts into the two venues when the teams weren't playing.

It was a terrific deal for MCA, since it required no investment on the part of the company and would give it control of three concert venues in Los Angeles. Now MCA could sign acts, manage the artists' careers, put out their records, and share in the profits from their live performances—what's known as vertical integration.

In October, MCA and another partner, PACE Entertainment Group, negotiated a forty-year lease with the city of Dallas to run the Starplex Amphitheater there. The controversial arrangement—which gave MCA/Pace ticket revenue, as well as all proceeds from concessions sales and parking fees at a city-built parking lot—was strongly supported by Dallas mayor Elizabeth Strauss, the sister-in-law of MCA board member Robert Strauss.

In November, Azoff and Atlanta mayor Andrew Young held a joint press conference to announce the construction of a twenty-thousand-seat amphitheater in South Atlanta, a joint venture of MCA Music Entertainment Group and Filmworks USA.

Coupled with MCA's belief that it had finally solved its problems with Marvin Rudnick, these successes prompted the record company to take out a self-congratulatory full-page color ad in the year-end edition of *Hits* magazine. "MCA . . . What a Year!" read the ad line, which ran with a photograph of MCA Records executives—including Azoff, Solters, Roth, and Palmese—standing in a line, laughing, and giving the finger to the world.

42

"... the most reprehensible person in the music business"

Valerie Tashjian was in the kitchen of her San Mateo home unpacking some new dishes when she heard the knock at the front door. Her husband, Ralph, was in his office, preparing to leave town on a business trip. Her three-year-old son, Michael, was playing with the babysitter in the family room. Seven-year-old Nicholas was at school.

It was 1:30 in the afternoon, Thursday, February 25. They were expecting a visit from the IRS. Kemp Schiffer had called them the day before to see if they were going to be home that afternoon. He said he needed to serve them with another grand jury subpoena.

Valerie listened from the kitchen as Ralph answered the door. She heard him greet Schiffer and then heard the agent say, "We have a warrant for your arrest."

By the time she reached the front hallway, Schiffer and three other IRS agents were already putting handcuffs on her husband, who was hollering for the babysitter to take Michael upstairs so he wouldn't see what was happening. Valerie's first instinct was to run to her son, but Schiffer stepped between them, blocking her way. "We have a warrant for your arrest, too," he said. One of the two female agents told her to go upstairs and change clothes. "Don't wear any jewelry and put on some warm socks; you're going to spend some time in jail," she said.

As the couple was led handcuffed from their home on the tree-lined, Ozzie-and-Harriet street, they noticed an NBC camera crew in a van at the curb, filming their humiliation for the evening news. Schiffer walked over and chatted amiably with the newsmen.

The Tashjians were caught in a game of government hardball. The plan was to try to hold them in jail over the weekend, thereby softening them up to cooperate in the investigation of Joe Isgro. "Why are you protecting him?" one of the female agents asked Valerie in the car on the way to jail. "Is he paying your attorney's fees? You don't have to be going through this, you know."

Valerie Tashjian's arrest was specifically intended as an arm twister, since Tashjian was known to dote on his attractive thirty-year-old wife. "If we put the cuffs on Valerie, Ralph will roll over in a minute," Schiffer had predicted on several occasions.

The next morning, U.S. Attorney Robert Bonner presided over a packed press conference in Los Angeles to announce what he called "the most significant payola case in fifteen years."

Flanked by the IRS's Richard Spiers, strike force chief Newcomer, and special attorney Rich Stavin, who'd recently taken over the investigation from Rick Small, Bonner said the payola investigation was "continuing here and throughout the country in several other cities—roughly half a dozen. Certainly, on the basis of the indictments returned today, it's fair to say there continues to be a significant payola problem in the recording industry."

Indicted along with the Tashjians were William Craig, a promoter from Scottsdale, Arizona, who was also a subcontractor of Isgro's, and George Wilson Crowell, the former vice president and general manager of KIQQ-FM, a Top 40 radio station in Los Angeles.

Ralph Tashjian and Craig were charged with making undisclosed payments of nearly $300,000 to nine radio station programmers around the country between 1980 and 1986. The nine program directors were named as recipients in the indictment but were not charged. Tashjian was also charged with conspiracy to distribute cocaine to three program directors, tax evasion, and obstruction of justice for providing false and altered business records to the grand jury under subpoena. His wife was charged with aiding in the preparation of a false tax return.

Crowell, who lost his job at KIQQ following a 1984 *Los Angeles Times* article alleging irregularities in his station's playlist, was charged with failing to file income tax returns on $450,000 of income, including more than $100,000 in undisclosed payments. An alcoholic with a bad gambling habit, Crowell was originally fingered in the investigation by Isgro's bodyguard David Michael Smith, who told agents in an initial telephone interview that he had regularly carried cash payments from the promoter to Crowell, passing the money to him in the restroom of a bar. When agents went to interview Crowell in Palm Springs in late 1986, he immediately admitted taking the money and not paying taxes on it.

Craig and Crowell were not arrested on the charges but were allowed to turn themselves in.

At the press conference, U.S. Attorney Bonner told reporters that virtually every major record company had hired Tashjian and Craig to get their records played on the radio, but he added that there was "no evidence" that the companies knew their money was being used for illegal payments to program directors.

Though peppered by repeated questions from reporters, both Bonner and Newcomer declined to comment on the Pisello investigation, except to say that it "did uncover some of the basic facts" that ultimately led to the payola indictments. They also refused to answer questions about why Marvin Rudnick had been removed from the case and why he wasn't present at the press conference.

Later in the day, a federal magistrate in San Francisco angrily turned down the government's request to have Ralph and Valerie Tashjian held without bail as possible flight risk, and the judge ordered the couple released on a property bond. "These people are no more of a flight risk than I am," he said, calling the agents' arrest of the pair in front of their child and the NBC News crew "reprehensible."

Marvin Rudnick learned of the indictments and press conference from reading the *Los Angeles Times* the next morning as he sat in McDonald's eating his breakfast Egg McMuffin. The news was a bitter pill for him to swallow. Neither Bonner, Newcomer, nor Stavin had anything to do with the development of the case, other than the decision to indict. Stavin had been assigned to the investigation just days earlier. Now here was Bonner—the man apparently behind the move to fire him for becoming "too high-profile" in the Pisello-MCA investigation—presiding over a dog-and-pony show for reporters that seemed designed to create the impression that Bonner himself was in charge of a national investigation when, technically at least, his office wasn't even in charge of the Los Angeles case. Rudnick doubted that Bonner had ever talked to any of the other strike force offices that were supposedly investigating payola. He had obviously reviewed the indictment and decided that payola was a good public relations horse to ride for awhile. Like many U.S. attorneys, Bonner was more of a politician than a prosecutor. Gather a bunch of reporters together and turn on a TV mini-cam and Bonner showed up to take credit—that was his reputation.

Rudnick was disgusted by the hypocrisy of it all. He laughed out loud at Bonner's statement that there was no evidence that the record companies had known what was going on. In fact, the grand jury had heard one witness, a former employee of Isgro's, testify about how a handful of record company vice presidents came to Isgro's office on a regular basis to receive cash kickback payments. And the IRS was holding thousands of dollars worth of canceled checks from Bill Craig to a catering company owned by the wife of Jheryl Busby, one of MCA's top promotion executives.

Bonner's gratuitous exoneration of the record companies meant he was either badly misinformed about the details of the investigation or was misleading the media to protect the companies' reputations. Otherwise, he could have just said "no comment" to reporter's questions about possible record company involvement in the payola scheme.

Rudnick's isolation within the strike force had worsened. Newcomer had taken him off the Mondavano investigation, saying it was to allow him more time to prepare for the Pisello trial. Rudnick was completely out of touch with what was going on in the payola investigation, partly out of choice. The fact that NBC had been on hand to record the Tashjians' arrest meant that someone was leaking information to the news media, and Rudnick didn't want to get blamed. The Tashjians' indictment was sealed until the day after their arrest, so NBC obviously had been given secret grand jury information, a clear violation of rule 6(e). He wasn't sure who the leaker was, but he had heard that Kemp Schiffer was going around the office pointedly mentioning that Rudnick's wife worked for the *Los Angeles Times*. He figured Kemp was covering his ass.

Rudnick likewise tried to remain ignorant about the other major investigation in the office, the Hollywood labor racketeering case that involved the bungled MCA wiretap attempt that the company was accusing him of instigating. He'd taken to closing his office door, something he never did before. He didn't mix with the agents or other lawyers in the office. He ate lunch by himself. He and Newcomer barely spoke, and when they did, the conversation was terse and fraught with tension.

Most of what he learned about other Justice Department activities during this period of time came from reading the newspaper. In January, *New York Newsday* broke the story about Reverend Al Sharpton being an FBI informant. In an interview with *Newsday* reporters, Sharpton denied informing on fight promoter Don King or other civil rights activists, but admitted that he'd helped the FBI gather incriminating evidence against one alleged mobster.

"It's 1984 and I'm threatening to boycott the [Jackson Five Victory Tour] concerts," he told the newspaper. "And one of these nice mobsters threatened to kill me—Sal Posillo [sic]. So right away I said, 'You guys want something? Here's a guy that wants to kill me and I would love to give this guy up.' They got a guy to sit in on a meeting with me and let him threaten me on behalf of one the biggest record company presidents in the business." He did not identify the company president, however, and Rudnick never heard anything from the FBI following the newspaper story.

In March, *Newsday* reported that Peter Thomas, the former assistant vice president of the Astoria Bank in Queens, had turned himself in to authorities and confessed to embezzling about $2 million over a five-year period to support a gambling habit that ran as high as $25,000 a week. Thomas was the "Peter" whose voice was picked up on the Newark wiretaps in 1985, warning Rocco Musacchia that the IRS was attempting to serve a lien on the Consultants for World Records account. Though the newspaper revealed that Thomas had testified before the Los Angeles grand jury the previous spring, no one from the government contacted Rudnick about the banker's role in the investigation.

Around the same time that *Newsday* wrote about Thomas, the *Los Angeles Times* reported that Joe Isgro's former bodyguard, David Michael Smith, had been placed in the government's Witness Protection Program and was cooperating in the investigation of the promoter. According to the *Times,* before contacting the authorities, Smith called lawyers for both Capitol Records and Warner Brothers Records from somewhere in Australia and offered to tell his story to them in exchange for money. "He indicated he would need financial support if he returned to the United States, and he was concerned about whether the government would prosecute him," one record company lawyer said. The record companies didn't pay Smith, but they did intercede on his behalf with the government. Warner intended to use the information they received from him to defend against Isgro's antitrust suit.

There was one article, published around the same time as the *Newsday* and *Times* articles, that Rudnick found intriguing mostly for what it didn't say. On February 8, *Newsweek* ran a feature on Irving Azoff that was headlined, "The Hit Man of the Record Biz." Calling Azoff "MCA's abrasive wizard," the magazine noted that he "loves to be hated" and described his recent finger-in-the-air photo in *Hits* magazine as a "gesture [that] summed up MCA's attitude toward the competition and the competition's opinion of Azoff."

It was a fairly balanced article, crediting Azoff with "having successfully revived the moribund music division" while at the same time reporting that he had "antagonized almost everyone" in the record industry. It quoted one record executive—"who knows him well"—as saying, "I think he's the most reprehensible person in the music business."

Rudnick found it curious that, despite its allusive headline, the *Newsweek* piece contained no mention of Sal Pisello, organized crime, or the cloud of scandal that had hung over MCA Records for the last three years.

"Part of being in the entertainment business is about clout," the magazine quoted Azoff as saying. Rudnick could certainly vouch for that.

43

". . . just a simple tax case"

arvin Rudnick woke up on March 29, 1988, with butterflies in his stomach. It was trial day, opening arguments in *U.S.* v. *Salvatore James Pisello*, CR-87-553. Pisello II, as he called it.

Rudnick had spent the last thirteen years of his life trying cases, and he'd loved every minute of it. But this time was going to be different. No matter what the outcome, he knew it probably would be his last hurrah as a prosecutor. This time, he was going to be on trial himself, right along with Sal Pisello. The stakes had never been higher. His reputation and future were on the line. More than ever before, he didn't want to lose.

Driving down the Pasadena Freeway on his way to the office, he thought about all that had happened in the forty-two months since he first opened those dust-covered boxes and began reading about Sal the Swindler. Working on a two-bit tax case, he'd stumbled into the labyrinth of record industry business practices—cutouts, cleans, free goods, returns, P&D deals, paper adds, and payola. A world where Irving Azoff, John LaMonte, Morris Levy, Gaetano Vastola, Fritzy Giovanelli, and Sal Pisello each played a part in the buying and selling of American music. He'd attempted to find out why all these characters had come together in a single record deal that went sour. His quest had thrust him into the eye of the national media, consumed his life, and ultimately derailed his career. And still there were enough unanswered questions to fill a book.

"Was it worth it?" he wondered. "Could I have done it another way?" He didn't know. He just knew he had to prevail in court one last time.

To do that, he would have to overcome some formidable obstacles. Pisello's lawyer, David Hinden, was one of the best defense attorneys in Los Angeles. Rudnick wondered where Sal got the money to hire him—at least $100,000, he figured. In pretrial motions and discussions, Hinden exhibited a keen intellect. "You know what I think?" he said to Rudnick one day. "Sal's the MacGuffin."

Rudnick laughed. "What the hell's a MacGuffin?"

Hinden explained that it was a term coined by Alfred Hitchcock to describe a sometimes meaningless object around which a movie plot turns. The Maltese Falcon was a MacGuffin. So was the child's sled named Rosebud in *Citizen Kane* and the wine bottle full of diamonds in Hitchcock's *Notorious*.

"Sal isn't the real issue here," he said. "You're not trying this case because Sal got money, but because he got it from MCA."

Hinden was right in a way. Pisello II was a righteous prosecution. Sal definitely was guilty of not paying taxes on the money he received in the various record deals. But the Justice Department never would have approved a second criminal investigation of a sixty-three-year-old man already sentenced to prison on a previous tax rap had it not been for the MCA connection. The original purpose of the investigation was to find out if Pisello's dealings in the record business constituted a racketeering conspiracy involving MCA Records executives. The plan had been to hold Sal's feet to the fire with the threat of another criminal prosecution, thereby getting him to cooperate and tell how he wound up inside the company.

Rudnick's former boss, Ted Gale, knew that was the strategy. He approved it, and so did Washington. Gale believed in the case, at least in the beginning, before his abrupt departure from Los Angeles. Afterwards, Gale's secretary told Rudnick, "Ted left because Washington asked him to do something he didn't want to do." But she didn't know what it was.

Based on the information gathered in the course of the investigation, Rudnick hoped he could prove that the cutout sales were a device for paying off Morris Levy on the Sugar Hill distribution deal—Sal was just the bag man—and MCA executives had prepared misleading documents to cover up the deal. If Rudnick could prove it was all part of a racketeering conspiracy, it was conceivable that MCA could lose its record company in a forfeiture. Under the RICO statute, the government could seize the division as the proceeds of an ongoing racketeering enterprise. MCA's lawyers no doubt were horrified at that prospect. Which is why they'd apparently gone to such lengths to keep him from going any further with the case.

Publically, the department had reversed itself to the point where John Newcomer was now saying that Pisello II was "just a simple tax case" all along, implying that Rudnick had recklessly and improperly tried to make it into something bigger. That was what MCA was saying. The government was taking the line that he was a rogue prosecutor, a loose cannon on the decks.

Going into court that morning, Rudnick knew he was up against a lot more than David Hinden. Newcomer was serving as cocounsel, which meant he would sit next to him all through the trial. Since Newcomer hadn't asked to question any witnesses or present any evidence, Rudnick assumed his function was that of a babysitter. He was there to make sure Rudnick didn't misbehave and use the trial as a grand jury proceeding to bring out more evidence.

Rudnick was convinced that Newcomer's agenda was to see that Rudnick didn't disclose any more damaging information about the company and its executives. Why else would the strike force chief spend an entire week of his time second-chairing a "simple tax case"?

Newcomer had already made one move that seriously affected Rudnick's strategy. The week before, Hinden had waived Pisello's right to a jury trial and requested a bench trial before Judge Rea instead. Newcomer immediately agreed, over Rudnick's objection. Rudnick preferred a jury trial mainly because judges tend to hand down stiffer sentences to defendants convicted by twelve of their peers. He was still hoping that Sal would roll over once he was convicted and realized he was facing considerable time in prison. Rudnick felt it was important to keep the heat turned up on Pisello; Newcomer had turned it down by agreeing to the bench trial.

Arriving at the Federal Court Building at 9:15, Rudnick was greeted by a group of reporters gathered in the corridor outside courtroom number 10. The usual suspects were there—*Rolling Stone, Variety,* the *Hollywood Reporter,* the *Los Angeles Times, Billboard,* NBC News, KCBS-TV.

Rudnick knew them all by now. He'd talked with them in the hallways on many occasions over the past three and a half years, and had fielded countless of their phone calls. Rudnick liked reporters. He felt comfortable in their company. Through his wife, he knew some of them personally. He'd met a few jerks among them, but for the most part they were an honorable bunch, he thought. Few of them were in it for the money; most were seeking the same thing he was after—truth, or at least some form of it. And every now and then they found it.

As Rudnick chatted with the reporters, Newcomer walked up to the group and began introducing himself with forced joviality, at the same time shooting Rudnick a hard look, as if to say, "Run along; I'll take over from here." As his boss familiarized himself with the newsmen's names and faces, Rudnick slipped into the courtroom to begin last-minute preparations.

His plan was to low-key his presentation and focus on the plumbing of the deals that caused money to flow to Pisello. Nothing inflammatory. He thought that Newcomer would be ready to step in at any moment and stop him. He had two main concerns— Ranji Bedi and Joe Robinson, his key witnesses.

Bedi's testimony would put $146,000 in Pisello's hands—$46,000 of it in cash—as a sort of finder's fee on the Scorpio cutout sale. Bedi was furious at Pisello for double-crossing him by not delivering the records Scorpio had ordered. He wanted to bury Sal. But Rudnick feared that Bedi was also holding back. According to John Gervasoni, Bedi told him that Pisello gave $130,000 of the front money on the Scorpio sale to MCA executives in order to secure the deal. Dan McGill testified in deposition in the Scorpio lawsuit that Bedi also had told him Sal claimed to have passed the money to company executives. Hinden was aware of Gervasoni's statements, so he could be expected to tear into Bedi on the witness stand, try-

ing to impeach his credibility and muddy the waters on the taxabil-
ity of the money that went to Pisello. If Sal were just passing the
money along, Hinden could argue, then it was not taxable to him.
Hinden planned to put Gervasoni on the stand to rebut Bedi, and
Gervasoni, Rudnick had seen, was a very convincing witness.

Joe Robinson, too, was a big question mark. Newcomer had
refused to let Rudnick travel to New Jersey to prepare Robinson for
his testimony. Newcomer said he'd take care of it himself, but he
never did, as far as Rudnick knew. So Rudnick had no idea what
Robinson was going to say on the stand. Rudnick knew there had
been some contact between MCA and Robinson and he was concerned that some unholy deal had been struck. Rudnick reckoned
that it was in MCA's interest to see Pisello get acquitted, since Sal
would then have no reason to cooperate in any further investigation.

Sugar Hill paid Pisello $156,000 in 1984 that Sal didn't report as
income. At Pisello's request, Robinson and Milton Malden had carried the payments on the company's books as loans. If Robinson
insisted on the stand that the payments were in fact loans, and not
advances on his commission for selling the Checker/Chess catalog
to MCA, it would raise doubt that the money was taxable.

That left the government with only the $80,000 that MCA had
paid Pisello in 1985—$30,000 on the Latin music deal and the
$50,000 that was either an advance on his Sugar Hill distribution
commissions or a payment for his help in obtaining the
Checker/Chess master tapes, depending on which version of MCA's
internal audit report you believed. The problem with the $80,000
was that the government didn't have any detailed memos from
MCA describing why the money was paid, just the internal audit
report, which was written after the fact. Dan McGill would testify
the money wasn't a loan, but his testimony on that point was in
effect hearsay, since he didn't make the deal with Pisello or approve
the payments. Myron Roth had done that, and he was beyond Rudnick's call. In a meeting a week before the trial, Rudnick had asked
Newcomer one last time to allow him to immunize Roth and call
him as a witness. "You don't need him," Newcomer replied.

So if David Hinden played his cards right and managed to raise
reasonable doubts in his cross-examination of Bedi, Robinson, and
McGill, Rudnick would have no rebuttal. He could lose the case.

Just before opening arguments were to begin, Rudnick was in the restroom washing his hands when a slightly built, gray-haired man walked in, nodded to him, and went about his business. Rudnick had seen the man moments earlier, talking chummily with Newcomer in the back of the courtroom.

"Hi, I'm Marvin Rudnick," he said, watching the man in the mirror.

"Bill Hundley," the man replied over his shoulder.

So, MCA brought its biggest legal gun all the way from Washington to watch over me, Rudnick thought.

"Welcome to the trial," he said.

Back in the courtroom, the opposing lawyers stood side by side before the judge.

"May it please the court, Marvin Rudnick representing the United States."

"May it please the court, David Hinden appearing on behalf of Salvatore Pisello, who is present."

The prosecution went first. Rudnick drew a picture of Sal as a glib wheeler dealer who for years had been able to convince legitimate businessmen to invest large sums of money in his business schemes, and then sought to make the money impossible for the IRS to trace, converting it to cashier's checks and running it through his girlfriend's checking account and various other shell corporation accounts he set up. Rudnick pointed out that Pisello didn't even have a bank account in his own name until 1985, after he was indicted on the first tax charges.

He said nothing about Pisello's alleged organized crime ties, nor did he mention Morris Levy. But twice he stressed to Judge Rea that Pisello had no prior experience in the record business when he began negotiating multimillion-dollar deals with MCA Records executives.

David Hinden countered with charts and graphs that he said would show that most of the money his client received was in the form of loans. And any taxes owed on the rest of the money was more than offset by business expenses—including the rent on a house in Los Angeles and an apartment in New York—that Pisello could have claimed if he had filed his tax returns for those years.

Rudnick's first witness was Joe Robinson, who took the oath apparently not realizing he was wearing sunglasses. He suddenly snatched them off as Rudnick began leading him through his first meeting with Sal Pisello in the fall of 1983: He was having breakfast with Rocco Musacchia, an old friend, in the Polo Lounge of the Beverly Hills Hotel, when Pisello happened by their table, Robinson said. Rocco and Sal were friends, and he knew Pisello, too, but just slightly, from years before in New York.

"Mr. Pisello asked me what I was doing out here in California and I told him . . . I was trying to get distribution for my records with Capitol, and Mr. Pisello said to me that he could get me a deal with MCA Records. . . . I said, 'Be my guest.'"

Robinson had said previously that Pisello quickly arranged for a meeting with Azoff, Roth, and Horowitz at MCA's offices in Universal City, and that Rocco had gone along with him. On the witness stand, however, his memory faltered. He was "confused" about the initial meeting, he said.

"I don't recall him going with me. . . . Azoff don't recall him being there either, and I asked Rocky and he said he did not come there."

"The question is, did Mr. Musacchia go to MCA with you?" Rudnick asked sharply.

"Nope. I don't recall him going with me."

Robinson was back-pedaling on his grand jury testimony, putting Rudnick in the position of having to cross-examine his own witness. Rudnick's face registered frustration and anger. He looked up at Judge Rea.

"I'm not quite at the 611-C stage, Your Honor," he said, referring to the rule of evidence that allows a prosecutor to declare a witness "adverse." He was signaling the judge that Robinson was not testifying as planned, but was, in effect, testifying for the defense.

Newcomer sat marine-rigid at the prosecution table, scribbling notes. MCA's lead outside counsel, Ron Olson, had slipped into a pew in the back of the courtroom and was listening intently to the testimony.

Rudnick pushed ahead. "Did Mr. Pisello give you any indication about how he was able to cut a deal with MCA?"

"No," Robinson replied. "He said he had friends there, that's all."

"Did he say what kind of friends?"

"Nope. Just friends."

Previously, Robinson had claimed that Pisello specifically said his friends were "in the Tower," meaning the executive offices of MCA. Rudnick wanted that in the trial record, but Robinson wasn't delivering. Rudnick tried again.

"Did Mr. Pisello tell you anything about what he did in Los Angeles to get the contract that would justify his fee?"

"No, we didn't discuss that."

"Did you ever discuss it with him?"

"Did I ever discuss what he did to get it?"

"That's correct."

"Yes."

"And when was that?"

"I had asked him a few times, 'How could you, how did you get this?' I said, 'My lawyer couldn't get it and you got it.' He said, 'Never mind.'"

"That was it?"

"Yeah. He said he had friends up at MCA. He did say that, that's right, 'I have friends up at MCA.'"

"Did he say who they were?"

"No."

"Did you ask him?"

"Yes."

"What did he say when you asked him?"

"He would never tell me."

Robinson testified that Pisello said he thought he could convince MCA to purchase Sugar Hill's Checker/Chess catalog for $8 million. In return for Sal's efforts, he agreed to pay him a 7 percent commission on the sale price—in advance.

"I loaned him money against this Chess catalog sale," he said.

There it was. He described it as a loan. Rudnick moved quickly to raise doubt about the true nature of the transaction.

"What kind of agreement did you have about the loan?" he asked.

"There was nothing written about the loan."

"How did you pay him this loan money?"

"By check."

"How much money did you loan him?" Judge Rea cut in.

"It was $214,000 totally."

"And it was never evidenced by a note or anything in writing?"

"Eventually, Mr. Pisello or his attorneys sent us a letter stating that this is the amount that he owed us and they was going to pay us 8 percent on this money. We did have that. That's all."

Rudnick was relieved—the judge wasn't buying the story. What kind of legitimate business loan had no written agreement or arrangement for repayment?

Rudnick showed Robinson two of the twenty-six checks—totaling $214,000—that Sugar Hill had written to Pisello in 1984. The checks were for $5,000 each and contained a hand-written notation on the bottom left corner that said "advance."

"What does the word *advance* mean?" Rudnick asked.

"That was put on there by Milton Malden, who is Yugoslavian." This nervous non sequitur of Robinson's caused Rudnick to smile against his will. "He had to write something down, and I guess he advanced it against a loan, or whatever. I don't know," Robinson said.

"Did you ever get repaid for either check?"

"No."

"Did you talk to Mr. Pisello about that?"

"No."

"Did you ever ask him for money?"

"No."

Hinden began his cross-examination of Robinson the next morning. He went straight to Sugar Hill's books and zeroed in on one of the $5,000 checks Rudnick introduced the day before.

"Would you please read aloud the entry in the ledger next to the credit?"

"Loan: S. Pisello," Robinson read.

Addressing the court, Hinden said. "Each and every entry reflects that the disbursements in question totaling $214,000 are recorded as loans."

"This is what my thinking was," Robinson said, turning to the judge. "What is in this book is a loan."

Rea looked incredulous. "All of the $214,000 was a loan?"

"Yes sir."

"Did you ask him for a receipt or a note or anything to protect you?"

"No sir. I didn't have that."

On redirect, Rudnick produced a transcript of Robinson's grand jury testimony. He directed him to page forty-seven, line fourteen, where Robinson had testified that long after Pisello asked him to "advance" the money on the promised Checker/Chess sale, "all of a sudden he sends a piece of paper to us saying it was a 'loan'—and on some of the checks it may have said 'loans.'"

"Did you say that to me?" Rudnick asked.

"Yes."

"In the grand jury?"

"Yes.

"Was it true then?"

"Yes.

"Is it true now?"

"Yes."

"Thank you. No more questions."

Rudnick felt confident he'd managed to blunt the testimony about the Sugar Hill "loans"—even if he had been forced to impeach his own witness to do it. But as he sat down at the prosecution table, Newcomer leaned over to him and hissed, "You did a lousy job preparing that witness."

"I did a lousy job?" Rudnick shot back. "You wouldn't let me go to New Jersey to talk to him, remember? You said you would go instead but you backed out of it. Robinson didn't come out here to Los Angeles till yesterday. So when was I supposed to prepare him?"

Rudnick slammed shut his trial book, got up, and walked away from the table. Sitting a dozen feet away, the reporters snapped to attention and began scribbling notes, exchanging glances among themselves. It's not often you see a prosecution team in a fight in the middle of a trial.

44

"They're playing my song"

anji Bedi took the witness stand Thursday morning, March 31, the third day of the trial. He identified himself as a "self-employed entertainer, composer, recording artist, and business-man." He had authored a number of Top 40 hits, he said, including "I'll Never Let You Go," by Bobby Sherman. From 1980 to 1986, he also owned a small company that bought cutouts from the major record companies and sold them to other companies around the country and in Europe. Betaco was an anagram for Bedi Tape Company, he said.

Rudnick led him through the chronology of how he became involved with Sal Pisello. It was in late March or early April 1984, Bedi recalled. He telephoned Sam Passamano at MCA Records to inquire about buying cutouts on behalf of his biggest customer, Scorpio Music.

"He said that he no longer handled the cutout product, but that if I gave him my phone number he would have the gentleman who's now in charge give me a call. The gentleman that was supposed to get in touch with me called me the following day. His name was Sal Pisello. We made an arrangement to meet at a coffee shop in Westwood. The appointment was made for noon the following day."

Pisello showed him an MCA cutout inventory list marked "Property of Sal Pisello," Bedi said. "Three and a half million units. He told me I could buy the total list for fifty cents a unit or 'cherry pick' it, using his term, for sixty-five cents a unit. It was a ten- to fifteen-minute meeting. He was recommended to me by MCA as their representative."

After conferring with Scorpio's owner, John Gervasoni, he agreed to purchase approximately 550,000 albums and cassettes, Bedi said. At a second meeting at the same coffee shop the next day, Pisello said that to secure the deal he needed a cashier's check for $100,000 made out to Roulette Records, plus $15,000 in cash for himself, with the balance to be paid after delivery of the records. Bedi said he questioned the check to Roulette.

"I said, 'I thought I was dealing with MCA.' He said, 'You are dealing with MCA, but Roulette has the option on the cutouts, so your purchase order has to go to them. But that's my business; that's not yours. It will be MCA that you're dealing with.'"

After some initial nervousness on the witness stand, Bedi was warming to his role as storyteller to a room full of people taking notes on what he said. Details, anecdotes, and remembrances began flowing out of him easily, requiring little or no prodding from Rudnick.

He said he handed over the $100,000 cashier's check during a third meeting at another Westwood restaurant, Gatsby's, several days later.

"I just remembered something. At that point, the music was playing on the restaurant sound system and they were playing the song from *The Godfather*. And he looked at me and said, 'They're playing my song.'"

Laughter erupted from the knot of reporters in the first two rows of spectator seats. Hinden was on his feet to object.

"We'd ask to strike that," Rudnick said quickly, fighting to keep a straight face.

"Your Honor, it's nonresponsive," Hinden said.

"It will be stricken," the judge replied.

Pleased with himself, Bedi continued. "I got home and that afternoon Mr. Pisello called me up and he says, 'Ranji, I want you to do me a favor.' I said, 'What is that?' He said, 'I want you to meet me tomorrow morning, and I want you to pick up your $100,000 check made out to Roulette Records, and I want you to substitute it with a check made out to MCA for $100,000.' Now I want to tell you, my reaction was I was ecstatic. Because now I knew that the money was going directly to MCA and that my original call had been heeded."

They met in the lobby of MCA Records. "He shook hands with me, introduced me to [MCA Manufacturing vice president] Dan Westbrook. At that time I gave him the $100,000 check. It was in an envelope. And I left.

"The following day . . . I called him and I asked him to meet me at my bank, at the parking lot of my bank, at ten o'clock in the morning, and said that I would have his cash available to him." Bedi turned over the cash while sitting in the front seat of Pisello's Eldorado in the parking lot of Santa Monica Bank. The money was in an envelope.

"It was pretty thick. It was a regular one of those bank envelopes, which are a little bigger than the normal mailing envelope. And there were a lot of hundred-dollar bills. $15,000 is a lot. He didn't count it all. You've got to understand they were precounted already, they were in bunches of a thousand dollars, so there were fifteen of them."

"A band around them?" Rudnick asked.

"Yeah, had a band around them."

"Fresh bills?"

"Very fresh. In fact, it looked like they were right off the press. As a matter of fact, Mr. Pisello made a comment to me that they were in sequence, and he asked me if I was trying to get funny because the bills were in sequence."

After the parking lot transaction, "the deal went like a hot knife through butter," Bedi said. MCA was paid the balance of $235,000, Gervasoni got the records he ordered, Sal and Ranji made their profits, and everyone was happy.

Everyone, that is, except John LaMonte, who was expecting those same records to be included in his shipment from MCA.

Rudnick intended to keep LaMonte out of the trial. It was too complicated and indefensibly prejudicial. Certainly Hinden would object. Rudnick began guiding Bedi through the second cutout deal.

Bedi said he heard from Pisello again in late September of 1984. Sal had another list of cutouts from MCA.

"The difference was that I was supposed to buy a minimum of a million units, and the payments would be different. The down payment would be larger. He said I would have to come up with at least $200,000 deposit to MCA, and that the purchase order had to be made out to MCA for fifty cents a unit, and he wanted a ten-cents-a-unit commission on top of that. But he didn't want it spelled out in the purchase order."

"Did he tell you why?"

"He told me that he was . . . as MCA's agent, he was going to make his commission on top of that, and they didn't care what he made. Therefore, he didn't want them to know. He told me to prepare the purchase order in the manner I described because he told me it was none of MCA's business what he made; that they had allowed him to make whatever he could as his commission. That's how he explained it to me."

He jumped at the deal, Bedi said, because the list contained so many "splendid LPs. I did not have to be an expert to see that those were splendid. The Who's double album, *Hooligans*, three or four other Who albums. Some of the best product that MCA had in previous years that went gold and platinum was in there. Olivia Newton-John product, Neil Diamond, Elton John, some more Lynyrd Skynyrd. There was a tremendous amount of catalog product in there. I couldn't believe my eyes—it was the best list I'd ever seen; it was that good."

"Did Mr. Pisello say anything to you about the quality of the list?"

"He was as excited as I was. He said, 'Isn't that great?' I said, 'Absolutely.'"

"Did he tell you where he got the list?"

"He got it from MCA."

"Did he tell you where at MCA he got the list?"

"He told me this is the list that MCA prepared. As far as I'm concerned, to me, in my mind, I visualized the executives of MCA giving him this list. That was my understanding."

Bedi said he gave Pisello a check made out to MCA on November 6, 1984. "I didn't foresee any problems whatsoever."

He also gave Pisello a $50,000 advance payment on his ten-cents-a-unit commission.

"He says, 'You'll get me $15,000 in cash, and you will get me a $35,000 wire transfer made out to General Enterprises in Las Vegas.' He told me it was one of his corporations."

Once again, he turned the cash over to Pisello in the parking lot of the Santa Monica Bank, Bedi said. Only this time he took his lawyer, Sam Galici, along to witness the transaction. It was just a legal precaution, since Pisello refused to sign a receipt for the money.

On December 18, Pisello invited him to lunch at the Palm, Bedi said. Again Galici went with him. "And at that meeting, Mr. Pisello asked me for another advance because he said he needed money for Christmas presents. I couldn't believe I had to come up with any more money. I hadn't received even one record."

Nonetheless, he agreed to give Pisello another $16,000 in cash. Same drill: front seat of Sal's Eldorado in the parking lot of the Santa Monica Bank; $100 bills in an envelope; no receipt; Galici as a witness.

MCA shipped about 130,000 cutouts to Scorpio in the middle of January 1985, Bedi said. "We got a mishmash of everything. There was no catalog product in there. And that caused my clients to be extremely aggravated with me."

After some pressure, Pisello agreed to get MCA to return the $200,000 deposit until the balance of the records was shipped. They met again at the bank.

"And he's holding my $200,000 made out to Betaco. He said, 'I brought you the check, but I'm going to need another $30,000.' And I said, 'What do you need another $30,000 for?' And he said, 'Because I need the money to do what I have to do with MCA to get your product.'"

Bedi said he gave Pisello the $30,000 in cash and later refunded $150,000 to John Gervasoni at Scorpio.

"Why did you only give him $150,000 instead of the $200,000?" Rudnick asked. After all, it was Scorpio's money that had gone to pay the deposit to MCA and Pisello's advances. Gervasoni was $350,000 into the deal and had received less than 150,000 cutouts. Bedi hadn't put up a penny and was still nearly $100,000 to the good.

"There was no rhyme or reason," Bedi replied. "I wasn't going to refund any more because I needed some cash reserves in case that MCA requested their money back."

After that, another month passed and still no more records were shipped, Bedi said. So he complained to Pisello again.

"And he says, 'Don't worry about it. I'm working with the people. I go to MCA every day. I'm talking to Irv, Myron. We're working.' For the first time I heard Horowitz, who is the legal guy over at MCA."

"Who did you know Irv and Myron to be?"

"Irv Azoff, Myron Roth."

"Mr. Pisello told you that he dealt with those people?"

"Many, many times. . . . He told me that he was very close to these people and he dealt with them directly on a one-to-one basis."

"Did you rely on that representation in making your decision to go forward with business with Mr. Pisello?"

"I had no other choice. MCA recommended him to me. The several opportunities that I had to meet with Mr. Pisello at MCA, or even go with him, the man could walk through those doors as if he was part of the company. I mean, no one would even question where he was going. Several times he would just walk by the receptionist and say, 'I'm on my way to see Myron' or 'McGill.' I mean, he just walked through as though he was a top employee there. So I had no reason to question him. I mean, he had authority. He showed authority."

At one point he phoned Dan Westbrook, Bedi testified. "I said, 'Dan, what the heck is going on?' He said, 'You've got the best guy working for you. He's up there with the big boys and he's really working to get your product for you.'"

But the records never came. Around the first week of April, Pisello "started to call me and tell me that in order for me to get all the product that I ordered, I had to perform one more time with cash," Bedi said.

"Now he needed $50,000 because he had to do what he had to do with MCA."

"Did he tell you what that was?"

"'If you want your product, I've got to do what I've got to do with MCA.'"

"Did he say who the people were?"

"As far as I'm concerned, it was MCA."

"Did you believe him?"

"Absolutely."

Bedi said he came up with another $30,000 in cash. Several days later, he said, "my lawyer called me and asked if I had read the morning paper, which had the story in the business section."

"Figure in Record Deal Tied to Crime Family," the *Times* headline read. That was how he first learned Sal had problems with the government, Bedi said.

"I called Mr. Pisello. I said, 'What's going on?' He wanted to meet with me, and we met. He told me he was being literally persecuted by the U.S. government, that the article wasn't true, that the people at MCA were behind him, and that his troubles were no different than anybody that has tax problems. I said, 'What's going to happen now? Am I going to get my product?' He said, 'I'm going to talk to Irv, and I'm going to make sure you get your stuff.'"

Bedi said he met with three MCA executives several days later—Roth, McGill, and Zach Horowitz.

"Did you tell Myron Roth that Mr. Pisello had received on the second cutout deal $133,000 from your own pocket?" Rudnick asked.

"Yes," Bedi replied emphatically.

Later, under cross-examination by David Hinden, Bedi denied John Gervasoni's version of events.

"Prior to the time that Mr. Gervasoni wired any money to you on the second cutout transaction, did you tell Mr. Gervasoni that you needed $50,000 in cash currency for Irving Azoff?" Hinden asked.

"No."

"Did you tell him you knew Irving Azoff?"

"No."

"Did you ever tell Mr. Gervasoni that $150,000 was in the system at MCA and could not be recovered?"

"I never said that."

45

"I'm going to recommend that you be removed from this office"

The government calls its next witness, Dan McGill."

Rudnick's words sent a jolt of electricity through the reporters in the courtroom. They'd been waiting more than two years for this: nitty gritty time—an officer of MCA Records finally testifying under oath about what happened inside that company when Sal Pisello was roaming the halls.

"Mr. McGill, do you recognize exhibits 56 and 57?" Rudnick asked.

"Yes, I do."

"Tell the court what those exhibits are."

"My understanding is, this is—I believe the term is a proffer—which my attorneys negotiated with the government prior to my testimony before the grand jury."

The reporters scribbled excitedly. Rudnick avoided saying it, but McGill was obviously testifying under a grant of immunity. The top financial officer at the record company was about to spill the beans, the reporters figured.

But it didn't turn out that way. By the end of the day, they were wondering why the government had bothered to make any deal at all with McGill. To hear him tell it, he knew next to nothing about what went on with Sal Pisello.

McGill said he was first introduced to Pisello by Myron Roth as a "representative of Sugar Hill Records." But he never asked anyone what Pisello's duties were at Sugar Hill.

McGill said he was "responsible for all the financial reporting of the companies within the MCA Music Group, the billing of sales, checks, receivables, and safeguarding the company's assets." Yet he never knew what Consultants for World Records was, or even where it was located.

He issued checks to Pisello totaling $100,000 for the break-dance mat venture. But he never knew specifically what the money was being used for.

It was Myron Roth who made the deals with Pisello and ordered the payments to Pisello, McGill said. He simply followed orders.

Rudnick showed him the $30,000 check MCA wrote to Pisello on the Latin music deal.

"It says on the voucher copy, 'If MCA Records does not accept the proposal, this advance will be returned,' does it not, sir?"

"Yes, it does."

"Do you know whether Mr. Pisello ever handed you a proposal?"

"He never handed me a proposal, no."

"Did he ever verbally give you a proposal?"

"No, he did not."

"Do you have any knowledge at all what Mr. Pisello did for the $30,000?"

"No, I don't."

"Is there a contract for the $30,000 payment?"

"No, there is not."

"Is there a letter of understanding to the $30,000 payment?"

"Not that I'm aware of."

"Did MCA ever get back the $30,000?"

"No, it did not."

"Did it ever get back any kind of a product or service from any third party for the $30,000?"

"No."

And so it went. McGill's answers were terse, clipped, offering nothing more than the bare minimum in response to Rudnick's questions. No elaboration, zero enlightenment.

Rudnick wasn't surprised. He'd met with McGill and his lawyer at MCA's offices the night before, to go over his testimony. He knew McGill had been well coached. He would give up just enough to put MCA's money in Pisello's hands. But any questions about how or why the money was put there elicited the same response. "I don't know; you'll have to ask Myron." He was a brick wall.

Still, Rudnick pressed McGill on the witness stand. If nothing else, he reasoned, it would give Judge Rea some of the flavor of how Pisello did business.

He showed McGill a check that MCA wrote Pisello on March 7, 1984, for $18,300.

"It doesn't have a mailing address on it. How would the check be able to get to Mr. Pisello?"

"He would either pick it up at our offices or have someone pick it up for him."

"Who is this person that would come by and pick it up?"

"There was a gentleman by the name of Spider who would come by and pick up checks for him."

"Spider?" Judge Rea interrupted, as a chorus of guffaws went up from the reporters present.

"Yes, sir," McGill said, stone-faced.

Rudnick made no attempt to hide his amusement this time. He turned toward the spectator seats and flashed a broad smile.

The humor was lost on Newcomer. A few minutes earlier, he had glared at Rudnick and silently mouthed the words, "Push ahead." Now he was doing a slow burn, tapping his right foot on the floor, rapping his pen sharply on his note pad and looking as if he might spring for the podium at any second.

Judge Rea adjourned at 2:00 P.M. that Friday, saying he had other court matters to attend to. Back at the strike force office a few hours later, Rudnick was standing by a secretary's desk when he overheard her put a call through to Newcomer, "from Mr. Hadl at MCA." Bob Hadl was MCA's newly appointed chief counsel.

Rudnick was standing in the same spot five minutes later when Newcomer emerged from his office. "I want to see you right now," he said.

In his office, Newcomer told Rudnick, "This weekend I want

you to work on preparing the Mondavano indictment; I want it ready Monday morning first thing."

Newcomer never ceased to astonish him. They were weeks, if not months, away from asking the grand jury to indict Mondavano, and here Newcomer was, putting him back on the case.

"I got a trial Monday, remember?" he said.

"Just do it," Newcomer replied.

Rudnick turned and walked out of the office. Newcomer got up from his desk and followed him into the foyer. "And another thing," he said. "If you treat that witness like that again on Monday, I'm taking over the case."

"What are you talking about?"

"You know what I'm talking about."

"Put it in writing." Rudnick spat out the words, turned on his heel, and walked away. He had no intention of working on Mondavano over the weekend. Let Newcomer build a case against him for insubordination, if that's what he was up to. He would deal with it later. Right now, he had to focus all his energies on convicting Sal Pisello.

The resumption of McGill's testimony on Tuesday was postponed so that Bedi's attorney, Sam Galici, could be called to the stand. Galici was not an eager witness. He'd been complaining for weeks that testifying at the trial would interfere with his work schedule. Rudnick agreed to have him appear first thing Tuesday morning so he could get back to work. His testimony was to be short, and David Hinden had no objection to moving him up in the witness order.

Moments before Galici's testimony was to begin, Rudnick was in the hallway conferring with IRS agent John Anderson. The two were leaning against the wall, talking quietly, in full view of a handful of reporters. Suddenly, Newcomer strode out of the courtroom, walked over to where they stood, and stepped between them, his back to Anderson, his face inches from Rudnick's.

"Who the hell is Galici?" he asked.

"He's Bedi's lawyer," said Rudnick, genuinely stunned by the question, and at Newcomer's obvious irritation.

"What do we need him for?"

"He saw the cash Ranji passed to Pisello."

"Why are you always interested in cash?" Newcomer queried.

Rudnick was at a complete loss. What was this all about? Surely he could see the need for having Galici back up Bedi's story about handing over cash in the front seat of Sal's Eldorado.

As he waited for Rudnick to respond, Newcomer noticed that two reporters were standing not five feet away, listening to the conversation and taking down notes.

Turning back to Rudnick, he snapped, "Stop trying this case in the hallway, Marvin. Do you like to give interviews with reporters?" He motioned for Rudnick to follow him to the other end of the hall, away from the reporters, where the argument continued for several more minutes, their angry voices echoing in the marble corridor.

"Watch my lips," Newcomer said. "You do not call witnesses without my approval."

"You've known about Galici all along," Rudnick argued back. "He's been on the witness list for weeks."

After the hallway drama, Galici's testimony was anticlimactic. He recalled seeing Bedi give Pisello $15,000 on one occasion, but didn't remember subsequent incidents that Bedi had related. He was off the stand in fifteen minutes.

McGill returned, and Rudnick started in going through each MCA-Pisello transaction.

"Do you recognize these checks?"

"Yes, I do."

"Could you tell the court what they are?"

"They are four checks from Mr. Salvatore Pisello, three in the amount of $60,000 and one in the amount of $52,109."

"Did you receive them from Mr. Pisello?"

"Yes, I did."

"They are undated, are they not?"

"They are."

"Now, what did you do with these checks when you received them?"

"I kept them in my desk at my office at MCA."

"In a drawer?"

"Yes."

"Did you ever attempt to cash the checks?"

"No, I did not."

"Why not?"

"Because whenever I would talk to Mr. Pisello about their col-
lectability, he would indicate there was not sufficient funds at the
time."

Asked about the January 1985 payment of $50,000 to Pisello,
McGill said that Myron Roth "agreed to advance the money."

"Did Mr. Pisello tell you anything about why he needed the
money?"

"Not specifically, no."

"Just said he needed it for business purposes?"

"Yes, sir."

"Did Mr. Roth ask Mr. Pisello to do anything in exchange for the
$50,000 in your presence?"

"Not in my presence, no."

"Did you ask him for anything?"

"No, I did not."

"Did Mr. Pisello promise anything in exchange for the $50,000?"

"No, he did not."

McGill testified that MCA later wrote off the $50,000 debt
because "we determined that it was not collectible."

Rudnick wondered if the judge or anyone else in the courtroom
picked up on the significance of that admission. According to previous testimony, MCA had already collected the $50,000 advanced
to Pisello by deducting it from what the company paid Joe Robinson on the Checker/Chess deal. They had forced Robinson to pay
the money and then took an arguably improper tax deduction on
the $50,000 as an uncollected debt. In essence, MCA collected
twice, once from the taxpayers.

"Was this a loan?" Rudnick asked.

"No, it wasn't."

"Why not?"

"It was an advance against future proceeds. It's different from a
loan."

"How is it different from a loan?"

"In my opinion, a loan has specific repayment terms, usually stated with interest, and there is a policy at MCA that all loans in
excess of $10,000 require Mr. Sheinberg's approval."

"Was that approval received on this $50,000?"

"It was not."

McGill testified that his last meeting with Pisello was "sometime
in the early part of 1985. February or March of that year, I believe."

"And where was that meeting?"

"At La Serre."

Rudnick knew La Serre was one of the priciest restaurants in Los Angeles, a favorite spot for studio executives to "do lunch."

"Who was present?" he asked.

"Myself, Mr. Pisello, and Mr. Roth."

"Would you tell us what happened in that meeting?"

"He advised us of his problems with the government. We asked him, I believe at that meeting, to help us retrieve our records from Out of the Past from the first cutout transaction."

"And did he agree to do that?"

"Yes, he did."

"And did he do that?"

"Yes, he did."

As a truth seeker, Rudnick wanted to press McGill on the La Serre meeting. For one thing, the lunch took place after March 20, 1985, when he first informed MCA that the Organized Crime Strike Force was conducting a criminal investigation of Sal Pisello. Yet, armed with that information, Roth and McGill had gone ahead and assigned Pisello the task of retrieving MCA's cutouts from Out of the Past. That chronology contradicted MCA's oft-printed protest that its executives never knowingly did business with an organized crime figure.

After a few more questions, he yielded the floor to Hinden for cross-examination. He'd gotten all he was going to get out of McGill—the money went to Pisello from business transactions, and it was not a loan. "Nothing further, Your Honor."

Hinden went right to it. "Do you believe that you committed any criminal acts in connection with your dealings with Mr. Pisello on the MCA matters?" he asked McGill.

"I do not."

"And you have never taken any money for yourself from Mr. Pisello, have you?"

"I have not."

"And now it's a fact, is it not, that overall, with respect to all of these transactions, MCA has made well over a million dollars in connection with these matters?"

"I'd say that is correct, yes."

Hinden's spin on the Pisello-MCA story was that all the transactions were legitimate, both sides were making money, and everything was hunky-dory until the Los Angeles strike force and the *Los Angeles Times* articles caused MCA to unilaterally cancel all its agreements with Pisello, thereby making it impossible for him to repay the money the company had advanced to him as loans. MCA changed the rules in the middle of the game and that's what put Pisello in tax trouble, he argued.

"Now, when you asked for the three checks from Mr. Pisello, did you tell him that it was in connection with an annual review being done by Price Waterhouse?"

"I believe the essence of the conversation was that I indicated that we were being audited by Price Waterhouse. We had these amounts on the books and I'd like to have something to be able to demonstrate to Price Waterhouse that I was in the process of getting these funds returned."

"You weren't taking these checks from Mr. Pisello as some kind of sham to put over on your auditors, were you?"

"Absolutely not."

"Did your auditors at any time in January or February or March of 1985 ever ask to look at those checks?"

"I don't recall if they did or not."

Judge Rea appeared fascinated by the testimony. He was leaning forward on his elbow, with his chin resting in his hand, staring at McGill. When testimony turned to the January 1985 payment of $50,000 to Pisello, he interrupted Hinden and began questioning McGill himself.

"What investigation or efforts do you make to recover this amount of money before you write it off as uncollectable?" he asked.

"I review it with various executives who might be involved in the situation," McGill replied.

"Do you do a credit check?"

"On this specific item we had a lot of information as to the gentleman's whereabouts, advice from counsel as to what, if any, collection efforts we could pursue. It wasn't just something I did in my own mind."

"When you say advice from counsel, which counsel?"

"Our outside counsel, as to whether or not we had sufficient grounds to pursue a lawsuit to attempt to collect the monies."

"And they advised you that you didn't have grounds?"

"They advised that we may have had grounds, but we felt that there wasn't sufficient assets to go after, even if we wanted to undertake that, to warrant the attempt."

"But did you ever, to your knowledge, run a credit check to see if he owned property?"

"To my knowledge, we did not, Your Honor."

"Okay, all right." Rea said, shaking his head as if in disbelief.

Rudnick loved it. Rea was doing what he couldn't—questioning MCA's behavior.

On redirect, Rudnick had one aim—to show that both Pisello and MCA were weaving a phony story around the January 1985 $50,000 payment and the checks kept in McGill's desk drawer, and he wanted to bring that point home to Judge Rea, who was obviously suspicious of the whole scenario.

Rudnick went to the checks kept in McGill's desk drawer.

"Did you know that the checks that he gave you—the undated checks—were worthless when he gave them to you?"

"Yes, I did."

"What made you think that those were security?"

"I felt they were more security than nothing."

"At the time you accepted the three $60,000 checks, had Mr. Pisello already owed you $300,000 for one of the cutout deals?"

"At the time he gave me the three checks for $60,000, I think the balance on the first cutout transaction was in excess of $300,000. That's my recollection."

"Was it almost $839,000?"

"It was at one point. I don't know if it was at this time now."

"If Mr. Pisello owed you $839,000 at one point, what made you think that his giving you worthless checks would be any more secure?"

"Objection, argumentative," Hinden called out.

"Overruled," said Rea, leaning forward to hear McGill's response.

"I believe I have testified as to my reasons for taking those checks, and I will state them again," McGill said stiffly. "I was going to use them as leverage or security for the other monies that he had agreed to pay. Those transactions had nothing to do with the cutout transaction which we were involved in collection and getting the records, which we subsequently did."

His answer made no discernible sense. Rudnick went to the matter of the $300,000 check that Pisello bounced to MCA on the first cutout deal. "Why would you take $180,000 in worthless checks from Mr. Pisello sometime in 1985 knowing he's given you a bad check in the past?"

Hinden objected, and Rea asked Rudnick to repeat the question.

"Why did you accept three $60,000 checks—worthless checks, undated, no funds to back them—as security, knowing that Mr. Pisello had given you a bad $300,000 check from his company just two months before?"

Hinden again objected that the question was argumentative.

Rea turned to Rudnick. "I think you better get on to another subject," he said. "I think you're beating a dead horse here. You are just going over and over and over the same thing."

Rea was right, Rudnick thought. McGill was just going to keep saying—using the most tortured logic—there was nothing unusual in what he did with the checks, and it had no connection to anything else that transpired between MCA and Pisello.

Rudnick hated giving up; it wasn't in his nature. After three and a half years of work, McGill was his last shot at the truth, the last MCA executive he'd ever be able to question. But he knew he couldn't push it any further. Then he would be using the trial improperly as a grand jury inquiry. He felt certain he'd accomplished what he set out to do with McGill's testimony—raise Rea's suspicions about the whole Pisello-MCA relationship, thereby making it more difficult for him to accept the defense being offered by Hinden.

After a few more questions, he cut it off. "Nothing further, Your Honor."

Shortly after noon on Thursday, April 7—the seventh day of the trial, the prosecution rested its case.

David Hinden's key witness was John Gervasoni, whom he hoped would discredit Ranji Bedi enough for him to win an acquittal. Once again, Sal Pisello would not take the stand in his own defense.

"Do you know the defendant, Sal Pisello?" Hinden asked Gervasoni.

"No, I don't."

"Have you ever spoken to him?"

"No, I haven't."

"Have you ever seen him before?"

"No, I haven't."

Hinden went right to the second Ranji Bedi cutout deal, and Gervasoni began pouring out his story, telling how Bedi had asked to meet him in Las Vegas.

"Did he say why he wanted you to meet him there?"

"He says, 'I have to meet you in Las Vegas, bring $50,000 cash, bring it in a brown paper bag.' And he chuckled and told me that it was for Irving Azoff."

"What did you say in response to that?"

"I said I couldn't do it. He said, 'Well, we have to do this if you want the deal.' And I said, 'Look, I can do the ordinary thing, wire transfer the money to your bank as I usually do. I am not going to meet you with $50,000 cash because I don't have access to cash like that.'"

"Did Mr. Bedi tell you at any time prior to the conversation about taking money to Las Vegas that he personally knew Irving Azoff?"

"Yes."

"What did he say in that regard?"

"He would call me from a ski lodge somewhere in Aspen or another one near Aspen, and he said Irving Azoff had a lodge and he was using it with the family and children—Irv's lodge. And he would call me from MCA and he acted like he was very close to Irving. He would say 'Irving.'"

"When Mr. Bedi asked you for this $50,000 to be taken to Las Vegas in a brown paper bag, did he mention anything about giving cash to a Mr. Pisello?"

"No."

Hinden asked him about trying to get his money back from Bedi after the deal fell through.

"I said to Mr. Bedi, 'Ranji, what are you telling me? You gave it to MCA and MCA handed it back to you and they said go down the block and give it to somebody else?' And he said, 'No, I gave it to MCA and what they did with it is not your business from that point, and don't be so naive.'

"At that point I was almost steamed, and I said, 'What do you mean? They used the money to buy cocaine for rock stars?' And he said, 'Don't be naive. Cash runs the record business, runs the film business. It's gone. You will get your records. MCA is too big of a company to screw you.'"

"Did you ever ask Mr. Bedi if he had given cash to Mr. Pisello?" Hinden inquired.

"Yes, I did."

"When?"

"When I read the article in the newspaper."

"What did you ask him and what did he say?"

"I said, 'Ranji, did you give my money to Sal Pisello?' and he said, 'No.' I said, 'Are you sure?' And he said, 'John, I told you one hundred times, I gave everything to MCA.'

"I believed him," Gervasoni said. "I believed him."

Hinden knew exactly when to quit. "I have nothing further, Your Honor."

Rudnick believed Gervasoni was telling the truth. But all that had little to do with the charges in the case, most of which involved actions prior to the second cutout sale to Bedi. Hinden was trying to confuse the two, suggesting that Pisello really didn't get any money, that it all went to MCA executives. Gervasoni's testimony was all hearsay on that point, and Rudnick could have objected. But he'd let it go on because it opened up an area he couldn't have gone into otherwise, namely that Pisello stiffed Gervasoni on the second deal, a further example of the fraudulent way he did business.

"Why did you believe Ranji Bedi when he told you he needed $50,000 cash to get the deal?" Rudnick asked.

"I believed him because, number one, if you look at it on the other end of the spectrum, there was no reason to have Ranji Bedi in there," Gervasoni replied. "I could have bought the product from MCA if they wanted to sell it to me; but they needed to shield the transaction through Ranji Bedi, so naturally Ranji Bedi is going to be in a position where he has to get cash to certain people. He doesn't want to touch his cash, so he wanted to get the cash from me, the end user."

"So when Mr. Bedi asked you for the $50,000 cash, you believed him and you agreed to pay him, but you didn't want to carry the cash in a suitcase, isn't that correct?"

"No, the reason was that if I withdrew $50,000 from Scorpio Music's bank account to make a $50,000 payoff to Ranji Bedi, I would feel like I was doing something criminal, because there is no reason to give him cash. . . . If I am handing him green, I am part of something illegal in my mind. Being Italian, I would never do anything illegal, because I grew up on the streets and I know better. So I just kept away from any cash dealings."

"As a result of this business deal, the second cutout deal, you lost some money, isn't that correct?"

"Yes, sir."

"And as a result of that you had further contact with Mr. Bedi to try to get the money back, is that correct?"

With that, Gervasoni was off and running, describing all his attempts over the period of a year to get his records or his money from Bedi and MCA.

"Finally it got to a point where I started not to believe him, and he said, 'Would you like to talk to the vice president of MCA?' And I said, 'Who?' And he said, 'Zach Horowitz. He's the vice president of finance or legal affairs.' I said, 'Fine.' So he put me on the phone to Zach Horowitz, who confirmed that MCA had my order and that I would get everything, but I have to keep my mouth shut. I have to keep my mouth shut because they are having problems at MCA because they did some transactions they weren't happy with, and the corporation was doing an audit on MCA Record Distributing, which is very small compared to the corporation, MCA corporation, and the government was up there asking questions and looking around, and he was concerned."

As Rudnick stood listening to Gervasoni rattle on, Newcomer got up from his seat, strode over to him, and placed a note directly in front of him on the podium. Rudnick did not look at Newcomer, but glanced down at the note: "Marvin, please wrap this up; it's not helping our case."

Gervasoni was still talking about Horowitz: "He said, 'You will get every record.' I said, 'Well, when, when? I have been patient. When am I going to get them?' He said, 'Look, I can't tell you you will get them next week or you will get them next month, but you will get every record we owe you. You just have to sit tight.' And I says, 'Okay.' And then he was very, very firm about me not telling a soul about the deal—he told me that two or three times in the conversation. And any problems, I could just call him. He said for me to just sit tight and be patient.

"So I was happy. I mean, this guy is a big guy. He's number three guy at MCA. It's Irving Azoff, Myron Roth, who is like the bagman for Irving Azoff, and Zach Horowitz, who keeps everybody away on the legal front."

"I move that be stricken," Hinden said. "We're getting terribly far afield."

"That will be stricken," Rea said.

Rudnick was afraid to look over at Newcomer. Gervasoni's "bagman" line was just the sort of inflammatory testimony he figured Newcomer was trying to prevent by handing him the note.

"Did you ultimately sue . . . " he started to ask, when Rea cut in.

"I'd like to know, did you ultimately get your product?"

"No." Gervasoni said. "They sued me for counterfeiting."

"So you didn't get your product?" Rea repeated.

"I didn't get my product and they did sue me for counterfeiting and they tried to put me out of business."

"By 'they,' you mean MCA?"

"Yes, Your Honor."

Rudnick was struck by an irony: He had the judge on his side, but not his own boss. He had educated Rea to the point where the judge was taking over the questioning—the judge had become the prosecutor.

Rudnick, too, knew when to quit. He could feel Newcomer, sitting ten feet away, staring a hole right through him.

"Did the fact that you lost [your] suit [against MCA] have any impact on whether you told the truth today?" he asked Gervasoni.

"Absolutely not."

"Nothing further."

Late Friday afternoon, April 8, after only an hour's recess for deliberation, Judge Rea returned to the bench and confirmed what Rudnick already knew in his gut. He found Pisello guilty of tax evasion.

Rudnick left the courthouse without talking to reporters. Newcomer left without saying anything to him. It wasn't until the following Tuesday, April 12, that Newcomer spoke. He called Rudnick into his office to talk about the Pisello sentencing memorandum Rudnick was preparing.

"I want to be sure you don't speculate or raise issues you can't prove," Newcomer said.

"About MCA's role in the case?" Rudnick responded.

"Yes. If there's another investigation, I'll make the decision. You will not be part of it. Do you understand that I don't want you to write about any MCA conspiracy in the sentencing memo?"

"But John, that goes to the heart of the question: How did Sal

Pisello get into the company? What did Sal Pisello do for the money he received?"

"You are hereby ordered not to conduct any investigation of MCA. Do you understand?"

"I understand."

"Also, I'm not happy with your work. You are an embarrassment to the office. You can't write. You did a lousy job at the trial."

"You wouldn't let me call witnesses."

"If you disagree with me, call Defeo or Margolis and go over my head. Others do."

"I don't want to go over your head. I just don't want you to be biased against me. Why do you dislike me?"

"I'm not biased. You're just impossible to manage. When I go back to Washington I'm going to recommend that you be removed from this office, from this job."

"I'm sorry you feel that way. I don't think you've given me a fair shake."

"I've given you plenty of time."

"You knew about the threat," Rudnick said. "I told Defeo and Margolis."

"What threat?"

"From Susman at MCA. Don't be stupid. Susman called me and told me if I persisted in the investigation, he had friends in the courthouse, too."

"When did this happen?"

"September."

"Why were you talking to him?"

"I was returning his call."

Newcomer ended the conversation. Back in his own office, Rudnick pondered the absurdity of the situation: He'd just won a big case and for his efforts he was going to be fired.

Over the next week, Newcomer badgered him constantly about the sentencing memo, going over it line by line and demanding changes be made. At the same time, Rudnick was told by the office secretaries that MCA lawyers Ron Olson and Bill Hundley were calling Newcomer frequently. The day the sentencing memo was filed with the court, someone left a photocopy of a phone message from Olson to Newcomer in Rudnick's office mail box. The message read, "Okay to proceed."

On April 19, Rudnick found an envelope in his office mail slot addressed to him from strike force headquarters in Washington. He opened it half expecting to find a pink slip and a severance check. Instead it was a copy of the report he filed on the Pisello conviction. Stapled to it was a note from strike force chief David Margolis in Washington: "Marvin," it read. "Congratulations. I know how hard you worked for this." Next to his signature, Margolis had drawn a small circular smiling face.

On May 9, 1988, Judge Rea sentenced Sal Pisello to four years in prison and a $250,000 fine.

46

"You'll hear harsh language"

On the day that Sal Pisello was sentenced in Los Angeles, Morris Levy, Dominick Canterino, and Howard Fisher (Levy's Roulette Records controller) stood in Federal Court in Newark, New Jersey, for the opening of their trial on charges of extorting John LaMonte.

Gaetano Vastola, Lew Saka, Sonny Brocco, and Rudy Farone were not present in court because U.S. District Court Judge Stanley S. Brotman had divided the twenty-one-defendant case into seven separate trials. Brotman's ruling was designed to make the case easier to manage; taken together, the trial of the twenty-one men on 114 different charges could have lasted as long as a year and would have taxed the stamina of a single jury.

Levy, Canterino, and Fisher went on trial first because they were originally named in only three counts of the indictment and, unlike Vastola and the others, they were not charged with racketeering under the federal RICO statue. By the morning of their trial, the number of charges against the trio had dropped by one. In a surprise move the previous day, May 8, Assistant U.S. Attorney Bruce Repetto asked the court to dismiss the extortion count against them. The government would proceed on the two remaining counts of extortion conspiracy, Repetto said, but without the testimony of John LaMonte. He didn't need LaMonte to prove the conspiracy charges—the defendants' own words on tape would do that.

The defense lawyers were stunned at the prosecutor's action. For more than a year they had organized their case around a single strategy—attacking the credibility of the government's purported star witness, John LaMonte. Levy's attorney—Martin London, from the high-powered New York firm of Paul, Weiss, Rifkind, Wharton and Garrison—had filed a series of pretrial motions, asking that the case be dismissed on the grounds that LaMonte was harassing witnesses and continuing to run a record-counterfeiting operation with the help of the FBI and the U.S. Marshals Service. The defense had a list of witnesses who were prepared to trash LaMonte's character and detail his past criminal exploits. The prosecution's eleventh-hour motion meant London and the others were forced to recast their whole case in less than twenty-four hours!

Repetto had struck a brilliant blow from which the defense would never recover. He'd actually made the decision months earlier, but didn't even tell LaMonte about it until the week before the trial. He'd done it partly because he was worried that London would be effective in discrediting LaMonte in the eyes of the jury. In recent months, juries had acquitted both Philadelphia mob boss Nicodemo ("Little Nicky") Scarfo and Gambino family boss John Gotti primarily because they were put off by the criminal histories of the government's cooperating witnesses. LaMonte was an ex-convict and an admitted drug user. If the jury decided they didn't like him and thought perhaps he got what he deserved, Repetto feared they might acquit Levy et al. in spite of the evidence.

Without LaMonte, Repetto felt sure he could still get a conviction on the conspiracy charges, which carried a maximum twenty-year sentence. That was good enough. It would take Levy and Canterino off the street for practically the rest of their lives. They would be very old men when they got out of prison. Putting La-

Monte on the stand was too big a risk to take just to add a few meaningless years to the sentences.

The real beauty of Repetto's motion was that it left the defense with nothing to cross-examine. Now the government's star witnesses would be the defendants themselves, speaking to each other in presumed confidence, talking their own peculiar business lingo—all on tape, transcribed, and neatly typed up for easy reading along.

"You'll hear harsh language," Repetto told the jury in his opening argument. "But this case is not about vulgar language. It's about control and agreeing to pull money out of someone else and control his business." He quoted Levy from the tapes: "We won't let anything in or out until we get our money."

The charges centered around the single sale of MCA cutouts to LaMonte in April 1985. "This deal is on the surface simple," Repetto said. "LaMonte was to pay $1.25 million and get about 4.7 million records and cassettes. The records came to LaMonte through Morris Levy and Roulette Records, and Levy was to collect the money for the records.

"For this deal, the people interested in collecting the money included Levy, Dominick Canterino, Howard Fisher, Gaetano Vastola, Elias [Lew] Saka, Nick Massaro, Fritzy Giovanelli, Rocco Musacchia, and Rudy Farone. There is no evidence that any of these men were a licensed collection agency, yet this vast group was interested in collecting the money."

From the start, it was "a controlled sale," Repetto said. LaMonte was picked by Brocco and Vastola to receive the records and everyone involved in the collection process expected to share in a profit. "But when LaMonte's payments did not come fast enough or plentiful enough, the control broke down, and that caused aggravation."

He quoted from a taped conversation between Vastola and Levy, in which Vastola said, "Why are we dealing with this guy? You knew from the start he was a cocksucker."

"Yeah," Levy replied. "But I thought he was a controllable cocksucker."

In addressing the jury, Repetto substituted the term "C-sucker" for cocksucker. It was a term that would be heard repeatedly on the tapes, he explained to them. And in the parlance of the men on trial, "C-sucker" meant "he who disappoints."

Martin London's opening argument bespoke the defense's

predicament. Like an actor who'd been handed a completely rewritten script just hours before his opening night performance, he struggled valiantly to make the scene work, despite the fact that his principal foil—John LaMonte—had been cut from the play.

The government's case was precariously balanced on a select set of taped telephone conversations, "most of which are not the voice of the defendants," he told the jury. In fact, "most of the conversations the government taped, you're not going to hear—thousands of them, months of surreptitious eavesdropping on people's homes and offices. But for the purposes of this trial, they have only forty conversations," he said, pointing to the prosecution table.

He would take those same set of conversations, plus a few not offered by the government, and be able to tell an entirely different story, London predicted. He held up his hand, palm toward the jury, and noted that though it was in plain sight right in front of them, "you can only see half my hand," he said, turning it slowly around to reveal the other side.

"You will hear several kinds of conversations," he went on. "Some are of a man working with the government and steering it the way he wants." Of LaMonte, he sneered, "He wrote the book when it comes to lying and deception."

"There are technical problems with the tapes," London said. "Some recordings are scratchy; some unclear. Some voices you won't recognize, so you will have transcripts. Those are not evidence! Only what you hear is evidence. These are transcripts of what the prosecutor thinks the tape says when he played it. But there are significant errors in those transcripts, things that seem to make the case work. We've prepared our own transcripts. The prosecution has chosen not to show you my copy. So when he plays the tapes, be aware there may be a disagreement."

The main disagreement, of course, was over the culpability of his client. "The real victim," London intoned, "was Morris Levy, whose $120,000 payment to MCA to square the cutout deal is the only evidence that anyone in this case lost a nickel. . . . There is no evidence that anyone on trial here engaged in a conspiracy to extort," London said. Rather, the defendants merely engaged in "unsuccessful efforts to get a deadbeat to pay for what he bought."

As trials go, *U.S.* v. *Morris Levy et al.* was hardly a crowd pleaser. It would not have made a good television drama. Most of the time, the courtroom was silent as the judge, jury, defendants, prosecutors, and spectators all sat listening to the tapes through headphones, reading along from printed transcripts handed out by the court clerk. Every few minutes, the room rustled with the sound of pages turning in unison. The scene looked more like a library study group than an episode of "Perry Mason."

During the government's presentation of its case, Martin London objected loudly to the introduction of every tape, as well as to nearly every statement and question from the prosecutor. The proceeding quickly degenerated into a contentious sparring match between London and Repetto, with Judge Brotman playing referee, struggling to separate two enraged fighters after the bell had sounded to end the round. For every five minutes of evidence presented, there seemed to be forty-five minutes of angry dialogue between the two attorneys—most of it outside earshot of the jurors, who may have set a record for miles walked at a trial as time and again they trudged back and forth between the courtroom and sound-proofed jury room.

London fought most fiercely to keep the jury from hearing references to organized crime, the Genovese family, Vincent Gigante, and Sal Pisello's legal problems.

In most instances he prevailed. But Repetto managed to introduce the bulk of the government's tapes, more than enough to paint an unattractive picture of the defendants. Levy on the phone to Brocco, for instance: "Drop your pants, get some Vaseline, and we'll stick it right in your ass."

And the jury heard plenty of how this group of supposedly legitimate businessmen went about collecting from creditors:

Levy telling Lew Saka on February 28, 1985, "Why don't you smack him [LaMonte] in the mouth for lying to you?"

Vastola saying to Sonny Brocco that same day, "You know what Morris just told me?" He said, 'You should make Sonny go smack this guy right in the mouth.' I says, 'Believe me that's just what Sonny is gonna do.'"

Levy ordering Saka to "go out to that place and take over that kid's business. You go into the books . . . you open up the mail every morning."

Vastola hollering to Brocco, "I tell ya, I'm gonna give him a fuckin' beating like you never saw in your fuckin' life. And it's gonna be in front of you that I'm gonna put him in the fuckin' hospital. Bet your fuckin,' fuckin' dollars on that."

And Vastola instructing Brocco, "Do me a favor. Walk in, don't say a word, walk in there and slap him in the mouth."

"Who? The kid?"

"Yeah."

"All right."

"Do me that favor, will you, please?"

"And then say that's from you?"

"No. From me he's gonna get the rest."

Repetto also prevailed in introducing FBI agent James Scanlon's surveillance photographs of Levy, Vastola, Musacchia, Sonny Brocco, and Fritzy Giovanelli arriving at LaMonte's warehouse in January 1985 to look over his MCA inventory.

The photographs were powerful ammunition for the prosecution. The jurors got to see the five hulking, grim-faced characters climb out of Levy's van, huddle for a moment, then enter John LaMonte's warehouse. Coupled with the phone conversations about putting LaMonte in the hospital or, as Vastola said, "in a fucking bucket," the pictures were convincing—if circumstantial—evidence that an extortion conspiracy was afoot. The jurors could imagine how they'd feel seeing the same fearsome-looking group coming through the front door of their home or business. Verbal threats would not be necessary; the mere presence of these particular visitors would suffice to scare the hell out of most people. The jurors' sympathy went to LaMonte.

Another damning piece of evidence was a phone conversation on October 23, 1986, between Levy and a *Los Angeles Times* reporter. The newspaper was getting ready to print its first article about the New Jersey investigation.

"I'm calling to tell you that we're going with a story in the next day or so," the reporter said.

"Excuse me," Levy interrupted, "I want to let you know that I'm recording this conversation."

Levy wasn't taping the conversation, of course. And he had no idea that the FBI was not only listening in, but also watching with hidden cameras as he sat at his desk in his office.

Levy listened as the reporter told him the gist of the article that was to be printed and asked for his comment: "Information gathered so far suggests that members of the Genovese and the DeCavalcante families have infiltrated the cutout record market.... According to law enforcement sources, you are a target of that investigation, along with a gentleman named Gaetano Vastola. . . . The investigation involves John LaMonte who is now in federal protective custody."

It was the first time Levy had heard any of this. He'd had Vastola and the boys looking for LaMonte for weeks, calling around to customers and even peeking into the windows of the LaMonte family's now-abandoned home. It must have made Levy's blood run cold to learn from a reporter that LaMonte was probably sitting in a room somewhere telling the FBI everything he knew about the Roulette Records operation. Still, he feigned nonchalance, saying "Whatever is going to be is going to be. I know that I'm clean. I've not done nothing wrong."

He cut off the conversation when the subject of Consultants for World Records came up.

"Whose company is that?" the reporter asked.

"I don't know," Levy said. "Okay, thank you for calling me." He hung up after saying, "I gotta go to a UJA [United Jewish Appeal] dinner, a UJA cocktail party."

The jury had already listened to the phone conversation in which Rocco Musacchia told Levy about the IRS attempt to place a lien on the Consultants for World Records bank account, and they had heard Levy order the money to be pulled out of the account. So in the mind of the jury, Levy's conversation with the reporter, in effect, proved he was a liar.

Levy did not take the witness stand to testify in his own defense. Neither did Canterino or Fisher. The tapes were left to speak for themselves. About the only "live" testimony during the trial came from detective Sgt. Bobby Jones and other law enforcement officers who monitored the wiretaps, swearing to the authenticity of the tapes.

After three tedious weeks, both sides rested their cases. During four hours of deliberations on May 24 and 25, the jury asked to review only two pieces of evidence—the photographs outside LaMonte's warehouse and Levy's conversation with the reporter. Shortly before noon on May 25, the jurors filed back into court and pronounced Canterino, Fisher, and Levy guilty on both counts of extortion conspiracy.

When the foreman read the verdict, Levy bent his head down slightly and stared at the table, the color drained from his face. Canterino looked at his lawyer and gave a disgusted shrug. Fisher turned to his wife, sitting in the first pew of the spectator section, and reached out and took her hand as she dabbed at her eyes with a handkerchief. The reporters in the courtroom were surprised Fisher had been found guilty along with the other two. The evidence against him had been the weakest. He barely factored in to the tapes.

Repetto immediately asked that bail for Levy and Canterino be doubled to $1 million, telling Brotman, "The stakes here are very different than they've ever been at any time in these men's lives." Brotman agreed, but continued Fisher's bail at $100,000.

Following the proceedings, London and the two other defense attorneys rushed past reporters, with little comment except to say they would appeal the convictions and seek a new trial.

Repetto was characteristically low-key in victory, saying, "We didn't offer a whole lot beyond the tapes." Asked about the organized crime aspects of the case that had been kept out of the trial, he noted wryly, "Mr. Canterino did not drop in from Mars."

For Repetto, it was three down and eighteen to go. Next up was Gaetano Vastola.

47

"You can't
fight City Hall"

With all the questions left unanswered in the wake of the Sal Pisello and Morris Levy trials, news coverage of the whole affair took an abrupt turn in the late spring of 1988. The media began questioning the government's role with regard to MCA.

The June issue of *Regardie's*, a slick, hotly read Washington, D.C., magazine, contained an article titled, "MCA and the Mob: Did the Justice Department cut Reagan's Hollywood pals a break?" Written by investigative reporter Dan E. Moldea, who had authored the book *Dark Victory: Ronald Reagan, MCA and the Mob* a year earlier, the *Regardie's* article revealed for the first time Bill Hundley's involvement in getting the MCA-Pisello investigation killed. The article contained the revelation that Marvin Rudnick had been called back to Washington in late 1987 and was told directly by Mike Defeo and David Margolis, the top two men in the

Organized Crime Strike Force, not to cause MCA "any embarrassment."

As he'd done in his book, Moldea strongly suggested that MCA
pulled Reagan's strings, and the president in turn had pulled
strings in the government on the company's behalf. "Ronald Reagan is an invention of MCA," Moldea wrote. "Every facet of his life,
from his career in acting and politics to his financial successes, have
been directed by MCA, which has been the most powerful force in
Hollywood since the mid 1940s."

Moldea's article was followed in July by a lengthy report in the
American Lawyer magazine, which was headlined, "Death of a Mob
Probe." Written by reporter Michael Orey, who sat through the
entire Pisello trial and spent several months investigating the government's handling of the case and MCA's successful campaign to
neutralize Rudnick, the article stated: "Troubling questions arise
from the strange behavior of Justice. Was a credible inquiry into
possible mob infiltration of an industry sabotaged by MCA pressure? If not, why did Justice—already reeling from allegations of
influence peddling (under the stewardship of Attorney General Ed
Meese)—call off the dogs?"

In the article, MCA counsel Allen Susman was quoted as not
exactly denying he told Rudnick that MCA had friends in the
courthouse. Susman said he didn't remember calling Rudnick and
that the statement didn't sound like one he would make. Rudnick
was quoted as saying he "reported the threat to the appropriate
authorities."

Orey's article included a statement of stupefying arrogance from
MCA president Sid Sheinberg. Asked how Pisello came to do business with the company, Sheinberg responded, "I don't know the
answer to that question and, more importantly, I don't care about
the answer to that question. How Pisello managed to get inside the
company and basically con the company out of its money isn't a
question we have decided needed investigating."

Among reporters who'd been covering the case, there was growing sentiment that the Justice Department felt the same way. For
whatever reasons, it appeared that the nation's top law enforcement
officers didn't want the questions about MCA answered, or even
asked.

Billboard magazine weighed in with a report that a congressional
subcommittee was considering looking into the Justice Depart-

ment's handling of the MCA-Pisello matter. The article reported the surprising claim by MCA attorneys Allen Susman and Dennis Kinnaird that they were unaware of Hundley's involvement in the affair until after the fact. It also quoted an angry-sounding strike force chief David Margolis, speaking in stiffly worded government-ese: "As to the Pisello case and any related matters involving MCA which may have been speculated about by some of the media recently, none of my superiors have given me any direction or suggestions of any kind at any time regarding the disposition thereof. This department makes prospective decisions strictly on the merits in all cases."

Margolis and other higher-ups in the Justice Department were furious at the negative media coverage, and they blamed Rudnick for all of it.

By midsummer, Rudnick was under siege on all fronts. MCA counsel Ron Olson was telling reporters MCA had hard evidence that Rudnick had leaked secret grand jury information to the media and was continuing to do so, in violation of federal law. In off-the-record interviews, Olson suggested inaccurately that the *Los Angeles Times*'s early jump on the Pisello story came from Rudnick through his wife, *Los Angeles Times* reporter Kathryn Harris. MCA Records executives were boasting that they'd succeeded in getting Rudnick pulled off the investigation because he'd become a rogue prosecutor.

In the Los Angeles strike force office, Rudnick was completely isolated, stripped by chief John Newcomer of all responsibilities except handling the barrage of Freedom of Information requests from the media for documents on the now-closed Pisello investigation—clerical work. As a suspected leaker who might be under investigation by the Office of Professional Responsibility, Rudnick was shunned by his colleagues, out of the loop on every investigation in the office. Normal shop talk ceased when he walked into a room.

Newcomer rode him constantly, criticizing everything he did, loudly and usually in front of other people. It quickly became clear to Rudnick and others in the office that Newcomer's plan was to drive him out of the department, make life so unbearable that he would resign. In July, Rudnick was told by another lawyer in the office that Newcomer was putting negative reports in his personnel file, building a case to have him fired. Shortly thereafter, Rudnick learned the Justice Department had instituted formal proceedings against him on the basis of an annual job performance review by Newcomer rating him so low that, if allowed to stand, it was grounds for termination. Among other things, the review said he was incompetent and insubordinate.

In mid-August, Newcomer immunized Pisello and put him before the grand jury without telling Rudnick, who learned about it from reporters, after the fact. Rudnick took it as another slap in the face. It was a cover-your-ass move on the part of the department, he thought, something to counter the bad publicity of recent weeks. If the department had really wanted to get at the truth, Rudnick reasoned, it would have had the prosecutor most knowledgeable about the case ask the questions. Newcomer was not up to speed enough to dance with a slick operator like Pisello. In later interviews with reporters, Pisello seemed to confirm that view, saying of the grand jury session, "They really didn't want to find out anything; they just asked me a bunch of questions like 'Do you know Lew Wasserman?'" Pisello denied that he did.

In the same situation, most prosecutors would resign in order to keep their record clean. Being fired from the Justice Department would not be a good way to launch a career in private practice. With little else to occupy his time, Rudnick spent countless hours agonizing over what to do. Friends and family advised him to throw in the towel and walk away. "You can't fight City Hall, Marvin," was the constant refrain. "It's time for you to get out of government and make some real money in the private sector."

"But I shouldn't have to quit," he'd reply. "I haven't done anything to warrant it. Why should I have to give up my career because they have a political problem?" In his mind, quitting meant admitting he'd done something wrong. Walking away would leave a black mark on his record forever. The department would never have to explain what really happened. Anything he said in his own defense after that would be dismissed as sour grapes from a disgruntled former employee.

In the end, he resolved to fight. He hired a lawyer—a daunting prospect on his $60,000-a-year public servant salary—and made a Privacy Act demand for all his personnel files. He was going to force the government to put its case against him on the public record and defend it. In effect, he declared war on the Justice Department.

It was not as easy as the telling. For Rudnick, the months of stress finally manifested in a case of walking pneumonia that hung on for weeks. At times, in his darker moments, he wondered about his mental health. Was he becoming paranoid? Crazy? Was he the only person in the Justice Department who thought something fishy had gone on inside MCA Records?

For months he'd suspected that his phones might be tapped and that he was under some sort of surveillance. It wasn't inconceivable that MCA would hire a private detective, or assign one of its own security men, to follow him and try to find out if he were talking to or meeting with reporters.

Rudnick's suspicions turned into conviction one evening in late August. On his way home from work about 6:30 P.M., he picked up his two-and-a-half-year-old daughter, Virginia, at the home of one of her friends. His wife was working on a late deadline at the newspaper, and he didn't feel like cooking or doing dishes, so he headed to a nearby McDonald's for a quick no-fuss dinner.

Halfway there, Virginia piped up from her safety seat in back, "Daddy, there's a bug in the car." He made a right turn on Grand Street in Pasadena and drove for less than a block, until Virginia's persistent complaints that the bug was bothering her could no longer be ignored. He checked his rear-view mirror to see if any cars were behind him. The street was deserted; his was the only car in sight in either direction. He pulled over to the curb, got out, opened the rear door, and leaned inside to shoo away the tiny bee that had been so vexing to Virginia.

While assuring her that the bug was all gone, he noticed through the rear window of the car that a gray pickup truck with a camper was parked at the curb about one hundred yards away, facing the same direction in which he'd been traveling. The driver's face was obscured by something, a newspaper or a map.

He climbed back into the driver's seat feeling queasy. Not sixty seconds earlier, there had been no cars parked on the street. The pickup had appeared out of nowhere. The driver must have turned the corner and pulled over, just as he had done. He put his aging Chrysler into gear and drove about two hundred feet down the street before whipping a quick U-turn, his tires squealing in protest.

As he drove back past the parked pickup, he got a look at the driver: white male; brown hair; high forehead; wide face, with a sharp, pointed nose; glasses. He hung a left at the corner and watched in his rear-view mirror to see if the pickup followed. Seconds later, it did. He put his foot down on the accelerator and roared away. The pickup kept pace. He drove through the residential area for eight to ten blocks, with the pickup following through left turns and right. He pulled into a driveway, watched the pickup pass by, then backed out into the street and headed back in the other direction. In his rear-view, he saw the pickup stop, then make a U-turn. Rudnick hung a left, then a right, then another left and waited for the pickup to appear again. It didn't. Had he lost him? Or had the driver simply backed off, realizing his quarry had spotted the tail?

Rudnick's heart was still pounding ten minutes later as he sat in McDonald's with Virginia, thinking, "How did I get my little girl mixed up in this?"

48

"What are they afraid of?"

I f Marvin Rudnick felt under siege in the summer of 1988, it was nothing compared with what Joe Isgro was feeling. In the two and a half years since the NBC News report on "The New Payola," Isgro's life had taken a turn worthy of a Greek tragedy.

His record promotion business, which pulled in at least $10 million a year in its heyday, was all but gone. Only a skeleton staff of loyalists remained and his once bustling Universal City offices were eerily empty. He still managed to get some promotion work, but mostly from smaller, independent record companies or from artists' managers, and at one-tenth of his former fee. He'd been forced to unload his Encino mansion in favor of a more modest dwelling in Glendale. The yellow Rolls was gone, too.

Isgro spent most of his time dealing with his two lawyers—one handling his $25 million antitrust lawsuit against MCA Records and Warner Brothers Records, the other dealing with the criminal investigation of him by the Justice Department. In the latter case, the government's building blocks included David Michael Smith, Isgro's former bodyguard and near-constant companion; Ralph Tashjian and Bill Craig, the two promoters who'd formerly handled virtually all of Isgro's contact with radio stations; and Dennis DiRicco, Isgro's former tax accountant, the man who'd accompanied him to his interview with Marvin Rudnick at the strike force office in April 1986.

All four men were cooperating with authorities, spilling their guts before the Los Angeles grand jury, now directed by strike force attorney Richard Stavin. Smith had provided the information that led to the indictment of George Wilson Crowell, the former vice president and general manager of the Los Angeles Top 40 radio station KIQQ. Among other things, Smith told the grand jury that he had carried regular cash payoffs from Isgro to Crowell, passing the money to him in the men's room of a Los Angeles restaurant. Tashjian and Craig, both under indictment themselves, said they had made payoffs to a score of radio programmers around the country, at Isgro's behest. Tashjian confessed to providing some programmers with cocaine. DiRicco had been indicted by a federal grand jury in San Francisco on unrelated charges of conspiracy to distribute cocaine and setting up phony tax shelters for a number of clients, including Joe Isgro and Ralph and Valerie Tashjian. In an attempt to curry favor with the government, DiRicco was now providing Los Angeles investigators with a road map through Isgro's Byzantine financial dealings.

The stress of it all was visibly taking its toll on Isgro. His once jet-black hair was now thinning and streaked with gray, making him look older than his forty years. Never a font of gaiety even in the best of times, he was now a brooding, angry presence, a man at once haunted and obsessed by the forces that were arrayed against him. Practically every conversation he had would at some point veer off into a diatribe against the media, the government, or the big record companies.

"Within thirty-six hours of Brian Ross's report, I was accused, tried, found guilty, and executed. . . . I find it real difficult to believe the head of an organized crime family would hold a summit meeting in the lobby of a downtown hotel. . . . No two ways about it, if the FBI was there, it must be very obvious that I did not meet with these guys. We did not meet! . . . I've never been arrested for a parking ticket. In the last ten years I've been investigated by the FCC, FTC, and '60 Minutes,' and I find it curious that the only people mentioned in Brian Ross's story just happened to be the Italian guys."

Isgro was particularly offended by the media's characterization of his relationship with one particular Italian guy, Joseph ("Joe Piney") Armone. "I have known him for sixteen years," Isgro told anyone who'd listen. "He is my uncle's closest friend. When I go to New York, I always have a spaghetti dinner with his wife and two daughters and him. I call him my Uncle Joe and I ain't ashamed of it. But I have never done business with him. That day, he came to the Helmsley hotel with two bags of Christmas gifts for the girls at my office. He called me up and said he was going to stop by. I gave him a big hug, but I was not introduced to John Gotti."

(Isgro's "Uncle Joe" had also undergone some life changes since that fateful day at the Helmsley. First, Gotti had elevated him to the position of Gambino family underboss after the previous holder of that title, fellow Helmsley "summit" attendee Frank DeCicco, was blown to bits by a car bomb. More recently, in February, the seventy-year-old Armone had been convicted of drug dealing and sentenced to fifteen years in prison.)

Isgro complained, "When Joe Armone was indicted, NBC was there and asked, 'What's your relationship with Joe Isgro?' At a press conference for Michael Jackson, they asked 'What's his relationship with Joe Isgro?' They have me down as Don Vito Corleone. I got cars following me, people asking me about suitcases full of thousand-dollar bills. I go out with a girl and the next day the FBI is following her. City, state, federal, you name it. It's a nightmare! I wish they'd go ahead and indict me."

They were working on it. And in the process they were royally screwing up Isgro's antitrust suit against MCA and Warner.

The two companies were all that remained from Isgro's original lawsuit. All the others had settled out of court on undisclosed terms, leaving Warner and MCA on the hook for the whole $25 million if Isgro won. And if that happened, MCA and Warner expected to be hit with a host of similar lawsuits from other promoters whose businesses had been devastated by the cutback in the wake of the NBC report. To keep that from happening, the two companies were apparently willing to fight to the death. Both had countersued Isgro, charging violations of the federal racketeering statute.

The gist of Isgro's suit was that all the major record companies had conspired to use the NBC News report as a pretext for lowering the cost of independent promotion. As he testified in a sworn deposition: "After the chain of events took place, I felt the entire purpose of this was to divert their cost and charge it back to their artists' royalties. They have accomplished lowering the rates; they have accomplished charging it back against the artist royalties, and they are in the best of both worlds. It was a brilliant strategy. But the object was not to rid themselves [of payola]. The object was to lower the cost."

The gist of the MCA and Warner counterclaims was that Isgro had defrauded them by signing an antipayola agreement and then violating the agreement in a pattern of racketeering that included mail fraud, wire fraud, and violations of payola and drug laws.

As evidence of those alleged transgressions, MCA's suit listed many of the same statements that cooperating witnesses Ralph Tashjian, Bill Craig, and David Michael Smith had given to strike force investigators working on the payola probe. The specificity of MCA's suit was stunning, right down to the names of the program directors and radio stations allegedly involved in the payoffs. Clearly, someone was making information gathered in the grand jury investigation available to the record companies to help them in their legal battle with Isgro.

"How do I know that?" Isgro said to a reporter. "Because right now [record company lawyers] are asking me the same questions in depositions, word for word, that I was asked when I spoke to the prosecutor. They are asking me things that could only come from the grand jury, names that don't appear in any of my books and records.

"You know what they are asking about? This is an antitrust case, right? And the lawyers are asking me if I ever had $13,000 in a suitcase in San Francisco, and have I ever been to a record industry party where drugs or prostitutes were present. I said the real headline news would be if I ever attended a record industry party where drugs and prostitutes weren't present."

He was off and running again: "I have never offered anyone drugs or prostitutes in my life. The record companies terminated independents based on allegations in TV news reports that prostitutes and drugs were being given out in exchange for radio airplay. One of those reports showed film of a party with young women prancing around and some guy licking champagne out of a girl's navel. But that was a party thrown by a record company. It wasn't my party; I wasn't even there. So where do they get off terminating my services? The hypocrisy is just unbelievable."

Just as unbelievable to some observers was Isgro's notion that the Justice Department was knowingly conspiring with MCA lawyers to do him in—in flagrant violation of federal laws governing grand jury secrecy. "A key person at MCA told me the government said it would not look upon MCA favorably if they settled the case with me," Isgro said. "MCA is in a position to play ball with the government, and settlements are not helpful to the government."

Conversely, a grand jury indictment of Isgro on payola charges would be helpful to the record companies' case. As one Warner attorney told the *Los Angeles Times*, "His only chance is if he gets the antitrust trial out of the way before he's indicted. After he's charged, there's not a jury in the country that would award him damages. So we wish the government would get off its butt and indict him."

'It's a total setup," Isgro complained.

Isgro's lawyer in the civil suit, Steve Cannata, was a little more subtle with his accusations. "I think the interests of the record companies and the government are pretty well aligned right now," he told the *Los Angeles Times*.

Just how well aligned became apparent to all in April, the week before Isgro's suit was set for trial in U.S. District Court in Los Angeles. During a pretrial hearing before Judge Consuelo Marshall, strike force attorney Richard Stavin walked into the courtroom with a surprise motion on the part of the Justice Department. The government asked the court to put off the civil trial for three months and quash all outstanding subpoenas for depositions because the civil case was interfering with the grand jury investigation. Stavin explained to a perplexed Judge Marshall that Isgro was the target of that investigation and was likely to be indicted in the near future.

After a brief discussion in chambers, with only Stavin and Marshall present, the judge returned to the bench and said she would consider the government's request. Three days later, on the very eve of the trial, Judge Marshall said she was reluctantly agreeing to postpone the civil trial for three months, in deference to the government.

As Stavin explained it to reporters after Marshall's ruling: "The problem for us is, there are witnesses still to testify before the grand jury, and for them to surface now in a civil case and have their testimony be made public could have a chilling effect on future grand jury testimony. If prospective grand jury witnesses see that people going before the grand jury are also being called in a civil proceeding, it will make people less likely to cooperate with us."

Isgro and his attorney were livid. The way they saw it, the government was trying to scuttle their lawsuit. Several weeks earlier, Michael Jackson's manager, Frank DiLeo, had been about to give a deposition in the civil case in the Beverly Hills office of Warner Brothers Records outside counsel, Milton Rudin. "We expected Mr. DiLeo's deposition to be helpful to our case," Steve Cannata said. "But before it could begin, two federal agents showed up and handed him a subpoena to appear before the grand jury. I think that has a chilling effect on anyone who gets involved in the civil case."

In June, after publication of Dan Moldea's "MCA and the Mob" article in *Regardie's* magazine, Cannata filed a motion in court seeking to depose MCA Records executives Irving Azoff, Myron Roth, and Dan McGill about their dealings with Sal Pisello. Cannata attached a copy of the *Regardie's* article to the motion for Judge Marshall to read, stating "the foregoing information is highly relevant to this litigation.

"First, MCA's extensive business dealings with a high-ranking Mafioso severely undermines the veracity of its contention in this action that MCA terminated plaintiff's independent promotion services due to plaintiff's possible ties to members of organized crime," Cannata wrote in his motion. "Indeed, MCA's substantial business relationships with an organized crime figure nullifies the plausibility of this contention.

"Parenthetically," Cannata continued, "the close working (and highly questionable) relationship between the Justice Department and MCA, which is currently the subject of intense publicity, may have also precipitated this action by the Justice Department [in] successfully requesting this Court to continue the April 26, 1988 trial date."

Judge Marshall was not moved. She denied the motion to depose the MCA Records executives.

Said an aggrieved Isgro: "I've been waiting more than two years for my day in court. The only fair ground I have is in the courtroom, not in the press, not with the politicians. I've been warned about the clout these companies have. I don't have their kind of money and I have only one lawyer out there. But I'm prepared. Let's go. I'm not afraid of anything that's going to come out. What are they afraid of?"

Isgro knew very well what MCA was afraid of—the testimony of his planned first witness, the vice president of promotion at MCA Records, Jheryl Busby.

The grand jury was in possession of just under $50,000 worth of canceled checks written by Bill Craig to Busby, Busby's wife, Caroline, and a catering company owned by Caroline Busby. On their face, the checks had the appearance of kickbacks. Why else would a promoter be paying money back to the record company executive who was in charge of hiring him to promote records? On the strength of the checks, Busby was at the top of the strike force's list of potentially indictable record executives in the payola investigation. MCA knew it, so did Busby, and so did lawyers for Craig, Tashjian, and Isgro.

More disturbing—from MCA's point of view at least—was that Warner Brothers attorney Milton Rudin knew it and he intended to make use of it if and when Busby was put on the witness stand. Seventy-year-old "Mickey" Rudin was something of a legend in show business circles. As Frank Sinatra's lawyer and principle mouthpiece for more than thirty years, the gnomelike, cigar-smoking Rudin had faced down more than his share of government inquisitors and nosy reporters in his time. He was Marilyn Monroe's lawyer at the time of her death and had represented Sinatra rat packers Dean Martin and Sammy Davis, Jr. He'd also represented Warner Brothers Records chairman Mo Ostin since Ostin launched Reprise Records, originally Sinatra's own label, in the early 1960s.

As counsel for Ostin's Warner Brothers Records, Rudin had become one of the record industry's most ardent opponents of independent promotion. It was at his urging that the Warner labels suspended the use of independents in 1981; and it was over his objection that the company had resumed the practice six months later.

In Rudin's view, the Network posed a huge threat to the record companies because of its potential for breeding executive corruption. The way he saw it, placing company promotion executives in charge of handing out tens of millions of dollars worth of business to outsiders like Joe Isgro and Fred DiSipio provided more temptation than human nature could withstand.

Rudin intended to prove that it was fear of just that possibility—not an attempt to lower the price of promotion—that moved Warner to terminate Isgro's service. And he intended to use Busby and the checks from Bill Craig as a perfect example of what could happen when a company dealt with the Network.

Isgro and his attorney were sure that MCA would settle with the promoter and drop its countersuit against him rather than have the existence of the Busby checks revealed in court, thereby provoking another media field day at MCA's expense.

They were still certain MCA would fold and run when they appeared in Judge Marshall's courtroom on August 22 for another pretrial hearing in the case. With the long-delayed trial set to begin the following week, Marshall was expected to rule on a number of "housekeeping motions," including MCA's and Warner's repeated request that Isgro's suit be dismissed because he'd failed to prove there had been an antitrust conspiracy among the record companies.

Since Marshall had previously denied that motion on several occasions, no one in the courtroom expected her to do anything different this time. Which is why an audible gasp went up from the spectators—mostly reporters—when Marshall announced that after reading the record companies' arguments one more time she decided that she'd been "incorrect" in her earlier denials and was hereby reversing herself by dismissing Isgro's lawsuit.

Isgro and Steve Cannata sat slack-jawed and speechless at the witness table. In less than five minutes, Judge Marshall had tossed out more than two years of hard work, comprising more than one hundred depositions and thousands of pages of testimony and legal briefs. Walking out of the courtroom moments later, the normally garrulous Cannata appeared bewildered when he said to a reporter, "I don't get it. It was the same motion, word for word, that she already denied."

Isgro's reaction was typically bitter: "If she was gonna throw it out of court, she could have done it months ago. It cost me all this money because she made a mistake?"

Isgro and Cannata made half-hearted noises about appealing the ruling, and lawyers for MCA and Warner spoke boldly about pursuing their racketeering lawsuits to their righteous conclusion. But it would never happen. For all intents and purposes, the war between the Network and the major record companies ended that day, though it would be months before all sides quietly agreed to let matters drop.

The biggest winner, of course, was MCA. Thanks to Judge Marshall's ruling, no MCA executives were questioned under oath about the company's dealings with Sal Pisello, and the potentially embarrassing matter of Bill Craig's checks to Jheryl Busby was not made public.

The strike force ultimately decided not to indict Busby. It turned out that he had not pocketed the payments from Craig but rather had used the money to buy satin tour jackets and airline tickets for MCA artists, and to pay for vacations, bonuses, and even office computers for some of his MCA promotion staffers. The payments still smacked of a kickback from an independent promoter, but given that Busby hadn't profited personally and at the time held the distinction of being the highest-ranking black executive in the record industry, strike force attorney Richard Stavin doubted whether any jury would ever convict him. (Several months later, Busby rose to an even higher rank when MCA bought Motown Records for $61 million and named him president.)

The war between Isgro and the record companies was over, but the government's war on Joe Isgro was just starting to heat up.

49

"To say this was a legitimate business deal is just crazy"

On Friday, October 28, 1988, Marvin Rudnick heard some encouraging words from an unexpected source—Assistant U.S. Attorney Bruce Repetto in New Jersey.

It was sentencing day for Morris Levy and Dominick Canterino in Camden. Judge Stanley Brotman had overturned Howard Fisher's conviction in late August, ruling that the government failed to prove the accountant knew about the plan to use force to collect LaMonte's debt. But Brotman denied Levy's and Canterino's request for a new trial on the same grounds, and now it was time for them to pay the piper.

Levy was represented at the sentencing hearing by a new lawyer. He'd fired Marty London and retained John Barry, the husband of U.S. District Court Judge Maryanne Trump Barry and the brother-in-law of Donald Trump.

Barry's main task at the hearing was to convince Brotman to disregard the government's presentencing report in determining his client's punishment. The report contained allegations that Levy operated his record business through force and intimidation, that he had longstanding and extensive business ties to Vincent Gigante and the Genovese family, and that he was deeply involved in the trafficking of heroin in the New York City area.

Barry attacked the allegations as "unattributed hearsay."

"With respect to the force and intimidation in the record industry, we make the point that the presentence report preparer interviewed no one in the record industry," Barry told the judge. "And in the letters submitted on behalf of Mr. Levy from virtually everybody of any significance in the record industry, that allegation is flatly denied. They say that Mr. Levy is a man of honor and integrity in the record industry, and that he conducts his business as a respectable businessman."

Repetto argued back that "there was enough in this trial to put the government in a position to recommend the sternest possible sentence in this case."

"There were various things we could not put before the jury," Repetto said, "but the charade that this somehow was a legitimate business deal that somehow went awry and somebody got hurt, that charade is over. It was an organized crime concept from day one."

To buttress the drug allegations in the presentencing report, Repetto called FBI agent Jeff Dossett to the witness stand to relate an interview he'd conducted with convicted Philadelphia heroin kingpin Roland Bartlett.

"He stated that Mr. Levy told him that he could supply him the heroin at a better quality and quantity," Dossett testified. "He stated that initially Mr. Levy set him up with a purchase of an eighth of a kilo and that he took the eighth of a kilo, and he stated that he didn't receive the drugs from Mr. Levy personally, but that Mr. Levy directed him to meet with individuals on the pickup points in Manhattan and, most often, at the Holland Tunnel in New Jersey, and that he would meet with these individuals and he described them as young Italian individuals.

"He stated that he would deliver the money to Mr. Levy's office in a suitcase, and the only discussion he ever had with Mr. Levy was in his offices or in the hallway. He stated that, however, he did deliver the money in a briefcase or suitcase to Mr. Levy."

"Deliver personally to him?" Brotman asked.

"Yes."

"In Levy's office?"

"That is correct."

"Where is Roland Bartlett today?"

"He's presently incarcerated. He's presently on trial for murder."

Repetto went on. "This trial was about operating in the music business with force and intimidation, institutionalized force and intimidation," he said. "It's never been satisfactorily explained how Sal Pisello ended up in MCA. . . . When the publicity about his involvement with organized crime came out he was moved out of MCA. How did he get there in the first place? To say this was a legitimate business deal is just crazy. It wasn't."

Ordinarily, such a statement would not have been remarkable. But it was the first time in the three-year course of the investigation that Repetto had publicly addressed the California end of the case. In raising the question as to how Pisello had managed to penetrate MCA, he was taking a page right out of Marvin Rudnick's book. Rudnick's whole career had been jeopardized by his uttering almost the exact same words in a Los Angeles courtroom. Finally, it appeared he wasn't the only prosecutor who suspected the whole truth about Pisello and MCA had not yet been told.

After listening to Repetto and Barry argue back and forth for more than two hours about the presentencing report, Judge Brotman said he would not take the organized crime and drug allegations into account when passing sentence. After a short recess, both sides took their last shots, with Barry painting a glowing portrait of his client, St. Morris of the music business: "Morris Levy has given money to all kinds of people. He buys wheelchairs for paralyzed children. He donates millions to charities. Is Morris Levy a generous man? Yes, he is a generous man.

"He has been a major force in American music. He has started numerous young artists off on their careers. He has achieved national stature in the business. He has achieved it by virtue of his honesty, his integrity, his genius, his work, his energy. . . . Mr. Levy is a good, decent human being."

"Mr. Levy, I'll hear from you now," Brotman said.

Levy stood up and faced the judge. "I just want to say another thing, that I accept the fact . . . " He stopped in midsentence, then said simply, "I feel I'm innocent."

"Do you want to say anything other than what your lawyer has said on your behalf?" Brotman asked. "It's your opportunity to tell me what you want to tell me."

"I am innocent, Your Honor," Levy replied. "That's all I can say. I believe I am innocent."

"Thank you very much," Brotman said curtly, as Levy sat back down in his chair. "Mr. Repetto, I'll hear from you now."

Once again, Repetto hit hard on the MCA-Pisello connection. "The characterization of the MCA transaction as a normal business transaction is not so," he said. "It wasn't. It was a controlled transaction from the MCA side. It was a controlled transaction going to LaMonte, and it was a controlled transaction with the attempts to make LaMonte pay.

"The person who is engineering this from the inside of MCA is a man by the name of Sal Pisello. Sal Pisello, who does not have a background in the music business, a man whom the internal audit of MCA discusses, with numerous amounts of money going to Sal Pisello without MCA receiving any benefit from that. Sal Pisello was the person on the inside.

"It is not known, has never been developed, how Sal Pisello got to the inside. But these records come out. And when these records come out a whole host of people are going to take a part of the deal. They will get a profit on this deal.

"This is interesting because Sal Pisello is now on both sides of the deal. He is in MCA making the records available, and also on the other end paying back to MCA from a company called Consultants for World Records. Who is this company? Has anybody heard of them before?

"There are some unanswered questions in the case, one of which is how did Sal Pisello end up in MCA in the first place. What this case was about is these records were coming out at either a loss to MCA or nobody cared about it, but as a gain to a whole host of people. Everybody was to get a cut of this pie."

Again and again Repetto repeated the unanswered questions. "Why does Levy have to guarantee the deal at all? Why is the sale to Mr. Levy? If Sal Pisello is creating the deal on the inside of MCA, then it's either sold to Morris Levy or it's not sold to him. Why is Mr. Levy there as a guarantor? Because the whole thing was a sham. . . . If you look at who received and who got it, it doesn't make any sense. If Sal Pisello is on one end, the receiving end, and on the paying end, none of it makes any sense."

The defendants "conspired over a year's period of time," he said, "threatening to take the business and to do all kinds of things to [John LaMonte] to accomplish what they wanted.

"That is not our system. If that becomes the norm, if that is the norm in the music industry or if that's the norm in this country, then God help us."

When Repetto was done, Brotman took a short recess "to think something out," he said. He returned to the bench ten minutes later and got right to it. "This is not an easy case to sentence," he said. "Mr. Levy is an individual who has made it by himself. He has been a very successful individual and I have received many, many letters from people who spoke very, very highly of Mr. Levy. There is no question in my mind that Mr. Levy has done a lot of good, has been helpful to a lot of people. But that in and of itself does not excuse the crime that has been committed for which the jury has found him guilty."

He looked directly at Levy, who was standing before him. "I know it is very difficult for you as a man who has been a very driving person, who had control of his opportunities and of his businesses and has been a successful businessman, to be in a position such as this. But here you are, and I am satisfied that you could have controlled the situation to the extent that you would have not been here had you said. 'Well, okay, all this money is out there, I am not getting it. This guy LaMonte is no good; to hell with it.' But you didn't do that. There is no need to lecture. I think we understand each other.

"It is adjudged that the defendant is hereby committed to the custody of the attorney general or his authorized representative for a term of imprisonment of ten years, and to pay a fine of $200,000."

Brotman set bail for Levy at $3 million, secured by his farm in upstate New York, valued at $16 million. Repetto had argued for immediate incarceration, saying to Brotman, "Your Honor, if I haven't made it clear today that I consider Mr. Levy a danger to our society, then I'm taking up farming tomorrow."

Brotman then sentenced Dominick Canterino to twelve years in prison.

Following the sentencing, *Billboard* magazine published an editorial headlined, "Sadly, No Tears for Morris Levy." It read: "If Morris Levy were a simple crook in a cops-and-robbers world, he could be regarded as just a rare bad apple in the music business. But Levy is anything but simple.

"Levy, always known as a tough, resourceful operator, was suspected of mob ties through most of his career. As a wiretap transcript furnished at his trial indicates, he felt comfortable with gangsters, and they with him.

"Levy's sentencing is a warning that music industry-ites had better be careful how they operate. In both his case and the related trial of Sal Pisello, federal prosecutors suggested that organized crime may have infiltrated certain areas of the music business. The government is clearly watching this glamour industry, and it would behoove all concerned to avoid even the appearance of links with mob-connected individuals."

But was the government still watching the record business? Marvin Rudnick wondered as he waded through all the articles printed in the wake of the Levy sentencing. The investigation he launched was dead. Pisello had been immunized and apparently didn't tell the grand jury anything. As far as Rudnick could tell from his isolated perspective, the payola investigation was stalled; no indictment of Isgro was imminent. According to the Hollywood trade papers, Myron Roth was leaving MCA Records to become senior vice president and general manager of the West Coast operations of CBS Records, and Richard Palmese was being promoted to the newly created position of executive vice president and general manager of MCA Records.

The *Hits* magazine article reporting Palmese's elevation contained a quote from Irving Azoff: "It was important to promote Richard because he's the only one left around here whose name ends in a vowel, and we needed a new target for the *Los Angeles Times*." *Hits* accompanied the article with a photograph of Azoff in his Front Line Management days, standing on his desk, smiling broadly and giving the finger.

Rudnick thought Azoff looked and sounded like a man who knew he had won.

Still, what Repetto said at the Levy sentencing hearing gave Rudnick hope. Repetto wasn't the sort of guy to go against the company line publicly, and it seemed as if he'd gone out of his way to point the finger of suspicion at MCA in court. What did that mean? Rudnick hoped that it meant someone someplace high up in Washington believed that he had tried to do the right thing with the MCA-Pisello investigation, and that there still might be a chance that his career in the Justice Department could be salvaged.

It turned out to be a false hope.

50

"I'm not gonna answer nothing"

In the weeks leading up to his November trial date, Gaetano Vastola tried desperately to cop a plea. He'd seen what happened to his old friend "Moishe" Levy, and he knew that he stood even less of a chance of beating the rap in court. It was his voice, after all, that the jury would hear on tape threatening to put John La-Monte right where he ended up—"in the fuckin' hospital."

Vastola's cousin, Sonny Brocco, and Sal Pisello's buddy Rudy Farone had already pleaded guilty to reduced charges and had accepted eight-year prison sentences without trial. That left Vastola and Lew Saka as the last of the original twenty-one defendants in the case.

Though Vastola was technically facing two-hundred-plus years in prison if convicted on all counts, he knew that, realistically, he was looking at a twenty-to-thirty-year sentence if found guilty, which was likely. Plus, a racketeering conviction meant the government could seize his assets.

Through his lawyers—Michael Rosen and his own daughter, Joy—Vastola offered to plead guilty to a number of the charges without a trial, and to accept a ten-year sentence. But with no racketeering conviction, no forfeiture of his property. His offer would save the government a lot of time and money spent on a trial and a lengthy appeals process. On a ten-year sentence, he'd have to do only six years behind bars. He'd be sixty-six years old when he got out, and he'd still have his assets. He could live out the remainder of his life in comfort.

But Bruce Repetto was granite. The government would accept nothing less than a twenty-year sentence, he said, with a racketeering conviction. The plea bargain discussions continued until minutes before the trial began at 9:30 A.M. November 28. Repetto held fast to his hard line.

In opening arguments, Assistant U.S. Attorney Donald Davidson, subbing for Repetto, described Vastola as the head of a "secret criminal enterprise that used fear and intimidation to generate hundreds of thousands of dollars of illegitimate income." Vastola was a man who "had no respect for any law other than the law of force, the law that the stronger will prevail," Davidson told the jury. He described Lew Saka as Vastola's "left-hand man."

Defense attorney Michael Rosen countered that his client was simply a "businessman" who had been "betrayed by his former associates" in the MCA cutout deal. Referring to Vastola by the cuddly sounding nickname "Tommy," Rosen said he intended to prove that the accused was "not an intimidator but a victim of lies and duplicity by those who sold the records to LaMonte and of LaMonte himself."

If Rosen had that evidence, he wasn't able to present it. The Vastola trial turned out to be a replay of the Levy trial, with the government presenting little more than the wiretapped conversations, the testimony of a handful of FBI agents and police officers confirming their legitimacy, and the surveillance photographs taken by FBI agent James Scanlon outside John LaMonte's Darby warehouse in January 1985. Like Martin London before him, Rosen was hard pressed to rebut what the jury saw and heard; he couldn't cross-examine tapes.

As before, the jury listened to hours of coarse discussion among the defendants, 118 separate conversations in all. What they heard painted an audio portrait of a world few outsiders ever glimpse. But for their age and wealth, the men talking could have been a neighborhood street gang of eighth-grade dropouts sitting on a stoop in Brooklyn.

There was sixty-six-year-old Sonny Brocco laughingly telling LaMonte how, on his way to a "sit-down with the Galoot" in New York City, he got a quickie blow job from a street-corner prostitute: "I whistled to her and asked, 'You give head?' She said, 'Yeah.' So I popped it off right there in the car."

In another phone conversation, Brocco talked excitedly about his purchase of a "new machine. . . . This one has heat." He was apparently referring to a vibrator.

As in the Levy trial, the prosecution's most damning tape was of the meeting between Morris Levy, Dominick Canterino, Vastola, and Saka in the Roulette Records office on September 23, 1985. The three-and-a-half-hour sit-down was a textbook lesson in the banality of evil.

"You want me to tell you what this all boils down to?" Vastola said. "This guy fucked everybody."

"No shit, no shit, no shit," Levy replied. "He fucks everybody. You ain't giving me no news."

Vastola turned to Saka, "Moishe said he was no fucking good right from the beginning."

"As far as I'm concerned," Levy went on, "the one that fucked us with him was Sonny Brocco. I say that flat out, too. What do you think of that? Because he was the one who sat in that fucking chair at the first meeting with me last year looking to him for what to say. And that's the first time this kid ever, ever, ever got up on his, on his ass and got the nerve to even talk back."

"Sonny Brocco's dying," Vastola said.

"Fuck him," Levy replied.

"He's dying. I went to see him at the hospital in isolation. He's in isolation."

Levy was unmoved. "What's he done nice things for people, Sonny Brocco? A lot of people are dying. Let me tell you something about me. If a guy's a cocksucker in his life, when he dies he don't become a saint."

"Yeah," said Vastola.

"The only difference is, he was a live cocksucker Monday and he's a dead cocksucker Tuesday."

"That's a good philosophy, huh?" Saka piped up.

"You're right," Vastola said. "You're absolutely, 100 percent right."

(Vastola's cousin, Sonny, was still a live cocksucker at the time of the trial. He had pulled through his illness and was a relatively healthy prison inmate on this particular Tuesday.)

At one point in the tape, the jury got to listen in on Levy conducting legitimate record business. In the midst of his discussion with Vastola and Saka, he took a call from Maurice Starr, the lead singer of New Edition, whose five members had been discovered in 1979, legend had it, as they were vocalizing on the sidewalk in Boston's Orchard Park housing project. The youngsters were immediately signed to a small New York label called Streetwise Records, which Levy owned in part. They now recorded for MCA.

"Hi Maurice, how are you?" Levy said. "Did you ever get that check? Good, good, very good. Are you up to date on what's happening in court? Well, I said I'd settle for two million. How do you feel about that? You go along with that, I will, too. Okay, that's it. Take a walk. To hell with it, I'd settle for two million. Okay? All right, Maurice. All right, pal. I'll see you in Boston. Bye."

Levy hung up and turned back to Vastola and Saka. "All right, you know what this is," he said. "The New Edition. We own the name; we won the name in court."

"New Edition?" Vastola repeated.

"Yeah, and I'm going to give the name back to MCA. I'm gonna charge them two million. This is another thing with MCA."

"Who's New Edition? Who's that?" Vastola asked.

"The black group that recorded Maurice Starr. That was Maurice Starr. They recorded on a record company called Streetwise."

"How you doing with that company? Anything much?"

"Good, good." Levy replied.

As it turned out, the most incriminating statement on the September 23 tape wasn't uttered by either Vastola or Levy. It came from the mouth of Lew Saka. The three were marveling at LaMonte's chutzpah in not paying what they demanded for the MCA cutouts. In the past, LaMonte had always complied when Levy threatened him.

"It's completely out of character," said Levy.

"Yeah, but then he went and did two and a half years and he got brave in jail," Vastola responded. "You know, Federal. He became an ex-con."

"Let me tell you," Saka interjected. "After what happened to him at, ah, Hightstown and he still has the balls not to come up with the money like he was supposed to! He promised that he would come up every week. He busted his jaw; he broke it!"

It was the only time in all the 118 taped conversations that any of the defendants acknowledged what had happened to LaMonte. And the mere mention of the punch heard round the Justice Department set Vastola to worrying out loud.

"I don't want to be sitting in the can doing twenty years and saying, 'Well, sure, they all wanted to collect the money and I'm sitting in the fucking joint here.'"

"Nobody should go to the joint," Levy soothed. "I want to tell you something. You've done nothing wrong; I've done nothing wrong. We're trying to collect what we sold; we're trying to get the goods returned."

"That's right," said Vastola, as the two men launched into a confidence-bolstering exchange that played like a rehearsal for their ultimate defense in court.

"We're acting in a peaceable manner," Levy said.

"Right," Vastola agreed.

"I could stand up with this here and show it to whatever and there's nothing wrong. There's only one beef here, one thing."

"John LaMonte," Vastola said.

"That's it," said Levy. "There's only one beef. This thing could go, I don't give a fuck if they took this to a grand jury. They can't do no, I won't go. I wouldn't even take the Fifth. I wouldn't even need an immunity."

The issues of the Fifth Amendment and immunity came up in the testimony of the government's only two outside witnesses in the trial—MCA Records vice president Dan McGill and Rocco Musacchia. McGill took the stand on December 8. It was the fifth time in three years that he'd been called to testify about the cutout deal—first during the Scorpio Music case, then before the Los Angeles grand jury, and afterward at the Pisello and Levy trials. As in the two previous trials, the government needed someone from MCA to simply swear to the fact that there had been a cutout sale from the company in April 1984. To that end, McGill had become MCA's designated witness, giving the prosecution the bare minimum in exchange for immunity.

After Repetto elicited the boilerplate testimony he needed from McGill, Michael Rosen practically bounded from his seat to the witness stand. He finally had a chance to cross-examine someone, and he promptly tore into the MCA executive.

"You testified that these cutouts were sold to Sal Pisello, am I correct?" Rosen asked.

"That is my understanding, yes."

Rosen handed him a copy of the now famous MCA internal audit report. "And your document purports to analyze this transaction, am I correct, sir?"

"Yes, sir."

"You see the caption, '1984 cutout sale to Roulette Records Inc'? You see those words?"

"Yes."

"There was no sale to Roulette Records Inc., was there?"

"No, the sale was to Sal Pisello."

"So that is incorrect, is it not?"

"That is incorrect, yeah."

"And if you look down at the bottom of the page where it says, 'As a result, Pisello arranged a sale of cutouts by MCA Records to Roulette Records,' that is also incorrect, isn't it, sir?"

"It is my understanding it is incorrect, yes."

Rosen went through the cutout section of the report line by line, getting McGill to admit that the company's description of what happened was inaccurate. It wasn't clear what purpose the lawyer's line of questioning served, except perhaps to impeach McGill by casting doubt on the MCA internal audit report.

It's unlikely any member of the jury fully understood the significance of what they'd just heard. The chief financial officer of MCA Records had admitted under oath that, in a report purportedly leveling with MCA's board of directors about the record company's dealings with Sal Pisello, the record company executives had, in fact, lied and covered up.

On the afternoon of December 14, Repetto called Rocco Musacchia to the witness stand. The government wanted him to confirm the authenticity of the books that had been subpoenaed from Consultants for World Records, the company he operated in partnership with Fritzy Giovanelli, Sal Pisello, and Morris Levy.

Musacchia didn't come to court willingly. He was taken into custody as a material witness the previous day as he checked out of Wyckoff Heights Hospital in Brooklyn. He'd checked into the hospital seeking treatment for a purported heart condition after receiving a subpoena to testify.

Musacchia was led into the courtroom by a pair of U.S. marshals. He staggered, moaned, panted, rolled his eyes wildly, and clutched his chest as if he were in the throes of a coronary. But Repetto told Judge Brotman that the two doctors who'd treated Musacchia at the hospital "have been able to find no physical evidence that he is suffering any kind of physical ailment at all. They state to me, categorically, he has not had a heart attack. Dr. Vechai opined to me that Mr. Musacchia was, in his word, 'pretending.'"

After being sworn in, Musacchia slumped into the witness chair.

"Mr. Musacchia, were you connected to Consultants for World Records during the years 1984 and 1985?" Repetto asked.

Musacchia turned to Brotman. "Your Honor, my condition, I . . . "

"The question is directed to you," Brotman said. "Respond to it."

"I refuse to answer," Musacchia responded.

"I'm suggesting and directing, sir, you answer the question," Brotman said sharply.

"My condition," Musacchia mumbled, sagging in his seat. "I'll take the Fifth Amendment."

"Pardon me?" Brotman responded.

"I'll take the Fifth."

"What do you mean, take the Fifth? You refuse to answer any questions on the grounds that you would incriminate yourself, is that it?"

"Due to my condition."

"Not due to your condition," Brotman retorted. "The question is, sir, do you refuse to answer any questions on the basis of your constitutional right to remain silent?"

"Yes."

Repetto immediately moved that Musacchia be granted immunity and be compelled to testify. Brotman granted the motion and turned to Musacchia again. "If you still refuse to testify, this court can hold you in contempt and incarcerate you, put you in jail, until such time as you decide to testify. Do you understand that, sir?"

"I'm not gonna answer nothing; I'm having another episode," Musacchia replied. By this time he was almost completely out of the chair, draped over the railing in front of it. Suddenly he burped, long and loud. "Excuse me," he said.

Exasperated, Brotman ordered that Musacchia be held overnight and returned to court the next day. "Maybe in the quietness of a room somewhere, he may discuss with his lawyer and have a little more reason and possibly recognize that this court can send him to jail for six months and fine him up to a thousand dollars. Maybe he'll have second thoughts."

But he didn't. The next day, Musacchia still refused to answer any questions and Brotman ordered the marshals to take him directly to New York's Metropolitan Correction Center "for flagrant contempt of this court."

Repetto and Donald Davidson were far from upset with Musacchia's antics. The questions they had intended to ask him would not have placed him in jeopardy of prosecution, nor would they have injured Vastola's defense, such as it was. Musacchia apparently decided it was safer to maintain the code of silence than to answer even the most innocuous line of inquiry. As a result, the prosecution got an unexpected bonus—without even bringing charges, they got another bad guy off the streets for six months.

(Within days of his release from jail, Musacchia was working as a technical consultant during the filming of the Mafia-themed comedy *The Freshman*, starring Marlon Brando in a send-up of his Oscar-winning performance as Don Vito Corleone in *The Godfather.*)

Three days after Musacchia's comic performance in court, Gaetano Vastola checked himself into the hospital, complaining of severe headaches. Preliminary tests indicated he had contracted encephalitis. Judge Brotman called a recess that would ultimately last two months.

The trial resumed on February 16, 1989, and three weeks later, on March 5, the jury found Vastola and Saka guilty of racketeering, extortion, and eighteen other charges.

Vastola would appeal his conviction all the way to the U.S. Supreme Court, to no avail. On October 28, 1991, six and a half years after he put John LaMonte in the hospital with a single punch, Vastola was sentenced by Judge Brotman to seventeen years in prison. The prediction Vastola made to Morris Levy in the Roulette Records offices on September 23, 1985, finally came true: "We're going to wind up in the joint here—me, I know, definitely."

51

"My guy
is bigger
than their guy"

The trial of Gaetano Vastola didn't get much ink outside of New Jersey, primarily because another startling mob-in-show-business story completely diverted the Hollywood media's attention. On Thursday, December 15, the *Los Angeles Times* published an article headlined, "MCA Official Suspected of Funneling Funds to the Mafia."

The official was Eugene F. Giaquinto, the fifty-seven-year-old president of MCA's Home Entertainment division. According to the article, the FBI believed Giaquinto had passed a large amount of MCA funds on an annual basis to Edward ("the Conductor") Sciandra, the underboss of Pennsylvania's Bufalino crime family. The FBI also believed that Giaquinto had a longstanding relationship with Gambino family boss John Gotti and may have called upon Gotti for help in an intramural battle with MCA Music Entertainment chairman Irving Azoff.

Those beliefs were based on information gathered in the course of the two-year FBI–strike force investigation into suspected labor racketeering in the movie business. It was Giaquinto's MCA office phone that agents were attempting to tap back in September 1987 when MCA security officers discovered the plan and wrongly blamed it on Marvin Rudnick. In fact, the racketeering investigation was overseen by strike force attorney Richard Stavin.

Though Stavin and his investigators failed to tap Giaquinto's office phone, they had managed to install one on the telephone of a Giaquinto confidante named Marty Bacow. A self-styled labor negotiator with ties to Teamster president Jackie Presser, Bacow was suspected of trying to extort Hollywood film companies in exchange for labor peace. But based on what investigators overheard on Bacow's phone, they concluded that labor extortion was just the tip of the iceberg.

One of the people Bacow talked to the most was Gene Giaquinto. And what the two men talked about convinced Stavin and FBI case agent Tom Gates that the nation's two largest organized crime families—the Gambinos and the Genoveses—were engaged in a dispute over control of MCA's Home Entertainment division.

Gates laid out the bare bones of it in a sworn affidavit in support of extending the wiretaps in the case: "On June 30, 1987, at around 11:19 A.M., Bacow made an outgoing call to Giaquinto at 777-4302 (MCA Home Entertainment). Giaquinto told Bacow that 'A' (a reference to Irving Azoff, in charge of the record division of MCA) was planning to take over the whole thing (a possible reference to Azoff taking over the entire MCA/Universal operation). Bacow told Giaquinto to 'wait, it's warfare.'

"On July 7, 1987, at about 8:56 P.M., Bacow received another incoming call from Giaquinto. . . . Giaquinto said if they wanted war that he had had a meeting in New York and he had anything he wanted and it came from 'Number One.' Bacow asked if it was the 'G guy' and Giaquinto said, 'Yes.' Giaquinto said if he made one phone call he could have them (a possible reference to La Cosa Nostra figures around the country) all on planes."

Gates and Stavin believed that the "G guy" was Gotti, whom Giaquinto referred to in other conversations as "the guy with the suits."

In a July 8 conversation, Giaquinto told Bacow "he had carte blanche with 'G' (Gotti) in New York and that he had known him all his life."

In a later telephone conversation with Michael Villano, a New

York man the FBI believed was a contact for Gotti, "Giaquinto said they (Genovese members) were 'all over the place.' Villano said 'shame on them, then.' Giaquinto said they had managed to keep it out of the newspapers because of certain contacts they had."

On December 15, a *Los Angeles Times* article revealed the federal indictment of another organized crime figure and Bacow associate, Angelo Commito, on labor racketeering charges. The day after the *Times* story ran, MCA announced that Giaquinto had been relieved of all his responsibilities pending a company investigation into his activities.

As the Giaquinto story broke nationally, MCA counsel Ron Olson responded to calls from the media with the by-now-familiar refrain, "MCA has been advised repeatedly that it is not a target or a subject of this Department of Justice investigation." However, a spokesman for the Justice Department in Washington flatly denied Olson's statement, saying MCA had been told it wasn't a target of the Pisello investigation, not that it wasn't a target of the Giaquinto investigation. At best, Olson was playing a game of semantics when he told reporters, "There is no association with MCA here at all." He added that MCA executives had "no knowledge" of company funds being passed to Edward ("the Conductor") Sciandra.

If they didn't, they should have. According to the government, the money supposedly flowed to Sciandra through a Clifton, New Jersey–based company called Northstar Graphics, which had a longstanding contract for packaging MCA's home videos that was worth an estimated $5 million a year.

In 1981, Sciandra was implicated along with Northstar Graphics and its president, Michael Del Gaizo, in a $68,000 false billing scam that victimized MCA's Universal 8 Films division, which would later become MCA's Home Entertainment division. Sciandra and Del Gaizo were convicted on tax evasion charges in connection with the scheme. In a background report prior to Sciandra's sentencing, the prosecutor stated: "Although he was neither an employee nor an authorized agent, Sciandra was able—because of his organized crime connections—to dictate to which companies Universal sent its film processing and film editing work." Northstar president Michael Del Gaizo was characterized in court documents as "a close friend and associate of Sciandra."

Despite the public nature of those documents and the fact that MCA executives were made aware of the Sciandra–Del Gaizo case at the time, seven years later MCA was still doing its home video packaging business on an exclusive basis with Northstar Graphics. And at the time the Giaquinto story broke, Northstar was gearing up for its most lucrative job ever for MCA—the packaging of the home video version of *E.T.: The Extra Terrestrial.*

The Northstar contract had been the subject of internal debate at MCA for some time. As one company executive told the *Los Angeles Times,* "I did an internal audit years back showing some irregularities, between a $400,000 and $500,000 difference in things we were paying for and not getting. Prices on boxes were thirty-four cents when we could have gotten them for eighteen cents." In addition, since Northstar was located in New Jersey and MCA manufactured its videocassettes in Newberry Park, California, the company had to ship the cassette boxes clear across the continent to complete the packaging.

From the wiretaps in the FBI–strike force investigation, it appeared that Edward ("the Conductor") Sciandra collected regular payments on Northstar's contract with MCA and that the crime boss was concerned the future of the contract was in question because of a new internal audit that Azoff was using in his attempt to wrest control of the Home Entertainment division from Giaquinto. As FBI agent Tom Gates wrote in his affidavit: "On July 7, 1987 at about 11:16 A.M., Bacow made an outgoing call to Giaquinto at 213-278-3538. Bacow and Giaquinto spoke about what I believe to be their meeting with Edward Sciandra on June 18, 1987, at the Bistro Gardens.

"The conversation and the meeting between Bacow, Giaquinto and Sciandra all relate to the MCA/Universal internal audit which was critical of Giaquinto and his awarding of a multimillion-dollar contract to Northstar Graphics and Michael Del Gaizo. It is the opinion of [Gates] that Giaquinto indicated to Sciandra that something might happen to cancel the contract."

In a July 8 conversation with Bacow, "Giaquinto said that he went to dinner with Michael (Del Gaizo) the next night (this is a possible reference to the night after the June 18 Bistro Gardens dinner). Giaquinto was told that he should tell [MCA president] Sidney Sheinberg to 'get a pillow and lean on it.' Giaquinto was concerned that they (Sciandra and Del Gaizo) may have mentioned something to 'G' (Gotti).

"Gates interpreted the conversation to mean that "Del Gaizo

might carry out some type of threat or violence against Sheinberg to retain the [Northstar] contract."

Later in that same July 8 conversation, "Bacow said the younger guys are taking over. Giaquinto agreed and said that they wanted to retire Eddie (Sciandra) and 'send him to Istanbul.' He said that Eddie (Sciandra) wanted to meet Azoff in the open. Bacow indicated that Eddie said he wanted to go to [MCA chairman Lew] Wasserman and Sheinberg and tell them who they were up against. Giaquinto said that he had received a call from Chicago yesterday. He then added that maybe Sheinberg would break a toe and end up in the hospital for a couple of days, 'maybe he'll break a leg.'

"This conversation in part stems from the problem with the Northstar contract and Sciandra's reaction to the news," Gates wrote. "It appears that Sciandra's reaction to this news was irrational and is of concern to various La Cosa Nostra members. The La Cosa Nostra may be concerned that Sciandra may attract attention and should be 'retired.'"

In another taped conversation, Bacow and Giaquinto wondered if members of the Genovese family—perhaps under orders from Vincent Gigante himself—were trying to get Giaquinto ousted from his position at MCA. "I don't care who their guy is," Giaquinto said. "My guy is bigger."

FBI agent Gates and strike force attorney Stavin concluded that such talk "may indicate the manner in which [La Cosa Nostra] has different people as overseers in certain industries throughout the country. These people usually have no criminal records so as not to attract law enforcement attention . . . so they can operate secretly on behalf of La Cosa Nostra and its interests."

The Giaquinto-Bacow investigation was to Rich Stavin what the MCA-Pisello investigation was to Marvin Rudnick. Stavin was confident that he was on to the biggest case of Mafia infiltration of legitimate business in the history of the country. He had a twenty-seven-year employee of MCA, a president of a multimillion-dollar division, who was able to pick up the phone and call Edward Sciandra and confer with him over dinner, who met with John Gotti on at least one occasion, and who regularly spoke to a man the FBI believed was his "liaison" to Gotti. When Giaquinto wanted to find out what was happening "upstairs" at his own company in California, he would call Northstar's Michael Del Gaizo in New Jersey, and Del Gaizo—identified as an associate of a Pennsylvania crime family boss—would later call him back with the information. And through it all, Stavin and his investigators were listening in! In his ten years as a prosecutor, Stavin had never had anything approaching it. This could be the biggest case of his career.

There were times, however, when Stavin worried that the case was bigger than his superiors would have liked. He'd seen what happened to Marvin Rudnick and couldn't believe that Mike Defeo and David Margolis had yanked him back on the MCA-Pisello investigation when they were fully aware of what was on the Giaquinto-Bacow wiretaps. Stavin liked Rudnick and sympathized with his predicament, but he steered clear of him nonetheless for fear of being painted with the same brush, another "loose cannon." He didn't want his case to end up in the same trash can as Rudnick's.

Stavin was having his own problems with Rudnick's nemesis, L.A. strike force chief John Newcomer. Though the theory of the planned racketeering prosecution had been discussed and approved all the way up the line to Defeo and Margolis, as far as Stavin could tell, Newcomer either didn't like the case or didn't understand it. By early 1989, Stavin had presented 95 percent of his evidence to the grand jury and was long past ready to ask for the indictments of Giaquinto and Bacow, for starters. But before Stavin could ask for indictments, he had to get Washington's approval of his "pros memo" (prosecution memo), a written outline of the evidence and charges. And to get to Washington, Stavin's pros memo first had to go through Newcomer, who kept kicking it back with what Stavin considered niggling objections. As a result, months had passed and the memo still had not cleared Newcomer's desk.

Stavin knew that Newcomer was in frequent telephone contact with Bill Hundley, MCA's outside counsel in Washington. Hundley had even called Stavin on a number of occasions, inquiring whether there was anything the prosecutor needed from the company. "We want to cooperate fully," Hundley kept saying. But when Stavin asked for MCA's notes on its attorneys' interviews with Giaquinto, Hundley refused, saying, "That's privileged; the company will not give it up." As happened in Rudnick's investigation, Stavin believed MCA was making a claim that it was cooperating, while not really cooperating at all.

It was clear to Stavin that MCA had a lot to be concerned about in the investigation. Giaquinto constantly hinted to Bacow and others over the phone that he had something either on the company or on Wasserman that would be his ace in the hole when push came to shove with his rival Irving Azoff. Stavin and Gates wondered what it could be.

Giaquinto also talked frequently about some secret "connections" he supposedly had inside the government that would protect him in the end.

The Gates affidavit noted that in a July 12 conversation, "Bacow and Giaquinto were heard to talk of the top executives at MCA. Bacow asked if Azoff had something on 'S.S.' [MCA president Sidney Sheinberg]. Giaquinto said it had been bandied about and he would know more when those other documents came in.

"Giaquinto told Bacow he was getting some interesting things off the computers. Giaquinto said they (possibly government agents) were coming from Washington to meet with him next week and they had a master plan. Giaquinto didn't know if Lew (Wasserman) was with them or not. He said Bacow wouldn't believe 'what they have in those machines—companies we own, stockholders.' Giaquinto said that they didn't think Azoff would get indicted and there was nothing in writing. Giaquinto said he would show him reports coming out of Washington, that he had them just working on his company. He said they had him as 'an Italian thing' (no further clarification) and a very good manager."

Later, according to the affidavit, "Giaquinto told Bacow that he had the inside story but that they didn't have all the facts. In a cryptic manner, Giaquinto said they think S.S. (Sheinberg) is trying to take over the company (MCA). Giaquinto said that he got it from his people. Bacow responded that it was from 'your friends that you don't know.' Giaquinto added that they said 'Azoff's out,' that the 'government had him.' He said they told him that timing is of the essence and he (Giaquinto) should go to Lew (Wasserman) when he gets out of the hospital and name his position (possibly a new position within the top management of MCA)."

Gates wrote that these conversations made it appear that Giaquinto had "an association with government employees in Washington who are furnishing [him] with confidential law enforcement information" and who "may be obstructing justice."

Gates and Stavin constantly wondered who those government employees might be, what branch of the government employed them. Whoever they were, they seemed to have information about

MCA and its executives that neither the FBI nor the strike force in Los Angeles had.

An incident that occurred on July 15, 1987, led Stavin and Gates to suspect that "they" were members of the intelligence community, perhaps the CIA. On that date, according to the Gates affidavit, "FBI surveillance agents observed Giaquinto exit Le Dome Restaurant on Sunset Blvd. with an unidentified male and walk to Giaquinto's automobile. The male retrieved a box from Giaquinto's trunk and drove to the Beverly Hills Hotel where the surveillance was terminated."

The car the man was driving bore a Hawaiian license plate, CAP-648. A check with the Department of Motor Vehicles in Hawaii showed that the car was registered to the Wells Fargo Bank at 528 Hakaka Place in Honolulu, Hawaii. But a utilities check revealed that a Harold Okimoto resided at that address, not the Wells Fargo Bank. A records check with the Honolulu Police Department indicated that Okimoto had been arrested for gambling in 1977. Agents went back to the DMV and discovered that more than fifty cars were registered to the Wells Fargo Bank at various Hawaiian addresses. But they found that, of the thirty individuals supposedly living at those addresses, only one had a valid Hawaiian driver's license. From there, investigators learned that Wells Fargo had no auto-leasing operations in Hawaii, nor did it have any banking facilities in the state.

As FBI agent Gates wrote in his affidavit, "The method of registration of the aforesaid vehicles leads me to believe that some type of covert activity was involved."

The individual seen with Giaquinto was subsequently identified as Robert Nichols, described in FBI investigative files as "allegedly an international money launderer for money generated through narcotics trafficking and organized crime activities." Nichols also claimed to have CIA connections, though the agency denied any knowledge of him. Still, when Stavin contacted Nichols's lawyer and asked why his client was meeting with Giaquinto, the lawyer responded, "It's none of your business; it's a matter of national security."

In a wiretapped phone conversation with Nichols on July 20, 1987, Giaquinto discussed "the rift among the top executives at MCA," according to the Gates affidavit. "Giaquinto indicated that he might be the one to lose his job and stated that they (MCA) would be in for trouble. He then laughed and asked Nichols if Nichols knew what he (Giaquinto) was saying."

As Gates and Stavin pondered the implications of what they'd learned, they found themselves wondering aloud if it all had something to do with the story that was dominating the news at the time—the Iran-contra scandal. Was it possible that Reagan administration officials were using mobsters and the far-flung international operations of MCA, a company run by the president's old friend Lew Wasserman, to funnel money to the contras? Was former senator Howard Baker's recent jump from the MCA board of directors to the position of Ronald Reagan's White House chief of staff somehow connected?

No, they told themselves. It was too wild, too far-fetched, too much like something out of a John le Carré spy novel. They were just being paranoid. They dismissed the idea, sort of. But they couldn't shake the feeling that there was some hidden power out there somewhere, some dark secret, that was affecting things. Stavin had felt it the first week in December when, almost a year to the day after Rudnick was called back to Washington, he himself was summoned to meet with Defeo and Margolis in Margolis's Justice Department office.

At that meeting, Defeo and Margolis read him the riot act because he'd committed a technical violation of the U.S. Attorney's Manual in the course of the labor-racketeering investigation. What he'd done was grant informal, or "pocket," immunity to Sylvester Stallone without first getting written permission from his supervisor, John Newcomer. Stallone was neither a subject nor a target of that investigation, but he apparently knew Bacow, and his production company, White Eagle, had employed Bacow as a consultant on the movie *Over the Top*. When the strike force approached Stallone for information, the actor's lawyer, Donald Santorelli, a formerly high-ranking Justice Department attorney, asked for informal immunity for his client. So Stavin granted it without checking with Newcomer. Prosecutors gave pocket immunity all the time without going through channels. Everyone knew it, including Defeo and Margolis.

Stavin argued that he hadn't gone through Newcomer in order to save time. "He takes three days to decide whether to go to the bathroom," he complained. He couldn't believe they'd called him all the way back to Washington at taxpayers' expense for this, something that could have been handled in a phone call or a memo.

They told him that in the future, "Everything goes through Newcomer." And in the next breath they talked about what a bright future he had with the Justice Department.

It was clear to Stavin what was really going on. He was being told, in the most circumspect way possible, that his days of independence were over and that, henceforth, even the smallest details of the investigation would be controlled by Washington through their appointed babysitter, John Newcomer. The way Stavin saw it, they were setting up a process that would thwart the progress of the case. From that moment on, Stavin suspected his investigation was going the same way Rudnick's had gone—nowhere.

His suspicions hardened into conviction on January 31, 1989, when he read in *Daily Variety* that Ronald Reagan, newly returned to the private sector, had taken a suite of offices in the plush Fox Plaza building in Century City, and that the former president's first luncheon guest there was none other than MCA chairman Lew Wasserman. A Reagan spokesman described the meeting as "just conversation with an old friend."

"Right," Stavin thought. And a Republican administration was going to let him go after Gene Giaquinto and risk having Giaquinto roll over and tell investigators what he knew that could embarrass the "old friend" of the Republican Party's grand old man?

"It will never happen," Stavin thought.

He was right. It never did.

52

"I wasn't going to let that happen to me"

Whatever his doubts about the Giaquinto investigation, Rich Stavin was confident that he had a dead-bang payola case against Joe Isgro.

In the two years since he'd taken over the case from Rick Small, Stavin had become at least as knowledgeable as Rudnick and Dubois had been. And Stavin was pursuing it in much the same way. His plan was to get the lower people—Ralph Tashjian, Bill Craig, George Wilson Crowell, Dennis DiRicco, and David Michael Smith—to roll over on Isgro, convict Isgro on racketeering charges, and then get him to roll over on the industry to lighten his sentence. IRS investigators had information that at least eight record company promotion executives had taken cash kickbacks from Isgro.

Like Rudnick and Dubois before him, Stavin believed the major record companies were, by and large, willing victims of Isgro and the Network. He, too, felt that the government was acting as an accomplice to the record companies in going after Isgro. He had no doubt that Azoff in particular was trying to deflect attention from his own problems by pointing the finger at payola and the independents. But Stavin didn't intend to just do the industry's bidding and stop there. He planned to bring it back around full circle to bite the hands that fed the promoters in the first place—the record companies themselves.

The next major step in Stavin's game plan was to nail down guilty pleas from Ralph and Valerie Tashjian. So on February 14, 1989, a year after their indictment and arrest, the couple appeared in U.S. District Court in Los Angeles for a hearing on their plea bargain agreements with the government.

After months of negotiations, Ralph Tashjian was to plead guilty to two counts of the original indictment—making undisclosed payments to radio program directors, a misdemeanor, and filing a false income tax return, a felony. In exchange for his plea, the government dropped the other six counts in the indictment and agreed not to prosecute him "for any crimes rising out of the facts of this case or related investigations." Tashjian also agreed to cooperate with the ongoing investigation.

It was a good deal for the promoter, considering the case the government had put together against him. As Stavin laid it out in a court brief: "Tashjian would generally receive two checks personally from Isgro Enterprises Inc. and deposit those checks through his secretary, Lucretia D'Amore, into one or more corporate or personal accounts he maintained. Tashjian, through his secretary, would then write checks for cash made out in an amount equivalent to one of the deposited checks. The cash would then be divided up, put into cassette-tape plastic holders, and sent via Federal Express to radio station program directors. This money would be paid to the program directors so that they would play the records promoted by Ralph Tashjian.

"John Walker was one such program director. He had been employed as an announcer and program director at radio station KYNO in Fresno, California, for approximately nine years. As part of his duties, Walker determined what records were included on the playlist of KYNO.

"Walker first met Tashjian in 1980. Walker was told by Tashjian that he (Walker) could make money by doing nothing more than adding records he (Walker) would normally add anyway. Tashjian told Walker it was a white collar crime and that no one got hurt. Tashjian also offered him drugs.

"An agreement was reached between them that for every record added, Walker would receive $200 in cash or drugs. Tashjian would call him on Monday with a list of thirty or forty records and instruct him to listen to them. Tashjian would call him on Tuesday, find out which records were to be added and then pay him for those adds. Walker received $200 per record added to the playlist either in person or by mail. Tashjian also mailed him cocaine via Federal Express. The cash was placed in a record sleeve and the cocaine, approximately $300 worth each time, was placed in a cassette case. Neither Walker nor Tashjian ever informed either the management or licensee of KYNO of the payments. This arrangement lasted about five or six years."

The Tashjian plea was a good deal for the government as well. Stavin figured that with Tashjian's cooperation and his testimony that all this was done with Joe Isgro's knowledge and encouragement, Isgro was dead meat on the payola charges.

The case against Valerie Tashjian was far less dramatic. As secretary and bookkeeper for her husband's in-home business, she agreed to plead guilty to one count of aiding in the preparation of a false tax return. It seems she had allowed about $7,000 worth of personal and home-improvement expenses—including some landscaping and two shower doors—to be claimed as business expenses. Though the charge was a felony punishable by a maximum three years in prison, neither the prosecution nor the defense expected the judge in the case, Pamela Rymer, to sentence the young mother of two to any jail time on a first offense.

Everyone expected the February 14 hearing to go off without a hitch. But when Valerie Tashjian stood up before Judge Rymer to enter her guilty plea, the best-laid plans of all those male attorneys quickly went awry.

Dressed adorably in a floral print dress with a white lace collar, the young woman stoically admitted that she'd written the checks, that she knew it was wrong, and that she "accepted full responsibility" for her actions. But as she went on, her composure started to crumble and tears began streaming down her cheeks. She hadn't really meant to cheat the government, she explained to Rymer, she had just been distracted by "taking care of my two kids and not being used to keeping books, and I thought our tax accountant would sort it all out at the end of the year."

Then why, with that sort of defense available to her, was she pleading guilty? Rymer asked. At that point, Valerie broke down completely. "Because they told me they will file more serious charges against my husband if I don't," she sobbed.

Rich Stavin felt his stomach turn over. This was no act, the tears and emotion were real. He could see it and so could the judge.

Rymer reacted immediately. "I cannot accept this plea," she said angrily. Claiming that she had not been told by the prosecution or the defense that the two guilty pleas were contingent upon one another, Rymer said such a package deal smacked of "coercion" and ordered both sides back in court the next day to explain themselves.

Overnight the two sides composed a joint letter to Rymer apologizing for "any confusion in the proceeding yesterday morning." The letter said that the Tashjians were pleading guilty of their own free will because they are guilty as charged and because they believed the agreement was in each of their best interests. And the letter acknowledged that "the government plea agreement with Mr. Tashjian is contingent on Mrs. Tashjian's agreement and vice versa."

The next day, Rymer's anger had not subsided. She once again refused to accept Valerie Tashjian's guilty plea because of her belief that "the reason for Mrs. Tashjian's willingness to forgo a trial in which she has been advised of a viable defense was that unless she did, there would be subsequent charges brought against Mr. Tashjian."

The judge then launched into a stern rebuke of the prosecution: "Nothing that's said in this letter alleviates my concerns. I have concerns about the intrinsic propriety of the package deal under the special circumstances of this case, where it is clear the primary focus of the government's case is Mr. Tashjian. It is an implicitly coercive situation. It is not right and I cannot accept it."

Rymer eventually threw out the case against Valerie Tashjian, accusing the government of "reprehensible" behavior. "It is clear that the course of conduct of the strike force lawyers falls well below the standard of conduct expected of government prosecutors," she said.

Rymer's action in the Valerie Tashjian plea bargain naturally scuttled the deal between Ralph Tashjian and the government, setting back the planned indictment of Isgro. Moreover, the judge's tongue-lashing of the prosecution provoked news reports that characterized the Justice Department's vaunted payola investigation as being in disarray.

Newcomer was furious with Stavin, and within days of the Tashjian hearing he arranged to have a big gun sent out from Washington to take over the payola case—William Lynch, the Justice Department's senior counsel for litigation. A white-haired, florid-faced Irishman, the fifty-eight-year-old Lynch was a former chief of the Organized Crime Strike Force, Bill Hundley's hand-picked successor in that post.

Lynch's quiet arrival in Los Angeles was greeted with a noisy banner headline in *Variety:* "Payola Probe Gets A New Boss." Pointing out that Lynch was the fifth chief prosecutor on the case in three years, *Variety* said his assignment was "to help bring some semblance of order to the chaotic investigation, which has produced only four indictments so far, resulting in just one conviction—on tax charges."

For Rich Stavin, the arrival of Lynch was the last straw. He'd begun looking for a job in private practice after his dressing down by Mike Defeo and David Margolis back in December. Now he was determined to get out fast.

Stavin would resign in May. He hated leaving the strike force with the two cases he'd worked so hard on—payola and Giaquinto—unresolved, but he felt he had no choice. "I was convinced I was about to become the next Marvin Rudnick," he told friends and colleagues. "And I wasn't going to let that happen to me."

53

"The government is full of shit"

On August 20, 1990—four years, six months, and thirteen days after Marvin Rudnick sent out the first subpoena in what would become the longest and costliest payola investigation in U.S. history—Joe Isgro was finally brought to trial in U.S. District Court in Los Angeles.

Isgro had been indicted the previous November, charged with fifty-one counts of payola, racketeering, drug trafficking, and tax fraud. He faced a maximum sentence of two hundred years in prison. "That's sixty more years than Manuel Noriega," Isgro complained to reporters, "and they invaded a whole country to get him."

Indicted along with Isgro were Ray Anderson, a former vice president of promotion at Columbia Records who was accused of taking $70,000 in kickbacks from Isgro, and Jeffrey Monka, a convicted drug trafficker who was charged with helping Isgro cheat the IRS through a bogus company called Star Promotions.

It is interesting that, after an unprecedented examination of record industry business practices, countless man-hours expended, and untold millions in tax dollars spent, the Justice Department was throwing the proverbial book at three men who were not employed by record companies. Monka wasn't connected to the record industry in any way.

The media turned out big time for the long-awaited event. Every Los Angeles TV station and all the networks had correspondents doing stand-ups outside the federal courthouse. Even the *New York Times*, which had printed barely a word about the MCA-Pisello-Levy investigation during its entire four years in the news, had a reporter in the courtroom and weighed in with an opening-day "curtain-raiser" article describing the trial as "Sex, drugs and rock with a racketeering slant." Most of the news report played up the salacious allegations of drugs and prostitutes for airplay, even though the prostitution angle had long since disappeared from the government's case and the quantity of cocaine involved probably amounted to less than was consumed in a single day at the record industry's annual NARM convention.

Joe Isgro showed up for trial sporting a new look. His once thinning, graying, slicked-back hair was newly dyed jet-black and was woven into a curly pompadour. Gone was the dangling crucifix earring he'd taken to wearing in recent months, and his flashy-casual Hollywood sports jacket and baggy silk slacks were replaced by a conservative business suit. The makeover made him appear less ominous.

The judge in the case, James M. Ideman, was a stern conservative with a reputation for leaning toward the government in criminal cases. Among Los Angeles defense attorneys, Ideman had earned the nickname "Maximum Jim."

He'd already disdainfully rejected a defense motion to dismiss the charges against the three defendants on account of prosecutorial misconduct. Isgro's attorney, Donald Re, had argued that Marvin Rudnick was ordered by the Justice Department—against his will—to steer away from the MCA-Pisello investigation and focus instead on Isgro. To which Ideman responded, "I don't intend to use this court to investigate the Justice Department." As far as Isgro and Re were concerned, Ideman was a hanging judge.

The chief prosecutor, William Lynch, wasted little time putting the building blocks of the government's payola charges into place for the jury.

George Wilson Crowell testified that between 1980 and 1985 Isgro paid him more than $100,000 a year for adding records to the playlist of KIQQ-FM in Los Angeles, where Crowell was general manager and his wife, Paula Matthews, was program director.

"He would give me a list, usually on Monday on the phone," Crowell said. "The records that he was working that I added, I would be paid for."

Crowell testified that he was usually paid $750 for each add, but sometimes received a "double," a $1,500 payment, for records Isgro was pushing particularly hard. The money was always in $50 or $100 bills and was usually passed to him by David Michael Smith in the men's room of a popular record industry lunch spot, Crowell said.

"One of his employees would meet me either at Martoni's Restaurant or the Jolly Roger Restaurant, hand me a record envelope with the money, and I'd go back to the bar."

David Michael Smith backed up Crowell's testimony about the payoffs in the men's room, estimating that he handed Crowell between $3,000 and $5,000 every week.

According to Smith, the source of cash for the payoffs was Isgro's tax accountant, Dennis DiRicco. Smith testified that he made regular trips to San Francisco in 1984 and 1985 to pick up suitcases full of cash from DiRicco. Smith said DiRicco would meet him at the San Francisco airport and hand him a suitcase containing approximately $100,000 in $100 bills. Smith would then fly back to Los Angeles and deliver the money to Isgro's house or office.

Smith claimed he once watched as part of that money was divvied up by one of Isgro's assistants and placed in album jackets for mailing to radio stations. "She was lining the sleeves of the LPs with cash, different amounts," he said.

Smith also testified that he witnessed Isgro making cash payments to mobster Joseph ("Joe Piney") Armone on "three different occasions" and to Fred DiSipio twice.

Ralph Tashjian testified that he set up a system of regular payola payments to three radio programmers between 1983 and 1985, paying them an average of $200 per add. Tashjian said he sent either cash or the equivalent in cocaine to the programmers each week via

Federal Express. When he informed Isgro of the payments, Tashjian testified, Isgro told him, "If that's what it takes, do what you gotta do. But be careful."

All three of the program directors confirmed Tashjian's version of the payment system, but said they never spoke to Isgro about it. One of them, Johnny Walker, the program director of KYNO in Fresno, said under direct questioning by Lynch that Tashjian didn't want Isgro to know about the payments.

"He told me that if I ever met Joe Isgro, to not mention anything to him about this because Joe didn't know anything about it and for me to make sure I never mention anything to him if I ever met him at a convention or any sort of radio event."

"Did you ever in fact meet Mr. Isgro?" Lynch asked.

"No, sir."

Judge Ideman apparently wanted clarification on the previous point.

"What did Tashjian say you should not discuss with Isgro?" he asked Walker. "The cocaine, or the fact that you were receiving any type of payment at all?"

"The fact that I received any kind of payment at all," Walker replied.

Prosecutor Lynch could not have been pleased with the exchange.

In his cross-examination, Donald Re sought to discredit the prosecution's key witnesses by portraying them as, in his words, "people who are bought and paid for by the government for their testimony."

He got Crowell to admit that he was an alcoholic and compulsive gambler who was fired from KIQQ in 1985. He also elicited the fact that in exchange for Crowell's testimony, the government reduced felony tax charges against him to a single misdemeanor and dropped payola charges altogether.

The three program directors confirmed that they failed to pay taxes on the tens of thousands of dollars they collected in payoffs from Tashjian, but the government agreed not to prosecute them for criminal tax evasion, again in exchange for their testimony.

Tashjian acknowledged that while he once faced 175 counts carrying a maximum penalty of two hundred years in prison, he was allowed to plea bargain down to just two counts and was ultimately sentenced to only sixty days in a halfway house.

Re intended to take the same tack with Dennis DiRicco, Isgro's former tax lawyer and the witness Re figured could be most damaging to his client. For all their headline value, the payola charges remained misdemeanors. The drug-trafficking charges were laughable, Re thought. The jury was unlikely to convict on those counts based solely on Tashjian's testimony that Isgro knew he was providing cocaine to the programmers. The heart of the government's case, the basis for the racketeering and fraud charges that could send Isgro to prison for years, was DiRicco. Among other things, the lawyer was expected to testify that he'd helped Isgro set up a scheme to exchange checks from Isgro Enterprises for cash from Monka's bogus company, Star Promotions. The cash supposedly came from a cocaine-dealer client of DiRicco's and was passed through Star Promotions disguised as legitimate business expenses. DiRicco was also expected to testify that prior to Isgro's meeting with Marvin Rudnick in the strike force offices in April 1986, he and the promoter shredded ten linear feet of business records that would have revealed the cash-for-checks scam.

But DiRicco was bringing a lot of baggage to the witness stand, both for himself and the government. After all, he'd been found guilty of laundering hundreds of thousands of dollars for a Colombian drug operation, a conviction that could have landed him in prison a lot of years. And yet the government was willing to let him off in exchange for his testimony against Isgro, a man charged with merely knowing about the distribution of less than one thousand dollars' worth of cocaine over a two-year period by a subordinate working in a city four hundred miles away. Re believed that the juxtaposition of those facts would do more than anything else to convince the jury that the government was out to get his client at all cost. "And isn't this the same government, ladies and gentlemen of the jury, that has been boasting for years about its war on drugs?" He couldn't wait to get DiRicco under cross-examination.

As it turned out, however, DiRicco didn't get a chance to testify against Isgro, due to a prosecutorial blunder that will be talked about in the halls of the Justice Department and the executive suites of the record industry for years to come. On the morning of August 29, just before the fifth day of testimony was to begin, Judge Ideman announced that he was considering a motion made in chambers the previous afternoon by Jeffrey Monka's attorney, Gerson Horn. The motion was to dismiss the indictment against all three defendants on the grounds of prosecutorial misconduct.

Ideman said he was disturbed by what Horn had told him: that just three days earlier, the defense attorney had obtained a transcript of DiRicco's testimony at his own trial in December 1988. In that testimony, DiRicco denied practically everything he later admitted to before the Los Angeles grand jury—after he made a deal with the government. Among other things, DiRicco denied at his trial that he ever made cash deliveries to Isgro through David Michael Smith and said he'd never conspired with Isgro to defraud the IRS.

According to Horn, there were seventy striking inconsistencies between DiRicco's trial testimony and his subsequent grand jury testimony, inconsistencies that indicated he'd committed perjury on one witness stand or the other.

Ideman glared down from the bench to where William Lynch and his prosecution team were sitting. In the months leading up to the trial, the prosecution had repeatedly assured the defense and the court that it possessed no "exculpatory" material that tended to exonerate the defendants. Prosecutors are required by law to turn over such material to the defense. It now appeared that the prosecution had possessed such material all along and had lied about it to Ideman. Moreover, Lynch had not made DiRicco's trial testimony available to the Los Angeles grand jury that returned the payola indictments. Ideman looked to Lynch for an explanation.

Clearly uncomfortable, Lynch denied there was any inconsistency between the two sets of testimony and said he had not turned over a transcript of DiRicco's trial testimony because he didn't think it was exculpatory.

Ideman wasn't buying it. "The integrity of the indictment itself might be in question," he said. "To put it frankly, I'm wondering if dismissal of the indictment with prejudice might not be appropriate." He adjourned the trial and ordered both sides to prepare a brief on the matter.

They were back in court on September 4, and judging by the looks on their faces, they knew what was coming. Lynch and his prosecution team appeared grim; the three defense attorneys were laughing and talking among themselves.

Ideman gazed out over the courtroom. He'd gone over both briefs, he said, and was now prepared to read his ruling. What followed was a blistering fifteen-minute rebuke of the chief prosecutor the likes of which no reporter present had ever heard.

Having read DiRicco's trial testimony, Ideman said he'd come to the conclusion that it "constituted a complete and detailed denial of any wrongdoing not only by himself but also by any of the defendants in this case." As he read aloud, Ideman punched the underlined words in his ruling for emphasis.

"Among other things, DiRicco *denied* in sworn testimony before his trial jury acquiring cash from drug dealers, *denied* taking that cash to Isgro personally, and *denied* sending it to him via Isgro's employees. Furthermore, DiRicco ... *denied* conspiring with Isgro and others to defraud the government of income tax, and *denied* conspiring with Isgro or anyone else to commit any crime. Evidently, that testimony had considerable effect on *his* jury, since it only convicted him of two counts and acquitted him of eight counts.

"Four months later, in August 1989, Mr. Lynch called Mr. DiRicco before the grand jury in this case as a witness. Personally handling the questioning of Mr. DiRicco, Mr. Lynch extracted a story from him that was diametrically opposed to his prior testimony in every important respect. Yes, DiRicco now swore, he *had* received cash from drug dealers, yes, he *had* supplied said cash to Isgro personally and by way of Mr. Smith ... and yes, he *had* conspired with Mr. Isgro and others to defraud the government and record companies. Moreover, DiRicco described phony paper transactions set up by himself, Isgro, and others which were false and part of the criminal scheme. And yes, Anderson and Monka were in on it.

"Despite this dramatic 180-degree switch from DiRicco's former sworn trial testimony, Mr. Lynch failed to reveal any of that prior testimony to the grand jury. He neither asked DiRicco about it before the grand jury, nor read the prior testimony to the grand jury.

"Consider the situation here," Ideman said. "The charges are very serious, particularly with regard to Isgro, including a RICO claim with severe criminal and civil penalties. The witness, DiRicco, is probably the only one who can prove much, or all, of the RICO violations alleged, as well as numerous other counts against Isgro. Codefendants Anderson and Monka probably could not have been indicted at all absent the testimony of DiRicco. Furthermore, the witness is already in a suspect category: He has been convicted of felonies and has made a plea agreement with the government whereby the government has something to say about his eventual testimony. Thus, DiRicco has great motivation to attempt to please the government.

"Contrary to the Government's assertion that dismissal of the indictment is not the remedy for its misconduct, the court finds that dismissal with prejudice is precisely the remedy called for."

At the crack of the gavel, a chorus of cheers went up from Isgro's supporters in the courtroom and a score of reporters bolted to the pay phones in the hallway.

Ideman's dismissal of the indictment with prejudice meant the government could not refile the charges unless an appeals court overturned his ruling, which was not likely. As he brushed past the television camera crews following the worst public scolding of his career, a seething William Lynch fairly spat out the words, "We believe the judge is wrong and we will make the appropriate recommendation for appeal."

"They got caught with their hand in the cookie jar," Donald Re told the crush of reporters that swarmed around him on the courthouse steps. "They focused on the wrong guy when it came to payola."

Despite his new scott-free status, Isgro displayed little joy in his victory, saying only that he was "relieved and happy" with Ideman's ruling. "The last five years have been very difficult," he added.

The government might have said the same thing. Its much ballyhooed payola investigation had been a near-total bust. In their zeal to nail Isgro, the prosecutors had let everyone else off the hook, even Fred DiSipio. As a result, the only jail time handed out in the entire case was Ralph Tashjian's sixty days in a halfway house.

The investigation that once promised to enhance careers, garner promotions, and shower glory on the Justice Department in the end produced only embarrassment.

As one Isgro juror summed it up to *Billboard* reporter Chris Morris following Ideman's ruling, "The government is full of shit."

54

"Does this have to be so undignified?"

On the morning of March 30, 1989, Marvin Rudnick returned to the office after being out sick for two days with a bad cold. John Newcomer spotted him in the hallway and called from his office, "I have to see you right away, Marvin."

"Be right there," Rudnick called back. He went into his office, dropped his briefcase on the desk, and, instinctively, picked up his pocket tape recorder and slapped in a blank tape. He didn't know what was coming, but he figured it had to be some sort of show-down and he wanted to have a record of what was said.

He and Newcomer hadn't spoken to each other for several weeks, not since Rudnick filed a twenty-thousand-word statement with the department, laying out his side of the story in copious detail. In the statement, he accused Newcomer of placing misleading documents in his personnel file to make him look like a leaker. One such document was a copy of a phone message taken by one of the office secretaries. It indicated that on July 7, 1988, a reporter from a London newspaper had called him. Beneath the reporter's name, two boxes were checked—"will call again" and "returned your call." Newcomer had sent the slip to Washington as proof that Rudnick had been placing phone calls to reporters. But Rudnick had never called that reporter. What Newcomer didn't know when he sent the message slip to Washington was that Rudnick kept the original copies of all his messages, just in case he later had to reconstruct a series of events for an affidavit. On the original, only the box "will call again" was checked. Someone had doctored the copy to make it look as if he had initiated the call to the reporter.

All of that was in the back of his mind when he walked into New-comer's office a few minutes later carrying his tape recorder.

"I think I'd better tape this, John, because of all the problems we've had lately," he said, holding up the recorder for Newcomer to see.

Newcomer handed him a piece of paper. "I want you to read this letter from the department," he said. Standing off to the side was a new secretary who'd just transferred in from the Las Vegas strike force. Rudnick didn't know her name and Newcomer didn't intro-duce her. She looked stricken and kept her eyes on the floor. She was Newcomer's witness.

Rudnick sat down, turned on the tape recorder, and began read-ing the letter aloud. It was from Ed Dennis, chief of the criminal division in Washington. "You are hereby placed on temporary duty status, with pay, pending determination of your full-time employ-ment with the department," he read. It meant he was being sus-pended, the first step toward being fired.

Rudnick stopped reading and looked up at Newcomer. "When do you want this to start, John?"

"Right now," Newcomer replied. "I'll need your key to the office, your department ID, and your security card for the parking lot."

Rudnick stood up, unfastened the key from his key ring, and plopped it on Newcomer's desk. Then he fished his security card out of his wallet and placed it on top of the key. "I don't have my department ID anymore," he said sheepishly. "I lost it about two years ago." Newcomer arched an eyebrow, but didn't comment. He took a few steps toward the door, then turned, waiting for Rudnick to follow.

"You're not to take any documents out of your office, except what's personal in nature," he said.

The three of them walked the thirty feet down the hall to Rudnick's office. Newcomer positioned himself just inside the door, like a guard. He stood and watched as Rudnick fetched an empty cardboard box from the corner of the room.

"Does this have to be so undignified, John?" Rudnick protested. "I've never been accused of stealing anything before. Can't I do this by myself?"

"No, you can't," Newcomer replied.

Rudnick filled the box with his personal effects—pictures of his family, books, a Justice Department dedicated service plaque that hung on the wall above his desk, along with a framed certificate announcing his appointment to the strike force in 1980, signed by then-attorney-general Griffin Bell.

Newcomer let him take his Rolodex, but not his research files containing the pleadings from all the cases he'd worked on over the years. The pleadings would be invaluable later on in private practice. Usually, attorneys leaving the strike force were allowed to take them when they left. Not this time.

For Rudnick, the whole scene seemed surreal, like he was being booked and fingerprinted. He half expected Newcomer to confiscate his shoes and belt. As he walked out of his office—cardboard box tucked under his arm, Newcomer and the nameless secretary on either side of him—he felt like a prisoner being escorted to lockup. The only detail lacking was handcuffs.

The outer office was deserted as he was paraded through; not a single colleague came out of his quarters to say good-bye. He walked down the long corridor to the elevators feeling numb. After all the months of waiting for the axe to fall, it was all happening so fast. His mind filled with inane thoughts. He wondered how many times he'd made this same walk before: at least 5 times a day, 250 times a year, for nine years? What did that come to—11,250?

In silence, the trio rode the elevator down four levels to the underground parking garage. Approaching his banged-up Chrysler, Rudnick's attention was drawn to the locked, fenced-off area fifty feet away, where the black, bullet-proof presidential limousine was kept, the one Ronald Reagan had used on his countless vacation trips to the West Coast. There was an irony in the moment that he couldn't quite put his finger on.

He dropped the cardboard box into his trunk and got into the car.

"Good luck, Marvin," Newcomer said, without emotion.

Looking straight ahead, Rudnick replied, "Thank you."

The whole thing had taken less than an hour. It was not yet 10:00 A.M. when he drove up the dark tunnel of the parking garage into the bright sunlight of Temple Street. It was a beautiful spring day. He turned on the radio and, for the first time in years, didn't feel like listening to the all-news station. Instead, he punched in a pop music station and began tapping time on the steering wheel. Pulling onto the Pasadena Freeway, headed for home, he felt the first twinge of an as-yet-undefined new beginning, a vague sense that he was traveling from the shadows into the light.

55

"It's a big loss"

During the last week of June 1989, MCA Records held the top three slots on the *Billboard* album chart—the Fine Young Cannibals' *The Raw and the Cooked* at number one, Bobby Brown's *Don't Be Cruel* at number two, and Tom Petty's *Full Moon Fever* at number three.

The following week, MCA took out a full-page ad in *Billboard* consisting of a picture of the chart and a reproduction of a letter ostensibly written to Azoff. "Dear Irving," the letter read. "For the first time in MCA Records' long history, we have the top three albums. Congratulations to you and all your team. We are thrilled with the achievement and proud of your accomplishments."

The letter was signed "Lew" and "Sid."

That same week, on July 6, Marvin Rudnick received a letter in the mail, delivered overnight from Washington, D.C. Signed by Edward Dennis, the acting deputy attorney general of the U.S. Justice Department, the correspondence was two sentences long: "Dear Mr. Rudnick," it read. "This is to inform you that pursuant to the authority set forth in 28 C.F.R. 0.15 you are hereby removed from your position as trial attorney (general), organized crime and racketeering section, criminal division. This action is effective immediately upon your receipt of this letter."

After thirteen years of public service, Marvin Rudnick was fired as he stood in the driveway of his Pasadena home.

Two months later, on September 5, Irving Azoff resigned from MCA to form his own record company. In a farewell address to his staff, he thanked them for helping him "rape and pillage" the competition and, in a trademark cruel aside, he hailed Dan McGill as "the financial community's brightest media star since Barry Minkow, Jim Bakker, and Mike Milken."

In an interview with the *Los Angeles Times*, Azoff characterized the strike force's investigation of the Pisello affair as "a witch hunt beyond my wildest dreams. The fact that it could happen is another reason not to hold a corporate job." (It is interesting that the *Times*, which had broken almost all the stories about Pisello's dealings with MCA over a four-year period, devoted only four sentences to the scandal in its twenty-five-hundred-word article about Azoff's resignation.)

Despite the fact that MCA Records was still only marginally profitable, the *Times* quoted Wall Street analyst Mara Balsbaugh as saying of Azoff's departure, "It's a big loss. My impression is, Irving single-handedly engineered a turnaround at MCA Records."

In truth, Azoff may have left MCA with far more money in his own pockets than the record company earned during his six-year tenure—including an estimated $30 million worth of MCA stock. By year's end he'd lined up a reported $50 million in financing from Time-Warner to launch a new record label. He called his new company Giant Records.

As he had said, "Either I win, or I win."

Rock 'n' roll rules.

Epilogue

Since he was booted out of the strike force, **Marvin Rudnick** has built a successful private law practice in Pasadena, California. The Justice Department still will not comment on his firing other than to say that it was a "personnel matter" having to do with his rocky relationship with his former boss, John Newcomer. However, in October 1990, Rudnick's reputation as a public servant got a boost from a congressional committee investigating misconduct by senior managers of the Internal Revenue Service. In its final report on the investigation, the House Committee on Government Operations noted that when an IRS Internal Security investigator called Newcomer in 1986 to ask if the Justice Department would be interested in prosecuting Ron Saranow for attempting to interfere with Rudnick's case against an IRS agent, Newcomer responded, "Rudnick's not playing with a full deck."

According to the committee's report, "This description of Mr. Rudnick by Mr. Newcomer was contrary to the opinions of almost every individual interviewed on this matter. The overwhelming consensus was that Mr. Rudnick was a dedicated, effective and hardworking prosecutor whose honesty and integrity were beyond reproach."

John Newcomer is the deputy chief of the Justice Department's bank fraud unit in Tampa, Florida.

Richard Stavin is in private practice in Santa Monica, California. He's convinced that someone high up in the Justice Department obstructed justice in the killing of his Hollywood labor racketeering investigation.

Bruce Repetto is still an assistant U.S. attorney in Newark, New Jersey.

Irving Azoff is the chairman of Giant Records, which scored hits in 1991 with the soundtrack to *New Jack City* and the rap group Color Me Badd but, because it doesn't report publicly, its profitability is unknown. In a December 7, 1991, article in *Billboard,* Azoff was quoted as saying: "Giant Records had a stellar year, and in the first year with its own marketing and promotion staff, it turned a profit."

MCA, Inc., was sold to the Japanese electronics conglomerate Matsushita in 1990 for $6.1 billion. **Lew Wasserman,** who made more than $300 million on the sale, remains chairman of the American subsidiary. **Sidney Sheinberg,** who pocketed about $86 million in the buyout, remains as president and chief executive officer.

Richard Palmese is now president of MCA Records and **Zach Horowitz** is executive vice president. **Dan McGill** and **John Burns** retain their former positions with the company.

Myron Roth is now president of Scotti Bros. Records, a small, Los Angeles–based label.

Sam Passamano is retired and living in Arcadia, California. He settled his wrongful termination lawsuit against MCA out of court in 1991.

George Collier settled his wrongful termination lawsuit against MCA in June 1992, after eight years of litigation. He now operates his own country music entertainment company in Nashville, Tennessee.

Gene Froelich is chief financial officer of Maxi-Care Health Plans, Inc., in Los Angeles.

Al Bergamo runs his own talent agency in Colorado Springs, Colorado.

Joe Robinson settled his lawsuit against MCA out of court in 1991. "No money changed hands," he says. "We just shook hands and walked away. I couldn't afford the lawyers no more." He is now the president of SHR Inc., a New Jersey–based company that repackages and markets recordings of the now-defunct Sugar Hill Records.

Eugene Giaquinto operates his own video production and duplication firm in the San Fernando Valley. He has never been prosecuted in the Hollywood labor racketeering case, and the wiretaps of his telephone conversations with Marty Bacow remain sealed.

Joe Isgro has broadened his business interests beyond independent record promotion. He is the executive producer of the Twentieth Century Fox movie *Hoffa* starring Jack Nicholson and directed by Danny DeVito.

In September 1992, the U.S. Ninth Circuit Court of Appeals "reluctantly" reversed Judge James Ideman's dismissal of the fifty-seven-count indictment against Isgro, saying he went too far in throwing the case out of court with prejudice. However, noting that Ideman was "justifiably frustrated with the government prosecutors in the case," the court recommended that the Justice Department consider disciplining chief prosecutor William Lynch for his misconduct in the case and took the unusual step of criticizing Lynch by name in its published opinion. The ruling cleared the way for the Justice Department to re-indict Isgro and his co-defendants, but as of this writing the government has not done so.

Sal Pisello was released from prison in the summer of 1991 after serving two years of his four-year sentence for tax evasion. He is living in Los Angeles but is no longer working in the record business. In May 1990, the Justice Department responded to repeated Freedom of Information requests from the *Los Angeles Times* for all of its files on the Pisello investigation by releasing a memo from Pisello's prison chaplain. It read: "I would like to take this opportunity to commend inmate Salvatore Pisello for the extra effort that he has put forth to enhance the appearance of the chapel area.

"In addition to his regular duties as Visiting Room Orderly, he has painted the chapel tower as well as the exterior trim of the window sashes and eaves. In addition, he has assisted in caring for the flower beds and the lawn area.

"Through such generous efforts, the chapel area has become a most attractive entrance to the institution."

In the fall of 1992, Pisello was trying to sell two scripts he'd co-written to Hollywood; a drama and a comedy, both are about the Mafia.

Sonny Brocco was released from prison in the fall of 1991, after serving four years of his eight-year sentence.

Federico ("Fritzy") Giovanelli is serving a life sentence for the murder of detective Anthony Venditti.

Dominick ("Baldy Dom") Canterino is still serving his twelve-year sentence for the extortion of John LaMonte.

Morris Levy sold all of his music business holdings in 1990 for a reported $70 million. Before he could begin his ten-year prison sentence, Levy died of liver cancer in May 1991.

Vincent ("the Chin") Gigante was indicted on massive racketeering charges in 1991, but after he was examined by four court-appointed psychiatrists, the sixty-two-year-old boss of the Genovese crime family was declared mentally unfit to stand trial. He is now considered virtually immune from prosecution.

Gaetano ("Corky") Vastola is just one year into his seventeen-year prison sentence for the extortion of John LaMonte. In March 1992, he became the subject of another highly publicized Mafia trial when Gambino boss John Gotti was convicted in New York of murdering Big Paul Castellano and a host of other crimes. Among those other crimes was conspiring to murder Gaetano Vastola.

John LaMonte is operating a new budget cassette and compact disc business in a new city under a new name. His new life is good, but his old life is never far behind. "Sometimes I'll be playing racquetball or something and I'll look up and see some guy watching me from across the way, and the fear will hit me," he says. He still sleeps every night on the sofa in his living room "because that way, if they ever come for me, they won't accidentally get my wife and kids, too."

Does he really think that's still a possibility, with Levy gone and Vastola in prison possibly for the rest of his life?

"Yeah. These guys don't ever forget."

Index